Ranked Set Sampling Models and Methods

Carlos N. Bouza-Herrera
Universidad de La Habana, Cuba

A volume in the Advances in Data
Mining and Database Management
(ADMDM) Book Series   .

Published in the United States of America by
    IGI Global
    Engineering Science Reference (an imprint of IGI Global)
    701 E. Chocolate Avenue
    Hershey PA, USA 17033
    Tel: 717-533-8845
    Fax: 717-533-8661
    E-mail: cust@igi-global.com
    Web site: http://www.igi-global.com

Library of Congress Cataloging-in-Publication Data

Names: Bouza Herrera, Carlos Narciso, 1942- editor.
Title: Ranked set sampling models and methods / Carlos Bouza-Herrera,
  editor.
Description: Hershey, PA : Engineering Science Reference, [2021] | Includes
  bibliographical references and index.
Identifiers: LCCN 2020048009 (print) | LCCN 2020048010 (ebook) | ISBN
  9781799875567 (hardcover) | ISBN 9781799875574 (paperback) | ISBN
  9781799875581 (ebook)
Subjects: LCSH: Sampling (Statistics) | Ranking and selection (Statistics)
Classification: LCC QA276.6 .R3288 2021 (print) | LCC QA276.6 (ebook) |
  DDC 519.5/2--dc23
LC record available at https://lccn.loc.gov/2020048009
LC ebook record available at https://lccn.loc.gov/2020048010

This book is published in the IGI Global book series Advances in Data Mining and Database
Management (ADMDM) (ISSN: 2327-1981; eISSN: 2327-199X)

British Cataloguing in Publication Data
A Cataloguing in Publication record for this book is available from the British Library.

All work contributed to this book is new, previously-unpublished material.
The views expressed in this book are those of the authors, but not necessarily of the publisher.

For electronic access to this publication, please contact: eresources@igi-global.com.

Advances in Data Mining and Database Management (ADMDM) Book Series

ISSN:2327-1981
EISSN:2327-199X

Editor-in-Chief: David Taniar, Monash University, Australia

MISSION

With the large amounts of information available to organizations in today's digital world, there is a need for continual research surrounding emerging methods and tools for collecting, analyzing, and storing data.

The **Advances in Data Mining & Database Management (ADMDM)** series aims to bring together research in information retrieval, data analysis, data warehousing, and related areas in order to become an ideal resource for those working and studying in these fields. IT professionals, software engineers, academicians and upper-level students will find titles within the ADMDM book series particularly useful for staying up-to-date on emerging research, theories, and applications in the fields of data mining and database management.

COVERAGE

- Text Mining
- Database Security
- Profiling Practices
- Predictive Analysis
- Data Mining
- Neural Networks
- Data Warehousing
- Enterprise Systems
- Data Quality
- Cluster Analysis

IGI Global is currently accepting manuscripts for publication within this series. To submit a proposal for a volume in this series, please contact our Acquisition Editors at Acquisitions@igi-global.com or visit: http://www.igi-global.com/publish/.

The Advances in Data Mining and Database Management (ADMDM) Book Series (ISSN 2327-1981) is published by IGI Global, 701 E. Chocolate Avenue, Hershey, PA 17033-1240, USA, www.igi-global.com. This series is composed of titles available for purchase individually; each title is edited to be contextually exclusive from any other title within the series. For pricing and ordering information please visit http://www.igi-global.com/book-series/advances-data-mining-database-management/37146. Postmaster: Send all address changes to above address. Copyright © 2022 IGI Global. All rights, including translation in other languages reserved by the publisher. No part of this series may be reproduced or used in any form or by any means – graphics, electronic, or mechanical, including photocopying, recording, taping, or information and retrieval systems – without written permission from the publisher, except for non commercial, educational use, including classroom teaching purposes. The views expressed in this series are those of the authors, but not necessarily of IGI Global.

Titles in this Series

For a list of additional titles in this series, please visit:
http://www.igi-global.com/book-series/advances-data-mining-database-management/37146

New Opportunities for Sentiment Analysis and Information Processing
Aakanksha Sharaff (National Institute of Technology, Raipur, India) G. R. Sinha (Myanmar Institute of Information Technology, Mandalay, Myanmar) and Surbhi Bhatia (King Faisal University, Saudi Arabia)
Engineering Science Reference • © 2021 • 315pp • H/C (ISBN: 9781799880615) • US $245.00

Transforming Scholarly Publishing With Blockchain Technologies and AI
Darrell Wayne Gunter (Gunter Media Group, USA)
Information Science Reference • © 2021 • 336pp • H/C (ISBN: 9781799855897) • US $205.00

Political and Economic Implications of Blockchain Technology in Business and Healthcare
Dário de Oliveira Rodrigues (Instituto Politécnico de Santarém, Portugal)
Business Science Reference • © 2021 • 389pp • H/C (ISBN: 9781799873631) • US $225.00

Data Preprocessing, Active Learning, and Cost Perceptive Approaches for Resolving Data Imbalance
Dipti P. Rana (Sardar Vallabhbhai National Institute of Technology, Surat, India) and Rupa G. Mehta (Sardar Vallabhbhai National Institute of Technology, Surat, India)
Engineering Science Reference • © 2021 • 309pp • H/C (ISBN: 9781799873716) • US $225.00

Data Science Advancements in Pandemic and Outbreak Management
Eleana Asimakopoulou (Independent Researcher, Greece) and Nik Bessis (Edge Hill University, UK)
Engineering Science Reference • © 2021 • 255pp • H/C (ISBN: 9781799867364) • US $225.00

Industry Use Cases on Blockchain Technology Applications in IoT and the Financial Sector

For an entire list of titles in this series, please visit:
http://www.igi-global.com/book-series/advances-data-mining-database-management/37146

701 East Chocolate Avenue, Hershey, PA 17033, USA
Tel: 717-533-8845 x100 • Fax: 717-533-8661
E-Mail: cust@igi-global.com • www.igi-global.com

Table of Contents

Detailed Table of Contents

Chapter 1

> *Vishal Mehta, Department of Agricultural Statistics, College of
> Agriculture, Acharya Narendra Deva University of Agriculture and
> Technology, Azamgarh, India*

In this chapter, the authors suggest some improved versions of estimators of Morgenstern type bivariate exponential distribution (MTBED) based on the observations made on the units of ranked set sampling (RSS) regarding the study variable Y, which is correlated with the auxiliary variable X, where (X,Y) follows a MTBED. In this chapter, they firstly suggested minimum mean squared error estimator for estimation of $\theta 2$ based on censored ranked set sample and their special case; further, they have suggested minimum mean squared error estimator for best linear unbiased estimator of $\theta 2$ based on censored ranked set sample and their special cases; they also suggested minimum mean squared error estimator for estimation of $\theta 2$ based on unbalanced multistage ranked set sampling and their special cases. Efficiency comparisons are also made in this work.

Chapter 2

> *Beatriz Cobo, University of Granada, Spain
> Elvira Pelle, University of Modena and Reggio Emilia, Italy*

In situations where the estimation of the proportion of sensitive variables relies on the observations of real measurements that are difficult to obtain, there is a need to combine indirect questioning techniques. In the present work, the authors will focus on the item count technique, with alternative methods of sampling, such as the ranked set sampling. They are based on the idea proposed by Santiago et al., which combines the randomized response technique proposed by Warner together with ranked set sampling. The authors will carry out a simulation study to compare the item count technique under ranked set sampling and under simple random sampling without replacement.

In this chapter, the authors consider the problem of estimating the population means of two sensitive variables by making use ranked set sampling. The final estimators are unbiased and the variance expressions that they derive show that ranked set sampling is more efficient than simple random sampling. A convex combination of the variance expressions of the resultant estimators is minimized in order to suggest optimal sample sizes for both sampling schemes. The relative efficiency of the proposed estimators is then compared to the corresponding estimators for simple random sampling based on simulation study and real data applications. SAS codes utilized in the simulation to collect the empirical evidence and application are included.

Chapter 4

This chapter introduced basic elements on stratified simple random sampling (SSRS) on ranked set sampling (RSS). The chapter extends Singh et al. results to sampling a stratified population. The mean squared error (MSE) is derived. SRS is used independently for selecting the samples from the strata. The chapter extends Singh et al. results under the RSS design. They are used for developing the estimation in a stratified population. RSS is used for drawing the samples independently from the strata. The bias and mean squared error (MSE) of the developed estimators are derived. A comparison between the biases and MSEs obtained for the sampling designs SRS and RSS is made. Under mild conditions the comparisons sustained that each RSS model is better than its SRS alternative.

Shravya Jasti, Texas A&M University – Kingsville, Kingsville, USA
Stephen A. Sedory, Texas A&M University – Kingsville, Kingsville, USA
Sarjinder Singh, Texas A&M University – Kingsville, Kingsville, USA

In this chapter, the authors investigate the performance of the Gjestvang and Singh randomized response model for estimating the mean of a sensitive variable using ranked set sampling along the lines of Bouza. The proposed estimator is found to be unbiased, and a variance expression is derived. Then a simulation study is carried out to judge the magnitude of relative efficiency in various situations. At the end, the proposed model is assessed based on real secondary data applications. A set of SAS codes is also included.

Shivacharan Rao Chitneni, Texas A&M University – Kingsville,
    Kingsville, USA
Stephen A. Sedory, Texas A&M University – Kingsville, Kingsville, USA
Sarjinder Singh, Texas A&M University – Kingsville, Kingsville, USA

In the chapter, the authors consider the problem of estimating the population means of two sensitive variables by making use of ranked set sampling. The final estimators are unbiased and the variance expressions that they derive show that ranked set sampling is more efficient than simple random sampling. A convex combination of the variance expressions of the resultant estimators is minimized in order to suggest optimal sample sizes for both sampling schemes. The relative efficiency of the proposed estimators is then compared to the corresponding estimators for simple random sampling based on simulation study and real data applications. SAS codes utilized in the simulation to collect the empirical evidence and application are included.

Carmen Elena Viada- Gonzalez, Gestión de la Información, Clínica
    Centro de Inmunología Molecular, Cuba
Sira María Allende-Alonso, Facultad de Matemática y Computación,

Universidad de La Habana, Cuba

In this chapter, the authors develop stratified ranked set sampling (RSS) under missing observations. Imputation based of ratio rules is used for completing the information for estimating the mean. They introduce the needed elements on imputation and on the sample selection procedures. They extend RSS models to imputation in stratified populations. A theory on ratio-based imputation rules for estimating the mean is presented. Some numerical studies, based on real-world problems, are developed for illustrating the behaviour of the accuracy of the estimators due to their proposals.

Chapter 8

Arpita Chatterjee, Georgia Southern University, USA
Santu Ghosh, Augusta University, USA

This chapter provides a brief review of the existing resampling methods for RSS and its implementation to construct a bootstrap confidence interval for the mean parameter. The authors present a brief comparison of these existing methods in terms of their flexibility and consistency. To construct the bootstrap confidence interval, three methods are adopted, namely, bootstrap percentile method, bias-corrected and accelerated method, and method based on monotone transformation along with normal approximation. Usually, for the second method, the accelerated constant is computed by employing the jackknife method. The authors discuss an analytical expression for the accelerated constant, which results in reducing the computational burden of this bias-corrected and accelerated bootstrap method. The usefulness of the proposed methods is further illustrated by analyzing real-life data on shrubs.

Chapter 9

Bekir Cetintav, Burdur Mehmet Akif Ersoy University, Turkey
Selma Gürler, Dokuz Eylul University, Turkey
Neslihan Demirel, Dokuz Eylul University, Turkey

Sampling method plays an important role for data collection in a scientific research. Ranked set sampling (RSS), which was first introduced by McIntyre, is an advanced method to obtain data for getting information and inference about the population of interest. The main impact of RSS is to use the ranking information of the units in the sampling mechanism. Even though most of theoretical inferences are made based on exact measurement of the variable of interest, the ranking process is done with an expert judgment or concomitant variable (without exact measurement) in practice. Because of the ambiguity in discriminating the rank of one unit with another, ranking the units could not be perfect, and it may cause uncertainty. There are some studies focused on the modeling of this uncertainty with a probabilistic perspective in the literature. In this chapter, another perspective, a fuzzy-set-inspired approach, for the uncertainty in the ranking mechanism of RSS is introduced.

The authors develop the estimation of the difference of means of a pair of variables X and Y when we deal with missing observations. A seminal paper in this line is due to Bouza and Prabhu-Ajgaonkar when the sample and the subsamples are selected using simple random sampling. In this this chapter, the authors consider the use of ranked set-sampling for estimating the difference when we deal with a stratified population. The sample error is deduced. Numerical comparisons with the classic stratified model are developed using simulated and real data.

Preface

The need of using samples is present, both in scientific research as in managing official statistics, in order to answer the research questions. It is doubtful that researcher should be able to currently collect data from all the cases. Thus, often there is a need to select a sample. The entire set of cases from which researcher sample is drawn in called the population. The part of the population observed is a sample

Intuitive application of the principles of sampling in science has been taking place for a long time in the history of humanity. However, initially it was not called sampling, but inductive reasoning. Many scientific results are based on observations of a few experiments. Apparently, it was possible to generalize experimental results. Although inductive reasoning has been commonly applied, both in everyday life and in science for a long time, sampling as a well-defined statistical method is fairly young. Its history started just only in the year 1895.

English merchant John Graunt (1620-1674), in his famous tract described a method to estimate the population of London based on partial information. The second time of application of a survey-like method was applied was more than a century later. Pierre Simon Laplace (1749 – 1827) realized that it was important to have some indication of the accuracy of the estimate of the French population in 1812.

The census in its modern form can be closely associated with the rise of democracy, because a periodic count of the population was essential for a truly representative government. According to Porter (1986), that is the reason why the modern periodic censuses, were first introduced in the most advanced states of Europe and America. This took place around the beginning of the nineteenth century, at the end of the industrial revolution (1750-1840). The use of censuses spread over much of the world in subsequent years.

In the second half of the 19th century so called monograph studies or surveys became popular. They were based on Quetelet's idea of the average man. According to this idea, it suffices to collect information only on typical people. Investigation on the behavior of extreme people was avoided. This type of inquiry was still applied widely at the beginning of the 20th century. It was an "officially" accepted method.

The roots of survey sampling are more in official statistics and social statistics than in the probability theory and experimental design.

The starting point for thinking statistically in sampling is to be placed in 1895. Many reasons sustain the claim that 1895 marks the beginning of modern survey sampling. If there is a man who should merit to be credited for that start of the widespread use of sampling as a scientific method, it is Anders Kiaer. Many respected authors share this view, but different views also exist (see e.g. Stephan 1948). Anders Kiaer (1838-1919) was the founder and the first director of Statistics Norway. He advocated for the use sampling methods. The presentation of his ideas started the development of modern survey sampling theory and methods. He was ahead of other official statisticians his time. His proposal raised oppositions at the International Statistical Institute (ISI) meeting in Bern in 1895. Despite the criticism, some statisticians, as professor Arthur Bowley of the University of London, became attracted to the Representative Method proposed by Kiaer. He carried out several large-sample survey research in Norway. Bowley played a decisive role on behalf of Kiaer's ideas. Finally ISI endorsed a resolution in 1901 for considering the possible niceties of sampling. Bowley advocated for random sampling with equal probabilities. At the ISI Berlin's meeting, in 1903, Lucien March suggested that random sampling might objectivize "partial investigations" as statisticians could compute the accuracy of the estimates. Representative and random methods coexisted for a number of years. Bowley also was the first to consider stratification and proposed selecting at random and with equal proportion the units within each stratum for achieving more efficient results.

Neyman's article in 1934 opened a new era in sampling by presenting evidences that probability based sampling produced not only bias-free estimates but allowed measuring sampling errors. His paper was an attack to the purposive survey conducted by Gini and Galvani in 1929. Neyman demonstrated that their inferences were inappropriate, as the Central Limit Theorem did not work. The ideas were adapting Fisher`s methods used in agricultural experiments to social surveys.

In practice the use of random selection was supported in using simple random sampling (SRS). This procedure became the touchstone in survey sampling.

Although random sampling was theoretically attractive, it was not easy to apply it in social research. Several extensions of sampling models were developed by practitioners. They solved real life problems by developing new models. A frequent practical solution was to use systematic sampling, instead of SRS. Multistage sampling theory was developed by Hansen and Hurwitz in 1943. In a first stage, primary sampling units are randomly selected and a fixed number of secondary units are selected from the selected groups. These two methods are an example of early alternatives to purely using SRS.

Therefore, classical survey sampling theory was developed by modeling real life situations, mainly in governmental institutions. Academicians were involved in large scale surveys and the theoretical body of the theory of sampling was basically completed by the end of the first half of the 20th century. The randomization approach was almost unanimously accepted. Sampling was a matter taught in universities and the first text-books were edited by that time (Cochran, 1953; Deming, 1950; Hansen, Hurwitz, & Madow, 1953; Yates, 1949, for example).

In 1952 Horvitz and Thompson published a paper that provided a broader view of the theory of sampling. It was the basis of a general theory for constructing unbiased estimate. Whenever the selection probabilities of the units of the population be known and positive, it is always possible to construct an unbiased estimate. Horvitz and Thompson completed the classical theory and was a challenge for theoreticians to improve the basic SRS procedure. It represented a turning point.

Godambe in 1955 with his nonexistence theorem and his proposal was a challenge to the prevalent orthodox point of view. It established the non-existence of any uniformly best estimator within the work frame of sampling. Classes of estimators may be considered and the statistical properties were shared by all its members. Horvitz Thompson estimator was the token in the defined classes. A key rest was the proof that random sampling produced a probability measure and by this way the estimation, based on random samples, was only a particular case of the theory of point estimation, but with certain particularities. This proposal met with a lot of resistance in its beginnings. The establishment by Hanurav in 1968 that exists a one-to-one relationship between the sampling designs (the probability measure) and the selection procedures (algorithms for selecting samples) started the end of the reluctance of practitioners. This approach is known as Unified Sampling Theory.

Another breaking point was due in the decade of the seventies by Royall and his co-authors. They introduced the concept of model unbiasedness instead of the classic design unbiasedness. In this context ratio estimators became more relevant than Horvitz-Thompson estimator. Having balanced samples was better, in the framework of model-based inference, than pure random samples. This approach is called Model Assisted Survey Sampling.

Unified Sampling Theory and Model Assisted Survey Sampling were mainly academic topics of research in sampling. Practitioners proved the models cautiously using them in some applications. Some of the new models developed started to be used in some real-life problems.

In other context a new design, called Ranked Set Sampling (RSS), started to be a method used by some practitioners, in agricultural research mainly. It is an alternative to the sovereignty of SRS. It also came from real life needs, as in early stages of the development of sampling. In my experience clients rarely accepted working with "bad samples". "Why not use these plots instead of the selected ones if I see infected plants in unselected plots?" was argued frequently by biologists, for example. I had no sound answers for that. McIntyre, working with pastures proposed to select independently and provisionally n sets of n plots, with SRS with replacement (SRSWR). They were ranked and was selected only one plot in each set. The selection was made in such a way that each order statistic was observed only once. He argued that the method worked better. The n order statistics conform an independent random sample . His claim was ignored by theoreticians. He was a practitioner working in agriculture in Australia. RSS began to be used by other persons involved with similar agricultural problems and provided evidence on the gains in efficiency of estimating means and totals. A mathematical proof of the superiority of RSS to SRS was provided in 1968 by Takeushi-Wakimoto. It was followed by other theoretical papers that provided a mathematical support of the righteous of the claims of McIntire. Establishing the effect of ranking using auxiliary variables opened the doors to a profusion of new studies.

Statisticians are facing the development of RSS counterparts to the existent theories based on SRS. This book follows other oeuvres where statisticians presented their research which are new result to the estimation theory based on RSS.

If we look to the development of sampling theory after 1940, is to be noted the similitudes of the rise of RSS with the early improvements of SRS with extensions (systematic, multistage, unequal probabilities etc.). Particular models are being developed and they are structuring the basis for a future estimation theory alternative with the actual based on SRS.

This book presents some particular models of RSS and are contributions to the corresponding theory. A detailed description of the chapters is given in the sequel.

Chapter 1 presented an improvement of some previous estimators when RSS is used. It works more efficiently than other ones.

Chapter 2 is concerned with a particular problem present in many applications: dealing with qualitative variables in the context of RSS. The majority of the existent models developed methods for quantitative variables.

Chapter 3 studies the behavior of RSS under the knowledge of the auxiliary variable in a stratified population .

Chapter 4 studies the behavior of RSS under the knowledge of the auxiliary variable in a stratified population . It extends results obtained for un-stratified populations.

Chapter 5 presents strong results in the estimation when dealing with sensitive questions for a particular scrambling procedure.

Chapter 6 presents a model for estimating the population means of two sensitive variables using RSS. The efficiency of the proposal is significatively high.

Chapter 7 considers the existence of missing observations in the case of using RSS and proposes ratio based methods for imputation in the context o stratified populations.

Chapter 8 gives a description of resampling methods for RSS. The authors implemented some methods to construct bootstrap confidence interval for the mean.

Chapter 9 is concerned with using a fuzzy perspective for modeling the uncertainty in the ranking process for implementing RSS. Ranking uses fuzzy tools and ideas.

Chapter 10 extends common ratio-scrambling procedures for dealing with sensitive questions and expands them to stratified sampling

All the papers develop detailed proofs of the theoretical results. Studies on the behavior of the proposals are generally illustrated with empiric examples using data from real-life or simulated.

The authors are well-known specialists. The papers, as a whole, proportionate RSS counterparts to actual challenging problems in classical sampling theory. Therefore, the book is opening areas of research for academicians and providing tools for applications to practitioners decided to use RSS modeling instead of classic models.

The interested readers may obtain more information on historical issues of sampling theory in the bibliography listed at the end of this prologue.

REFERENCES

Bethlehem, J. (2009). *The rise of survey sampling*. Statistics Netherlands.

Bouza-Herrera, C. N., & Al-Omari, A. I. F. (2019). *Ranked Set Sampling: 65 Years Improving the Accuracy in Data Gathering*. Elsevier Inc.

Brewer, K. (2013). Three controversies in the history of survey sampling. *Survey Methodology*, *39*, 249–262.

Brewer, K. R. W., & Gregoire, T. G. (2009). Introduction to survey sampling. In Handbook of Statistics 29A, Sample Surveys: Design, Methods and Applications. Elsevier. doi:10.1016/S0169-7161(08)00001-1

Chen, Z., Bai, Z., & Sinha, B. K. (2004). Ranked set sampling: theory and applications. In Lectures Notes in Statistics (vol. 176). Springer. doi:10.1007/978-0-387-21664-5

Desrosières, A. (1998). *The Politics of Large Numbers; A History of Statistical Reasoning*. Harvard University Press.

Fowler, F. J. Jr. (2002). *Survey Research Methods (3rd ed.)*. Sage Publications.

Godambe, V. P. (1955). A unified theory of sampling from finite populations. *Journal of the Royal Statistical Society. Series B. Methodological*, *17*(2), 269–278. doi:10.1111/j.2517-6161.1955.tb00203.x

Groves, R. M. (2011). Three eras of survey research. *Public Opinion Quarterly*, *75*(5), 861–871. doi:10.1093/poq/nfr057

Horvitz, D. G., & Thompson, D. J. (1952). A generalization of sampling without replacement from a finite universe. *Journal of the American Statistical Association*, *47*(260), 663–685. doi:10.1080/01621459.1952.10483446

Kiaer, A. N. (1997). *Den repräsentative undersökelsesmetode*. Christiania Videnskabsselskabets Skrifter.

Neyman, J. (1934). On the two different aspects of the representative method: The method of stratified sampling and the method of purposive selection. *Journal of the Royal Statistical Society*, *97*(4), 558–606. doi:10.2307/2342192

Porter, T. M. (1986). *The Rise of Statistical Thinking 1820-1900*. Princeton University Press. doi:10.1515/9780691210520

Stephan, F. F. (1948). History of the uses of modern sampling theory and practice. *Journal of the American Statistical Association*, *43*(241), 12–39. doi:10.1080/016 21459.1948.10483247

Wright, T. (2001). Selected moments in the development of probability sampling: Theory and practice. Survey research methods section newsletter. American Statistical Association.

Acknowledgment

The only true heritage is to transmit your knowledge, then teach.

I devote my work in this oeuvre

To the last two pillars of my existence,

My daughter and my wife

Carlos N. Bouza-Herrera

Chapter 1
An Improved Estimation of Parameter of Morgenstern-Type Bivariate Exponential Distribution Using Ranked Set Sampling

Vishal Mehta

Department of Agricultural Statistics, College of Agriculture, Acharya Narendra Deva University of Agriculture and Technology, Azamgarh, India

ABSTRACT

In this chapter, the authors suggest some improved versions of estimators of Morgenstern type bivariate exponential distribution (MTBED) based on the observations made on the units of ranked set sampling (RSS) regarding the study variable Y, which is correlated with the auxiliary variable X, where (X,Y) follows a MTBED. In this chapter, they firstly suggested minimum mean squared error estimator for estimation of θ2 based on censored ranked set sample and their special case; further, they have suggested minimum mean squared error estimator for best linear unbiased estimator of θ2 based on censored ranked set sample and their special cases; they also suggested minimum mean squared error estimator for estimation of θ2 based on unbalanced multistage ranked set sampling and their special cases. Efficiency comparisons are also made in this work.

DOI: 10.4018/978-1-7998-7556-7.ch001

1.1. INTRODUCTION

Ranked set sampling (RSS) is a method of sampling that can be advantageous when quantification of all sampling units is costly but a small set of units can be easily ranked, according to the character under investigation, without actual quantification. The technique was first introduced by McIntyre (1952) for estimating means pasture and forage yields. The theory and application of ranked set sampling given by Chen *et al.* (2004). Suppose the variable of interest say Y, is difficult or much expensive to measure, but an auxiliary variable X correlated with Y is readily measureable and can be ordered exactly. In this case as an alternative to McIntyre (1952) method of ranked set sampling, Stokes (1977) used an auxiliary variable for the ranking of sampling units. If $X_{(r)r}$ is the observation measured on the auxiliary variable X from the unit chosen from the rth set then we write $Y_{[r]r}$ to denote the corresponding measurement made on the study variable Y on this unit, then $Y_{[r]r}$, $r=1,2,\ldots,n$, form the ranked set sample. Clearly $Y_{[r]r}$ is the concomitant of the rth order statistic arising from the rth sample.

A striking example for the application of the ranked set sampling as proposed by Stokes (1977) is given in Bain (1978, p. 99), where the study variate Y represents the oil pollution of sea water and the auxiliary variable X represents the tar deposit in the nearby sea shore. Clearly collecting sea water sample and measuring the oil pollution in it is strenuous and expensive. However the prevalence of pollution in the sea water is much reflected by the tar deposit in the surrounding terminal sea shore. In this example ranking the pollution level of sea water based on the tar deposit in the sea shore is more natural and scientific than ranking it visually or by judgment method.

Stokes (1995) has considered the estimation of parameters of location-scale family of distributions using RSS. Lam et al. (1994, 1995) have obtained the BLUEs of location and scale parameters of exponential distribution and logistics distribution. The Fisher information contained in RSS have been discussed by Chen (2000) and Chen and Bai (2000). Stokes (1980) has considered the method of estimation of correlation coefficient of bivariate normal distribution using RSS. Modarres and Zheng (2004) have considered the problem of estimation of dependence parameter using RSS. Robust estimate of correlation coefficient for bivariate normal distribution have been developed by Zheng and Modarres (2006). Stokes (1977) has suggested the ranked set sample mean as an estimator for the mean of the study variate Y, when an auxiliary variable X is used for ranking the sample units, under the assumption that (X, Y) follows a bivariate normal distribution. Barnett and Moore (1997) have improved the estimator of Stokes (1977) by deriving the Best Linear Unbiased Estimator (BLUE) of the mean of the study variate Y, based on ranked set sample obtained on the study variate Y. For current references in this context the reader is referred to Bouza (2001), Singh and Mehta (2013, 2014a, b, 2015, 2016a, b, c, 2017), Mehta and Singh (2015, 2014), and Mehta (2017, 2018a, b), Deka et. al (2021), Alawady (2021), Scaria and Mohan (2021), Abd Elgawad et. al (2020) and Irshad et. al (2019).

1.2. BACKGROUND

Chacko and Thomas (2008) have tried to estimate the mean of the population; under a situation where in measurement of observations are strenuous and expensive. Bain (1978, p. 99) has proposed an exponential distribution for the study variate Y, the oil pollution of the sea samples. Chacko and Thomas (2008) assumed a Morgenstern type bivariate exponential distribution (MTBED) corresponding to a bivariate random variable (X, Y), where X denotes the auxiliary variable (such as tar deposit in the sea shore) and Y denotes the study variable (such as the oil pollution in the sea water).

A random variable (X, Y) follows MTBED if its probability density function (*pdf*) is given by (see, Kotz *et al.* 2000, p. 353)

$$
f(x,y) = \begin{cases} \dfrac{1}{\theta_1\theta_2}\exp\left\{\dfrac{-x}{\theta_1}-\dfrac{y}{\theta_2}\right\}\left[1+\alpha\left[1-2\exp\left\{-\dfrac{x}{\theta_1}\right\}\right]\left[1-2\exp\left\{-\dfrac{y}{\theta_2}\right\}\right]\right] \\ \qquad\qquad\qquad\qquad\quad ;(x,y)>;-1\le\alpha\le1,(\theta_1,\theta_2)>0 \\ 0 \qquad\qquad\qquad\qquad ;Otherwise \end{cases}
$$

$$(1)$$

In this chapter motivated by Searls (1964), Singh *et al.* (1973) and Searls and Intarapanich (1990), we have suggested some improved estimators of the parameter $\theta2$ involved in (1) using ranked set sampling and obtained their biases and mean squared errors. Efficiencies comparisons have been made with Chacko and Thomas (2008) estimators. Numerical illustrations are given in support of the present study.

1.3. MAIN FOCUS OF THE CHAPTER

1.3.1. Minimum Mean Squared Error Estimator for Estimation of $\theta 2$ Based on Censored Ranked Set Sample

Let $Y_{[m_i]m_i}, i = 1, 2, ..., (n - k)$, be the ranked set sample observations on the study variate Y resulting out of censoring and ranking applied on the auxiliary variable X. Then an unbiased estimator of $\theta 2$ based on the ranked set sample mean $\dfrac{\sum\limits_{i=1}^{(n-k)} Y_{[m_i]m_i}}{(n - k)}$ is given by [See, Chacko and Thomas (2008)].

$$\theta_2^* (k) = \frac{2(n+1) \sum\limits_{i=1}^{(n-k)} Y_{[m_i]m_i}}{\left[2(n+1)(n-k) - \alpha \sum\limits_{i=1}^{(n-k)} (n - 2m_i + 1) \right]}, \tag{2}$$

and its variance is given by

$$Var\left[\theta_2^*(k)\right] = MSE\left[\theta_2^*(k)\right] = \theta_2^2 \frac{4(n+1)^2 \sum\limits_{i=1}^{(n-k)} \delta_{m_i}}{\left[2(n+1)(n-k) - \alpha \sum\limits_{i=1}^{(n-k)} (n - 2m_i + 1) \right]^2} = \theta_2^2 V, \tag{3}$$

where

$$V = \frac{4(n+1)^2 \sum\limits_{i=1}^{(n-k)} \delta_{m_i}}{\left[2(n+1)(n-k) - \alpha \sum\limits_{i=1}^{(n-k)} (n - 2m_i + 1) \right]^2}$$

and

$$\delta_{m_i} = 1 - \alpha \frac{\left(n - 2m_i + 1\right)}{2\left(n+1\right)} - \alpha^2 \frac{\left(n - 2m_i + 1\right)^2}{4\left(n+1\right)^2}.$$

We propose a class of estimators for the parameter $\theta 2$ as

$$t\left(k\right) = \lambda \theta_2^*\left(k\right), \tag{4}$$

Where λ is a suitably chosen constant, such that mean squared error (MSE) of t(k) is minimum.

The bias and mean squared error (MSE) of $t(k)$ are respectively given by

$$B[t(k)] = (\lambda - 1)\theta 2, \tag{5}$$

$$MSE\left[t\left(k\right)\right] = \theta_2^2\left[\lambda^2\left(1+V\right) - 2\lambda + 1\right]. \tag{6}$$

The $MSE[t(k)]$ is minimum when

$$\lambda = (1 + V)^{-1}. \tag{7}$$

Now substitution of (7) in (4) yields the minimum MSE estimator of $\theta 2$ as

$$t_m\left(k\right) = \left(1+V\right)^{-1} \frac{2\left(n+1\right) \displaystyle\sum_{i=1}^{\left(n-k\right)} Y_{[m_i]m_i}}{\left[2\left(n+1\right)\left(n-k\right) - \alpha \displaystyle\sum_{i=1}^{\left(n-k\right)}\left(n - 2m_i + 1\right)\right]}. \tag{8}$$

The bias and mean squared error (MSE) of $t_m(k)$ are respectively given by

$$B\left[t_m\left(k\right)\right] = \theta_2\left(-\frac{V}{1+V}\right), \tag{9}$$

$$MSE\left[t_{m}\left(k\right)\right]=\theta_{2}^{2}\left(\frac{V}{1+V}\right).$$ (10)

From (3) and (10) we have

$$Var\left[\theta_{2}^{*}\left(k\right)\right]-MSE\left[t_{m}\left(k\right)\right]=\theta_{2}^{2}\left(\frac{V^{2}}{1+V}\right)>0.$$

Thus the proposed estimator $t_{m}(k)$ is more efficient than $\theta_{2}^{*}\left(k\right)$.

1.3.1.1. Special Case

Let $Y_{[r]r}$, $r=1,2,\ldots,n$, be the ranked set sample observations on a study variate Y obtained out of ranking made on an auxiliary variable X, when (X,Y) follows MTBED as defined in (1). If we put $k=0$ and $m_{i}=i$ in (2) and (3) respectively, we get ranked set sample mean [see, Chacko and Thomas (2008)] based on complete sample as

$$\theta_{2}^{*}=\frac{\sum_{r=1}^{n}Y_{[r]r}}{n},$$ (11)

is unbiased estimator of $\theta2$ and its variance is given by

$$Var\left(\theta_{2}^{*}\right)=MSE\left(\theta_{2}^{*}\right)=\frac{\theta_{2}^{2}}{n}\left[1-\frac{\alpha^{2}}{4n}\sum_{r=1}^{n}\left(\frac{n-2r+1}{n+1}\right)^{2}\right]=\theta_{2}^{2}V_{1},$$ (12)

where

$$V_{1}=\frac{1}{n}\left[1-\frac{\alpha^{2}}{4n}\sum_{r=1}^{n}\left(\frac{n-2r+1}{n+1}\right)^{2}\right].$$

Now substitution of $k=0$ and $m_{i}=i$ in (8), we get a minimum MSE estimator of $\theta2$ based on complete sample in the class of estimators $t=\lambda_{1}\theta_{2}^{*}$, where $\lambda1$ being the suitably chosen scalar such that MSE of t is minimum. So we have

$$t_m = \left(1 + V_1\right)^{-1} \frac{\sum\limits_{r=1}^{n} Y_{[r]r}}{n}.$$

(13)

The bias and mean squared error (MSE) of t_m are respectively given by

$$B\left[t_m\right] = \theta_2 \left(-\frac{V_1}{1 + V_1}\right),$$

(14)

$$MSE\left[t_m\right] = \theta_2^2 \left(\frac{V_1}{1 + V_1}\right).$$

(15)

From (3) and (10) we have

$$Var\left[\theta_2^*\right] - MSE\left[t_m\right] = \theta_2^2 \left(\frac{V_1^2}{1 + V_1}\right) > 0.$$

Thus the proposed estimator t_m is more efficient than θ_2^*.

1.3.2. Minimum Mean Squared Error Estimator for Best Linear Unbiased Estimator of $\theta2$ Based on Censored Ranked Set Sample

Chacko and Thomas (2008) proposed the BLUE of $\theta2$ based on the censored ranked set sample, resulting out of ranking of observations on X as:

$$\hat{\theta}_2\left(k\right) = \frac{\sum\limits_{r=1}^{(n-k)} \left(\frac{\xi_{m_i}}{\delta_{m_i}}\right) Y_{[m_i]m_i}}{\sum\limits_{r=1}^{(n-k)} \left(\frac{\xi_{m_i}^2}{\delta_{m_i}}\right)},$$

(16)

and

$$Var\left[\hat{\theta}_2\left(k\right)\right] = MSE\left[\hat{\theta}_2\left(k\right)\right] = \theta_2^2 \frac{1}{\displaystyle\sum_{r=1}^{(n-k)}\left(\frac{\xi_{m_i}^2}{\delta_{m_i}}\right)} = \theta_2^2 V_2 , \tag{17}$$

where

$$V_2 = \frac{1}{\displaystyle\sum_{r=1}^{(n-k)}\left(\frac{\xi_{m_i}^2}{\delta_{m_i}}\right)}, \quad \xi_{m_i} = 1 - \frac{\alpha\left(n - 2m_i + 1\right)}{2\left(n+1\right)}$$

and

$$\delta_{m_i} = 1 - \frac{\alpha\left(n - 2m_i + 1\right)}{2\left(n+1\right)} - \frac{\alpha^2\left(n - 2m_i + 1\right)^2}{4\left(n+1\right)^2} .$$

We consider a class of estimators for the parameter $\theta2$ as

$$t_1\left(k\right) = \lambda_2 \hat{\theta}_2\left(k\right), \tag{18}$$

Where $\lambda2$ is a suitably chosen constant, such that mean squared error of $t1 k)$ is minimum.

The bias and mean squared error (MSE) of $t_1(k)$ are respectively given by

$$B[t_1(k)] = (\lambda2 - 1)\theta2, \tag{19}$$

$$MSE\left[t_1\left(k\right)\right] = \theta_2^2\left[\lambda_2^2\left(1 + V_2\right) - 2\lambda_2 + 1\right]. \tag{20}$$

The $MSE[t_1(k)]$ is minimum when

$$\lambda2 = (1 + V2)^{-1.} \tag{21}$$

Now substitution of (21) in (18) yields the minimum MSE estimator of $\theta2$ as

$$t_{1m}(k) = \left(1 + V_2\right)^{-1} \frac{\sum\limits_{r=1}^{(n-k)} \left(\frac{\xi_{m_i}}{\delta_{m_i}}\right) Y_{[m_i]m_i}}{\sum\limits_{r=1}^{(n-k)} \left(\frac{\xi_{m_i}^2}{\delta_{m_i}}\right)}.$$

(22)

The bias and mean squared error (MSE) of $t_{1m}(k)$ are respectively given by

$$B\left[t_{1m}(k)\right] = \theta_2 \left(-\frac{V_2}{1 + V_2}\right),$$

(23)

$$MSE\left[t_{1m}(k)\right] = \theta_2^2 \left(\frac{V_2}{1 + V_2}\right).$$

(24)

From (17) and (24) we have

$$Var\left[\hat{\theta}_2(k)\right] - MSE\left[t_{1m}(k)\right] = \theta_2^2 \left(\frac{V_2^2}{1 + V_2}\right) > 0.$$

Thus the proposed estimator $t_{1m}(k)$ is more efficient than $\hat{\theta}_2(k)$.

1.3.2.1. Special Case

If we put $k=0$ and $m_i=i$ in (16) and (17) respectively, we get BLUE $\hat{\theta}_2$ of $\theta 2$ [see, Chacko and Thomas (2008)] based on complete sample as

$$\hat{\theta}_2 = \frac{\sum\limits_{r=1}^{n} \left(\frac{\xi_r}{\delta_r}\right) Y_{[r]r}}{\sum\limits_{r=1}^{r} \left(\frac{\xi_r^2}{\delta_r}\right)},$$

(25)

and

$$Var\left[\hat{\theta}_2\right] = MSE\left[\hat{\theta}_2\right] = \theta_2^2 \frac{1}{\displaystyle\sum_{r=1}^{n}\left(\frac{\xi_r^2}{\delta_r}\right)} = \theta_2^2 V_3, \tag{26}$$

where

$$V_3 = \frac{1}{\displaystyle\sum_{r=1}^{n}\left(\frac{\xi_r^2}{\delta_r}\right)}, \; \xi_r = 1 - \frac{\alpha\left(n - 2r + 1\right)}{2\left(n+1\right)}$$

and

$$\delta_r = 1 - \frac{\alpha\left(n - 2r + 1\right)}{2\left(n+1\right)} - \frac{\alpha^2\left(n - 2r + 1\right)^2}{4\left(n+1\right)^2}.$$

Putting $k=0$ and $m_i=i$ in (22) we get the minimum MSE estimator of $\theta2$ based on complete sample of size n in the class of estimators $t_1 = \lambda_3\hat{\theta}_2$, where $\lambda3$ being suitably chosen constant such that MSE of $t1$ is minimum. So we have

$$t_{1m} = \left(1 + V_3\right)^{-1} \frac{\displaystyle\sum_{r=1}^{n}\left(\frac{\xi_r}{\delta_r}\right)Y_{[r]r}}{\displaystyle\sum_{r=1}^{r}\left(\frac{\xi_r^2}{\delta_r}\right)}. \tag{27}$$

The bias and MSE of t_{1m} are respectively given as

$$B\left[t_{1m}\right] = \theta_2\left(-\frac{V_3}{1 + V_3}\right), \tag{28}$$

$$MSE\left[t_{1m}\right] = \theta_2^2\left(\frac{V_3}{1 + V_3}\right). \tag{29}$$

From (26) and (29) we have

$$Var\left[\hat{\theta}_2\right] - MSE\left[t_{1m}\right] = \theta_2^2 \left(\frac{V_3^2}{1+V_3}\right) > 0 \,.$$

Thus the proposed estimator t_{1m} is more efficient than $\hat{\theta}_2\left(k\right)$.

1.3.3. Minimum Mean Squared Error Estimator for Estimation of θ2 Based on Unbalanced Multistage Ranked Set Sampling

In this section we deal with the MSRSS by assuming that the random variable (X, Y) has MTBED as defined in (1), where Y is the variable of primary interest and X is an auxiliary variable.

Al-Saleh and Al-Kadiri (2000) have extended first the usual concept of RSS to double stage ranked set sampling (DSRSS) with an objective of increasing the precision of certain estimators of the population when compared with those obtained based on usual RSS or using random sampling. Al-Saleh and Al-Omari (2002) have further extended DSRSS to multistage ranked set sampling (MSRSS) and shown that there is increase in the precision of estimators obtained based on MSRSS when compared with those based on usual RSS and DSRSS.

Abo-Eleneen and Nagaraja (2002) have shown that in a bivariate sample of size n arising from MTBED the concomitant of largest order statistic possess the maximum Fisher information on θ2 whenever $\alpha>0$ and the concomitant of smallest order statistic possess the maximum Fisher information on θ2 whenever $\alpha<0$. Hence in this section, first we consider $\alpha>0$ and carry out an unbalanced MSRSS with the help of measurements made on an auxiliary variate to choose the ranked set and then estimate θ2 involved in MTBED based on the measurement made on the variable of primary interest. At each stage and from each set we choose an unit of a sample with the largest value on the auxiliary variable as the units of ranked sets with an objective of exploiting the maximum Fisher information on the ultimately chosen ranked set sample.

Chacko and Thomas (2008) proposed the BLUE of θ2 based on the unbalanced multistage ranked set sampling, resulting out of ranking of observations on X. Let $U_i^{(r)}, i = 1, 2, ..., n$, be the units chosen by the (r stage) MSRSS. Since the measurement of auxiliary variable on each unit $U_i^{(r)}$ has the largest value, we may write $Y_{[n]i}^{(r)}$ to denote the value measured on the variable of primary interest on $U_i^{(r)}, i = 1, 2, ..., n$. Then it is easy to see that each $Y_{[n]i}^{(r)}$ is the concomitant of the largest order statistic of nr independently and identically distributed (i.i.d.) bivariate random variables with MTBED. Moreover $Y_{[n]i}^{(r)}, i = 1, 2, ..., n$, are also independently distributed with *pdf* given by [see, Scaria and Nair (1999)]

$$f_{[n]i}^{(r)}(y; \alpha) = \frac{\exp\left(\dfrac{-y}{\theta_2}\right)}{\theta_2}\left[1 + \alpha\left(\frac{n^r - 1}{n^r + 1}\right)\left\{1 - 2\exp\left(\frac{-y}{\theta_2}\right)\right\}\right]; y > 0, \theta_2 > 0.\qquad(30)$$

The BLUE of $\theta2$ is obtained as

$$\hat{\theta}_2^{n(r)} = \frac{\displaystyle\sum_{i=1}^{n} Y_{[n]i}^{(r)}}{n\xi_{n^r}}\qquad(31)$$

with variance given by

$$Var\left(\hat{\theta}_2^{n(r)}\right) = \theta_2^2 \frac{\delta_{n^r}}{n\left(\xi_{n^r}\right)^2} = \theta_2^2 V_{(r)},\qquad(32)$$

where

$$V_{(r)} = \frac{\delta_{n^r}}{n\left(\xi_{n^r}\right)^2}, \quad \xi_{n^r} = 1 + \frac{\alpha}{2}\left(\frac{n^r - 1}{n^r + 1}\right)$$

and

$$\delta_{n^r} = 1 + \frac{\alpha}{2}\left(\frac{n^r - 1}{n^r + 1}\right) - \frac{\alpha^2}{4}\left(\frac{n^r - 1}{n^r + 1}\right)^2.$$

We propose a class of estimators for the parameter $\theta2$ as

$$t^{(r)} = \lambda_{(r)}\hat{\theta}_2^{n(r)},\qquad(33)$$

where $\lambda_{(r)}$ is a suitably chosen constant such that mean squared error of $t^{(r)}$ is minimum.
The bias and mean squared error (MSE) estimator of $t^{(r)}$ are respectively given as

$$B\left(t^{(r)}\right) = \theta_2 \left(\lambda_{(r)} - 1\right) \tag{34}$$

$$MSE\left(t^{(r)}\right) = \theta_2^2 \left[\lambda_{(r)}^2 \left(V_{(r)} + 1\right) - 2\lambda_{(r)} + 1\right]. \tag{35}$$

The optimum value of $\lambda_{(r)}$ which will minimize the MSE of $t^{(r)}$ is given as

$$\lambda_{(r)} = (1 + V_{(r)})^{-1}. \tag{36}$$

Now using (36) in (33) we have

$$t_m^{(r)} = \frac{\left(1 + V_{(r)}\right)^{-1} \sum_{i=1}^{n} Y_{[n]i}^{(r)}}{n\xi_{n^r}}. \tag{37}$$

The bias and MSE of $t_m^{(r)}$ are respectively given by

$$B\left(t_m^{(r)}\right) = \theta_2 \left(-\frac{V_{(r)}}{1 + V_{(r)}}\right) \tag{38}$$

$$MSE\left(t_m^{(r)}\right) = \theta_2^2 \left(\frac{V_{(r)}}{1 + V_{(r)}}\right). \tag{39}$$

Also from (32) and (39) we have

$$Var\left(\hat{\theta}_2^{n(r)}\right) - MSE\left(t_m^{(r)}\right) = \theta_2^2 \left(\frac{V_{(r)}}{1 + V_{(r)}}\right) > 0.$$

Thus the proposed estimator $t_m^{(r)}$ is more efficient then $\hat{\theta}_2^{n(r)}$.

1.3.3.1. Special Case - (1)

Chacko and Thomas (2008) proposed the BLUE of $\theta 2$ based on the unbalanced single stage ranked set sampling, resulting out of ranking of observations on X, by putting r=1 in (31), (32) the MSRSS method, one can get the usual single stage unbalanced RSS.

Then the BLUE $\hat{\theta}_2^{n(1)}$ of $\theta 2$ is given by

$$\hat{\theta}_2^{n(1)} = \frac{\sum_{i=1}^{n} Y_{[n]i}}{n\xi_n} \tag{40}$$

with variance given by

$$Var\left(\hat{\theta}_2^{n(1)}\right) = \theta_2^2 \frac{\delta_n}{n\left(\xi_n\right)^2} = \theta_2^2 V_{(1)}, \tag{41}$$

where

$$V_{(1)} = \frac{\delta_n}{n\left(\xi_n\right)^2}, \; \xi_n = 1 + \frac{\alpha}{2}\left(\frac{n-1}{n+1}\right)$$

and

$$\delta_n = 1 + \frac{\alpha}{2}\left(\frac{n-1}{n+1}\right) - \frac{\alpha^2}{4}\left(\frac{n-1}{n+1}\right)^2.$$

Putting $r=1$ in (37) we get the minimum MSE estimator of $\theta 2$ based on complete sample of size n in the class of estimators $t^{(1)} = \lambda_{(1)}\hat{\theta}_2^{n(1)}$, where $\lambda_{(1)}$ being suitably chosen constant such that MSE of $t^{(1)}$ is minimum. So we have

$$t_m^{(1)} = \frac{\left(1 + V_{(1)}\right)^{-1} \sum\limits_{i=1}^{n} Y_{[n]i}}{n\xi_n}.$$

(42)

The bias and MSE of $t_m^{(1)}$ are respectively given by

$$B\left(t_m^{(1)}\right) = \theta_2 \left(-\frac{V_{(1)}}{1 + V_{(1)}}\right)$$

(43)

$$MSE\left(t_m^{(1)}\right) = \theta_2^2 \left(\frac{V_{(1)}}{1 + V_{(1)}}\right).$$

(44)

Also from (41) and (44) we have

$$Var\left(\hat{\theta}_2^{n(1)}\right) - MSE\left(t_m^{(1)}\right) = \theta_2^2 \left(\frac{V_{(1)}}{1 + V_{(1)}}\right) > 0.$$

Thus the proposed estimator $t_m^{(1)}$ is more efficient then $\hat{\theta}_2^{n(1)}$.

Further Chacko and Thomas (2008) have $Var\left(\hat{\theta}_2^{1(1)}\right) = Var\left(\hat{\theta}_2^{n(r)}\right)$. Hence $Var\left(\hat{\theta}_2^{1(1)}\right) = Var\left(\hat{\theta}_2^{n(r)}\right)$, where $\hat{\theta}_2^{1(1)}$ are the BLUE of $\theta2$ for $\alpha<0$ based on the usual unbalanced single stage RSS observations $Y[1_{ji,}\ i=1,2,...,n$.

Thus the proposed estimator $t_{m_1}^{(1)}$ is more efficient than $\hat{\theta}_2^{1(1)}$, where $t_{m_1}^{(1)}$ represent the MMSE of $\hat{\theta}_2^{1(1)}$ for $\alpha<0$.i.e.

$$MSE\left(t_m^{(1)}\right) = MSE\left(t_{m_1}^{(1)}\right) \text{ for } \alpha<0.$$

(45)

15

1.3.3.2. Special Case – (2)

Al-Saleh (2004) has considered the steady-state RSS by letting r to $+¥$. Chacko and Thomas (2008) applied the steady-state RSS, then the asymptotic distribution of $Y_{[n]i}^r, i = 1, 2, ..., n$ is given by

$$f_{[n]i}^{\infty}(y; \alpha) = \frac{\exp\left(-\dfrac{y}{\theta_2}\right)\left[1 + \alpha\left\{1 - 2\exp\left(-\dfrac{y}{\theta_2}\right)\right\}\right]}{\theta_2}; y > 0, \theta_2 > 0. \tag{46}$$

From the definition of our unbalanced MSRSS it follows that $Y_{[n]i}^{\infty}, i = 1, 2, ..., n$ are independent and identically distributed random variables each with *pdf* as defined in (46). Then $Y_{[n]i}^{\infty}, i = 1, 2, ..., n$ may be regarded as unbalanced steady-state ranked set sample of size n.

Let $\mathbf{Y}_{[n]}^{(\infty)} = \left(Y_{[n]1}^{(\infty)}, Y_{[n]2}^{(\infty)}, ..., Y_{[n]n}^{(\infty)}\right)'$. Then the BLUE $\hat{\theta}_2^{n(\infty)}$ based on $\mathbf{Y}_{[n]}^{(\infty)}$ and the variance of $\hat{\theta}_2^{n(\infty)}$ is obtained by taking the limits as $r®¥$ in (31) and (32) respectively and are given by

$$\hat{\theta}_2^{n(\infty)} = \frac{\sum\limits_{i=1}^{n} Y_{[n]i}^{(\infty)}}{n\left(1 + \dfrac{\alpha}{2}\right)} \tag{47}$$

and

$$Var\left(\hat{\theta}_2^{n(\infty)}\right) = \theta_2^2 \frac{\left(1 + \dfrac{\alpha}{2} - \dfrac{\alpha^2}{4}\right)}{n\left(1 + \dfrac{\alpha}{2}\right)^2} = \theta_2^2 V_{(\infty)}. \tag{48}$$

where

$$V_{(\infty)} = \frac{\left(1 + \dfrac{\alpha}{2} - \dfrac{\alpha^2}{4}\right)}{n\left(1 + \dfrac{\alpha}{2}\right)^2}.$$

Putting $r \to \infty$ in (37) we get the minimum MSE estimator of $\theta 2$ based on complete sample of size n in the class of estimators $t^{(\infty)} = \lambda_{(\infty)} \hat{\theta}_2^{n(\infty)}$, where $\lambda_{(\infty)}$ being suitably chosen constant such that MSE of $t^{(\infty)}$ is minimum. So we have

$$t_m^{(\infty)} = \frac{\left(1 + V_{(\infty)}\right)^{-1} \sum\limits_{i=1}^{n} Y_{[n]i}^{(\infty)}}{n\left(1 + \dfrac{\alpha}{2}\right)}. \tag{49}$$

The bias and MSE of $t_m^{(\infty)}$ are respectively given as

$$B\left(t_m^{(\infty)}\right) = \theta_2 \left(-\frac{V_{(\infty)}}{1 + V_{(\infty)}}\right), \tag{50}$$

$$Var\left(t_m^{(\infty)}\right) = \theta_2^2 \left(\frac{V_{(\infty)}}{1 + V_{(\infty)}}\right). \tag{51}$$

From (48) and (51) we have

$$Var\left(\hat{\theta}_2^{n(\infty)}\right) - MSE\left(t_m^{(\infty)}\right) = \theta_2^2 \left(\frac{V_{(\infty)}}{1 + V_{(\infty)}}\right) > 0.$$

Thus the proposed estimator $t_m^{(\infty)}$ is more efficient then $\hat{\theta}_2^{n(\infty)}$.

Also the proposed estimator $t_{m_1}^{(\infty)}$ is more efficient then $\hat{\theta}_2^{1(\infty)}$, where $t_{m_1}^{(\infty)}$ is represent the MMSE estimator of $\hat{\theta}_2^{1(\infty)}$ for $\alpha<0$ i.e.

$$MSE\left(t_m^{(\infty)}\right) = MSE\left(t_{m_1}^{(\infty)}\right) \text{ for } \alpha<0. \tag{52}$$

1.4. SOLUTIONS AND RECOMMENDATIONS

To throw some light on the performances of various estimators $\theta_2^*, \hat{\theta}_2, \hat{\theta}_2^{n(1)}, \hat{\theta}_2^{n(\infty)}$; $t_m, t_{1m}, t_m^{(1)}$ and $t_m^{(\infty)}$ of the parameter $\theta 2$, we have computed the relative efficiencies by using the formulae:

$$e_1 = RE\left(t_m, \theta_2^*\right) = \left(1 + V_1\right); \; e_2 = RE\left(t_m, \hat{\theta}_2\right) = \frac{V_3\left(1 + V_1\right)}{V_1};$$

$$e_3 = RE\left(t_{1m}, \theta_2^*\right) = \frac{V_1\left(1 + V_3\right)}{V_3}; \; e_4 = RE\left(t_{1m}, \hat{\theta}_2\right) = \left(1 + V_3\right);$$

$$e_5 = RE\left(t_m^{(1)}, \hat{\theta}_2^{n(1)}\right) = \left(1 + V_{(1)}\right); \; e_6 = RE\left(t_m^{(\infty)}, \hat{\theta}_2^{n(1)}\right) = \frac{V_{(1)}\left(1 + V_{(\infty)}\right)}{V_{(\infty)}};$$

$$e_7 = RE\left(t_m^{(1)}, \hat{\theta}_2^{n(\infty)}\right) = \frac{V_{(\infty)}\left(1 + V_{(1)}\right)}{V_{(1)}}; \; e_8 = RE\left(t_m^{(\infty)}, \hat{\theta}_2^{n(\infty)}\right) = \left(1 + V_{(\infty)}\right).$$

For $n=2(2)10(5)20$ and $\alpha=\pm0.25(0.25)1$.
Findings are shown in Table 1 and Table 2.

1.5. DISCUSSION

It is observed from Table 1 and Table 2 that

(i) for fixed α, the values of REs decrease as n increases.
(ii) for large value of n, there is marginal gain in efficiency. Similar trend of relative efficiencies is observed for fixed sample size n and varying α.

In general the values of $e_i's, i = 1, 2, ..., 8$ are greater than 'unity' for all values of (n, α). Thus the proposed minimum MSE estimators $t_m, t_{1m}, t_m^{(1)}$ and $t_m^{(\infty)}$ of the parameter $\theta 2$ are more efficient than Chacko and Thomas (2008) estimators $\theta_2^*, \hat{\theta}_2, \hat{\theta}_2^{n(1)}$ and $\hat{\theta}_2^{n(\infty)}$ respectively .

1.6. CONCLUSION

In this chapter, we have suggested some improved versions of estimators of Morgenstern type bivariate exponential distribution (MTBED) based on the

Table 1. The values of e_i's, $i = 1, 2, 3, 4 \ldots$

n	α	$e_1^{\oplus}$	e_2	e_3	e_4	α	e_2	e_3	e_4
2	0.25	1.4991	1.4992	1.4991	1.4991	-0.25	1.4992	1.4991	1.4992
2	0.50	1.4965	1.4966	1.4965	1.4966	-0.50	1.4966	1.4965	1.4966
2	0.75	1.4922	1.4921	1.4922	1.4922	-0.75	1.4921	1.4923	1.4921
2	1.00	1.4861	1.4861	1.4861	1.4861	-1.00	1.4861	1.4861	1.4861
4	0.25	1.2492	1.2492	1.2492	1.2492	-0.25	1.2493	1.2492	1.2492
4	0.50	1.2469	1.2468	1.2469	1.2469	-0.50	1.2468	1.2469	1.2469
4	0.75	1.2430	1.2422	1.2435	1.2428	-0.75	1.2421	1.2437	1.2428
4	1.00	1.2375	1.2347	1.2398	1.2370	-1.00	1.2347	1.2398	1.2370
6	0.25	1.1660	1.1661	1.1660	1.1660	-0.25	1.1661	1.1660	1.1661
6	0.50	1.1642	1.1641	1.1643	1.1642	-0.50	1.1640	1.1643	1.1642
6	0.75	1.1611	1.1598	1.1622	1.1609	-0.75	1.1598	1.1622	1.1609
6	1.00	1.1567	1.1519	1.1610	1.1561	-1.00	1.1520	1.1609	1.1561
8	0.25	1.1245	1.1244	1.1245	1.1245	-0.25	1.1245	1.1245	1.1245
8	0.50	1.1230	1.1228	1.1231	1.1230	-0.50	1.1228	1.1231	1.1230
8	0.75	1.1204	1.1189	1.1218	1.1203	-0.75	1.1189	1.1218	1.1203
8	1.00	1.1169	1.1107	1.1225	1.1163	-1.00	1.1107	1.1225	1.1163
10	0.25	1.0996	1.0995	1.0996	1.0996	-0.25	1.0996	1.0996	1.0996
10	0.50	1.0983	1.0981	1.0985	1.0983	-0.50	1.0981	1.0985	1.0983
10	0.75	1.0962	1.0944	1.0977	1.0960	-0.75	1.0944	1.0978	1.0960
10	1.00	1.0932	1.0860	1.0998	1.0926	-1.00	1.0860	1.0998	1.0926
15	0.25	1.0664	1.0663	1.0664	1.0664	-0.25	1.0664	1.0664	1.0664
15	0.50	1.0655	1.0652	1.0657	1.0654	-0.50	1.0651	1.0657	1.0654
15	0.75	1.0639	1.0620	1.0658	1.0638	-0.75	1.0618	1.0659	1.0638
15	1.00	1.0618	1.0531	1.0701	1.0613	-1.00	1.0530	1.0701	1.0613
20	0.25	1.0498	1.0498	1.0498	1.0498	-0.25	1.0498	1.0497	1.0498
20	0.50	1.0491	1.0487	1.0494	1.0490	-0.50	1.0487	1.0494	1.0490
20	0.75	1.0479	1.0457	1.0499	1.0478	-0.75	1.0456	1.0501	1.0478
20	1.00	1.0462	1.0366	1.0555	1.0458	-1.00	1.0366	1.0555	1.0458

$\oplus e_i$ is same for $\alpha < 0$

observations made on the units of ranked set sampling (RSS) regarding the study variable Y which is correlated with the auxiliary variable X, where (X, Y) follows a MTBED. In this chapter we firstly suggested Minimum mean squared error (MMSE) estimator for estimation of $\theta 2$ based on censored ranked set sample and their special

Table 2. The values of The values of e_i's. i=5,6,7,8

n	$\alpha^{\otimes}$	e_5	e_6	e_7	e_8
	0.25	1.4792	1.5726	1.3529	1.4383
	0.50	1.4586	1.6654	1.2086	1.3800
	0.75	1.4383	1.7808	1.0713	1.3264
	1.00	1.4184	1.9245	0.9417	1.2778
	0.25	1.2313	1.2870	1.1664	1.2191
	0.50	1.2131	1.3349	1.0814	1.1900
	0.75	1.1956	1.3943	0.9975	1.1632
	1.00	1.1790	1.4678	0.9148	1.1389
	0.25	1.1519	1.1916	1.1079	1.1461
	0.50	1.1376	1.2238	1.0473	1.1267
2	0.75	1.1240	1.2637	0.9862	1.1088
4	1.00	1.1113	1.3129	0.9248	1.0926
6	0.25	1.1129	1.1437	1.0797	1.1096
8	0.50	1.1013	1.1681	1.0325	1.0950
10	0.75	1.0904	1.1981	0.9844	1.0816
15	1.00	1.0802	1.2351	0.9353	1.0694
20	0.25	1.0899	1.1150	1.0631	1.0877
	0.50	1.0801	1.1345	1.0244	1.0760
	0.75	1.0710	1.1586	0.9847	1.0653
	1.00	1.0625	1.1882	0.9439	1.0556
	0.25	1.0594	1.0767	1.0415	1.0584
	0.50	1.0526	1.0898	1.0148	1.0507
	0.75	1.0461	1.1059	0.9871	1.0435
	1.00	1.0402	1.1256	0.9583	1.0370
	0.25	1.0444	1.0576	1.0308	1.0438
	0.50	1.0391	1.0674	1.0105	1.0380
	0.75	1.0341	1.0795	0.9893	1.0326
	1.00	1.0296	1.0943	0.9670	1.0278

$\otimes$ The values of e_i's, $i = 5,6,7,8$ are same for $\alpha < 0$

case, further we have suggested MMSE Estimator for Best Linear Unbiased Estimator (BLUE) of $\theta 2$ based on censored Ranked Set Sample and their special cases, we also suggested MMSE Estimator for Estimation Of $\theta 2$ Based On Unbalanced Multistage Ranked Set Sampling and their special cases. Efficiency comparisons are also made in this work. In General our all proposed minimum MSE estimators $t_m, t_{1m}, t_m^{(1)}$ and $t_m^{(\infty)}$ of the parameter $\theta 2$, are more efficient than Chacko and Thomas (2008) estimators $\theta_2^*, \hat{\theta}_2, \hat{\theta}_2^{n(1)}$ and $\hat{\theta}_2^{n(\infty)}$ respectively.

Remark: If we have a situation with unknown, we introduce an estimator (moment type) for α as follows. For MTBED the correlation coefficient between the two variables is given by $\frac{\alpha}{4}$. If r is the sample correlation coefficient between $X_{(i)i}$ and $Y_{[i]i}$, $i=1,2,\ldots,n$ then the moment type estimator for α is obtained by equating with the population correlation coefficient ρ and is obtained as [see, Chacko and Thomas (2008)]:

$$\hat{\alpha} = \begin{cases} -1; \ if \ r < \dfrac{-1}{4} \\ 4r; \ if \ \dfrac{-1}{4} \leq r \leq \dfrac{1}{4} \\ 1 \ ; \ if \ r > \dfrac{1}{4} \end{cases} . \tag{53}$$

ACKNOWLEDGMENT

The author is highly thankful to Prof. H. P. Singh, School of Studies in Statistics, Vikram University, Ujjain, Madhya Pradesh, India, for the guidance and constructive suggestions and Prof. C. N. Bouza, Department of Applied Mathematics, University of Havana, Havana, Cuba, for choosing my chapter in this book. Last, but not the least, I am also thankful to all teaching and nonteaching staff members of the Department of Agricultural Statistics, College of Agriculture Campus, Kotawa, Azamgarh, Acharya Narendra Deva University Of Agriculture And Technology (ANDUA & T), Kumarganj, Ayodhya, Uttar Pradesh, India, for providing all the necessary facilities.

REFERENCES

Abd Elgawad, M. A., Alawady, M. A., Barakat, H. M., & Xiong, S. (2020). Concomitants of generalized order statistics from Huang–Kotz Farlie–Gumbel–Morgenstern bivariate distribution: Some information measures. *Bulletin of the Malaysian Mathematical Sciences Society, 43*(3), 2627–2645. doi:10.100740840-019-00822-9

Abo-Eleneen, Z. A., & Nagaraja, H. N. (2002). Fisher information in an order statistic and its concomitant. *Annals of the Institute of Statistical Mathematics, 54*(3), 667–680. doi:10.1023/A:1022479514859

Al-Saleh, M. F. (2004). Steady-state ranked set sampling and parametric inference. *Journal of Statistical Planning and Inference, 123*(1), 83–95. doi:10.1016/S0378-3758(03)00139-3

Al-Saleh, M. F., & Al-Kadiri, M. (2000). Double ranked set sampling. *Statistics & Probability Letters, 48*(2), 205–212. doi:10.1016/S0167-7152(99)00206-0

Al-Saleh, M. F., & Al-Omari, A. (2002). Multistage ranked set sampling. *Journal of Statistical Planning and Inference*, *102*(2), 273–286. doi:10.1016/S0378-3758(01)00086-6

Alawady, M. A., Barakat, H. M., & Abd Elgawad, M. A. (2021). Concomitants of Generalized Order Statistics from Bivariate Cambanis Family of Distributions Under a General Setting. *Bulletin of the Malaysian Mathematical Sciences Society*, *44*(5), 3129–3159. Advance online publication. doi:10.100740840-021-01102-1

Bain, L. J. (1978). *Statistical analysis of reliability and life testing models: theory and methods*. Marcel Dekker.

Barnett, V., & Moore, K. (1997). Best linear unbiased estimates in ranked-set sampling with particular reference to imperfect ordering. *Journal of Applied Statistics*, *24*(6), 697–710. doi:10.1080/02664769723431

Bouza, C. N. (2001). Model assisted ranked survey sampling. *Biometrical Journal. Biometrische Zeitschrift*, *43*(2), 249–259. doi:10.1002/1521-4036(200105)43:2<249::AID-BIMJ249>3.0.CO;2-U

Chacko, M., & Thomas, P. Y. (2008). Estimation of parameter of Morgenstern type bivariate exponential distribution by ranked set sampling. *Annals of the Institute of Statistical Mathematics*, *60*(2), 301–318. doi:10.100710463-006-0088-y

Chen, Z. (2000). The efficiency of ranked-set sampling relative to simple random sampling under multi-parameter families. *Statistica Sinica*, *10*, 247–263.

Chen, Z., & Bai, Z. (2000). The optimal ranked set sampling scheme for parametric families. *Sankhya Series A*, *46*, 178–192.

Chen, Z., Bai, Z., & Sinha, B. K. (2004). *Lecture notes in statistics, ranked set sampling, theory and applications*. Springer. doi:10.1007/978-0-387-21664-5

Deka, D., Das, B., Deka, U., & Baruah, B. K. (2021). Bivariate transmuted exponentiated Gumbel distribution (BTEGD) and concomitants of its order statistics. *J. Math. Comput. Sci.*, *11*(3), 3563–3593.

Irshad, M. R., Maya, R. K., & Arun, S. P. (2019). Estimation of a Parameter of Morgenstern Type Bivariate Lindley Distribution by Ranked Set Sampling. *ISTATISTIK: Journal of the Turkish Statistical Association*, *12*(1-2), 25–34.

Kotz, S., Balakrishnan, N., & Johnson, N. L. (2000). *Distributions in statistics:continuous multivariate distributions*. Wiley. doi:10.1002/0471722065

Lam, K., Sinha, B. K., & Wu, Z. (1994). Estimation of a two-parameter exponential distribution using ranked set sample. *Annals of the Institute of Statistical Mathematics, 46*(4), 723–736. doi:10.1007/BF00773478

Lam, K., Sinha, B. K., & Wu, Z. (1995). Estimation of location and scale parameters of a logistic distribution using ranked set sample. In: H. N. Nagaraja, P. K. Sen, & D. F. Morrison (Eds.), Statistical theory and applications: papers in honor of Herbert A. David. New York: Springer.

McIntyre, G. A. (1952). A method for unbiased selective sampling, using ranked sets. *Australian Journal of Agricultural Research, 3*(4), 385–390. doi:10.1071/AR9520385

Mehta, V. (2017). Shrinkage estimator of the parameters of normal distribution based on K-record values. *Int. J. Sci. Res. Math. Stat. Sci., 4*(1), 1–5.

Mehta, V. (2018a). A New Morgenstern Type Bivariate Exponential Distribution With Known Coefficient Of Variation By Ranked Set Sampling. In Ranked Set Sampling: 65 years improving the accuracy in Data Gathering. Elsevier.

Mehta, V. (2018b). Shrinkage Estimators Of Scale Parameter Towards An Interval Of Morgenstern Type Bivariate Uniform Distribution Using Ranked Set Sampling. In Ranked Set Sampling: 65 years improving the accuracy in Data Gathering . Elsevier.

Mehta, V., & Singh, H. P. (2014). Shrinkage estimators of parameters of Morgenstern type bivariate logistic distribution using ranked set sampling. *J. Basic Appl. Eng. Res., 1*(13), 1–6.

Mehta, V., & Singh, H. P. (2015). *Minimum mean square error estimation of parameters in bivariate normal distribution using concomitants of record values. In Statistics and Informatics in Agricultural Research*. Indian Society of Agricultural Statistics, Excel India Publishers.

Modarres, R., & Zheng, G. (2004). Maximum likelihood estimation of dependence parameter using ranked set sampling. *Statistics & Probability Letters, 68*(3), 315–323. doi:10.1016/j.spl.2004.04.003

Scaria, J., & Mohan, S. (2021). Dependence Concepts and Reliability Application of Concomitants of Order Statistics from the Morgenstern Family. *Journal of Statistical Theory and Applications: JSTA, 20*(2), 193. Advance online publication. doi:10.2991/jsta.d.210325.001

Scaria, J., & Nair, N. U. (1999). On concomitants of order statistics from Morgenstern family. *Biometrical Journal. Biometrische Zeitschrift, 41*(4), 483–489. doi:10.1002/(SICI)1521-4036(199907)41:4<483::AID-BIMJ483>3.0.CO;2-2

Searls, D. T. (1964). The utilization of a know coefficient of variation in the estimation procedure. *Journal of the American Statistical Association, 59*(308), 1225–1226. doi:10.1080/01621459.1964.10480765

Searls, D. T., & Intarapanich, P. (1990). A note on the estimator for the variance that utilizes the kurtosis. *The American Statistician, 44*, 295–296.

Singh, H. P., & Mehta, V. (2013). An improved estimation of parameters of Morgenstern type bivariate logistic distribution using ranked set sampling. *Statistica, 73*(4), 437–461.

Singh, H. P., & Mehta, V. (2014a). Linear shrinkage estimator of scale parameter of Morgenstern type bivariate logistic distribution using ranked set sampling. *Model Assisted Statistics and Applications: An International Journal, 9*(4), 295–307. doi:10.3233/MAS-140301

Singh, H.P. & Mehta, V. (2014b). An alternative estimation of the scale parameter for Morgenstern type bivariate log-logistic distribution using ranked set sampling. *J. Reliab. Stat. Stud., 7*(1), 19-29.

Singh, H. P., & Mehta, V. (2015). Estimation of scale parameter of a Morgenstern type bivariate uniform distribution using censored ranked set samples. *Model Assisted Statistics and Applications: An International Journal, 10*(2), 139–153. doi:10.3233/MAS-140315

Singh, H. P., & Mehta, V. (2016a). Improved estimation of scale parameter of Morgenstern type bivariate uniform distribution using ranked set sampling. *Communications in Statistics. Theory and Methods, 45*(5), 1466–1476. doi:10.10 80/03610926.2013.864767

Singh, H. P., & Mehta, V. (2016b). Some classes of shrinkage estimators in the Morgenstern type bivariate exponential distribution using ranked set sampling. *Hacettepe Journal of Mathematics and Statistics, 45*(2), 575–591. doi:10.15672/ HJMS.201611415693

Singh, H. P., & Mehta, V. (2016c). A class of shrinkage estimators of scale parameter of uniform distribution based on K-record values. *National Academy Science Letters, 39*(3), 221–227. doi:10.100740009-016-0438-0

Singh, H. P., & Mehta, V. (2017). Improved estimation of the scale parameter for log-logistic distribution using balanced ranked set sampling. *Stat. Trans: New Ser., 18*(1), 53-74.

Singh, J., Pandey, B. N., & Hirano, K. (1973). On the utilization of known coefficient of kurtosis in the estimation procedure of variance. *Annals of the Institute of Statistical Mathematics, 25*(1), 51–55. doi:10.1007/BF02479358

Stokes, S. L. (1977). Ranked set sampling with concomitant variables. *Communications in Statistics. Theory and Methods, 6*(12), 1207–1211. doi:10.1080/03610927708827563

Stokes, S. L. (1980). Inference on the correlation coefficient in bivariate normal populations from ranked set samples. *Journal of the American Statistical Association, 75*(372), 989–995. doi:10.1080/01621459.1980.10477584

Stokes, S. L. (1995). Parametric ranked set sampling. *Annals of the Institute of Statistical Mathematics, 47*, 465–482.

Zheng, G., & Modarres, R. (2006). A robust estimate of correlation coefficient for bivariate normal distribution using ranked set sampling. *Journal of Statistical Planning and Inference, 136*(1), 298–309. doi:10.1016/j.jspi.2004.06.006

Chapter 2
Item Count Technique in Ranked Set Sampling

Beatriz Cobo

(iD) https://orcid.org/0000-0003-2654-0032
University of Granada, Spain

Elvira Pelle
University of Modena and Reggio Emilia, Italy

ABSTRACT

In situations where the estimation of the proportion of sensitive variables relies on the observations of real measurements that are difficult to obtain, there is a need to combine indirect questioning techniques. In the present work, the authors will focus on the item count technique, with alternative methods of sampling, such as the ranked set sampling. They are based on the idea proposed by Santiago et al., which combines the randomized response technique proposed by Warner together with ranked set sampling. The authors will carry out a simulation study to compare the item count technique under ranked set sampling and under simple random sampling without replacement.

INTRODUCTION

In human population surveys that involve sensitive or stigmatizing attributes, it can be difficult to obtain a real measure that reflects the true status of the survey participants. In fact, especially when sensitive questions are asked directly, survey participants may refuse to answer or provide false responses that can compromise the reliability of the survey results.

DOI: 10.4018/978-1-7998-7556-7.ch002

One possibility to improve the cooperation of respondents, and thus obtain more reliable answers, is to protect their privacy by taking an indirect questioning approach. The rationale for this approach is that survey participants are not asked questions about the sensitive topic directly, so their privacy is protected.

In this context, an important role is placed by the so-called randomized response technique (RRT), designed to reduce non-response and obtain more frank and reliable answers to sensitive questions. Among RRT, the present work focuses on the item count technique (ICT). In particular, the objective is to improve the estimation of a sensitive proportion under the ICT, using an alternative sampling method that is the ranked set sampling (RSS).

The rest of the chapter is organized as follows: since both RSS and ICT are central in this chapter, the next section provides background on both topics. Then, the use of the ICT in a RSS framework is proposed for the estimation of a sensitive attribute. A simulation study is presented to compare, under different scenarios, the efficiency of the proposed estimator under RSS with its counterpart under simple random sampling (SRS) without replacement. Finally, a conclusion section ends the chapter with a final discussion.

BACKGROUND

Ranked Set Sampling

Ranked set sampling is an ingenious statistical sampling scheme first proposed by McIntyre (1952) useful in situations where the variable of interest is difficult to measure (for example, because it is too expensive, time-consuming or destructive), but observations can be easily ranked at no additional cost or at very low cost. Although this assumption may seem prohibitive, many real situations have fulfilled this requirement, improving the diffusion of the method in the literature (among others, see Chen et. al, 2004).

The rationale for RSS is to obtain a sample of units "that are more likely to cover the entire range of values in the population and, therefore, is more representative of it than the same number of observations obtained by simple random sampling" (Wolfe, 2012).

Let $U=\{1, …, N\}$ be a finite population of N units and let Y be the variable under study. Suppose that Y cannot be easily measured, but potential sampled units can be classified according to an economic classification criterion (such as visual inspection, personal judgment, expert opinion). Suppose that the parameter of interest, say ϑ_Y, is unknown and must be estimated on the basis of a ranked set sample.

The original procedure proposed by McIntyre consists of a *balanced* RSS. The procedure can be described in terms of *cycles*. A cycle can be summarized in the following steps:

1. draw a sample of size k from the population of interest according to simple random sampling (SRS);
2. rank the selected units in each sample, without measuring the variable of interest (by any cheap classification criteria);
3. from the j-th sample, $j=1,..., k$, select the unit with rank j to be included in the ranked sample.

Then, the complete cycle (steps 1-3) is repeated m times, in order to obtain a final ranked set sample of size $n=km$. Therefore, in each cycle, m^2 units are observed, but only m are selected in the final ranked set sample. McIntyre's proposal assumes that the ranking is perfect, that is, the rank of the units reflects the order that would be obtained with respect to the variable of interest, if it is measured. Consequently, the measured values of Y are called *order statistics*. Many contributions on imperfect ranking have been proposed in the literature (see Chen et al. 2004 for a review). In this work the perfect ranking is assumed.

Note that the term balanced refers to the fact that the final sample is made up of the same number of units for each of the ranks. Many authors have proposed the use of *unbalanced* RSS for the estimation of the parameter of interest (see, for example, Chen et al., 2004 and Wolfe, 2012 for a review).

The reason for the success of RSS can be traced to the fact that, as is known, estimation through RSS is more efficient than estimation through SRS (see, among others, Dell and Clutter, 1972, Patil, 2002, Chen et al., 2004). In fact, since McIntyre seminal article, the literature on the subject has grown rapidly, as several methodological variants and extensions of the original procedure have been proposed, for example, Haq et al. (2015) were based on the linear unbiased estimators obtained under ordered ranked set sampling and ordered imperfect ranked set sampling to obtain improved exponentially weighted moving average control charts for monitoring process mean and dispersion, Omari and Zamanzade (2017) suggested some new goodness-of-fit tests based on the sample entropy and empirical distribution function for the Laplace distribution using ranked set sampling, and Zamanzade and Vock (2018) developed parametric and location-scale free tests of perfect judgment ranking based on ordered ranked set samples (see, Al-Omari and Bouza, 2014, Wolfe, 2012, and Bouza and Omari 2018 for a review).

Let us consider the procedure described above and suppose that the interest is in estimating the unknown population mean. Let $y_{(j)r}$ be the j-th smallest unit in sample $j, j=1, ..., k$, in the r-th cycle, $r=1, ..., m$, that is, the unit included in the final ranked set sample for the measurement of the variable under study. The RSS estimator of the population mean μ_Y is defined as

$$\bar{y} = \frac{1}{mk} \sum_{r=1}^{m} \sum_{j=1}^{k} y_{(j)r}.$$

Stokes (1997) proposed ordering the sample units on the basis of the value of the auxiliary variable, say X rather than a subjective judgment on the variable of interest Y. A common assumption when the units are ordered with respect to an auxiliary variable is that the ranking is perfect with respect to X, while it may be imperfect with respect to Y. In recent years, an increasing number of estimators that exploit additional information from auxiliary variables have been re-proposed and adapted in the context of RSS. It should be taken into account that if the ranking is based on an auxiliary variable and this is closely related to the sensitive characteristic, then it can reduce the cooperation of the respondents because they will see their privacy violated (see, for example, Pelle and Perri, 2018, and the references therein).

RSS can be successfully adopted also for the estimation of the unknown population proportion. Now suppose that the character of study Y is a binary variable and that the interest is in estimating the proportion of the unknown population, say p. As is well known, in such cases the proportion of the population is equal to the mean of the population, but calculated on a binary variable. Consequently, the RSS estimator for the proportion takes the form

$$\bar{p} = \frac{1}{mk} \sum_{r=1}^{m} \sum_{j=1}^{k} y_{(j)r}$$

where $y_{(j)r}$ can assume only 0 or 1 value.

When dealing with dichotomous variables in a RSS framework, a crucial issue concerns the ranking of units in the sampling procedure. Chen et al. (2005) proposed the use of a logistic regression model to estimate the probability of success of the possible sampling units. They used these probabilities as criteria for ordering the sample units to select a ranked set sample (as described above). In this scenario, Chen (2008) has shown that the variance can be expressed as:

$$Var\left(\bar{p}_{RSS}\right) = \frac{1}{nm} \sum_{r=1}^{m} p_{(r)}\left(1 - p_{(r)}\right)$$

where $p_{(r)}$ represents the probability of success for the r-th order statistic.

Item Count Technique

Indirect questioning techniques arose from the need to protect the privacy and maintain the anonymity of the respondents. Among them are the randomized response techniques, introduced by Warner in 1965, which emerged as techniques for estimating binary qualitative variables. In its original version, this non-standard survey approach adopts a randomization device such as a deck of cards, dice, coins, colored numbered balls, spinning wheels, or even a computer to hide the true answer, in the sense that the respondents answer one of two or more questions selected according to the result of the device. Randomization is performed by the interviewee and the interviewer is not allowed to observe the result of the randomization. The interviewee answers the question selected by the randomization device and the interviewer only knows the answer provided. The privacy or anonymity of the respondent is fully protected because no one other than the respondent knows which question was answered. Since many studies are based on quantitative sensitive variables, randomized response techniques were subsequently developed for these variables.

Despite the good reputation of RRTs, they have some limitations, which is why over the years other techniques have emerged such as the nominative technique (Miller, 1985), the three-card method (Droitcour and Larson, 2002), the non-randomized response technique (Tian and Tang, 2014) and the item count technique, (Raghavarao and Federer, 1979; Miller, 1984). We focus on ICT for simplify implementation.

The goal of the item count technique, also known as "unmatched count technique", "block total response" or "list experiment"', is to determine the prevalence of a sensitive attribute A in a population. The ICT consists of drawing two independent samples from the target population.

Without loss of generality, the units belonging to long list (LL) sample, s_{ll}, are given with a LL of items containing $(G+1)$ dichotomous questions, G of which are not sensitive, while the remaining refers to the sensitive attribute A. Sample units are instructed to consider the LL and count and report the number of items that apply to them (i.e., the number of "yes" responses) without answering each question individually.

Consequently, the privacy of respondents is protected, as their true sensitive status remains undisclosed unless they report that none or all of the items on the list apply to them. Therefore, the items included in the ICT list should be chosen carefully to minimize the possibility of floor and ceiling effects, that is, that participants prefer all or none of the items. Such effects can be problematic because they effectively reveal the participant's attitude towards the sensitive item (Blair and Imai 2012, Glynn 2013). In Gibson et al. 2018 propose a solution to this problem. In this article they focused on previous research to mitigate floor / ceiling effects, and selected four items so that one item was expected to be unpopular, another to be popular, and two items to be considered incompatible.

On the contrary, the units that belong to the short list (SL) sample, s_{sl}, are asked to give a response similar to a SL of items, which contain only the G innocuous questions that are identical to those present in the LL.

Innocuous items should be chosen and written in sufficient quantity to ensure the necessary variability in their application to the population units and should be measured in the same units as sensitive variables to maintain privacy.

Consider a finite population $U=\{1,\ldots,N\}$ consisting of N different and identifiable units. Let y_i be the value of the sensitive character under study, say Y, for the ith population unit. Suppose that the population proportion $\bar{Y} = \dfrac{1}{N}\sum_{i\in U}^{N} y_i$ is unknown and must be estimated in an ICT environment.

Suppose that s_{ll} and s_{sl}, are selected from U according to the generic sampling designs $p_{ll}()$ and $p_{sl}()$ with positive first and second order inclusion probabilities

$$\pi_{i(ll)} = \sum_{s_{ll}\ni i} p_{ll}\left(s_{ll}\right), \pi_{ij(ll)} = \sum_{s_{ll}\ni i,j} p_{ll}\left(s_{ll}\right), \pi_{i(sl)} = \sum_{s_{sl}\ni i} p_{sl}\left(s_{sl}\right),$$

and $\pi_{ij(sl)} = \sum_{s_{sl}\ni i,j} p_{sl}\left(s_{sl}\right)$ with $i,j\in U$. Let

$$d_{i(ll)} = \pi_{i(ll)}^{-1}, d_{ij(ll)} = \pi_{ij(ll)}^{-1}, d_{i(sl)} = \pi_{i(sl)}^{-1},$$

and $d_{ij(sl)} = \pi_{ij(sl)}^{-1}$ denote the known sampling design-basic weight for unit $i\in U$ in each sampling design.

Without loss of generality, let T be the variable that denotes the total score applicable to the G non-sensitive questions, and $Z=Y+T$ the total score applicable to the non-sensitive questions and the sensitive question. Therefore, the answer given by the ith respondent will be

$$z_i = \begin{cases} y_i + t_i, if\ i \in s_{ll} \\ t_i, if\ i \in s_{sl} \end{cases}$$

In order to introduce the estimator of $\bar{Y}$ under ICT framework, let consider the Horvitz-Thompson (HT) estimator (Horvitz and Thompson, 1952) for the T and Z variables. The use of the HT estimator is motivated by its well-known properties, such as its unbiasedness and applicability to any probability sampling design, which have ensured a central role in sampling theory. Furthermore, it enables to directly estimate the parameter of interest and to obtain an unbiased estimator for its variance. Thus, under the sampling designs $p_{ll}(),p_{sl}()$ let:

$$\widehat{\bar{Z}}_{HT} = \frac{1}{N}\sum_{i \in s_{ll}} d_{i(ll)} z_i, \widehat{\bar{T}}_{HT} = \frac{1}{N}\sum_{i \in s_{sl}} d_{i(sl)} t_i$$

be the unbiased HT estimators of $\bar{Z} = N^{-1}\sum_{i \in U}\left(y_i + t_i\right)$ and $\bar{T} = N^{-1}\sum_{i \in U} t_i$, respectively.

Therefore, a HT-type estimator of $\bar{Y}$ under the ICT can be easily obtained as:

$$\widehat{\bar{Y}}_{HT} = \widehat{\bar{Z}}_{HT} - \widehat{\bar{T}}_{HT}$$

From the unbiasedness of $\widehat{\bar{Z}}_{HT}$ and $\widehat{\bar{T}}_{HT}$, it follows easily that the estimator $\widehat{\bar{Y}}_{HT}$ is unbiased for $\bar{Y}$. Furthermore, as long as the two samples are independent, the variance of $\widehat{\bar{Y}}_{HT}$ can be expressed as:

$$V\left(\widehat{\bar{Y}}_{HT}\right) = V\left(\widehat{\bar{Z}}_{HT}\right) + V\left(\widehat{\bar{T}}_{HT}\right) = \frac{1}{N^2}\left[\sum_{i,j \in U}\sum\Delta_{ij(ll)} d_{i(ll)} z_i d_{j(ll)} z_j + \sum_{i,j \in U}\sum\Delta_{ij(sl)} d_{i(sl)} t_i d_{j(sl)} t_j\right],$$

where $\Delta_{ij(a)} = \pi_{ij(a)} - \pi_{i(a)}\pi_{j(a)}$ with $a=ll,sl$. An unbiased estimator of $V\left(\widehat{\bar{Y}}_{HT}\right)$ is given by:

$$\hat{V}\left(\widehat{\bar{Y}}_{HT}\right) = \frac{1}{N^2}\left[\sum_{i,j \in s_{ll}}\sum d_{ij(ll)}\Delta_{ij(ll)} d_{i(ll)} z_i d_{j(ll)} z_j + \sum_{i,j \in s_{sl}}\sum d_{ij(sl)}\Delta_{ij(sl)} d_{i(sl)} t_i d_{j(sl)} t_j\right]$$

Item Count Technique in a Ranked Set Sampling Framework

The present work aims at combining ICT with RSS. To the best of our knowledge, there are no contributions in literature that propose the use of ICT in a RSS framework, so that the suggested approach represents an original algorithm that can be used for the estimation of the unknown proportion of a sensitive issue.

Suppose that the interest is in estimating the prevalence of a sensitive attribute, say Y, in the population under study. The attribute Y is a dichotomous variable, which takes a value of 1 if the unit in the population has the sensitive characteristic (with probability p) and 0 otherwise. In other words, p represents the prevalence to be estimated.

In order to perform ICT in the context of RSS, two different samples are selected according to the RSS procedure described in the background section. In particular, the units of the first sample, say $s_{ll(RSS)}$, will be given a LL of items containing $(G+1)$ dichotomous questions, G of which are not sensitive, while the remainder will be refers to the sensitive attribute Y. By contrast, the units in the second sample, say $s_{sl(RSS)}$, will receive a SL of items containing the same G dichotomous harmless questions present in LL.

Let $\pi_{i(llRSS)}, \pi_{ij(llRSS)}, \pi_{i(slRSS)}$, and $\pi_{ij(slRSS)}$ with $i,j \in U$ be first and second order inclusion probabilities and let $d_{i(llRSS)} = \pi^{-1}_{i(llRSS)}, d_{ij(llRSS)} = \pi^{-1}_{ij(llRSS)}, d_{i(slRSS)} = \pi^{-1}_{i(slRSS)}$, and $d_{ij(slRSS)} = \pi^{-1}_{ij(sl)}$ denote the known RSS weight for unit $i \in U$.

Similar to section 2, let T be the variable that denotes the total score applicable to the G non-sensitive questions, and $Z=Y+T$ the total score applicable to the non-sensitive questions and the sensitive question. Therefore, the answer given by the ith respondent will be

$$z_i = \begin{cases} y_i + t_i, if\ i \in s_{ll(RSS)} \\ t_i\ if\ i \in s_{sl(RSS)} \end{cases}$$

Thus, it is possible to define:

$$\widehat{\overline{Z}}_{HTRSS} = \frac{1}{N} \sum_{i \in s_{llRSS}} d_{i(llRSS)} z_i, \qquad \widehat{\overline{T}}_{HTRSS} = \frac{1}{N} \sum_{i \in s_{slRSS}} d_{i(slRSS)} t_i$$

What are the unbiased HT estimators of $\overline{Z} = N^{-1} \sum_{i \in U} (y_i + t_i)$ and $\overline{T} = N^{-1} \sum_{i \in U} t_i$, respectively.

Therefore, a HT-type estimator of $\overline{Y}$ under ICT in a RSS framework can be easily obtained as:

$$\widehat{\overline{Y}}_{HTRSS} = \widehat{\overline{Z}}_{HTRSS} - \widehat{\overline{T}}_{HTRSS}$$

Its variance can be expressed as:

$$V\left(\widehat{\overline{Y}}_{HTRSS}\right) = V\left(\widehat{\overline{Z}}_{HTRSS}\right) + V\left(\widehat{\overline{T}}_{HTRSS}\right) = \frac{1}{N^2}\left[\sum_{i=1}^{N}\left(1 - \pi_{i(llRSS)}\right)z_i^2 d_{i(llRSS)}\right.$$

$$\left. + 2\sum_{i<j}\Delta_{ij(llRSS)}\, d_{i(llRSS)}\, z_i d_{j(llRSS)}\, z_j + \sum_{i=1}^{N}\left(1 - \pi_{i(slRSS)}\right)t_i^2 d_{i(slRSS)} + 2\sum_{i<j}\Delta_{ij(slRSS)}\, d_{i(slRSS)}\, t_i d_{j(slRSS)}\, t_j\right]$$

where $\Delta_{ij(a)} = \pi_{ij(a)} - \pi_{i(a)}\pi_{j(a)}$ with $a=llRSS, slRSS$.

The next section analyzes a simulation study designed to compare the proposed estimator in the RSS framework with the corresponding estimator in SRS without replacement.

SIMULATION STUDY

In this section, a simulation study is presented to evaluate the performance of the method discussed above. The simulation makes it possible to compare ICT when the sample is drawn by simple random sampling without replacement (SRSWOR) and ICT in a ranked set sampling.

For this, $N=50000$ artificial observations are generated for the sensitive variable Y and the innocuous T, and two auxiliary variables Y_{aux}, X correlated with Y. It is assumed that Y, Y_{aux}, X are observed from a multivariate Bernoulli distribution with probability of success $ps= (0.4, 0.5, 0.6)$ and different values of the correlation coefficients, $\rho_{\{Y, Yaux\}} = 0.8, \rho_{\{Y, X\}} = 0.5$, and T is a Bernouilli distribution with $ps=0.5$. The generated values are used to define the total score variable in the long list $Z=Y+T$ and the short list $Z=T$.

In this first case, the samples are selected according to SRSWOR, in the second case according to RSS and a logistic regression model is adjusted to calculate the probability of having the sensitive attribute for each population unit. These computed probabilities represent the ordering criterion that allows obtaining the indices of the individuals that will be part of the sample. In particular, the logistic regression model takes the form:

$$\text{logit}\left(p\right) = \log\left(\frac{p}{1-p}\right) = \alpha + \mathbf{\beta}'X$$

where α represents the intercept parameter, $X = \left(Y_{aux}, X\right)$ is the vector of auxiliary variables and β is the vector of slope parameters (Chen et al., 2005). Therefore, the probability of having Y for unit i in the population can be estimated as

$$\widehat{p}_i = \frac{e^{\hat{\alpha} + \widehat{\beta}'X_i}}{1 + e^{\hat{\alpha} + \widehat{\beta}'X_i}} \qquad \text{for } i = 1, \dots, n.$$

Once these probabilities have been estimated for each unit of the population, a ranked set sample can be selected according to the following procedure:

1. a sample of size k is drawn from the entire population according to SRS;
2. the units selected in each sample are ranked according to the estimated probabilities p_j, $j=1,\dots,k$;
3. from the j-th sample, $j=1,\dots,k$; select the unit with rank j to be included in the ranked sample.

Then, the complete cycle (steps 1-3) is repeated m times, in order to obtain a final ranked set sample of size $n=km$.

Therefore, for each possible scenario, the estimated proportion and variance of the estimators in the case of ICT are evaluated, using $B=1000$ runs and different sample sizes, from n=50, 100, 150,..., 500, considering the set size k=50 and number of cycles m=n/k.

To evaluate the performance of ICT in SRSWOR and RSS, the absolute relative bias (ARB), the relative mean square error and the relative efficiency (RE) are calculated as

$$ARB = \frac{1}{B}\sum_B \frac{\left|\hat{P}_{method} - P_T\right|}{P_T}$$

$$RMSE = \frac{1}{B}\sum_B \frac{\left(\hat{P}_{method} - P_T\right)^2}{P_T^2}$$

where $method = ICT_{SRSWOR}, ICT_{RSS}$ and P_T is the theoretical proportion,

$$RE_{ICT} = \frac{\hat{V}_{ICT_{SRSWOR}}}{\hat{V}_{ICT_{RSS}}}$$

with

$$\hat{V}_{method} = \frac{1}{B}\sum_{B}\hat{V}_{method}$$

where $method = ICT_{SRSWOR}, ICT_{RSS}$

The results are shown in Figures 1, 2 and 3.

Figure 1. Absolute relative bias (own elaboration)

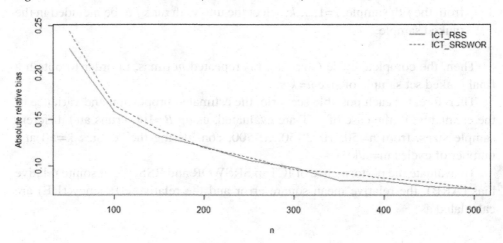

As expected, the absolute relative bias and the relative mean square error in SRSWOR are higher than RSS when the sample size is low, but the difference becomes negligible as the sample size increases.

In the case of relative efficiency, it is possible to notice that two methods are very similar, although the variance in the case of RSS is slightly higher. This loss of efficiency is offset by obtaining estimators closer to the real one.

The following table shows the values of the absolute relative bias and the relative mean square error in the two sampling schemes considered.

Figure 2. Relative mean square error (own elaboration)

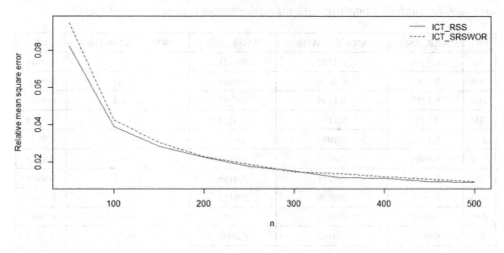

Figure 3. Relative efficiency (own elaboration)

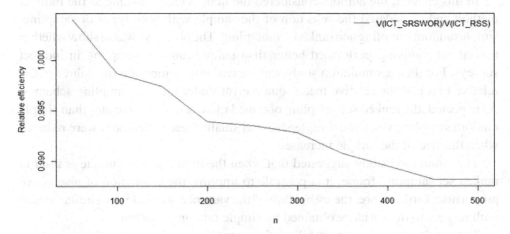

CONCLUSION

In the case of direct surveys, it is a well-known fact that the ranked set sampling works better than simple random sampling. However, when conducting a survey on sensitive topics, researchers have to grapple with an additional problem, known as social desirability bias. The way to avoid this type of bias is through indirect surveys, as many authors have shown since the seminal article proposed by Warner in 1965.

Table 1. Absolute relative bias and relative mean square error in ranked set sampling and simple random sampling without replacement and relative efficiency

n	ARB_RSS	ARB_SRSWOR	RMSE_RSS	RMSE_SRSWOR	RE
50	0.2260	0.2442	0.0821	0.0947	1.0041
100	0.1581	0.1648	0.0388	0.0425	0.9987
150	0.1318	0.1394	0.0281	0.0304	0.9974
200	0.1204	0.1196	0.0224	0.0227	0.9939
250	0.1063	0.1093	0.0176	0.0186	0.9935
300	0.0984	0.0964	0.0151	0.0146	0.9928
350	0.0845	0.0931	0.0116	0.0137	0.9908
400	0.0840	0.0876	0.0113	0.0121	0.9895
450	0.0782	0.0832	0.0093	0.0107	0.9882
500	0.0761	0.0768	0.0091	0.0093	0.9882

Source: (own elaboration)

In this chapter, the authors considered the item count technique as the indirect method and considered the selection of the sample with both types of sampling, simple random sampling and ranked set sampling. The objective was to show whether ranked set sampling performed better than simple random sampling in indirect surveys. For this, a simulation study was carried out, comparing the values of the relative bias and the relative mean square error under the two sampling schemes. As expected, the ranked set sampling obtained more accurate estimates than simple random sampling when the sample size was small; these differences were reduced when the size of the sample increased.

The simulation study suggested that when the item count technique is used in ranked set sampling frame, it is possible to improve the estimation of a sensitive proportion; furthermore, the estimation of the variance showed very similar values with respect to the variance obtained by simple random sampling.

The results showed the suitability of the proposal for estimating the proportion of sensitive variables.

Finally, it is important to note that the proposed approach offers some advantages that facilitate its use in real studies, particularly in the social sciences and medicine applications. Indeed, it is easily applicable to all situations where the interest is in the estimation of a sensitive proportion of a population; furthermore, the RSS framework eases its implementation, since it would allow researchers to save time and money when putting it into practice.

ACKNOWLEDGMENT

This research was supported by the Ministry of Education and Science [grant numbers MTM2015-63609-R, Spain].

REFERENCES

Al-Omari, A. I., & Bouza, C. N. (2014). Review of ranked set sampling: Modifications and applications. *Investigación Operacional*, *35*(3), 215–235.

Al-Omari, A. I., & Zamanzade, E. (2017). Goodness of-fit-tests for Laplace distribution in ranked set sampling. *Revista Investigación Operacional*, *38*(4), 366–276.

Blair, G., & Imai, K. (2012). Statistical analysis of list experiments. *Political Analysis*, *20*(1), 47–77. doi:10.1093/pan/mpr048

Bouza, C. N., & Al-Omari, A. I. (2018). *Ranked Set Sampling, 65 Years Improving the Accuracy in Data Gathering*. Elsevier.

Chen, H. (2008). Alternative ranked set sample estimators for the variance of a sample proportion. *Applied Statistics Research Progress*, 35.

Chen, H., Stasny, E. A., & Wolfe, D. A. (2005). Ranked set sampling for efficient estimation of a population proportion. *Statistics in Medicine*, *24*(21), 3319–3329. doi:10.1002im.2158 PMID:16100735

Chen, Z., Bai, Z., & Sinha, B. K. (2004). *Ranked Set Sampling. Theory and Applications*. Springer. doi:10.1007/978-0-387-21664-5

Dell, T. R., & Clutter, J. L. (1972). Ranked set sampling theory with order statistics Background. *Biometrika*, *28*(2), 545–555. doi:10.2307/2556166

Droitcour, J. A., & Larson, E. M. (2002). An innovative technique for asking sensitive questions: The three-card method. *Bulletin of Sociological Methodology*, *75*(1), 5–23. doi:10.1177/075910630207500103

Gibson, M. A., Gurmu, E., Cobo, B., Rueda, M. M., & Scott, I. M. (2018). Indirect questioning method reveals hidden support for female genital cutting in Southern Ethiopia. *PLoS One*, *13*(5), e0193985. doi:10.1371/journal.pone.0193985 PMID:29718908

Glynn, A. N. (2013). What can we learn with statistical truth serum? Design and analysis of the list experiment. *Public Opinion Quarterly*, *77*(S1), 159–172. doi:10.1093/poq/nfs070

Haq, A., Brown, J., Moltchanova, E., & Al-Omari, A. I. (2015). Improved exponentially weighted moving average control charts for monitoring process mean and dispersion. *Quality and Reliability Engineering International*, *31*(2), 217–237. doi:10.1002/qre.1573

Horvitz, D. G., & Thompson, D. J. (1952). A generalization of sampling without replacement from a finite universe. *Journal of the American Statistical Association*, *47*(260), 663–685. doi:10.1080/01621459.1952.10483446

McIntyre, G. A. (1952). A method of unbiased selective sampling using ranked sets. *Australian Journal of Agricultural Research*, *3*(4), 385–390. doi:10.1071/AR9520385

Miller, J. D. (1984). *A New Survey Technique for Studying Deviant Behavior* [Ph.D. Thesis]. The George Washington University.

Miller, J. D. (1985). The Nominative Technique: A New Method of Estimating Heroin Prevalence. *NIDA Research Monograph*, *57*, 104–124. PMID:3929108

Patil, G. P. (2002). Ranked Set Sampling. In A. H. El-Shaarawy & W. W. Piegorsch (Eds.), *Encyclopedia of Environmetrics*. John Wiley and Sons.

Pelle, E., & Perri, P. F. (2018). Improving mean estimation in ranked set sampling using the Rao regression-type estimator. *Brazilian Journal of Probability and Statistics*, *32*(3), 467–496. doi:10.1214/17-BJPS350

Raghavarao, D., & Federer, W. F. (1979). Block total response as an alternative to the randomized response method in survey. *Journal of the Royal Statistical Society. Series B. Methodological*, *41*(1), 40–45. doi:10.1111/j.2517-6161.1979.tb01055.x

Santiago, A., Sautto, J. M., & Bouza, C. N. (2019). Randomized estimation a proportion using ranked set sampling and Warner's. *Investigação Operacional*, *40*(3), 356–361.

Stokes, S.L. (1977). Ranked set sampling with concomitant variables. *Communications in Statistics – Theory & Methods A*, *6*(12), 1207-1211.

Tian, G.L., & Tang, M.L. (2014). *Incomplete Categorical Data Design: Non-Randomized Response Techniques for Sensitive Questions in Surveys*. Chapman & Hall/CRC (Statistics in the Social and Behavioral Sciences).

Warner, S. L. (1965). Randomized response: A survey technique for eliminating evasive answer bias. *Journal of the American Statistical Association, 60*(309), 63–69. doi:10.1080/01621459.1965.10480775 PMID:12261830

Wolfe, D. A. (2012). Ranked set sampling: Its relevance and impact on statistical inference. *ISRN Probability and Statistics*.

Zamanzade, E., & Vock, M. (2018). Parametric tests of perfect judgment ranking based on ordered ranked set samples. *Revista de Statistica, 16*(4), 463–474.

Chapter 3
On Estimating Population Means of Two-Sensitive Variables With Ranked Set Sampling Design

Agustin Santiago Moreno
Universidad Autónoma de Guerrero, Mexico

Khalid Ul Islam Rather
iD https://orcid.org/0000-0002-4631-5652
Sher-e-Kashmir University of Agricultural Sciences and Technology of Jammu, India

ABSTRACT

In this chapter, the authors consider the problem of estimating the population means of two sensitive variables by making use ranked set sampling. The final estimators are unbiased and the variance expressions that they derive show that ranked set sampling is more efficient than simple random sampling. A convex combination of the variance expressions of the resultant estimators is minimized in order to suggest optimal sample sizes for both sampling schemes. The relative efficiency of the proposed estimators is then compared to the corresponding estimators for simple random sampling based on simulation study and real data applications. SAS codes utilized in the simulation to collect the empirical evidence and application are included.

DOI: 10.4018/978-1-7998-7556-7.ch003

1. INTRODUCTION

The theory of ratio estimation is recommendable when the sampler has a complete knowledge of an auxiliary variable X which is highly correlated with the studied variable Y. The theory appears in text books as Cochran (1977), Wu and Thompson (2020). Some basic notation is needed. The sampler has all the information on the auxiliary variable and is able to compute

$$\bar{X} = \frac{\sum_{i=1}^{N} X_i}{N}, \ \sigma_X^2 = \frac{\sum_{i=1}^{N}(X_i - \bar{X})^2}{N}$$

the population mean and variance of the auxiliary variable X;

$$\bar{Y} = \frac{\sum_{i=1}^{N} Y_i}{N}, \ \sigma_Y^2 = \frac{\sum_{i=1}^{N}(Y_i - \bar{Y})^2}{N}$$

The population mean and variance of the study variable Y are unknown. The correlation coefficient between X and Y

$$\rho = \frac{Cov(X,Y)}{\sqrt{V(X)V(Y)}} = \frac{\sigma_{XY}}{\sigma_X \sigma_Y}$$

plays a key role in the theory of ratio estimation.

Commonly is used sampling design simple random sampling (SRS). The differences between using replacement or not is not important when the sampling fraction is small. Note that are unbiased estimators of the means and variances, of a sample of size n selected from a population $U=\{u_1,\ldots,u_N\}$,

$$\bar{z} = \frac{\sum_{i=1}^{n} z_i}{n}, \ s_X^2 = \frac{\sum_{i=1}^{n}(z_i - \bar{z})^2}{n-1}, \ z_i = x_i, y_i.$$

The sampling fraction is f=n/N. In many inquires is acceptable that f is not far from zero.

Ratio type estimators appear as good alternatives for improving the niceties of the usual ratio estimators. Some recent contributions are Al-Omari et al. (2008), Singh et al. (2010, 2014), Bouza- Al-Omari (2011), Al-Omari and Al-Nasser (2018).

Singh et al . (2010) proposed using as auxiliary variable a function of the sampling and population means and X_m (the minimum of $\{X_1,\ldots,X_N\}$) or X_M (the maximum of $\{X_1,\ldots,X_N\}$). The sampling design considered was SRS.

Section 2 is concerned with introducing basic elements on Stratified Simple Random Sampling (SSRS). We extend Singh et al. (2010) results to sampling a stratified population. The bias and mean squared error (MSE) are derived. SRS is used independently for selecting the samples from the strata.

Section 3 is devoted to introducing basic elements on Ranked Set Sampling (RSS). We extend Singh et al. (2010) results under the RSS design. They are used for developing the estimation in a stratified population. RSS is used for drawing the samples independently from the strata. The bias and mean squared error (MSE) of the developed estimators are derived. A comparison between the biases and MSE´s obtained for the sampling designs SRS and RSS is made. Under mild conditions the comparisons sustained that each RSS model is better than its SRS alternative

Section 4 presents numerical experiments for illustrating the behavior of the proposals. Data provided by a real-life study on the emission of contaminants are used. The results sustain the ideas obtained from the theoretical comparisons. Simulated data, where the sufficient conditions do not hold, generated the preference for RSS too.

2. EXTENDING SRSWR ESTIMATORS TO STRATIFICATION

We are considering that the population is divided into K strata. Formally

$$U = \bigcup_{k=1}^{K} U_k ; U_k \bigcap U_k = \varnothing;$$

$$\forall k = 1,..,K, |U_k| = N_k ; |U| = N = \sum_{k=1}^{K} N_k$$

Kadilar and Cingi (2003, 2005) developed some ratio estimators for stratified random .

We assumed that the sampler knows all the values of X for any unit. Hence, for each stratum we know the population mean $\bar{X}_k$ as well as the minimum and maximum X_{hm} and X_{hM}. From the proposal of Singh et al. (2010) we use as the transformed auxiliary variables for the i-th unit

$$u_{hi} = \frac{x_{hi} + X_{hm}}{X_{hm} + X_{hM}} \text{ or } w_{hi} = \frac{x_{hi} + X_{hM}}{X_{hm} + X_{hM}}$$

Their expectations are

$$E(u_{hi}) = \frac{E(x_{hi}) + X_{hm}}{X_{hm} + X_{hM}} = \frac{\bar{X}_h + X_{hm}}{X_{hm} + X_{hM}} = \bar{U}_h$$

$$E(w_{hi}) = \frac{E(x_{hi}) + X_{hM}}{X_{hm} + X_{hM}} = \frac{\bar{X}_h + X_{hM}}{X_{hm} + X_{hM}} = \bar{W}_h$$

Take the sample means

$$\bar{z}_h = \frac{1}{n_h} \sum_{i=1}^{n_h} z_{hi}; z_{hi} = x_{hi}, u_{hi}, w_{hi}, y_{hi}$$

They are unbiased estimators, when a sample of size n_h is selected from using U_h using SRS are simply derived by using the sample means of X. Explicitly we have

$$\bar{u}_h = \frac{\bar{x}_h + X_{hm}}{X_{hm} + X_{hM}}, \bar{w}_h = \frac{\bar{x}_h + X_{hM}}{X_{hm} + X_{hM}}$$

The proposed ratio type estimators within stratum are

$$\bar{y}_{h(u)} = \bar{y}_h \left(\frac{\frac{1}{N_h} \sum_{i=1}^{N_h} U_i}{\frac{1}{n_h} \sum_{i=1}^{n_h} u_i} \right) = \bar{y}_h \left(\frac{\bar{U}_h}{\bar{u}_h} \right) = r_{h(u)} \bar{U}_h$$

and

$$\bar{y}_{h(w)} = \bar{y}_h \left(\frac{\dfrac{1}{N_h} \sum_{i=1}^{N_h} W_i}{\dfrac{1}{n_h} \sum_{i=1}^{n_h} w_i} \right) = \bar{y}_h \left(\frac{\bar{W}_h}{\bar{w}_h} \right) = r_{h(uw)} \bar{W}_h$$

Denoting

$$R_h = \frac{\bar{Y}_h}{\bar{X}_h}, C_{Z_h} = \frac{\sigma_{Z_h}}{\bar{Z}_h}; Z = X, Y$$

and using Taylor Series expansions, their biases are approximated by

$$B\left(\bar{y}_{h(u)}\right) \cong \frac{R_h}{n_h} \left(\frac{\sigma_{X_h}^2}{\bar{X}_h + X_{hm}} \right) \left(\frac{\bar{X}_h}{\bar{X}_h + X_{hm}} - \rho_h C_{Y_h} C_{X_h} \right)$$

$$B\left(\bar{y}_{h(w)}\right) \cong \frac{R_h}{n_h} \left(\frac{\sigma_{X_h}^2}{\bar{X}_h + X_{hM}} \right) \left(\frac{\bar{X}_h}{\bar{X}_h + X_{hM}} - \rho_h C_{Y_h} C_{X_h} \right)$$

The mean squared errors of the population estimators

$$\bar{y}_q = \sum_{k=1}^{K} P_k \bar{y}_{k(q)}; q = u, v; P_k = \frac{N_k}{N}$$

are, approximately

$$MSE\left(\bar{y}_u\right) \cong M_u = \sum_{k=1}^{K} \frac{P_k^2 \bar{Y}_k^2}{n_k} \left(C_{Y_k}^2 + \frac{C_{X_k}^2}{C_{km}^2} - \frac{2\rho_k C_{X_k} C_{Y_k}}{C_{km}} \right); C_{km} = 1 + \frac{X_{km}}{\bar{X}_k}$$

$$MSE\left(\bar{y}_w\right) \cong M_w = \sum_{k=1}^{K} \frac{P_k^2 \bar{Y}_k^2}{n_k} \left(C_{Y_k}^2 + \frac{C_{X_k}^2}{C_{kM}^2} - \frac{2\rho_k C_{X_k} C_{Y_k}}{C_{kM}} \right); C_{kM} = 1 + \frac{X_{kM}}{\bar{X}_k}$$

These formulae are simply derived from the results of Singh at al. (2010).

3. RSS EXTENSION OF STRATIFIED SRSWR ESTIMATORS

Let us consider RSS. The Ranked Set Sampling (RSS) has its roots in the contribution of McIntyre (1952) . He considered that RSS produced more accurate estimations of the population mean than SRS. The mathematical proofs of his claims, were derived more than a decade after his paper. Basic contributions providing RSS of the adequate tools were Takahasi and Wakimoto (1968) and Dell and Clutter (1972).

The selection scheme is described as follows:

Basic Stratified RSS procedure:

Step 1: Fix m_k, r_k, K, $s_k = t_k = r_k = h = 0$
Step 2: $h=h+1$
Step 3: $s_k = s_k + 1$
Step 4: Randomly select m_k^2 independent units from each target stratum population.
These units are randomly allocated into m_k sets, each of size m_k.
Step 5: Rank the m_k units in each set using X.
Step 6: Measure Y in the *j-th* ranked unit of the *j-th* set.
Step 7: While $s_k < r_k$ go to Step 3.
Step 8: Evaluate the corresponding stratum units
Step 9: $h < K$ go to Step 2
END

It is well known, see Chen et al.(2004) that for any order of statistic

$$E\left[\xi_{(i:n)}\right] = \mu_{(i)} \ and \ V\left[\xi_{(i:n)}\right] = \sigma_{(i)}^2 = \sigma^2 - \Delta_{(i)}^2 ; \Delta_{(i)}^2 = \left(\mu_{(i)} - \mu\right)^2$$

and

$$\frac{1}{n}\sum_{i=1}^{n}\mu_{(i)} = \mu$$

These properties are to be used when analyzing the RSS estimators within strata.

Kadilar et al. (2009) developed a ratio estimator for studying the population mean using RSS.

In the stratification context we have to deal with a stratified sample of order statistics

$$\left\{ \left(X_{(j:j)t}, Y_{(j:j)t} \right)_k ; k = 1,..,K, j = 1,..,m_k, \right\}$$

Let us denote the RSS means by

$$\overline{z}_{RSS(k)} = \frac{1}{r_k m_k} \sum_{t=1}^{r_k} \sum_{i=1}^{m_k} z_{(j:j)t}, = \overline{Z}_k \left(1 + e_{ZRSS(k)} \right) z = x, y, u$$

The relative errors are denoted

$$e_{ZRSS(k)} = \frac{\overline{z}_{RSS(k)} - \overline{Z}_k}{\overline{Z}_k}$$

The expectations, variances and covariances have the same properties than in SRS

$$E \left(e_{ZRSS(k)} \right) = 0; V \left(e_{ZRSS(k)} \right) = \frac{V \left(\overline{z}_{RSS(k)} \right)}{\overline{Z}_k^2} = C_{z_k}^2 ; Cov \left(\overline{x}_{RSS(k)}, \overline{y}_{RSS(k)} \right) = \rho_k C_{x_k} C_{y_k}$$

The counterpart of $\overline{y}_u$ is

$$\overline{y}_{RSS,k(u)} = \left(\frac{\overline{y}_{RSS(k)}}{\overline{u}_{RSS(k)}} \right) \overline{U}_k = r_{RSS,k(u)} \overline{U}_k = \frac{\overline{Y}_k \left(1 + e_{yRSS(k)} \right)}{1 + \tau \left(u_k \right) e_{xRSS(k)}}$$

Take

$$\tau \left(u_k \right) = \frac{\overline{X}_k}{\overline{X}_k + X_m}$$

Developing the estimator in Taylor Series and assuming that $|\tau(uk_)|<1$ we have that

$$\left(\overline{y}_{RSS,k(u)} \right) \cong \overline{Y}_k E \left(\left(1 + e_{yRSS(k)} \right) \left(1 - \tau \left(u_k \right) e_{xRSS(k)} \right) \right)$$

$$E = \bar{Y}_k + \bar{Y}_k \left(\tau \left(u_k \right)^2 \left(\frac{V\left(\bar{x}_{RSS(k)} \right)}{\bar{X}_k^2} \right) - \tau \left(u_k \right) \rho_k C_{RSSx_k} C_{RSSy_k} \right)$$

Calculating the bias of $\bar{y}_{RSS,k(u)}$ and due to the properties of the RSS errors take $n_k = m_k r_k$

$$B\left(\bar{y}_{RSS,k(u)} \right) \cong \bar{Y}_k \left(\frac{\tau \left(u_k \right)^2}{\bar{X}_k^2} \left(\frac{\sigma_{X_k}^2}{n_k} - \frac{\sum_{j=1}^{m_k} {}^{''} X_{(j:j)k}^2}{m_k n_k} \right) - \tau \left(u_k \right) \rho_k \frac{\sqrt{\left(\frac{\sigma_{X_k}^2}{n_k} - \frac{\sum_{j=1}^{m_k} {}^{''} X_{(j:j)k}^2}{m_k n_k} \right)\left(\frac{\sigma_{X_k}^2}{n_k} - \frac{\sum_{j=1}^{m_k} {}^{''} X_{(j:j)k}^2}{m_k n_k} \right)}}{\bar{Y}_k \bar{X}_k} \right)$$

The bias derived for SSRS may rewritten as

$$B\left(\bar{y}_{h(u)} \right) \cong \frac{R_h}{n_h} \left(\frac{\sigma_{X_h}^2}{\bar{X}_h + X_{hm}} \right)\left(\frac{\bar{X}_h}{\bar{X}_h + X_{hm}} - \frac{\rho C_{Y_h}}{C_{X_h}} \right) = \frac{\bar{Y}_h}{n_h} \left(\frac{\sigma_{X_h}^2}{\left(\bar{X}_h + X_{hm} \right)^2} \right) - \frac{\rho_h C_{Y_h} C_{Y_h}}{\bar{X}_h + X_{hm}}$$

Note that

$$\frac{\tau \left(u_k \right)}{\bar{X}_k} = \frac{1}{\bar{X}_k + X_{km}}.$$

Then the difference between the biases is

$$B\left(\bar{y}_{RSS,k(u)} \right) - B\left(\bar{y}_{k(u)} \right) \cong \bar{Y}_k \left[\left(\frac{1}{\bar{X}_h + X_{hm}} \right)^2 \left[\left(\frac{\sigma_{X_k}^2}{n_k} - \frac{\sum_{j=1}^{m_k} {}^{''} X_{(j:j)k}^2}{m_k n_k} \right) - \left(\frac{\sigma_{X_h}^2}{\left(\bar{X}_h + X_{hm} \right)^2} \right) \right] \right.$$

$$\left. - \frac{\rho_k}{\bar{X}_h + X_{hm}} \left[\sqrt{\left(\frac{\sigma_{X_k}^2}{n_k} - \frac{\sum_{j=1}^{m_k} {}^{''} X_{(j:j)k}^2}{m_k n_k} \right)\left(\frac{\sigma_{Y_k}^2}{n_k} - \frac{\sum_{j=1}^{m_k} {}^{''} Y_{(j:j)k}^2}{m_k n_k} \right)} - \sqrt{\frac{\sigma_{X_k}^2}{n_k} \frac{\sigma_{X_k}^2}{n_k}} \right] \right]$$

The first term is negative, and the term between parenthesis in the second one is negative too. Hence, a sufficient condition for $B\left(\bar{y}_{RSS,k(u)}\right) - B\left(\bar{y}_{h(u)}\right) < 0$ is that $\rho_k > 0, \bar{Y}_k > 0$.

For calculating the MSE is to be noted that

$$MSE\left(\bar{y}_{RSS,k(u)}\right) = MSE_{RSSk(u)} = E\left(\bar{y}_{RSS,k(u)} - \bar{Y}_k\right)^2$$

Evaluating this expectation and neglecting the terms of order larger than 2 it is approximated by

$$SE\left(\bar{y}_{RSS,k(u)}\right) \cong M_{RSS,k(u)} \cong \bar{Y}_k^2 E\left(e_{yRSSy(u)}^2 + \tau\left(u_k\right)^2 e_{xRSSy(u)}^2 - 2\tau\left(u_k\right) e_{yRSSy(u)} e_{xRSSy(u)}\right)$$

$$M = \left(\frac{\sigma_{Y_k}^2}{n_k} - \frac{\sum_{j=1}^{m_k}{}'' Y_{(j:j)k}^2}{m_k n_k}\right) + R_k^2 \tau\left(u_k\right)^2 \left(\frac{\sigma_{X_k}^2}{n_k} - \frac{\sum_{j=1}^{m_k}{}'' X_{(j:j)k}^2}{m_k n_k}\right)$$

$$-2R_k \tau\left(u_k\right)\rho_k \left(\sqrt{\left(\frac{\sigma_{X_k}^2}{n_k} - \frac{\sum_{j=1}^{m_k}{}'' X_{(j:j)k}^2}{m_k n_k}\right)\left(\frac{\sigma_{X_k}^2}{n_k} - \frac{\sum_{j=1}^{m_k}{}'' X_{(j:j)k}^2}{m_k n_k}\right)}\right)$$

As $\tau\left(u_k\right) = \dfrac{1}{C_{km}}$ the difference between the MSE`s of both alternatives is

$$MSE_{RSS,k(u)} - MSE\left(\bar{y}_{k(u)}\right) \cong -\frac{\sum_{j=1}^{m_k}{}'' Y_{(j:j)k}^2}{m_k n_k} - R_k^2 \tau\left(u_k\right)^2 \frac{\sum_{j=1}^{m_k}{}'' X_{(j:j)k}^2}{m_k n_k}$$

$$-2R_k \tau\left(u_k\right)\rho_k \left(\sqrt{\left(\frac{\sigma_{X_k}^2}{n_k} - \frac{\sum_{j=1}^{m_k}{}'' X_{(j:j)k}^2}{m_k n_k}\right)\left(\frac{\sigma_{X_k}^2}{n_k} - \frac{\sum_{j=1}^{m_k}{}'' X_{(j:j)k}^2}{m_k n_k}\right)} + \sqrt{\frac{\sigma_{X_k}\sigma_{Y_k}}{m_k n_k}}\right)$$

The first two terms are negative and the expression between the parenthesis in the last term is negative unless $R_k\tau(uk_j\rho k<_0$. Hence, when this inequality holds for any k, we have a sufficient condition for preferring the use of RSS. Then, proposing the estimator

$$\bar{y}_{RSS(u)} = \sum_{k=1}^{K} P_k \bar{y}_{RSS,k(u)}$$

is a better decision that using SSRS because generally it is less biased than $\bar{y}_{(u)}$ and its MSE

$$MSE\left(\bar{y}_{RSS(u)}\right) \cong \sum_{k=1}^{K} P_k^2 \left[\left(\frac{\sigma_{Y_k}^2}{n_k} - \frac{\sum_{j=1}^{m_k} {}^{,,2}_{Y_{(j:j)k}}}{m_k n_k} \right) + R_k^2 \tau \left(u_k\right)^2 \left(\frac{\sigma_{X_k}^2}{n_k} - \frac{\sum_{j=1}^{m_k} {}^{,,2}_{X_{(j:j)k}}}{m_k n_k} \right) \right.$$

$$\left. -2R_k \tau \left(u_k\right) \rho_k \left(\sqrt{ \left(\frac{\sigma_{X_k}^2}{n_k} - \frac{\sum_{j=1}^{m_k} {}^{,,2}_{X_{(j:j)k}}}{m_k n_k} \right) \left(\frac{\sigma_{X_k}^2}{n_k} - \frac{\sum_{j=1}^{m_k} {}^{,,2}_{X_{(j:j)k}}}{m_k n_k} \right) } \right) \right]$$

is also expected to be smaller than $MSE\left(\bar{y}_{k(u)}\right)$ under a set of mild conditions.

Let us consider the RSS alternative of $\bar{y}_{k(w)}$. It is

$$\bar{y}_{RSSk(w)} = \left(\frac{\bar{y}_{RSSk}}{\bar{w}_{RSSk}} \right) \bar{W}_k$$

Developing an analysis to the case of using U, we have that $\tau\left(w_k\right) = \dfrac{\bar{X}_k}{\bar{X}_k + X_M}$

$$B\left(\bar{y}_{RSSk(w)}\right) \cong \frac{\bar{Y}_k}{n_k} \left(\tau\left(w_k\right)^2 \sigma_{X_k}^2 - \frac{\sum_{j=1}^{m_k} {}^{,,2}_{X_{(j)}}}{m_k} \right) - 2\frac{\tau\left(w_k\right)\rho_k}{n_k} \left(\sqrt{ \left(\sigma_{X_k}^2 - \frac{\sum_{j=1}^{m_k} {}^{,,2}_{X_{(j)}}}{m_k} \right) \left(\sigma_{Y_k}^2 - \frac{\sum_{j=1}^{m_k} {}^{,,2}_{Y_{(j)}}}{m_k} \right) } \right)$$

$$M\left(\bar{y}_{RSSk(w)}\right) \cong M_{RSSk(w)}$$

$$= \frac{\sigma_{Y_k}^2}{n_k} - \frac{\sum_{j=1}^{m_k} {}_{,,}^2 Y_{(j)}}{n_k m_k} + \tau \left(w_k \right)^2 R_k^2 \left(\frac{\sigma_{X_k}^2}{n_k} - \frac{\sum_{j=1}^{m_k} {}_{,,}^2 X_{(j)}}{n_k m_k} \right)$$

$$-2\tau \left(w_k \right) \rho_k R_k \left(\sqrt{\left(\frac{\sigma_{X_k}^2}{n_k} - \frac{\sum_{j=1}^{m_k} {}_{,,}^2 X_{(j)}}{n_k m_k} \right) \left(\frac{\sigma_{X_k}^2}{n_k} - \frac{\sum_{j=1}^{m_k} {}_{,,}^2 X_{(j)}}{n_k m_k} \right)} \right)$$

Now we have the differences of the biases and MSE`s are:

$$B \left(\bar{y}_{RSSk(w)} \right) - B \left(\bar{y}_{k(w)} \right)$$

$$\cong - \frac{\bar{Y}_k}{n_k} \left(\frac{\sum_{j=1}^{m_k} {}_{,,}^2 X_{(j)}}{m_k} \right) - 2\tau \left(w_k \right) \rho_k \left(\sqrt{\left(\frac{\sigma_{X_k}^2}{n_k} - \frac{\sum_{j=1}^{m_k} {}_{,,}^2 X_{(j)}}{n_k m_k} \right) \left(\frac{\sigma_{Y_k}^2}{n_k} - \frac{\sum_{j=1}^{m_k} {}_{,,}^2 Y_{(j)}}{n_k m_k} \right)} + \sqrt{\frac{\sigma_{X_k}^2}{n_k} \times \frac{\sigma_{Y_k}^2}{n_k}} \right)$$

and

$$M_{RSSk(w)} - M_{k(w)} \cong - \frac{\sum_{j=1}^{m_k} {}_{,,}^2 Y_{(j)}}{n_k m_k} - \tau \left(w_k \right)^2 R_k^2 \frac{\sum_{j=1}^{m_k} {}_{,,}^2 X_{(j)}}{n_k m_k}$$

$$-2\tau \left(w_k \right) \rho_k R_k \left(\sqrt{\left(\frac{\sigma_{X_k}^2}{n_k} - \frac{\sum_{j=1}^{m_k} {}_{,,}^2 X_{(j)}}{n_k m_k} \right) \left(\frac{\sigma_{X_k}^2}{n_k} - \frac{\sum_{j=1}^{m_k} {}_{,,}^2 X_{(j)}}{n_k m_k} \right)} + \sqrt{\frac{\sigma_{X_k}^2}{n_k} \frac{\sigma_{Y_k}^2}{n_k}} \right)$$

Note that the same conditions used for preferring RSS, when using u, support the preference of $\bar{y}_{RSSk(w)}$. Therefore, the bias of the weighed RSS-w means

$$\bar{y}_{RSS(w)} = \sum_{k=1}^{K} P_k \bar{y}_{RSSk(w)}$$

has a smaller bias than its SSRSWR alternative design. Its MSE is

$$MSE\left(\bar{y}_{RSS(w)}\right) = \sum_{k=1}^{K} P_k^2 \left(\frac{\sigma_{Y_k}^2}{n_k} - \frac{\sum_{j=1}^{m_k} Y_{(j)}^2}{n_k m_k} + \tau\left(w_k\right)^2 R_k^2 \left(\frac{\sigma_{X_k}^2}{n_k} - \frac{\sum_{j=1}^{m_k} X_{(j)}^2}{n_k m_k} \right) \right.$$

$$\left. -2\tau\left(w_k\right)\rho_k R_k \left(\sqrt{\left(\frac{\sigma_{X_k}^2}{n_k} - \frac{\sum_{j=1}^{m_k} X_{(j)}^2}{n_k m_k} \right)\left(\frac{\sigma_{X_k}^2}{n_k} - \frac{\sum_{j=1}^{m_k} X_{(j)}^2}{n_k m_k} \right)} \right) \right)$$

is also smaller than the MSE of the SRSWR model.

Remark: As $\tau(uk) > \tau(wk)$ using the transformed w-variables are the best altrantives.

4. NUMERICAL STUDIES

We evaluated the behavior of the analyzed estimators in terms of their MSE`s derived. A study of contaminating elements of solid waste compost provided the data. The grabs were prepared after coning and quartering the original wastes. The compost was collected from hospitals. The original particles were mechanically separated and then passed through a fine. Each batch was send for burning and the toxicity was measured by a laboratory. A qualification in the range 0-100 was given to each batch before being processed and was used for ranking. For the experiment a sensor was placed in the chimney for measuring the contents of plumb, magnesium, cadmium and other contaminants. The measurement was made for all the batch introduced in the furnaces. 1678 batches were measured.

10 000 samples were generated and were computed

$$\vartheta_Q = 100 \sum_{s=1}^{10000} \frac{\left|\bar{y}_Q - \bar{Y}\right|_s}{10000\bar{Y}}; \quad Q = u, w, RSSu, RSSv$$

Table 1. Mean relative differences

Q	Plumb	Magnesium	Cadmium	Other Contaminants
u	12,67	22,28	10,49	32,57
w	11,82	21,92	9,87	29,32
RSSu	11,02	18,03	8,25	18,10
RSSw	10,93	15,99	8,23	16,08

Large values of ϑQ suggest that the sampling strategy associated to Q has an inaccurate behavior for estimating the population mean. See the results in tables 1-4 below.

As is to be noted, SRSS based estimators behaved more accurate than the SSRS ones. The differences between $\overline{y}_{RSS(w)}$ and $\overline{y}_{RSS(u)}$ are small. The difference between $\overline{y}_{(w)}$ and $\overline{y}_{(u)}$ are considerable.

A set of simulation experiments were conducted using negative correlation coefficients between X and Y. We considered the following distributions on R^2.

Table 2. Distributions generated

Bivariate distributions	parameter
Exponential	1, 1
Gamma	$\vec{\alpha} = (1,1); \vec{\theta} = (1,1)$
Uniform	$\vec{\mu} = (1,-1); \vec{\sigma} = \left(1/\sqrt{6}, 1/\sqrt{6}\right)$
Beta	$\vec{\alpha} = (1,1); \vec{\beta} = (1,1)$
Weibull	$\vec{\alpha} = (1,1); \vec{\theta} = (1,1)$
Gaussian	$\vec{\mu} = (1,-1); \vec{\sigma} = (1,1)$

The same distribution was used for generating variables in each stratum .10000 vectors were generated with the same correlation coefficient in each stratum. The correlation coefficients were $\rho k_=$ -0.5, -0.7, -0.75, -0.9, -0.95. For each sample generated with the different distributions were computed. 5 strata where determined

$$\vartheta_{Q,F,\rho} = 100 \sum_{s=1}^{10000} \left| \frac{\overline{y}_{Q.F,\rho} - \overline{Y}}{10000\overline{Y}} \right|_s ; Q=u,w,RSSu,RSSw.$$

See the results in Table 3.

Looking to table 3 the empirical results in the analysis of the contents of plumb sustain the preferences suggested in the theoretical study. The increase of both the negative-ness of the correlation and the means implied a diminish of the accuracy of the estimators. For distributions with large negative means, the corresponding

Table 3. Mean relative differences $\vartheta_{Q,F,\rho}$ for the distributions generated: Plumb

Estimator	Distribution	$\rho = -0.50$	$\rho = -0.70$	$\rho = -0.90$
$\bar{y}_{(u)}$	Exponential	16,30	18,24	19,03
	Gamma	13,41	17,95	22,57
	Uniform	4,34	6,28	8,24
	Beta	17,21	17,51	17,55
	Weibull	15,98	16,02	16,06
	Gaussian	5,45	9,37	12,59
$\bar{y}_{(w)}$	Exponential	15,57	16,55	17,97
	Gamma	12,11	12,94	13,66
	Uniform	3,71	5,72	8,17
	Beta	17,03	17,03	17,06
	Weibull	14,75	15,98	16,04
	Gaussian	4,79	7,38	12,11
$\bar{y}_{RSS(u)}$	Exponential	14,79	17,38	18,11
	Gamma	11,82	11,96	12,09
	Uniform	3,39	4,73	7,18
	Beta	16,04	16,36	16,39
	Weibull	13,76	14,32	14,26
	Gaussian	4,52	6,10	10,48
$\bar{y}_{RSS(w)}$	Exponential	11,57	16,88	17,75
	Gamma	11,25	11,36	12,02
	Uniform	3,83	4,46	4,14
	Beta	14,99	15,48	15,86
	Weibull	11,57	11,63	11,97
	Gaussian	4,05	5,84	9,17

$\vartheta_{Q,F,\rho}$ is considerably larger. Under the $\beta\left[\vec{\alpha} = (1,1); \vec{\beta} = (1,1)\right]$ we observe small changes in the values of Mean Relative Differences in terms of the correlation.

Table 4 sustains the theoretical deductions. Again, the negative-ness of the correlation and the means generated smaller values of the increase of the Mean

Table 4. Mean relative differences $\vartheta_{Q,F,\rho}$ for the distributions generated: Magnesium

Estimator	Distribution	$\rho = -0.50$	$\rho = -0.70$	$\rho = -0.90$
$\bar{y}_{(u)}$	Exponential	31,63	32,20	32,93
	Gamma	23,42	27,95	28,57
	Uniform	4,34	6,28	8,24
	Beta	27,22	27,52	27,55
	Weibull	25,98	26,72	26,76
	Gaussian	5,45	9,37	12,59
$\bar{y}_{(w)}$	Exponential	28,57	28,95	29,07
	Gamma	22,22	28,54	29,96
	Uniform	3,72	4,72	5,27
	Beta	27,13	27,17	27,16
	Weibull	24,75	25,98	26,74
	Gaussian	4,79	7,38	12,22
$\bar{y}_{RSS(u)}$	Exponential	27,79	27,68	27,92
	Gamma	22,12	25,96	23,29
	Uniform	2,63	4,70	5,18
	Beta	26,54	26,36	26,39
	Weibull	23,76	24,32	25,26
	Gaussian	4,52	6,52	9,48
$\bar{y}_{RSS(w)}$	Exponential	22,57	22,88	23,15
	Gamma	22,05	25,36	23,11
	Uniform	2,33	4,46	4,94
	Beta	24,99	24,48	24,36
	Weibull	22,57	22,63	27,97
	Gaussian	4,25	5,84	8,27

Relative Differences. For the distributions $\beta \left[\vec{\alpha} = (1,1); \vec{\beta} = (1,1) \right]$ and $\vec{\alpha} = (1,1)$; $\vec{\theta} = (1,1)$ these measures are similar for all the correlations in the 4 estimators.

Table 5 also sustains the theoretical recommendations for preferring the estimators and the role of negative-ness of the correlation coefficients means in increasing the Mean Relative Differences of RSS procedures. More distributions exhibited similar

Table 5. Mean relative differences $\vartheta_{Q,F,\rho}$ for the distributions generated: Cadmium

Estimator	Distribution	$\rho= -0.50$	$\rho= -0.70$	$\rho= -0.90$
$\bar{y}_{(u)}$	Exponential	12,80	12,84	12,90
	Gamma	12,41	12,95	12,95
	Uniform	2,44	2,68	2,68
	Beta	12,21	12,51	12,55
	Weibull	15,98	16,02	19,96
	Gaussian	2,54	2,98	3,22
$\bar{y}_{(w)}$	Exponential	12,15	12,15	12,19
	Gamma	12,11	12,84	12,88
	Uniform	2,44	2,54	2,58
	Beta	12,04	12,04	12,06
	Weibull	14,45	15,98	18,04
	Gaussian	2,49	2,58	2,72
$\bar{y}_{RSS(u)}$	Exponential	12,09	12,14	12,17
	Gamma	12,02	12,09	12,09
	Uniform	2,16	2,25	2,28
	Beta	12,04	12,06	12,09
	Weibull	12,26	13,42	17,16
	Gaussian	2,45	2,51	2,58
$\bar{y}_{RSS(w)}$	Exponential	12,04	12,08	12,14
	Gamma	12125	12146	12202
	Uniform	2,14	2,24	2,26
	Beta	11,99	12,08	12,08
	Weibull	12,15	12,64	15,94
	Gaussian	2,40	2,34	2,47

values of the precision measures . It seems is due to the higher accuracy of estimates for cadmium, see table 3.

Table 6, as the other tables provides empirical support to the deductions made, on the gains in accuracy, of the SSSRS and SRSS estimators deduced.

Table 6. Mean relative differences $\vartheta_{Q2F,\rho}$ for the distributions generated: Other contaminants

Estimator	Distributions	$\rho=$ -0.50	$\rho=$ -0.70	$\rho=$ -0.90
$\bar{y}_{(u)}$	Exponential	32,63	32,82	32,93
	Gamma	32,34	32,60	32,96
	Uniform	12,43	12,68	12,74
	Beta	32,63	32,65	32,65
	Weibull	32,50	32,60	32,60
	Gaussian	12,54	12,96	13,92
$\bar{y}_{(w)}$	Exponential	32,55	32,65	32, 06
	Gamma	32,23	32,20	32,36
	Uniform	12,36	12,56	12,86
	Beta	32,60	32,63	32,63
	Weibull	32,45	32,58	32,60
	Gaussian	11,46	11,48	11,59
$\bar{y}_{RSS(u)}$	Exponential	32,46	32,38	32,33
	Gamma	32,02	32,10	32,10
	Uniform	11,63	11,84	12,08
	Beta	32,49	32,53	32,60
	Weibull	32,36	32,50	32,53
	Gaussian	11,42	11,48	11,50
$\bar{y}_{RSS(w)}$	Exponential	32,35	32,27	31,15
	Gamma	32,02	32,06	32,09
	Uniform	11,33	11,46	11,53
	Beta	32,40	32,45	32,49
	Weibull	32,35	32,46	32,50
	Gaussian	11,35	11,44	11,52

5. CONCLUSION

The Mean Relative Differences obtained for the different contaminant and the results of tables 3-6 give an idea of what is to be expected for setting some rules of preference. Variables with higher MSE`s have higher values of the Mean Relative Differences for all the distributions. In addition, we have evidence that when Y and X are negative correlated and the mean of Y is also negative the difference between the Mean Relative Differences of SSRS and SRSS may diminish seriously . In the experiments SRSS were preferred to their counterparts in all the cases, but in some practical problems they may have larger MSE`s then SSRS based ratio type models.

ACKNOWLEDGMENT

This paper has been benefited by the suggestions of Prof. A. I. Alomari. These results have been supported by the project PN223LH010-005, Desarrollo de nuevos modelos y métodos matemáticos para la toma de decisiones.

This paper has been developed under the advisory of Prof. Dr. Carlos Bouza-Herrera.

REFERENCES

Adatia, A. (2000). Estimation of parameters of the half-logistic distribution using generalized ranked set sampling. *Computational Statistics & Data Analysis*, *33*(1), 1–13. doi:10.1016/S0167-9473(99)00035-3

Al-Omari, A.I., Ibrahim, K., & JEMAIN, A.A. (2009). New ratio estimators of the mean using simple random sampling and ranked set sampling methods. *Revista Investigacion Operacional*, *30*, 97–108.

Al-Omari, A. I., & Al-Nasser, A. D. (2018). Ratio estimation using multistage median ranked set sampling approach. *Journal of Statistical Theory and Practice*, *12*(3), 512–529. doi:10.1080/15598608.2018.1425168

Al-Omari, A. I., Jaber, K., & Al-Omari, A. (2008). Modified ratio-type estimators of the mean using extreme ranked set sampling. *Journal of Mathematics and Statistics*, *4*(3), 150–155. doi:10.3844/jmssp.2008.150.155

Al-Saleh, M. F., & Al-Shrafat, K. (2001). Estimation of milk yield using ranked set sampling. *Environmetrics*, *12*(4), 395–399. doi:10.1002/env.478

Bai, Z. D., & Chen, Z. (2003). On the theory of ranked set sampling *and* its ramifications. *Journal of Statistical Planning and Inference*, *109*(1-2), 81–99. doi:10.1016/S0378-3758(02)00302-6

Bouza, C. N. (2001). Model assisted ranked survey sampling. *Biometrical Journal. Biometrische Zeitschrift*, *36*, 753–764.

Bouza Herrera, C. N., & Al-Omari, A. I. (2019). *Ranked Set Sampling, 65 Years Improving the Accuracy in Data Gathering*. Elsevier.

Chen, Z., Bai, Z., & Sinha, B. K. (2004). Ranked set sampling: theory and applications. In Lectures Notes in Statistics (vol. 176). Springer.

David, H. A., & Nagaraja, H. N. (2003). *Order Statistics* (3rd ed.). John Wiley & sons, Inc.

Dell, T. R., & Clutter, J. L. (1972). Ranked set sampling theory with order statistics background. *Biometrics*, *28*, 545–555.

Hall, L. K., & Dell, T. R. (1996). Trials of ranked set sampling for forage yields. *Forest Sc*, *121*, 22–26.

Kadilar, C. & Cingi, H. (2003). Ratio estimators in stratified random sampling. *Biometrical Journal. Biometrische Zeitschrift*, *45*, 218–225.

Kadilar, C., & Cingi, H. (2005). A new ratio estimator in stratified random sampling. Communications in Statistics. *Theory and Methods*, *34*, 597–602.

McIntyre, G. A. (1952). A method for unbiased selective sampling using ranked sets. *Australian Journal of Agricultural Research*, *3*, 385–390.

Ranked set estimation with imputation of the missing observations: The median estimator. (2011). *Revista Investigación Operacional, 32*, 30-37.

Singh, H. P., Tailor, R., & Singh, S. (2014). General procedure for estimating the population mean using ranked set sampling. *Journal of Simulation and Computation Statistics*, *84*, 931–945.

Singh, H. P., Tailor, R., & Tailor, R. (2010). On ratio and product methods with certain known population parameters of auxiliary variable in sample surveys. *SORT (Barcelona)*, *34*, 157–180.

Takahasi, K., & Wakimoto, K. (1968). On the unbiased estimates of the population mean based on the sample stratified by means of ordering. *Annals of the Institute of Statistical Mathematics*, *20*, 1–31.

Wu, C., & Thompson, M. E. (2020). *Sampling Theory and Practice*. Springer Nature, Switzerland AG.

Chapter 4
Ratio–Type Estimation Using Scrabled Auxiliary Variables in Stratification Under Simple Random Sampling and Ranked Set Sampling

Carlos N. Bouza-Herrera
Uiversidad de La Habana, Cuba

Jose M. Sautto
Universidad Autónoma de Guerrero, Mexico

Khalid Ul Islam Rather
iD https://orcid.org/0000-0002-4631-5652
Sher-e-Kashmir University of Agricultural Sciences and Technology of Jammu, India

ABSTRACT

This chapter introduced basic elements on stratified simple random sampling (SSRS) on ranked set sampling (RSS). The chapter extends Singh et al. results to sampling a stratified population. The mean squared error (MSE) is derived. SRS is used independently for selecting the samples from the strata. The chapter extends Singh et al. results under the RSS design. They are used for developing the estimation in a stratified population. RSS is used for drawing the samples independently from the strata. The bias and mean squared error (MSE) of the developed estimators are derived. A comparison between the biases and MSEs obtained for the sampling designs SRS and RSS is made. Under mild conditions the comparisons sustained that each RSS model is better than its SRS alternative.

DOI: 10.4018/978-1-7998-7556-7.ch004

1. INTRODUCTION

Commonly inferences are made by collecting sample data from a population $\{Z_1,...,Z_N\}$. Simple random sample (SRS) is usually the drawing method used for determining the sample from the population. Statistical theory considers that the underlying population is represented by a cumulative distribution function F. The sample provides a collection of independent random variables $\{Z_1,..,Z_{n_0}\}$. Each Z_i has the same probability distribution as the underlying population . There is no guarantee that $\{Z_1,..,Z_{n_0}\}$ provides a good representation of the population. The properties of the estimators and procedures depend of its evaluation of their behavior in average when repeating the sampling process over and over. The estimate computed from the observed sample might or might not be a good estimate.

Let us consider the estimation of the population mean

$$\mu_Z = \frac{1}{N}\sum_{i=1}^{N}Z_i$$

Under SRS the estimator

$$\bar{Z} = \frac{1}{n_0}\sum_{i=1}^{n}Z_i$$

is unbiased and its sample error is

$$Var\left(\bar{Z}\right) = \frac{\sigma_Z^2}{n_0}$$

Statisticians tried minimizing the possibility of having a "bad random sample" using some prior information. The ðrst idea was to divide the population and grouping similar units in subgroups. That was the idea of N. Kaier when proposed the "representative methods". Neyman (1934) provided mathematically concepts on representativeness. Determining subgroups and drawing independent random samples from them is the well-known Stratification sampling. Samplers consider that it ensures a broad representation across the entire population $U=\{u_1,....,u_N\}$. Stratification considers that U is divided into H strata, that is

$$U = \bigcup_{h=1}^{H} U_h; U_h \bigcap U_{h*} = \varnothing, \forall h \neq h*$$

Afterwards statistician developed other method as systematic sampling, probability-proportional-to-size sampling, etc. They are reðnements of simple random sampling and, under a set of appropriate conditions, increase the assurance of having a more representative data. Some of them assumed the knowledge of some correlated auxiliary variable.

According to the description of proportional sample allocation in Stratified Simple Random Sampling (SSRS), see Cochran (1977), we may take the number of sample units in the hth stratum ($h = 1, 2, \ldots, H$) as proportional to the stratum size, that is

$$\frac{n_{0h}}{n} = \frac{N_h}{N} = W_h$$

It is well known that if

$$\theta = \sum_{h=1}^{H} W_h \theta_h$$

A naïve estimator is the linear statistic

$$\hat{\theta} = \sum_{h=1}^{H} W_h \hat{\theta}_h$$

If the strata estimators are biased, that is if $E\left(\hat{\theta}_h - \theta\right) = B\left(h\right)$

$$E\left(\hat{\theta}\right) = \sum_{h=1}^{H} W_h \hat{\theta}_h = \theta + \sum_{h=1}^{H} W_h B_h$$

and the Mean Squared Error (MSE) is

$$MSE\left(\hat{\theta}\right) = E\left(\hat{\theta} - \theta\right)^2 = \sum_{h=1}^{H} W_h^2 E\left(\hat{\theta}_h - \theta_h\right)^2 = \sum_{h=1}^{H} W_h^2 MSE\left(\hat{\theta}_h\right)$$

McIntyre (1952) introduced the new concept of ranking preselected units and utilize this additional information for improving the representativeness of the random sample. His paper's proposal was an entirely new approach and provided an insightful introduction and its rationale. The theoretical interest in Ranked Set Sampling (RSS) was minimal for more than õfteen years. Takahashi and Wakimoto (1968) and K. Takahasi (1970) formally developed the needed basic statistical theory. Dell and Clutter (1972) and David and Levine(1972) provided important results. They sustained the unbiasedness of the proposed estimator of the population mean and that it was at least as precise as the SRS mean estimator . Stokes (1977) proposed the use of a concomitant variables X for ranking. She also developed inferential criteria on the population variance and the correlation coefficient. These papers developed innovative ideas and stimulated other statisticians to develop further research. These papers have developed a series of basic concepts and particular models to statistical inference based on RSS.

To select an RSS-sample of size $n_0 = m \times n$ units from U we use the following basic selection method.

Basic RSS Selection Procedure

Step 1. Randomly draw a sample of size n^2 units from the population.
Step 2. Allocate the n^2 selected units into n sets of size n.
Step 3. Rank the units within each set using an auxiliary variable X.
Step 4. Choose a sample for measurement with the unit ranked as the t-[th] in the t-[th] sample, t=1,…,n.
Step 5. Repeat steps 1 to 4 for m cycles until, $n_0 = m \times n$.

Denote $Z_{(i)j}$ as the ith-order statistic of ith sample from j[th] cycle (j = 1, 2, . . ., m) in RSS. The estimator of μ using RSS method for $n_0 = m \times n$ is given by:

$$\bar{Z}_{RSS} = \frac{1}{mn} \sum_{j=1}^{m} \sum_{i=1}^{n} Z_{(i)j}$$

Its variance is

$$Var\left(\bar{Z}_{RSS}\right) = \frac{\sigma^2}{mn} - \frac{1}{mn^2} \sum_{i=1}^{n} \left(\mu_{(i)} - \mu\right)^2 = \frac{1}{mn^2} \sum_{i=1}^{n} \sigma_{(i)}^2$$

$\mu_{(i)}$ and $\sigma^2_{(i)}$ are the mean and variance of the ith order statistic obtained in a random sample of size n, respectively. $\bar{Z}_{RSS}$ is called " balanced RSS estimator of μ". It is an unbiased estimator for the population mean μ also when the rankings are imperfect., Dell and Clutter (1972) results were obtained without conditions on the accuracy of the rankings based in prior information.

Remark. As $Var(\bar{Z}) - Var(\bar{Z}_{RSS}) = \dfrac{1}{mn^2}\sum_{i=1}^{n}\left(\mu_{(i)} - \mu\right)^2 \geq 0,$ RSS is to be preferred in terms of the sampling error and its efficiency is measured by

$$1 \leq eff\left(\bar{Z}_{SRS}\bar{Z}_{RSS},\right) = \frac{Var\left(\bar{Z}_{SRS}\right)}{Var\left(\bar{Z}_{RSS}\right)} \leq \frac{n+1}{2}$$

In many experimental problems is needed estimating **a** ratio. For example, in medicine the estimation of odds ratios, in economy, biology and engineering estimating rates, indexes and costs ratios are common problems. Ratio estimators are used for increasing the precision in the estimation of the population mean or total. The method is advantageous if exists a high correlation between the auxiliary and the study variables. The basic theory of ratio estimation is presented in standard text books as Cochran (1977) and Wu and Thompson (2020). The use of the ratio estimation method is present in the early works of J. Graunt and Laplace. They worked with the ratio between the number of habitants and the number of births. Laplace used it for estimating the population of France in 1820 introducing the use of random selection. See Cochran (1978) for details on these historical notes.

A ratio estimator of the population mean when SRS is used is

$$\bar{y}_R = \mu_X\left(\frac{\bar{y}}{\bar{x}}\right)$$

Its bias and MSE are derived using a Taylor Series expansion. Cochran (1940) seems to be the first paper pointing out that this estimator improved the efficiency of the estimations.

When RSS is used the corresponding ratio-estimator is

$$\bar{y}_{R(RSS)} = \mu_X\left(\frac{\bar{y}_{RSS}}{\bar{x}_{RSS}}\right)$$

The obtention of its bias and MSE used also Taylor Series expansions. It seems this estimator was suggested by Samawi and Muttlak (1966).

Ratio estimators are biased and different papers looked for diminishing the bias. The first paper, to my knowledge, was Hartley-Ross (1954) where an unbiased ratio estimator was developed. Other authors have proposed ratio type estimators. See for example Singh et al. (2010).

2. SSRS USING SCRAMBLED AUXILIARY VARIABLES

In some occasions the auxiliary variable is sensitive and the available data is not given to the sampler before scrambling it.

The population parameters used by the scrambler are

$$X_{kM} = Max\left\{X_{k1}, \ldots, X_{kN_k}\right\}$$

$$X_{km} = Min\left\{X_{k1}, \ldots, X_{kN_k}\right\}$$

The scrambling procedure produces as report for the ith selected unit from the kth stratum

$$a_{ki} = X_{kM}x_{ki} + X_{km}^2 ; i = 1, \ldots, n_k ; k = 1, .., K .$$

Let us propose the ratio type estimator

$$\bar{y}_{k(a)} = \bar{y}_k\left(\frac{\bar{A}_k}{\bar{a}_k}\right) = r_{k(a)}\bar{A}_k ; \bar{A}_k = X_{kM}\bar{X}_k + X_{km}^2 ; \bar{a}_k = X_{kM}\bar{x}_k + X_{km}^2$$

where

$$\bar{A}_k = \frac{1}{N_k}\sum_{i=1}^{N_k}A_{ki}$$

Its behavior is characterized in the next proposition

Proposition 2.1. Assume SSRS is used for selecting independent samples of size n_{0k} in each stratum U_k.

$$\bar{y}_a = \sum_{k=1}^{K} W_k r_{k(a)} \bar{A}_k$$

Has as bias and MSE

$$B\left(\bar{y}_a\right) = \sum_{k=1}^{K} W_k \left(\frac{\mu_{Y_k} C_{X_k}^2 \gamma\left(a_k\right)\left(\gamma\left(a_k\right) - \rho_k C_{Y_k} / C_{X_k}\right)}{n_k} \right)$$

$$MSE\left(\bar{y}_{(a)}\right) = M_a \cong \sum_{k=1}^{K} W_k^2 \frac{\mu_{Y_k}^{2}\left(C_{Y_k}^2 + C_{X_k}^2 \gamma\left(a_k\right)\right)\left(\gamma\left(a_k\right) - 2\frac{\rho_k C_{Y_k}}{C_{X_k}}\right)}{n_k}$$

Respectively.
Proof.
For developing the Taylor Series, we take the relative error

$$\bar{z}_k = \mu_{Z_k}\left(1 + e_{z_k}\right).$$

So

$$E\left(e_{z_k}\right) = 0, E\left(e_{z_k}^2\right) = \frac{C_{Z_k}^2}{n_k} = \frac{\sigma_{Z_k}^2 / \mu_{Z_k}^2}{n_k}, Z = X, Y; E\left(e_{X_k} e_{Y_k}\right) = \rho_k \frac{C_{Y_k} C_{X_k}}{n_k}$$

Hence, we may rewrite $\bar{y}_{k(a)}$ as

$$\bar{y}_{k(a)} = \mu_{Y_k}\left(1 + e_{Y_k}\right)\left(\frac{\bar{A}_k}{\bar{X}_{kM} \bar{X}_k\left(1 + e_{X_k}\right) + \bar{X}_{km}^2} \right) = \frac{\bar{Y}_k\left(1 + e_{Y_k}\right)}{\left(1 + \gamma\left(a_k\right) e_{X_k}\right)}$$

where

$$\gamma\left(a_k\right) = \frac{X_{kM} \bar{X}_k}{X_{kM} \bar{X}_k + X_{km}^2}$$

An expansion is possible when $|\gamma(ak_{\cdot}|<1$ holds. The terms of order larger than 2 are negligible and

$$\bar{y}_{k(a)} \cong \mu_{Y_k} \left(1 + e_{Y_k} - \gamma(a_k) e_{X_k} - \gamma(a_k) e_{Y_k} e_{X_k} + \gamma(a_k)^2 e_{X_k}^2 \right)$$

As $E\left(e_{X_k}\right) = E\left(e_{Y_k}\right) = 0$

$$E\left(\gamma(a_k) e_{Y_k} e_{X_k}\right) = \gamma(a_k) \rho_k \frac{C_{Y_k} C_{X_k}}{n_k}, E\left(\gamma(a_k)^2 e_{X_k}^2 \right) = \gamma(a_k)^2 \frac{C_{X_k}^2}{n_k}$$

the bias of the estimator in the stratum U_k is

$$E\left(\bar{y}_{k(a)} - \mu_{Y_k}\right) = B\left(\bar{y}_{k(a)}\right) \cong \frac{\mu_{Y_k} C_{X_k}^2 \gamma(a_k)\left(\gamma(a_k) - \rho_k C_{Y_k} / C_{X_k}\right)}{n_k}$$

The estimator of the population mean is the weighed sum of the strata estimators

$$\bar{y}_a = \sum_{k=1}^{K} W_k \bar{y}_{k(a)}$$

It is a linear statistical and the samples are independent. Therefore

$$B\left(\bar{y}_a\right) = \sum_{k=1}^{K} W_k \left(\frac{\mu_{Y_k} C_{X_k}^2 \gamma(a_k)\left(\gamma(a_k) - \rho_k C_{Y_k} / C_{X_k}\right)}{n_k} \right)$$

Calculating $E\left(\bar{y}_{k(a)} - \mu_{Y_k}\right)^2$ for each and eliminating the terms of order larger than 2 we have

$$E\left(\bar{y}_{k(a)} - \mu_{Y_k}\right)^2 \cong \left(\left(e_{Y_k}\right)^2 + \left(\gamma(a_k) e_{X_k}\right)^2 - 2\gamma(a_k) \rho_k e_{X_k} e_{Y_k}\right) = \bar{Y}_k^2 \left(C_{Y_k}^2 + C_{X_k}^2 \gamma(a_k)^2\right) - 2\gamma(a_k) \rho_k C_{X_k} C_{Y_k}$$

This result suggests that the sampler should prefer as auxiliary variable one with a small variation.

The approximation of the MSE of $\bar{y}_{(a)}$ may be written

$$MSE\left(\bar{y}_{(a)}\right) = M_a \cong \sum_{k=1}^{K} W_k^2 \frac{\mu_{Y_k}^2 \left(C_{Y_k}^2 + C_{X_k}^2 \gamma\left(a_k\right)\right)\left(\gamma\left(a_k\right) - 2\frac{\rho_k C_{Y_k}}{C_{X_k}}\right)}{n_k}.$$

Another transformation may be derived using the scramble report

$$b_{ki} = X_{km} x_{ki} + X_{kM}^2; i = 1, \ldots, n_k; k = 1, \ldots, K.$$

Mimicking the development of the study of $\bar{y}_{k(a)}$ the weight attached to b_k is

$$\gamma\left(b_k\right) = \frac{\bar{X}_{kM}\bar{X}_k}{\bar{X}_{kM}\bar{X}_k + X_{km}^2}$$

Take the population mean of the reports

$$\bar{B}_k = \frac{1}{N_k}\sum_{i=1}^{N_k} B_{ki}$$

The corresponding ratio type estimator is

$$\bar{y}_{k(b)} = \bar{y}_k\left(\frac{\bar{B}_k}{\bar{b}_k}\right) = r_{k(b)}\bar{B}_k;$$

With

$$\bar{B}_k = X_{km}\bar{X}_k + X_{kM}^2; \bar{b}_k = X_{km}\bar{x}_k + X_{kM}^2$$

We may rewrite the estimator as

$$\bar{y}_{k(b)} \cong \bar{Y}_k\left(1+e_{Y_k}\right)\left(\frac{\bar{B}_k}{\bar{X}_{kM}\bar{X}_k\left(1+e_{X_k}\right) + X_{km}^2}\right) = \bar{Y}_k\left(1+e_{Y_k} - \gamma\left(b_k\right)e_{X_k} - \gamma\left(b_k\right)e_{Y_k}e_{X_k} + \gamma\left(b_k\right)^2 e_{X_k}^2\right)$$

The bias and MSE are derived in the same way as in the previous case. The bias is

$$B\left(\bar{y}_{k(b)}\right) \cong \frac{\mu_{Y_k} C_{X_k}^2 \gamma\left(b_k\right)\left(\gamma\left(b_k\right) - \frac{\rho_k C_{Y_k}}{C_{X_k}}\right)}{n_k}$$

and the MSE is

$$MSE\left(\bar{y}_{k(b)}\right) \cong \frac{\mu_{Y_k}^2 \left(C_{Y_k}^2 + C_{X_k}^2 \gamma\left(a_k\right)\right)\left(\gamma\left(a_k\right) - 2\frac{\rho_k C_{Y_k}}{C_{X_k}}\right)}{n_k}$$

For the stratified model a biased estimator of the population mean of Y is

$$\bar{y}_b = \sum_{k=1}^{K} W_k \bar{y}_{k(b)}$$

Hence its bias and MSE are

$$B\left(\bar{y}_b\right) = \sum_{k=1}^{K} W_k \left(\frac{\mu_{Y_k} C_{X_k}^2 \gamma\left(b_k\right)\left(\gamma\left(b_k\right) - 2\frac{\rho_k C_{Y_k}}{C_{X_k}}\right)}{n_k}\right)$$

$$MSE\left(\bar{y}_{k(b)}\right) = M_b \cong \sum_{k=1}^{K} W_k^2 \left(\frac{\mu_{Y_k}^2 \left(C_{Y_k}^2 + C_{X_k}^2 \gamma\left(b_k\right)\right)\left(\gamma\left(b_k\right) - 2\frac{\rho_k C_{Y_k}}{C_{X_k}}\right)}{n_k}\right)$$

Then we have proved the following proposition.

Proposition 2.2. Assume SSRS is used for selecting independent samples of size n_{0k} in each stratum U_k. Take the scrambled variable is

71

$b_{ki} = X_{km}x_{ki} + X_{kM}^2; i = 1,\ldots,n_k; k = 1,..,K$. The proposed ratio type estimation procedure for the population mean of Y uses

$$\bar{y}_b = \sum_{k=1}^{K} W_k \bar{y}_{k(b)}$$

It has as bias and MSE

$$B(\bar{y}_b) = \sum_{k=1}^{K} W_k \left(\frac{\mu_{Y_k} C_{X_k}^2 \gamma(b_k)\left(\gamma(b_k) - 2\frac{\rho_k C_{Y_k}}{C_{X_k}}\right)}{n_k} \right)$$

and

$$MSE\left(\bar{y}_{k(b)}\right) = M_b \cong \sum_{k=1}^{K} W_k^2 \left(\frac{\mu_{Y_k}^2 \left(C_{Y_k}^2 + C_{X_k}^2 \gamma(b_k)\right)\left(\gamma(b_k) - 2\frac{\rho_k C_{Y_k}}{C_{X_k}}\right)}{n_k} \right)$$

Respectively.

3.2. SRSS Using Scrambled Auxiliary Variables

The ranked set sampling (RSS) has its roots in the contribution of McIntyre (1952) . Ranked set sampling (RSS) is a two-stage design and is well established that its use increases the precision of estimators, see a complete discussion in Chen et al. (2004). At the first stage, simple random samples are drawn and a low-cost ranking mechanism allows ranking the units in each simple random sample. At the second stage, measurements of the variable of interest are made on the units selected based on the ranking information obtained at the first stage RSS theory is growing in importance due to this fact and is being used in many application areas, see Alomari and Bouza (2014) for a review.

The probability model sustaining RSS uses the fact that once a sample of size n is drawn using SRS from a probability density function $f(z)$, with

$E(Z) = \mu_z, Var(Z) = \sigma_Z^{2\cdots}$. Assuming that n independent samples, each of size n, are selected using SRS are obtained the subsets

$$\{Z_1,\ldots,Z_n\}_1,\ldots,\{Z_1,\ldots,Z_n\}_n$$

The ordered samples are denoted

As is well known, David and Nagaraja (2003), the probability density function (pdf) and the cumulative distribution function (cdf) of the jth order statistics $Z_{(j)}$, for all the samples, are

$$f_{(j:n)}(z) = \frac{n!}{(n-j)!(j-1)!} \left[1 - F(z)\right]^{n-j} \left[F(z)\right]^{j-1} f(z)$$

$$F_{(j:n)}(z) = \frac{n!}{(n-j)!(j-1)!} \int_0^{F(z)} \left[1-v\right]^{n-j} \left[v\right]^{j-1} dv$$

Then

$$E\left(Z_{(j)}\right) = \mu_{Z_{(j:n)}} = \int_{-\infty}^{\infty} z f_{(j:n)} dz$$

$$Var\left(Z_{(j)}\right) = \sigma^2_{Z_{(j:n)}} = \int_{-\infty}^{\infty} (z - \mu_{Z_{(j:n)}})^2 f_{(j:n)}(z) dz$$

The upper bound of the efficiency of RSS is attained if and only if the parent distribution is rectangular. The lower bound is attained if and only if the parent distribution is degenerate. Dell and Clutter (1972) investigated the performance of RSS when ranking was subject to errors. Stokes (1977) studied the RSS with concomitant variables.

A selection procedure for stratified sampling is

Basic Stratified RSS Procedure

Step 1: Fix n_k, r_k, K, $s_k = t_k = m_k = h = 0$
Step 2. $h = h + 1$
Step 3. $s_k = s_k + 1$
Step 4: Randomly select independent units from each target stratum population. These units are randomly allocated into n_k sets, each of size n_k.

Step 5: Rank the n_k units in each set using X.
Step 6: Measure Y in the j-th ranked unit of the j-th set.
Step 7: While $s_k < m_k$ go to Step 3.
Step 8: Evaluate the corresponding stratum units
Step 9: $h < K$ go to Step 2
END

We have to deal with a stratified sample of order statistics

$$\left\{ \left(X_{(j:j)t}, Y_{(j:j)t} \right)_k; k = 1,..,K, t = 1,\ldots,m_k, j = 1,..,n_k, \right\}$$

The sample size in the kth stratum is $n_{0k} = m_k n_k$.
Let us denote the RSS Z-mean in U_k by

$$\overline{z}_{RSS(k)} = \frac{1}{n_k m_k} \sum_{t=1}^{m_k} \sum_{i=1}^{n_k} z_{(j:j)t}, = \overline{Z}_k \left(1 + e_{ZRSS(k)} \right) z = x, y, a, b$$

The RSS relative errors are denoted

$$e_{ZRSS(k)} = \frac{\overline{z}_{RSS(k)} - \mu_{Z_k}}{\mu_{Z_k}}$$

Their expected value and covariances are

$$E\left(e_{ZRSS(k)} \right) = 0; V\left(e_{ZRSS(k)} \right) = \frac{V\left(\overline{z}_{RSS(k)} \right)}{\mu_{Z_k}^2} = C_{z_k}^2; Cov\left(\overline{x}_{RSS(k)}, \overline{y}_{RSS(k)} \right) = \rho_k C_{x_k} C_{y_k}.$$

Then the counterpart of $\overline{y}_a$ is

$$a_{k(i)} = X_{kM} x_{k(i)} + X_{km}^2; i = 1,\ldots,n_k; k = 1,..,K$$

$x_{k(i)}$ is the ith order statistic of the auxiliary variable. Generally, we use it for ranking Y.

$$\bar{y}_{aRSS} = \left(\frac{\bar{y}_{RSS}}{\bar{a}_{RSS}} \right) \bar{A}$$

The within strata bias is given by

$$E\left(\bar{y}_{k(a)RSS} - \mu_{Y_k} \right) = B\left(\bar{y}_{k(a)RSS} \right) \cong \frac{\mu_{Y_k} C^2_{X_{kRSS}} \gamma\left(a_{kRSS} \right) \left(\gamma\left(a_{kRSS} \right) - 2\rho_k C_{Y_k RSS} / C_{X_{kRSS}} \right)}{n_k}$$

Then the bias of the estimator of the population mean

$$\bar{y}_a = \sum_{k=1}^{K} W_k \bar{y}_{k(a)RSS}$$

is

$$B\left(\bar{y}_{aRSS} \right) = \sum_{k=1}^{K} W_k \left(\frac{\mu_{Y_k} C^2_{X_{kRSS}} \gamma\left(a_{kRSS} \right) \left(\gamma\left(a_{kRSS} \right) - 2\rho_k C_{Y_{kRSS}} / C_{X_k RSS} \right)}{n_k} \right)$$

The MSE of $\bar{y}_{k(a)RSS}$ is approximated by

$$E\left(\bar{y}_{k(a)RSS} - \mu_{Y_k} \right)^2 \cong M_{k(a)RSS} = \mu_{Y_k}^2 \left(\left(e_{Y_{kRSS}} \right)^2 + \left(\gamma\left(a_{kRSS} \right) e_{X_k RSS} \right)^2 - \gamma\left(a_{kRSS} \right) \rho_k e_{X_{kRSS}} e_{Y_{kRSS}} \right)$$

$$= \frac{\mu_{Y_k}^2}{n_k} \left(\sigma^2_{Y_k} - \frac{1}{m_k} \sum_{j=1}^{n_k} \left(\mu_{Y_{k(j)}} - \mu_{Y_k} \right)^2 \right) + \frac{\mu_{Y_k}^2 \gamma\left(a_{kRSS} \right)^2}{n_k} \left(\sigma^2_{X_k} - \frac{1}{m_k} \sum_{j=1}^{n_k} \left(\mu_{X_{k(j)}} - \mu_{X_k} \right)^2 \right)$$

$$-2 \frac{\mu_{Y_{k(j)}} \gamma\left(a_k \right) \rho_k \sqrt{ \left(\sigma^2_{X_k} - \frac{1}{m_k} \sum_{j=1}^{n_k} \left(\mu_{X_{k(j)}} - \mu_{X_k} \right)^2 \right) \left(\sigma^2_{Y_k} - \frac{1}{m_k} \sum_{j=1}^{n_k} \left(\mu_{Y_{k(j)}} - \mu_{Y_k} \right)^2 \right) }}{\mu_{X_{k(j)}}}$$

The approximation of the MSE of $\bar{y}_{(a)}$ may be written

$$MSE\left(\bar{y}_{(a)RSS}\right) \cong M_{aRSS} = \sum_{k=1}^{K} W_k^2 \frac{\mu_{Yk}^2\left(C_{Y_k}^2 + C_{X_k}^2\gamma\left(a_k\right)\right)\left(\gamma\left(a_k\right) - 2\frac{\rho_k C_{Y_k}}{C_{X_k}}\right)}{n_k}$$

Then we have proved the following proposition.

Proposition 3.1 . Assume that SRSS is used for selecting samples of size n_{0k} in each stratum of U and take

$$a_{k(i)} = X_{kM}x_{k(i)} + X_{km}^2 ; i = 1,\ldots,n_k ; k = 1,..,K$$

$$\frac{\sigma_{Z_k}^2}{n_{0k}\mu_{Z_k}^2} = C_{Z_k}^2, Z = X, Y \, , \rho k\_Corr(Xj_{k,}Yj_{k)}.$$

The ratio type estimator of μY

$$\bar{y}_{aRSS} = \sum_{k=1}^{K} W_k \bar{y}_{k(a)RSS}$$

has approximate bias

$$B\left(\bar{y}_{aRSS}\right) = \sum_{k=1}^{K} W_k \left(\frac{\mu_{Y_k}C_{X_{kRSS}}^2\gamma\left(a_{kRSS}\right)\left(\gamma\left(a_{kRSS}\right) - 2\rho_k C_{Y_{kRSS}} / C_{X_k RSS}\right)}{n_k}\right)$$

and approximate MSE

$$M_{aRSS} = \sum_{k=1}^{K} W_k^2 \frac{\mu_{Yk}^2\left(C_{Y_{kRSS}}^2 + C_{X_{kRSS}}^2\gamma\left(a_k\right)\right)\left(\gamma\left(a_k\right) - 2\frac{\rho_k C_{Y_{kRSS}}}{C_{X_{kRSS}}}\right)}{n_k}.$$

Comparing this result with $MSE\left(\bar{y}_{k(a)}\right)$ suggests that the sampler should prefer RSS as commonly the first two terms of M_{aRSS} are smaller than their SRS counterparts. The last term of $M_{k(a)RSS}$ is expected to be larger . Only in some special cases in which $\mu_{Y_{k(j)}}\rho_k < 0$ it could not be not larger.

Note that

$$\sigma_{z_k}^2 - \frac{1}{m_k}\sum_{j=1}^{n_k}\left(\mu_{Z_{k(j)}} - \mu_{Z_k}\right)^2 \leq \sigma_{z_k}^2$$

$$\sqrt{\left(\sigma_{X_k}^2 - \frac{1}{m_k}\sum_{j=1}^{n_k}\left(\mu_{X_{k(j)}} - \mu_{X_k}\right)^2\right)\left(\sigma_{Y_k}^2 - \frac{1}{m_k}\sum_{j=1}^{n_k}\left(\mu_{y_{k(j)}} - \mu_{Y_k}\right)^2\right)} \leq \sigma_{X_k}\sigma_{Y_k}$$

Hence, the proposed RSS counterpart not necessarily has a smaller bias and/or MSE.

Take the scrambled auxiliary variable

$$b_{ki} = X_{km}x_{ki} + X_{kM}^2 ; i = 1,\ldots,n_k ; k = 1,..,K .$$

The RSS version uses the order statistics in a sample of size n_k

$$b_{k(i)} = X_{km}x_{k(i)} + X_{kM}^2 ; i = 1,\ldots,n_k ; k = 1,..,K$$

The ordering is perfect as X is known. The estimator in this case is

$$\bar{y}_{(b)RSS} = \sum_{k=1}^{K} W_k \left(\frac{\bar{y}_{kRSS}}{\bar{b}_{kRSS}}\right)\bar{B}_k ;$$

Let us denote

$$\bar{y}_{k(b)RSS} = \left(\frac{\bar{y}_{kRSS}}{\bar{b}_{kRSS}}\right)\bar{B}_k .$$

The corresponding Taylor Series approximation in the kth stratum is

$$\overline{y}_{k(b)RSS} = \mu_{Y_k}\left(1+e_{Y_k RSS}\right)\left(\frac{\overline{B}_k}{X_{kM}\overline{X}_k\left(1+e_{X_k RSS}\right)+X_{km}^2}\right)$$

$$\cong \mu_{Y_k}\left(1+e_{Y_k RSS}-\gamma\left(b_k\right)e_{X_k RSS}-\gamma\left(b_k\right)e_{X_k RSS}e_{Y_k RSS}+\gamma\left(b\right)^2 e_{X_k}^2\right);$$

Defining

$$\gamma\left(b_k\right) = \frac{\left(X_{kM}-X_{km}\right)\overline{X}_k}{\overline{B}_k}$$

The Taylor Series development allows to obtain that the approximations to the bias and the MSE for $\overline{y}_{k(b)RSS}$ are

$$B\left(\overline{y}_{k(a)RSS}\right) \cong \frac{1}{n_k}\left[\frac{\mu_{Y_k}\gamma\left(b_{kRSS}\right)^2\left(\sigma_{X_{kRSS}}^2-\frac{1}{m_k}\sum_{j=1}^{n_k}\left(\mu_{X_{k(j)}}-\mu_{X_k}\right)^2\right)}{\mu_{X_k}^2}\right.$$

$$\left.-\mu_{Y_k}\gamma\left(b_{kRSS}\right)\rho_k\sqrt{\left(\sigma_{X_k}^2-\frac{1}{m_k}\sum_{j=1}^{n_k}\left(\mu_{X_{k(j)}}-\mu_{X_k}\right)^2\right)\left(\sigma_{Y_k}^2-\frac{1}{m_k}\sum_{j=1}^{n_k}\left(\mu_{y_{k(j)}}-\mu_{Y_k}\right)^2\right)}\right]$$

and

$$E\left(\overline{y}_{k(b)RSS}-\mu_{Y_k}\right)^2 \cong M_{k(b)RSS}$$

$$= \frac{\mu_{Y_k}^2}{n_k}\left(\sigma_{Y_k}^2-\frac{1}{m_k}\sum_{j=1}^{n_k}\left(\mu_{Y_{k(j)}}-\mu_{Y_k}\right)^2\right)+\frac{\mu_{Y_k}^2\gamma\left(b_{kRSS}\right)^2}{n_k}\left(\sigma_{X_k}^2-\frac{1}{m_k}\sum_{j=1}^{n_k}\left(\mu_{X_{k(j)}}-\mu_{X_k}\right)^2\right)$$

$$-2\frac{\mu_{Y_{k(j)}}\gamma\left(b_k\right)\rho_k\sqrt{\left(\sigma_{X_k}^2-\frac{1}{m_k}\sum_{j=1}^{n_k}\left(\mu_{X_{k(j)}}-\mu_{X_k}\right)^2\right)\left(\sigma_{Y_k}^2-\frac{1}{m_k}\sum_{j=1}^{n_k}\left(\mu_{Y_{k(j)}}-\mu_{Y_k}\right)^2\right)}}{\mu_{X_{k(j)}}}$$

The SRSS model is characterized in the next proposition

Proposition 3.2. Assume that SRSS is used for selecting samples of size n_{0k} in each stratum of U and take

$$\frac{\sigma^2_{Z_k}}{n_{0k}\mu^2_{Z_k}} = C^2_{z_k}, Z = X, Y, \rho k_{\_} Corr(Xj_{k,} Yj_{k)}.$$

The ratio type estimator of μY

$$\overline{y}_{bRSS} = \sum_{k=1}^{K} W_k \overline{y}_{k(b)RSS}$$

has approximate bias

$$B\left(\overline{y}_{bRSS}\right) = \sum_{k=1}^{K} W_k \frac{1}{n_k} \left[\frac{\mu_{Y_k}\gamma\left(b_{kRSS}\right)^2\left(\sigma^2_{X_{kRSS}} - \frac{1}{m_k}\sum_{j=1}^{n_k}\left(\mu_{X_{k(j)}} - \mu_{X_k}\right)^2\right)}{\mu^2_{X_k}} \right.$$
$$\left. -\mu_{Y_k}\gamma\left(b_{kRSS}\right)\rho_k \sqrt{\left(\sigma^2_{X_k} - \frac{1}{m_k}\sum_{j=1}^{n_k}\left(\mu_{X_{k(j)}} - \mu_{X_k}\right)^2\right)\left(\sigma^2_{Y_k} - \frac{1}{m_k}\sum_{j=1}^{n_k}\left(\mu_{y_{k(j)}} - \mu_{Y_k}\right)^2\right)} \right]$$

and approximate MSE

$$M_{bRSS} = \sum_{k=1}^{K} W_k^2 \frac{\mu_{Y_k}^2}{n_k}\left(\sigma^2_{Y_k} - \frac{1}{m_k}\sum_{j=1}^{n_k}\left(\mu_{Y_{k(j)}} - \mu_{Y_k}\right)^2\right) + \frac{\mu_{Y_k}^2\gamma\left(b_{kRSS}\right)^2}{n_k}\left(\sigma^2_{X_k} - \frac{1}{m_k}\sum_{j=1}^{n_k}\left(\mu_{X_{k(j)}} - \mu_{X_k}\right)^2\right)$$

$$-2\frac{\mu_{Y_{k(j)}}\gamma\left(b_k\right)\rho_k \sqrt{\left(\sigma^2_{X_k} - \frac{1}{m_k}\sum_{j=1}^{n_k}\left(\mu_{X_{k(j)}} - \mu_{X_k}\right)^2\right)\left(\sigma^2_{Y_k} - \frac{1}{m_k}\sum_{j=1}^{n_k}\left(\mu_{Y_{k(j)}} - \mu_{Y_k}\right)^2\right)}}{\mu_{X_{k(j)}}}.$$

Proof:

The proof is obtained from the fact that $\overline{y}_{bRSS}$ is a linear statistic and the samples of the strata are mutually independent.

Note that the proposed RSS counterpart of $\overline{y}_a$ of not necessarily has a smaller bias and/or MSE than the SSSRS.

3. A NUMERICAL STUDY

Analytical comparisons of the different estimators depend of a series of parameters that may tune the preference due to the particular values of them. The behavior of the proposed estimators in terms of their Biases and MSE`s are studied numerically. They were conducted for detecting some regularities . Some real-life data were used .

We used data coming from 5 studies where the owner of the data considered that X was sensitive and f=n/N=0,1. The studies were:

1. A marketing study on the capacity of buyers. X was the state of their accounts to be obtained from a bank. K=6, N=2 349
2. A study on the quality of the water obtained from the wastes of some enterprises after purifying it was studied. X was the statistics in their files. K=7, N=8 000
3. The use of internet in the offices for personal purposes was studied. X was the last month reports of the employees . K=5, N=236
4. The local government is planning to give support to projects of small and medium business. The loans obtained by them from an ONG was X and was controlled by an association of the entrepreneurs. K=4, N=274.
5. Toxicity in horticulture farms was studied. The types of farms were K=10, N=379.

With the obtained data were computed the ratios

$$F\left(\bar{y}_\tau, \bar{y}_\omega\right) = \frac{B\left(\bar{y}_\tau\right)}{B\left(\bar{y}_\omega\right)}; \tau, \omega = a, b, aRSS, bRSS$$

$$G\left(\bar{y}_\tau, \bar{y}_\omega\right) = \frac{MSE\left(\bar{y}_\tau\right)}{MSE\left(\bar{y}_\omega\right)}; \tau, \omega = a, b, aRSS, bRSS$$

When $H(\tau,\omega)>1$, $H=F,G$ is preferred the sampling, strategy identified by τ. The results are reported in Tables 1-5. In all the cases the SRSS estimators were more efficient than the . The best estimator was by $\bar{y}_{bRSS}$. The scrambling using b was systematically the best option.

Table 1 sustains that the efficiency $\bar{y}_{bRSS}$ vs $\bar{y}_{baRSS}$ is rather small both for bias and MSE. In e case of water quality the efficiency of RSS estimators is very high in the case of the bias and $\bar{y}_{bRSS}$ vs $\bar{y}_{aRSS}$ behaves vey similarly. For the MSE of the estimators the increase in the gains are similar.

Table 1. $F\left(\bar{y}_\tau, \bar{y}_\omega\right)$ *in the marketing study*

	Estimator	$\bar{y}_a$	$\bar{y}_b$	$\bar{y}_{aRSS}$	$\bar{y}_{bRSS}$
	$\bar{y}_a$	1	0,9713	0,9154	0,8716
Bias	$\bar{y}_b$	-	1	0,9384	0,9285
	$\bar{y}_{aRSS}$	-	-	1	0,9899
	$\bar{y}_{bRSS}$	-	-	-	1
	$\bar{y}_a$	1	0,9781	0,9641	0,9362
MSE	$\bar{y}_b$		1	0,9858	0,9573
	$\bar{y}_{aRSS}$			1	0,9705
	$\bar{y}_{bRSS}$				1

The internet use study, reported in Table gives evidence that the four estimators have small gains. As in the rest of the cases $\bar{y}_{bRSS}$ is the best option.

Table 2. $F\left(\bar{y}_\tau, \bar{y}_\omega\right)$ *in the water quality study*

	Estimator	$\bar{y}_a$	$\bar{y}_b$	$\bar{y}_{aRSS}$	$\bar{y}_{bRSS}$
	$\bar{y}_a$	1	0,8714	0,7154	0,7014
Bias	$\bar{y}_b$	-	1	0,9808	0,7291
	$\bar{y}_{aRSS}$	-	-	1	0,7431
	$\bar{y}_{bRSS}$	-	-	-	1
	$\bar{y}_a$	1	0,8781	0,8441	0,8142
MSE	$\bar{y}_b$		1	0,9627	0,8454
	$\bar{y}_{aRSS}$			1	0,8994
	$\bar{y}_{bRSS}$				1

Table 3. $F\left(\bar{y}_\tau, \bar{y}_\omega\right)$ in internet use study

	Estimator	$\bar{y}_a$	$\bar{y}_b$	$\bar{y}_{aRSS}$	$\bar{y}_{bRSS}$
	$\bar{y}_a$	1	0,9513	0,9085	0,9013
Bias	$\bar{y}_b$	-	1	0,9593	0,9322
	$\bar{y}_{aRSS}$	-	-	1	0,9711
	$\bar{y}_{bRSS}$	-	-	-	1
	$\bar{y}_a$	1	0,9591	0,9331	0,9132
MSE	$\bar{y}_b$		1	0,9725	0,9364
	$\bar{y}_{aRSS}$			1	0,9615
	$\bar{y}_{bRSS}$				1

Table 4 presents de efficiencies in the Government Support to Projects Study. $\bar{y}_{bRSS}$ is considerably more efficient than $\bar{y}_a$ in terms of Bias and with the all other estimators in terms of MSE.

The results of the efficiency in the Toxicity in the Horticulture Farms Study $\bar{y}_{bRSS}$ is considerably more efficient than the other estimators.

4. CONCLUSION

The proposed ratio type estimators allow that the knowledge of auxiliary sensitive variables protects the privacy of the intervieweed. The use of RSS provides better estimators in terms of efficiency. Section 4 presented real life studies and they provided quantitative evidence sustaining that the efficiency may be negligable or important

ACKNOWLEDGMENT

This paper has been benefited by the suggestions of Prof. A. I. Alomari. These results have been supported by and project PN223LH010 Modelos epidemiológicos avanzados. Estrategias de modelación, resolución y aplicaciones.

Table 4. $F\left(\bar{y}_{\tau}, \bar{y}_{\omega}\right)$ *in Government Support to Projects Study*

	Estimator	$\bar{y}_a$	$\bar{y}_b$	$\bar{y}_{aRSS}$	$\bar{y}_{bRSS}$
	$\bar{y}_a$	1	0,8712	0,8172	0,7812
Bias	$\bar{y}_b$	-	1	0,9368	0,8336
	$\bar{y}_{aRSS}$	-	-	1	0,8895
	$\bar{y}_{bRSS}$	-	-	-	1
	$\bar{y}_a$	1	0,8781	0,8551	0,6152
MSE	$\bar{y}_b$		1	0,9738	0,6315
	$\bar{y}_{aRSS}$			1	0,6484
	$\bar{y}_{bRSS}$				1

Table 5. $F\left(\bar{y}_{\tau}, \bar{y}_{\omega}\right)$ *in Toxicity in the Horticulture Farms Study*

	Estimator	$\bar{y}_a$	$\bar{y}_b$	$\bar{y}_{aRSS}$	$\bar{y}_{bRSS}$
	$\bar{y}_a$	1	0,8912	0,6152	0,6014
Bias	$\bar{y}_b$	-	1	0,8704	0,6908
	$\bar{y}_{aRSS}$	-	-	1	0,7936
	$\bar{y}_{bRSS}$	-	-	-	1
	$\bar{y}_a$	1	0,8781	0,8441	0,6429
MSE	$\bar{y}_b$		1	0,9612	0,6684
	$\bar{y}_{aRSS}$			1	0,6953
	$\bar{y}_{bRSS}$				1

REFERENCES

Al-Omari, A. I., & Bouza, C. N. (2014). Review of Ranked Set Sampling: Modifications And Applications. *Revista Investigación Operacional*, *35*, 215–240.

Al-Omari, A. I., Ibrahim, K., & Jemain, A. A. (2009). New ratio estimators of the mean using simple random sampling and ranked set sampling methods. *Revista Investigacion Operacional*, *30*, 97–108.

Al-Omari, A. I., Jaber, K., & Al-Omari, A. (2008). Modified ratio-type estimators of the mean using extreme ranked set sampling. *Journal of Mathematics and Statistics*, *4*(3), 150–155. doi:10.3844/jmssp.2008.150.155

Bai, Z. D., & Chen, Z. (2003). On the theory of ranked set sampling *and* its ramifications. *Journal of Statistical Planning and Inference*, *109*(1-2), 81–99. doi:10.1016/S0378-3758(02)00302-6

Bouza, C. N. (2001). Model assisted ranked survey sampling. *Biometrical Journal. Biometrische Zeitschrift*, *36*, 753–764.

Bouza Herrera, C. N., & Al-Omari, A. I. (2011). Ranked set estimation with imputation of the missing observations: The median estimator. *Revista Investigación Operacional*, *32*, 30–37.

Chen, Z., Bai, Z., & Sinha, B. K. (2004). Ranked set sampling: theory and applications. In Lectures Notes in Statistics (vol. 176). Springer. doi:10.1007/978-0-387-21664-5

Cochran, W. G. (1940). Some properties of estimators based on sampling scheme with varying probabilities. *The Australian Journal of Statistics*, *17*, 22–28.

Cochran, W. G. (1977). *Sampling Techniques*. John Wiley and Sons.

Cochran, W. G. (1978). Laplace's ratio estimator. In Contributions to Survey Sampling and Applied Statistics. Academic Press. doi:10.1016/B978-0-12-204750-3.50008-3

David, H. A., & Levine, D. N. (1972). Ranked set sampling in the presence of judgment error. *Biometrics*, *28*, 553–555.

David, H. A., & Nagaraja, H. N. (2003). *Order Statistics* (3rd ed.). John Wiley & Sons, Inc. doi:10.1002/0471722162

Dell, T. R., & Clutter, J. L. (1972). Ranked set sampling theory with order statistics background. *Biometrics*, *28*(2), 545–555. doi:10.2307/2556166

Hall, L. K., & Dell, T. R. (1996). Trials of ranked set sampling for forage yields. *Forest Sc*, *121*, 22–26.

Hartley, H. O., & Ross, A. (1954). Unbiased ratio estimator. *Nature, 174*, 270–27.

Ibrahim, K., Syam, M., & Al-Omari, A. I. (2010). Estimating the Population Mean Using Stratified Median Ranked Set Sampling. *Applied Mathematical Sciences, 47*, 2341–2354.

Liu, L., & Tua, Y. (2006). Imputation for missing data and variance estimation when auxiliary information is incomplete. *Model Assisted Statistics and Applications: An International Journal, 1*(2), 83–94. doi:10.3233/MAS-2005-1204

McIntyre, G. A. (1952). A method of unbiased selective sampling using ranked sets. *Australian Journal of Agricultural Research, 3*(4), 385–390. doi:10.1071/AR9520385

Neyman, J. (1934). On the application of the representative methods, the method of stratified sampling and the purposive method. *Journal of the Royal Statistical Society, 97*, 558–606. doi:10.2307/2342192

Rueda, M., & González, S. (2004). Missing data and auxiliary information in surveys. *Computational Statistics, 10*(4), 559–567. doi:10.1007/BF02753912

Samawi, H. M., & Muttlak, H. A. (1996). Estimation of ratio using ranked set sampling. *Biometrical Journal. Biometrische Zeitschrift, 38*(6), 753–764. doi:10.1002/bimj.4710380616

Singh, H. P., Tailor, R., & Tailor, R. (2010). On ratio and product methods with certain known population parameters of auxiliary variable in sample surveys. *SORT (Barcelona), 34*, 157–180.

Stokes, S. L. (1977). Ranked set sampling with concomitant variables. *Communications in Statistics, 6*(12), 1207–1211. doi:10.1080/03610927708827563

Takahasi, K. (1970). Practical note on estimation of population means based on samples stratiðed by means of ordering. *Annals of the Institute of Statistical Mathematics, 22*(1), 421–428. doi:10.1007/BF02506360

Takahasi, K., & Wakimoto, K. (1968). On the unbiased estimates of the population mean based on the sample stratified by means of ordering. *Annals of the Institute of Statistical Mathematics, 20*(1), 1–31. doi:10.1007/BF02911622

Chapter 5
A Study of Gjestvang and Singh Randomized Response Model Using Ranked Set Sampling

Shravya Jasti
Texas A&M University – Kingsville, Kingsville, USA

Stephen A. Sedory
Texas A&M University – Kingsville, Kingsville, USA

Sarjinder Singh
Texas A&M University – Kingsville, Kingsville, USA

ABSTRACT

In this chapter, the authors investigate the performance of the Gjestvang and Singh randomized response model for estimating the mean of a sensitive variable using ranked set sampling along the lines of Bouza. The proposed estimator is found to be unbiased, and a variance expression is derived. Then a simulation study is carried out to judge the magnitude of relative efficiency in various situations. At the end, the proposed model is assessed based on real secondary data applications. A set of SAS codes is also included.

DOI: 10.4018/978-1-7998-7556-7.ch005

1. INTRODUCTION

Warner (1965) proposed an estimator for estimating the prevalence of a sensitive attribute in a population that utilized a device by implementing the idea of randomized response. The goal of his method was to reduce non-response and evasive-answer biases by maintaining the privacy of interviewees during an in person survey. While his procedure allowed for the estimation of the proportion of a population having or not having a stigmatizing characteristic, it does not address the issue of estimating the mean of a sensitive quantitative variable, such as the number of abortions, income, drug usage, etc. To overcome this limitation Horvitz *et al.* (1967) and Greenberg *et al.* (1971) extended the work of Warner and by considering quantitative variables rather than qualitative ones. Himmelfarb and Edgel (1980) introduced the concept of an additive scrambling randomization response model, which utilized a scrambling variable having a known distribution in order to estimate the mean of a quantitative sensitive variable. Later Eichhorn and Hayre (1983) developed the concept of a multiplicative randomized response model for the same purpose. Chaudhuri and Stenger (1992) suggested a way to incorporate both ideas of additive and multiplicative models in a single model. Bouza (2009) investigated use of Chaudhuri and Stenger (1992) randomized response technique in ranked set sampling, while Bouza *et al.* (2017) extended the Saha's randomized response technique for ranked set sampling. These two investigations by Bouza motivated the authors to work on similar lines for Gjestvang and Singh (2009) model. This later model was originally used by Gjestvang and Singh (2006) for estimating the proportion of a sensitive characteristic, further detail can be found in Singh (2020).

   In the next section, we propose a new estimator of the population mean of a sensitive variable, then show the unbiasedness of the proposed estimator and derive the variance expression.

2. PROPOSED ESTIMATOR

Consider a population Ω of N units with the values of the stigmatizing variable Y as $Y_1, Y_2, \ldots, Y_N$. Then our aim is to estimate the population mean $\overline{Y}$ of the sensitive variable Y defined as:

$$\overline{Y} = \frac{1}{N} \sum_{i=1}^{N} Y_i \tag{2.1}$$

It may be worth pointing out that Ranked Set Sampling (RSS) was first introduced by McIntyre (1952). Bouza (2009) considered selecting a sample s of n people from a population Ω by using Ranked Set Sampling. Let r be the overall number of replicates and then let $m \times m$ be the cumulative proportion of individuals specified for ranking through every replicate so that $n=mr$. One replication of ranked set sampling cycle is explained as follows. During the first step, choose a simple random sample of m individuals, ranking them by judgement assessment as $y_{(11)} < y_{(12)} < \ldots < y_{(1m)}$; over the next session, designate the next sample of individuals a random sample of m individuals, ranking these again based on a judgement assessment as $y_{(21)} < y_{(22)} < \ldots < y_{(2m)}$; and finally in the mth cycle, then choose a simple random sample of m individuals, classify these again as $y_{(m1)} < y_{(m2)} < \ldots < y_{(mm)}$. Table 1 provides a visual cycle analysis of such a RSS process.

Table 1. Cycle of ranked set sampling

$y_{(11)}$	$y_{(12)}$	...	$y_{(1m)}$
$y_{(21)}$	$y_{(22)}$	...	$y_{(2m)}$
$\vdots$	$\vdots$		$\vdots$
$y_{(m1)}$	$y_{(m2)}$	...	$y_{(mm)}$

Therefore, in the very first replicating composition of m cycles, m individuals have assigned shown in triangular listings of the $m \times m$ matrix. In certain expressions, during the first cycle an individual with a rank value of $y_{(11)}$ is chosen, in the second cycle an individual with a rank value of $y_{(22)}$ is chosen as well as in the mth cycle an individual with a ranking value of $y_{(mm)}$ is assigned. Replicating such m cycles r times would be a rank set sample of $n=mr$ with their predicted ranked and non-observed values such as $Y_{(1)}, Y_{(2)}, \ldots, Y_{(n)}$. Notice that $Y_{(1)}, Y_{(2)}, \ldots, Y_{(n)}$ are the real and non-observed rank set sample, s of n individuals with sensitive attributes. We were collecting scrambled responses as follows. -- respondent specified in the survey will draw a random number S from any known distribution, with known parameters, say mean θ and variance γ^2. Do not report this random number S to the interviewer. For a fixed values of α and β, we compute $P = \dfrac{\beta}{\alpha + \beta}$ then we make a deck of cards consisting of two types of cards. The proportion P of the cards bear the statement, "Please report the value Y+αS" and (1–P) be the proportion of cards bearing the statement, "Please report the value Y–βS". Then each respondent is asked to draw a card from the deck, and report the value to the interviewer as directed by the outcome from the deck. In short, the observed response from the ith respondent has the probability mass function as:

$$
Z_{(i)} = \begin{bmatrix} Y_{(i)} + \alpha S \text{ with probability } P = \dfrac{\beta}{\alpha + \beta} \\[2mm] Y_{(i)} - \beta S \text{ with probability } (1-P) = \dfrac{\alpha}{\alpha + \beta} \end{bmatrix} \tag{2.1}
$$

Now considering the Lemma expression:

Lemma 2.1. Each observed response $Z_{(i)}$ is an unbiased estimator of the population mean $\bar{Y}$ of the sensitive variable.

Proof. Let E_R denote the expected value over the randomization device, and E_d denote the expected value over the design which is Ranked Set Sampling. Then taking expected of $Z_{(i)}$, we have

$$
E\left(Z_{(i)}\right) = PE_d E_R\left[Y_{(i)} + \alpha S\right] + (1-P)E_d E_R\left[Y_{(i)} - \beta S\right]
$$

$$
= PE_d\left[Y_{(i)} + \alpha E_R(S)\right] + (1-P)E_d\left[Y_{(i)} - \beta E_R(S)\right]
$$

$$
= PE_d\left[Y_{(i)} + \alpha\theta\right] + (1-P)E_d\left[Y_{(i)} - \beta\theta\right]
$$

$$
= P\left[E_d\{Y_{(i)}\} + \alpha\theta\right] + (1-P)\left[E_d\{Y_{(i)}\} - \beta\theta\right]
$$

$$
= P\left[\bar{Y} + \alpha\theta\right] + (1-P)\left[\bar{Y} - \beta\theta\right]
$$

$$
= P\bar{Y} + (1-P)\bar{Y} + \alpha\theta P - (1-P)\beta\theta
$$

$$
= \bar{Y} + \alpha\theta\frac{\beta}{\alpha + \beta} - \frac{\alpha}{\alpha + \beta}\theta\beta = \bar{Y} \tag{2.2}
$$

which proves the Lemma.

Now we have the following theorem:

Theorem 2.1. For RSS, an unbiased estimator of the population mean $\bar{Y}$ is given by

$$\bar{y}_{sravi} = \frac{1}{n}\sum_{i=1}^{n} Z_{(i)} \tag{2.3}$$

Proof: Take expected value on both sides of (2.3), we get

$$E[\bar{y}_{sravi}] = E\left[\frac{1}{n}\sum_{i=1}^{n} Z_{(i)}\right]$$

$$= \frac{1}{n}\sum_{i=1}^{n} E\left(Z_{(i)}\right)$$

$$= \frac{1}{n}\sum_{i=1}^{n} \bar{Y} = \frac{n\bar{Y}}{n} = \bar{Y} \tag{2.4}$$

which proves the theorem.

Theorem 2 2. For the RSS, the variance of the estimator $\bar{y}_{sravi}$ is given by

$$V\left(\bar{y}_{sravi}\right) = \frac{\alpha\beta\left(\gamma^2 + \theta^2\right)}{n} + \frac{1}{n}\left[\sigma_y^2 - \frac{1}{m}\sum_{i=1}^{m}\left\{\mu_{y_{(i)}} - \bar{Y}\right\}^2\right] \tag{2.5}$$

Proof: Let V_R represent the randomizing variance, and let V_d define the variance across the RSS design. The variance of the $\bar{y}_{sravi}$ estimator is given by

$$V\left(\bar{y}_{sravi}\right) = E_d V_R\left[\bar{y}_{sravi}\right] + V_d E_R\left[\bar{y}_{sravi}\right]$$

$$= E_d V_R \left[\frac{1}{n} \sum_{i=1}^{n} Z_{(i)} \right] + V_d E_R \left[\frac{1}{n} \sum_{i=1}^{n} Z_{(i)} \right]$$

$$= E_d \left[\frac{1}{n^2} \sum_{i=1}^{n} V_R \left\{ Z_{(i)} \right\} \right] + V_d \left[\frac{1}{n} \sum_{i=1}^{n} E_R \left\{ Z_{(i)} \right\} \right] \qquad (2.6)$$

Now,

$$E_R \left(Z_{(i)} \right) = P E_R \left[Y_{(i)} + \alpha S \right] + (1-P) E_R \left[Y_{(i)} - \beta S \right]$$

$$= P \left[Y_{(i)} + \alpha E_R (S) \right] + (1-P) \left[Y_{(i)} - \beta E_R (S) \right]$$

$$= P Y_{(i)} + \alpha P \theta + (1-P) Y_{(i)} - (1-P) \beta \theta$$

$$= P Y_{(i)} + (1-P) Y_{(i)} + \frac{\alpha \beta}{\alpha + \beta} \theta - \frac{\alpha \beta}{\alpha + \beta} \theta = Y_{(i)} \qquad (2.7)$$

Also note that the $V_R(Z_{(i)})$ is given by

$$V_R \left(Z_{(i)} \right) = E_R \left[\left(Z_{(i)} \right)^2 \right] - \left[E_R \left(Z_{(i)} \right) \right]^2$$

$$= E_R \left[P \left\{ Y_{(i)} + \alpha S \right\}^2 + (1-P) \left\{ Y_{(i)} - \beta S \right\}^2 \right] - \left\{ Y_{(i)} \right\}^2$$

$$= E_R \left[P \left\{ Y_{(i)}^2 + \alpha^2 S^2 + 2\alpha Y_{(i)} S \right\} + (1-P) \left\{ Y_{(i)}^2 + \beta^2 S^2 - 2\beta Y_{(i)} S \right\} \right] - \left[Y_{(i)} \right]^2$$

$$= P \left[Y_{(i)}^2 + \alpha^2 E_R (S^2) + 2\alpha Y_{(i)} E_R (S) \right] + (1-P) \left[Y_{(i)}^2 + \beta^2 E_R (S^2) - 2\beta Y_{(i)} E_R (S) \right] - \left[Y_{(i)} \right]^2$$

$$= Y_{(i)}^2 + P\alpha^2 \left(\gamma^2 + \theta^2 \right) + 2\alpha Y_{(i)} \theta P + (1-P)\beta^2 \left(\gamma^2 + \theta^2 \right) - 2(1-P)\beta Y_{(i)} \theta - \left[Y_{(i)} \right]^2$$

$$= P\alpha^2\left(\gamma^2+\theta^2\right)+\left(1-P\right)\beta^2\left(\gamma^2+\theta^2\right)+\left[2\alpha\theta P-2\left(1-P\right)\beta\theta\right]Y_{(i)}$$

$$= \frac{\beta\alpha^2}{\alpha+\beta}\left[\gamma^2+\theta^2\right]+\frac{\alpha}{\left(\alpha+\beta\right)}\beta^2\left[\gamma^2+\theta^2\right]+2\theta\left[\alpha P-\left(1-P\right)\beta\right]Y_{(i)}$$

$$= \left(\gamma^2+\theta^2\right)\frac{\left(\beta\alpha^2+\alpha\beta^2\right)}{\left(\alpha+\beta\right)}+2\theta\left[\frac{\alpha\beta}{\alpha+\beta}-\frac{\alpha\beta}{\alpha+\beta}\right]Y_{(i)}$$

$$= \frac{\alpha\beta\left(\gamma^2+\theta^2\right)\left(\alpha+\beta\right)}{\left(\alpha+\beta\right)}+0$$

$$= \alpha\beta\left(\gamma^2+\theta^2\right) \tag{2.8}$$

From (2.6), (2.7) and (2.8) we have

$$V\left(\bar{y}_{sravi}\right)=E_d\left[\frac{1}{n^2}\sum_{i=1}^{n}\alpha\beta\left(\gamma^2+\theta^2\right)\right]+V_d\left[\frac{1}{n}\sum_{i=1}^{n}Y_{(i)}\right]$$

$$= E_d\left[\frac{\alpha\beta\left(\gamma^2+\theta^2\right)}{n}\right]+V_d\left[\frac{1}{n}\sum_{i=1}^{n}Y_{(i)}\right]$$

$$= \frac{\alpha\beta\left(\gamma^2+\theta^2\right)}{n}+\frac{1}{n}\left[\sigma_y^2-\frac{1}{m}\sum_{i=1}^{m}\left(\mu_{Y_{(i)}}-\bar{Y}\right)^2\right]$$

which proves the theorem

In the next section, we carried out a simulation study to investigate the performance of the proposed estimators for various distributions as well as for various choice of parameters of the randomization device.

3. SIMULATION STUDY

The variance of the Gjestvang and Singh (2009) estimator $\bar{y}_{GS}$ for the Simple Random and With Replacement Sampling (SRSWR) design is given by

$$V\left(\bar{y}_{GS}\right) = \frac{\alpha\beta\left(\gamma^2 + \theta^2\right)}{n} + \frac{\sigma_y^2}{n} \tag{3.1}$$

The variance of the proposed estimator $\bar{y}_{sravi}$ can be re-written as:

$$V\left(\bar{y}_{sravi}\right) = \frac{\alpha\beta\left(\gamma^2 + \theta^2\right)}{n} + \frac{1}{n}\left[\sigma_y^2 - \frac{\bar{Y}^2}{m}\sum_{i=1}^{m}\left(R_{(i)} - 1\right)^2\right] \tag{3.2}$$

where

$$R_{(i)} = \frac{\mu_{Y_{(i)}}}{\bar{Y}} \tag{3.3}$$

is the ratio of realized population mean value of the ith unit after ranking to the population mean.

The percent relative efficiency (RE) of the proposed estimator $\bar{y}_{sravi}$ with respect to the estimator $\bar{y}_{GS}$ is given by

$$RE = \frac{V\left(\bar{y}_{GS}\right)}{V\left(\bar{y}_{sravi}\right)} \times 100\%$$

$$= \frac{\alpha\beta\left[\gamma^2 + \theta^2\right] + \sigma_y^2}{\alpha\beta\left(\gamma^2 + \theta^2\right) + \sigma_y^2 - \frac{\bar{Y}^2}{m}\sum_{i=1}^{m}\left(R_{(i)} - 1\right)^2} \times 100\% \tag{3.4}$$

From (3.4), it is evident that the percent relative efficiency (RE) value is free from of the sample size value. It is a function of several other device parameters α, β, θ, γ and the research vector parameters $\bar{Y}, \sigma_y^2$ and $R_{(i)}$ for some other system parameters. In practice the $R_{(i)}$ value in fact less than one, or equivalent to one, or may be greater than one. We consider doing rank set sampling by selecting m=5, by choosing five values of $R_{(i)}$ as:

$$R_{(1)} = 0.50 + 0.08e_1 \tag{3.5}$$

$$R_{(2)} = 0.75 + 0.08e_2 \tag{3.6}$$

$$R_{(3)} = 1.00 + 0.08e_3 \tag{3.7}$$

$$R_{(4)} = 1.50 + 0.08e_4 \tag{3.8}$$

$$R_{(5)} = 1.75 + 0.08e_5 \tag{3.9}$$

where $e_i \sim N(0,1)$. Bollabonia *et al.* (2018), Salinas *et al.* (2018), Zong *et al.* (2018) and Singh *et al.* (2014) have also considered similar proportions for measuring percentage relative output values.

In the first simulation study, we simulated the values of the parameters of the scrambling variables for various distributions where the proposed estimator is showing the value of the percent relative efficiency more than 100%. We explain the simulation process with an illustration as follow. We generate the first population of size N=10,000 from a Gamma distribution with parameters a_y=2.0 and b_y=1.0 using the RAND function in SAS as: Y = RAND('GAMMA', AY, BY). Then from the observed 10,000 values, we computed the population mean $\bar{Y} = 1.996$, and $\sigma_y^2 = 2.0529$. Then we simulated the values of the randomization device parameters α, β, θ, and γ such that the value of the percent relative efficiency (RE) is greater than 100%. In the second simulated population we update the values of the Gamma parameters a_y=4.0 and b_y=1.0 and in the third population we varied the values of the Gamma parameters as parameters a_y=6.0 and b_y=1.0. The values of the parameters α were adjusted from 0.1 to 0.9 with a jump of 0.1; and the values of the parameter β was also modified from 0.1 to 0.9 with a skip of 0.1; the values of γ was varied by a skip of 1.5 from 1.5 to 4.5; and the values of θ was varied by a skip 2 between -10 to 10. It may be worth pointing out here that in the present study we are investigating the benefit of use of RSS thus the choice of device parameters is kept same for both sampling schemes, that is, for the SRS as well as for RSS. A thumb-rule in deciding the choice of scrambling variables is that the respondents should not feel threatened while responding. A summary of the results obtained from three populations is given in Table 2.

Table 2. Summary of percent relative efficiency (RE) values for the three populations generated from the Gamma distributions

	$Y\sim G(2,1)$	$Y\sim G(4,1)$	$Y\sim G(6,1)$
Mean	110.76	140.92	230.51
Median	107.53	129.93	174.86
Mode	110.39	140.30	207.32
Standard Deviation	9.49	39.93	144.28
Kurtosis	0.66	.42	3.24
Skewness	1.20	1.12	1.85
Minimum	100.62	102.47	105.68
Maximum	142.30	254.41	882.00
Count	2673	2673	2673

Thus in each one of the three populations we found there are 2673 cases where the proposed RSS estimator was more efficient than the SRSWR estimator. In the first population with $Y\sim G(2,1)$, the average value of the RE was 110.76% with a standard deviation of 9.49%; the median value was 107.53%, mode value was 110.39%, minimum value was 100.62% and maximum value was 142.31%; In the second population with $Y\sim G(4,1)$, the average value of the RE was 140.92%, with a standard deviation of 39.93%; the median value was 129.43%; the mode value was 140.30%, minimum value was 102.47% and maximum value was 254.41%. In the third population with $Y\sim G(6,1)$, the average value of the RE was 230.51% with a standard deviation of 144.28%, the median value was 174.86%, the mode value was 207.32%, the minimum value was 105.68%, and maximum value was 882.00%. The values of the coefficient of skewness and kurtosis of the RE value corresponding to the three populations are also given which are slightly positively skewed distributed in each situation and the kurtosis values are less than three for the first two populations indicating that the distributions are leptokurtic and greater than three for the third population indicating that the distribution is platykurtic.

For our second simulation study, we generate a population of N=10,000 values from a normal distribution with a mean of 1000 and a standard deviation of 25 by using the SAS function Y = RAND('NORMAL', 1000, 25). Now we simulate different values of the randomizing device parameters. The values of the parameters α were changed with a step of 5 between 5 and 25; and the values of the parameter β was also changed by a step of 5 between 5 and 25; the value of γ was changed by a step of 5 between 5 and 15; and the value of θ was changed by a step of 2 between 80 to 100. A summary of results from the normal population is in Table 3.

Table 3. Summary of the percent relative efficiency (RE) values for the population generated from the Normal distributions

	$Y \sim N(1000,25)$
Mean	136.3
Median	111.6
Mode	127.8
Standard Deviation	133.3
Kurtosis	140.2
Skewness	10.7
Minimum	102.5
Maximum	2334.4
Count	825

In the case of a population generated from normal distribution with a mean of 1000 and standard deviation 25 there were 825 cases simulated for different choices of randomization device parameters such that the RSS estimator was more efficient than the SRSWR estimator. It would be worth pointing out that a choice of device parameters is crucial. The average value of RE was 136.3% with a standard deviation of 133.3%, the median value was 111.6%, the mode value was 127.8%, a minimum value was 102.5% and maximum value of 2334.4%.Thus if a population has a normal distribution it is likely to have more gain from the use of RSS than the use of SRSWR with an appropriate choice of randomization response device parameters. The skewness value is 10.7 indicating the distribution of RE values is highly skewed towards right indicating a few values of RE will be large relative to majority of the RE values. A high value of the coefficient of Kurtosis being 140.2 indicates that the distribution of RE values is platykurtic. Thus the use of RSS is more productive for a normally distributed population.

In the next section, we address the proposed estimator's percentage relative efficiency with respect to the Gjestvang and Singh (2009) estimators for supplementary real data sets.

4. APPLICATIONS: REAL DATA SETS

We will evaluate the performance of the proposal estimator on several variables within a dataset labeled as the MU284 population found in the Särndal, Swenson, and Wretman (1992). The set of supplementary results consists of multiple variables from 284 Swedish districts and is also commonly accessible at the Swedish Statistics Agency. Table 4 lists some concise parameters of those variables.

Table 4. Summary of Descriptive Parameters of various variables in MU284

Variable	RMT85	P85	P75	S82	ME84	REV84
Pop. Size	284	284	284	284	284	284
Average	245.1	29.36	28.81	47.535	1779	3078
SD	596.3	51.56	52.87	11.052	4253	4746
Minimum	21	3	4	31	173	347
Quartile 1	67.3	10	10	41	485	1140
Median	113.5	16.00	15	47	808	1855
Quartile 3	230.8	31.0	29.0	51	1596	3366
Maximum	6720	653	671	101	47074	59877
Skewness	8.83	8.28	8.52	1.39	8.73	7.93
Kurtosis	87.75	87.79	90.82	2.88	86.18	83.53

For example the mean value of the variable RMT85 is 254.1 with a standard deviation of 596.3, min to be 21, max is 6720, the median is 113.5, the first quartile is 67.3, the value of the 3rd quartile is 230.8, the skewness would be 8.83 and that of kurtosis is 87.75. Likewise the associated parameter values for the other variables may be extracted from Table 4. We varied the α from 0.1 to 0.9 with a step of 0.1; the β-value from 0.1 to 0.9 with a step of 0.1; the γ-value from 0.5 to 3.5 with a step of 0.5; and the value of θ between -10 and +10 with a step of 2.

A summary of the values of RE for the five variables listed in Table 4 is given in the following Tables 5.

One conclusion is very interesting in that although we considered various 2673 combinations of the parameters, there was not much change in the value of REs for each one of these variables listed in Table 5. Thus the choice of the device parameter is not very important, but due to the use of RSS the average value of percent relative efficiencies for the five factors are 102.69%, 105.27%, 104.80%, 102.79% and 106.97%, respectively, with almost zero value of standard deviation

Table 5. Summary of the values of RE below 5 factors

	RMT85	P85	P75	ME84	REV84
Mean	102.69	105.27	104.80	102.79	106.97
Median	102.69	105.28	104.81	102.79	106.97
Mode	102.69	105.29	104.82	102.79	106.97
Standard Deviation	0.00	0.03	0.03	0.00	0.00
Kurtosis	-2.00	4.85	4.88	-2.00	-2.00
Skewness	1.00	-2.10	-2.11	-1.00	-1.00
Range	0.00	0.18	0.16	0.00	0.00
Minimum	102.69	105.11	104.66	102.79	106.97
Maximum	102.69	105.29	104.82	102.79	106.97
Count	2673	2673	2673	2673	2673

in each case. Note that the value of standard deviation is not exactly zero as can be seen from the values of kurtosis and skewness.

The behavior of the value of the RE for the variable S82 is different. For this variable, we varied the values of α from 1 to 9 by a step of 1; the value of β from 1 to 9 by a step of 1; the value of γ from 5.5 to 10.5 by step of 2.5; and the value of θ from 10 to 20 by a step of 5. A summary of the RE values obtained is presented in Table 6. One can easily see that over the 726 cases where the proposed estimator was more efficient, the average value of RE was 121.6% with a standard deviation of 79.8%, the median value was 106.8%, the mode value is 103.9%, the minimum value was 100.9% and maximum value was 1335.0%. A very high value of the coefficient of kurtosis of 149.6 was observed, and also a relatively higher coefficient value of skewness of 11.4 was noted.

Table 6. Summary of the values of RE for the S82 variable

Mean	121.6
Median	106.8
Mode	103.9
Standard Deviation	79.8
Kurtosis	149.6
Skewness	11.4
Minimum	100.9
Maximum	1335.0
Count	726

From the analysis based on real data sets, one can conclude a very useful result that while dealing with variables like RMT85, P85, P75, ME84 and REV84 the choice of device parameters in making the proposed estimator efficient is not important, however there is a gain due to the use of RSS. In contrast while dealing with a variable like S82 then a better choice of device parameters may lead to more fruitful results. SAS Codes used in the simulation study and the real data applications are given in the Appendix-A. The original version of this chapter can be had from Jasti (2020).

CONCLUSION

We conclude that the use of Ranked Set Sampling in the Gjestvang and Singh (2009) model can lead to efficient estimator of the population mean of a sensitive variable by making a proper use of the device parameters.

ACKNOWLEDGMENT

The authors are grateful to Prof. Bouza and to the referees for their comments on the original version of the manuscript.

REFERENCES

Bollabonia, V., Sedory, S. A., & Singh, S. (2018). *Forced Quantitative Randomized Response Model Using Ranked Set Sampling. In Ranked Set Sampling: 65 Years Improving the Accuracy in Data Gathering//Introduction and Schedule.* Elsevier.

Bouza, C., Bracho, R., Santiago, A., & Sautto, J. M. (2017). Saha's randomized response technique under ranked set sampling. *RevistaInvestigacionOperacional*, *38*(5), 537–544.

Bouza, C. N. (2009). Ranked set sampling and randomized response procedure for estimating the mean of a sensitive quantitative character. *Metrika*, *70*(3), 267–277. doi:10.100700184-008-0191-6

Chaudhuri, A., & Stenger, H. (1992). *Sampling Survey*. Marcel Dekker.

Eichhorn, B. H., & Hayre, L. S. (1983). Scrambled randomized response methods for obtaining sensitive quantitative data. *Journal of Statistical Planning and Inference,* *7*(4), 307–316. doi:10.1016/0378-3758(83)90002-2

Gjestvang, C., & Singh, S. (2009). An improved randomized response model: Estimation of mean. *Journal of Applied Statistics,* *36*(12), 1361–1367.

Gjestvang, C. R., & Singh, S. (2006). A new randomized response model. *J.R. Statist. B,* *68*, 523–530.

Greenberg, B. G., Kuebler, R. R. Jr, Abernathy, J. R., & Horvitz, D. G. (1971). Application of the randomized response technique in obtaining quantitative data. *Journal of the American Statistical Association,* *66*(334), 243–250. doi:10.1080/0 1621459.1971.10482248

Himmelfarb, S., & Edgell, S. E. (1980). Additive constant model: A randomized response technique for eliminating evasiveness to quantitative response questions. *Psychological Bulletin,* *87*(3), 525–530. doi:10.1037/0033-2909.87.3.525

Horvitz, D.G., Shah, B.V., & Simmons, W.R. (1967). The unrelated question randomized response model. *Proc. of Social Statistics Section, Amer. Stat. Assoc.,* 65-72.

Jasti, S. (2020). A study of Gjestvang and Singh randomized response model using ranked set Sampling [Unpublished MS project]. Department of Mathematics, Texas A&M University-Kingsville, Kingsville, TX.

McIntyre, G. A. (1952). A method of unbiased selective sampling using ranked sets. *Australian Journal of Agricultural Research,* *3*, 385–390.

Salinas, V. I., Sedory, S. A., & Singh, S. (2018). Calibrated estimator of population mean using two-stage ranked set sampling. In Ranked Set Sampling: 65 Years Improving the Accuracy in Data Gathering//Introduction and Schedule. Elsevier.

Särndal, C. E., Swensson, B., & Wretman, J. H. (1992). *Model Assisted Survey Sampling.* Springer-Verlag.

Singh, H. P., Tailor, R., & Singh, S. (2014). General procedure for estimating the population mean using ranked set sampling. *Journal of Simulation and Computation Statistics,* *84*(5), 931–945.

Singh, S. (2020). Reply to the correction by Grover and Kaur: A new randomized response model. *J.R. Statist., Series B,* *82*(3), 865–868.

Warner, S. L. (1965). Randomized response: A survey technique for eliminating evasive answer bias. *Journal of the American Statistical Association*, *60*, 63–69.

Zong, R., Sedory, S. A., & Singh, S. (2018). Construction of Strata Boundaries for Ranked Set Sampling. In Ranked Set Sampling: 65 Years Improving the Accuracy in Data Gathering//Introduction and Schedule. Elsevier.

APPENDIX-A

SAS Codes Used in the Simulation Study

```
DATA DATA1;
CALL STREAMINIT(1234);
AY = 6;
BY = 1.0;
DO I =1 TO 10000 BY 1;
Y = RAND('NORMAL', 1000, 25);
*Y = RAND('GAMMA', AY, BY);
OUTPUT;
END;
KEEP Y;
DATA DATA2;
SET DATA1;
KEEP Y;
PROC MEANS DATA = DATA2 NOPRINT;
VAR Y;
OUTPUTOUT = OUT1 MEAN=MEANY VAR=VARY N=NP;
DATA DATA3;
SET OUT1;
SIGMAY2 = VARY*(NP-1)/NP;
DATA RDY;
CALL STREAMINIT(1234);
R1 = 0.50 + 0.08*RAND('NORMAL',0,1);
R2 = 0.75 + 0.08*RAND('NORMAL',0,1);
R3 = 1.00 + 0.08*RAND('NORMAL',0,1);
R4 = 1.50 + 0.08*RAND('NORMAL',0,1);
R5 = 1.75 + 0.08*RAND('NORMAL',0,1);
RDY = ((R1-1)**2+(R2-1)**2+(R3-1)**2+(R4-1)**2+(R5-1)**2)/5;
KEEP RDY;
DATA DATA4;
SET DATA3;
DO ALPHA1 = 5 TO 25 BY 5;
DO BETA1 = 5 TO 25 BY 5;
DO GAMMA1 = 5 TO 15 BY 5;
DO THETA1 = 80 TO 100 BY2;
```

```
OUTPUT;
END;
END;
END;
END;
RUN;
DATA DATA5;
SET DATA4;
IF _N_ = 1THENSET RDY;
VAR_GS = ALPHA1*BETA1*(GAMMA1**2+THETA1**2)+SIGMAY2;
VAR_SH = ALPHA1*BETA1*(GAMMA1**2+THETA1**2)+SIGMAY2-
MEANY**2*RDY;
RE = VAR_GS/VAR_SH*100;
P = BETA1/(ALPHA1+BETA1);
DROP _TYPE_ _FREQ_;
KEEP MEANY SIGMAY2 ALPHA1 BETA1 P THETA1 GAMMA1 RE;
IF RE GT 100;
PROC PRINT DATA=DATA5;
VAR  ALPHA1 BETA1 P THETA1 GAMMA1 MEANY SIGMAY2 RE;
RUN;
```

Chapter 6

On Estimating Population Means of Two–Sensitive Variables With Ranked Set Sampling Design

Shivacharan Rao Chitneni
Texas A&M University – Kingsville, Kingsville, USA

Stephen A. Sedory
Texas A&M University – Kingsville, Kingsville, USA

Sarjinder Singh
Texas A&M University – Kingsville, Kingsville, USA

ABSTRACT

In the chapter, the authors consider the problem of estimating the population means of two sensitive variables by making use of ranked set sampling. The final estimators are unbiased and the variance expressions that they derive show that ranked set sampling is more efficient than simple random sampling. A convex combination of the variance expressions of the resultant estimators is minimized in order to suggest optimal sample sizes for both sampling schemes. The relative efficiency of the proposed estimators is then compared to the corresponding estimators for simple random sampling based on simulation study and real data applications. SAS codes utilized in the simulation to collect the empirical evidence and application are included.

DOI: 10.4018/978-1-7998-7556-7.ch006

1. INTRODUCTION

Warner (1965) presented a method for addressing the problem of evasive answer bias when asking questions about sensitive topics in a survey. In particular he created the technique called randomized response to estimate the proportion of a population possessing some sensitive characteristic, this model only dealt with qualitative variable, but was soon modified to handle quantitative variables by Horvitz *et al.* (1967), and Greenberg *et al.* (1971). Himmelfarb and Edgell (1980) introduced the idea of an additive scrambled randomized response model, which makes use of the known distribution of a scrambling variable for estimating the population means of sensitive quantitative variables. Eichhorn and Hayre (1983) studied in detail a technique in which every respondent is requested to report a multiplicative response obtained by multiplying the real value of the sensitive variable by a scrambling variable. These authors estimated mean of a single sensitive variable. Ahmed *et al.* (2018, 2020) considered the problem of estimating two population means by obtaining two responses from each respondent; one response is a scrambled response on the sensitive variables, and the second response is only about the value used in obtaining the scrambling response. Pampana *et al.* (2019) extended the Ahmed *et al.* (2018) estimators for Ranked Set Sampling (RSS) and showed the superior performance of RSS over the use of Simple Random and With Replacement Sampling (SRSWR). In this chapter, we considered a different approach for estimating the population means of two sensitive variables by collecting information from the respondents in two independent samples by using two different sampling schemes, that is, SRSWR and RSS.

Assume finite number N of individuals comprises a population Ω. Assume we are choosing of n_1 persons from Ω by SRSWR, which constitutes our first sample s_1. Assume Y_{1i} and Y_{2i} be the true values of the two sensitive quantitative variables attached to i^{th} unit in Ω. Assume μ_{Y_1} and μ_{Y_2} are the two population means of interest. Now every subject selected in S_1 is requested to randomly draw two values of the random variables S_1 and S_2 whose distributions are assumed to be known. More specifically assume that S_1 and S_2 are independent, and information on their parameters such, as $E(S_1)=\theta_1$, $V\left(S_1\right)=\gamma_1^2$, $E(S_2)=\theta_2$ and $V\left(S_2\right)=\gamma_2^2$, is assumed to be known.

In the proposed randomized response technique, each respondent selected in first sample is informed to report the scrambled answer as:

$$Z_{1i} = S_1 Y_{1i} + S_2 Y_{2i}, \; i=1,2,\ldots,n_1 \tag{1.1}$$

Consider selecting a second sample, s_2, of n_2 persons by SRSWR from the population Ω. Each respondent in the second sample is asked to generate two independent random numbers S_3 and S_4 from two different distributions. Assume information about the parameters of these scrambling variables, such as $E(S_3) = \theta_3$, $V(S_3) = \gamma_3^2$, $E(S_4) = \theta_4$ and $V(S_4) = \gamma_4^2$, is available.

Now again every subject selected in the second sample s_2 is asked to submit a scrambled reply in the proposed randomized response techniques as:

$$Z_{2i} = S_3 Y_{1i} + S_4 Y_{2i}, \ i=1,2,\ldots,n_2 \tag{1.2}$$

On taking expected values on both sides of (1.1) and (1.2), we get

$$E(Z_{1i}) = E[S_1 Y_{1i} + S_2 Y_{2i}] = \theta_1 \mu_{Y1} + \theta_2 \mu_{Y2} \tag{1.3}$$

and

$$E(Z_{2i}) = E[S_3 Y_{1i} + S_4 Y_{2i}] = \theta_3 \mu_{Y1} + \theta_4 \mu_{Y2} \tag{1.4}$$

By the methods of moments, from (1.3) and (1.4), we have

$$\theta_1 \hat{\mu}_{Y1} + \theta_2 \hat{\mu}_{Y2} = \frac{1}{n_1} \sum_{i=1}^{n_1} Z_{1i} \tag{1.5}$$

and

$$\theta_3 \hat{\mu}_{Y1} + \theta_4 \hat{\mu}_{Y2} = \frac{1}{n_2} \sum_{i=1}^{n_2} Z_{2i} \tag{1.6}$$

The system of equations (1.5) and (1.6) can be written as

$$\begin{bmatrix} \theta_1 & \theta_2 \\ \theta_3 & \theta_4 \end{bmatrix} \begin{bmatrix} \hat{\mu}_{Y1} \\ \hat{\mu}_{Y2} \end{bmatrix} = \begin{bmatrix} \dfrac{1}{n_1} \displaystyle\sum_{i=1}^{n_1} Z_{1i} \\ \dfrac{1}{n_2} \displaystyle\sum_{i=1}^{n_2} Z_{2i} \end{bmatrix} \tag{1.7}$$

By the Cramer's rules, we have

$$\Delta = det \begin{bmatrix} \theta_1 & \theta_2 \\ \theta_3 & \theta_4 \end{bmatrix} = \theta_1\theta_4 - \theta_2\theta_3 \tag{1.8}$$

$$\Delta_1 = det \begin{vmatrix} \dfrac{1}{n_1}\sum_{i=1}^{n_1}Z_{1i}, & \theta_2 \\ \dfrac{1}{n_2}\sum_{i=1}^{n_2}Z_{2i}, & \theta_4 \end{vmatrix} = \dfrac{\theta_4}{n_1}\sum_{i=1}^{n_1}Z_{1i} - \dfrac{\theta_2}{n_2}\sum_{i=1}^{n_2}Z_{2i} \tag{1.9}$$

$$\Delta_2 = det \begin{vmatrix} \theta_1, & \dfrac{1}{n_1}\sum_{i=1}^{n_1}Z_{1i} \\ \theta_3, & \dfrac{1}{n_2}\sum_{i=1}^{n_2}Z_{2i} \end{vmatrix} = \dfrac{\theta_1}{n_2}\sum_{i=1}^{n_2}Z_{2i} - \dfrac{\theta_3}{n_1}\sum_{i=1}^{n_1}Z_{1i} \tag{1.10}$$

From (1.8), (1.9) and (1.10), the values of $\hat{\mu}_{Y_1}$ and $\hat{\mu}_{Y_2}$ are given by

$$\hat{\mu}_{Y_1} = \frac{\Delta_1}{\Delta} = \frac{\left[\dfrac{\theta_4}{n_1}\sum_{i=1}^{n_1}Z_{1i} - \dfrac{\theta_2}{n_2}\sum_{i=1}^{n_2}Z_{2i} \right]}{\theta_1\theta_4 - \theta_2\theta_3} \tag{1.11}$$

and

$$\hat{\mu}_{Y_2} = \frac{\Delta_2}{\Delta} = \frac{\dfrac{\theta_1}{n_2}\sum_{i=1}^{n_2}Z_{2i} - \dfrac{\theta_3}{n_1}\sum_{i=1}^{n_1}Z_{1i}}{\theta_1\theta_4 - \theta_2\theta_3} \tag{1.12}$$

Now we establish the following theorems.

Theorem 1.1. The estimators $\hat{\mu}_{Y_1}$ and $\hat{\mu}_{Y_2}$ are unbiased estimators of the population means μ_{Y_1} and μ_{Y_2} respectively.

Proof. Assume E_1 stands for the expected value over the SRSWR design while E_2 stands for the expected value over the proposed randomization device.

Now taking expected values on the both sides of $\hat{\mu}_{Y_1}$ and $\hat{\mu}_{Y_2}$, we get

$$E\left(\hat{\mu}_{Y_1}\right) = E_1 E_2[\hat{\mu}_{Y_1}] = E_1 E_2\left[\frac{\dfrac{\theta_4}{n_1}\sum_{i=1}^{n_1}Z_{1i} - \dfrac{\theta_2}{n_2}\sum_{i=1}^{n_2}Z_{2i}}{\theta_1\theta_4 - \theta_2\theta_3}\right]$$

$$= E_1\left[\frac{\dfrac{\theta_4}{n_1}\sum_{i=1}^{n_1}E_2(Z_{1i}) - \dfrac{\theta_2}{n_2}\sum_{i=1}^{n_2}E_2\left(Z_{2i}\right)}{\theta_1\theta_4 - \theta_2\theta_3}\right]$$

$$= E_1\left[\frac{\dfrac{\theta_4}{n_1}\sum_{i=1}^{n_1}\{Y_{1i}\theta_1 + Y_{2i}\theta_2\} - \dfrac{\theta_2}{n_2}\sum_{i=1}^{n_2}\{Y_{1i}\theta_3 + Y_{2i}\theta_4\}}{\theta_1\theta_4 - \theta_2\theta_3}\right]$$

$$= E_1\left[\frac{\dfrac{\theta_4\theta_1}{n_1}\sum_{i=1}^{n_1}Y_{1i} + \dfrac{\theta_2\theta_4}{n_1}\sum_{i=1}^{n_1}Y_{2i} - \dfrac{\theta_2\theta_3}{n_2}\sum_{i=1}^{n_2}Y_{1i} - \dfrac{\theta_2\theta_4}{n_2}\sum_{i=1}^{n_2}Y_{2i}}{\theta_1\theta_4 - \theta_2\theta_3}\right]$$

$$= \left[\frac{\theta_4\theta_1\mu_{Y_1} + \theta_2\theta_4\mu_{Y_2} - \theta_2\theta_3\mu_{Y_1} - \theta_2\theta_4\mu_{Y_2}}{\theta_1\theta_4 - \theta_2\theta_3}\right]$$

$$= \frac{(\theta_4\theta_1 - \theta_2\theta_3)\mu_{Y_1}}{(\theta_4\theta_1 - \theta_2\theta_3)} = \mu_{Y_1} \tag{1.13}$$

So the estimator $\hat{\mu}_{Y_1}$ is proved to be an unbiased estimator for the population mean, μ_{Y_1}.

Now taking the expected value of $\hat{\mu}_{Y_2}$, we get

$$E\left(\hat{\mu}_{Y_2}\right) = E_1 E_2[\hat{\mu}_{Y_2}] = E_1 E_2 \left[\frac{\dfrac{\theta_1}{n_2}\sum_{i=1}^{n_2} Z_{2i} - \dfrac{\theta_3}{n_1}\sum_{i=1}^{n_1} Z_{1i}}{\theta_1\theta_4 - \theta_2\theta_3} \right]$$

$$= E_1 \left[\frac{\dfrac{\theta_1}{n_2}\sum_{i=1}^{n_2} E_2(Z_{2i}) - \dfrac{\theta_3}{n_1}\sum_{i=1}^{n_1} E_2\left(Z_{1i}\right)}{\theta_1\theta_4 - \theta_2\theta_3} \right]$$

$$= E_1 \left[\frac{\dfrac{\theta_1}{n_2}\sum_{i=1}^{n_2}\{Y_{1i}\theta_3 + Y_{2i}\theta_4\} - \dfrac{\theta_3}{n_1}\sum_{i=1}^{n_1}\{Y_{1i}\theta_1 + Y_{2i}\theta_2\}}{\theta_1\theta_4 - \theta_2\theta_3} \right]$$

$$= E_1 \left[\frac{\dfrac{\theta_1\theta_3}{n_2}\sum_{i=1}^{n_2}Y_{1i} + \dfrac{\theta_1\theta_4}{n_2}\sum_{i=1}^{n_2}Y_{2i} - \dfrac{\theta_1\theta_3}{n_1}\sum_{i=1}^{n_1}Y_{1i} - \dfrac{\theta_2\theta_3}{n_1}\sum_{i=1}^{n_1}Y_{2i}}{\theta_1\theta_4 - \theta_2\theta_3} \right]$$

$$= \left[\frac{\theta_1\theta_3\mu_{Y_1} + \theta_1\theta_4\mu_{Y_2} - \theta_1\theta_3\mu_{Y_1} - \theta_2\theta_3\mu_{Y_2}}{\theta_1\theta_4 - \theta_2\theta_3} \right]$$

$$= \frac{(\theta_1\theta_4 - \theta_2\theta_3)\mu_{Y_2}}{(\theta_1\theta_4 - \theta_2\theta_3)} = \mu_{Y_2} \tag{1.14}$$

So the estimator $\hat{\mu}_{Y_2}$ is also proved to be an unbiased for μ_{Y_2}. From (1.13) and (1.14), and hence the theorem holds.

Theorem1.2. The variance of the estimator $\hat{\mu}_{Y_1}$ is given by

$$V(\hat{\mu}_{Y_1}) = \frac{1}{\left(\theta_1\theta_4 - \theta_2\theta_3\right)^2} \left[\frac{\theta_4^2 \sigma_1^2}{n_1} + \frac{\theta_2^2 \sigma_2^2}{n_2} \right] \qquad (1.15)$$

where

$$\sigma_1^2 = \gamma_1^2\left(\sigma_{Y1}^2 + \mu_{Y1}^2\right) + \gamma_2^2\left(\sigma_{Y2}^2 + \mu_{Y2}^2\right) + \theta_1^2\sigma_{Y1}^2 + \theta_2^2\sigma_{Y2}^2 + 2\theta_1\theta_2\sigma_{Y_1Y_2} \qquad (1.16)$$

and

$$\sigma_2^2 = \gamma_3^2\left(\sigma_{Y1}^2 + \mu_{Y1}^2\right) + \gamma_4^2\left(\sigma_{Y2}^2 + \mu_{Y2}^2\right) + \theta_3^2\sigma_{Y1}^2 + \theta_4^2\sigma_{Y2}^2 + 2\theta_3\theta_4\sigma_{Y_1Y_2} \qquad (1.17)$$

Proof. Since both samples are taken independently, so the variance of $\hat{\mu}_{Y_1}$ is obtained as

$$V[\hat{\mu}_{Y_1}] = V\left[\frac{\frac{\theta_4}{n_1}\sum_{i=1}^{n_1} Z_{1i} - \frac{\theta_2}{n_2}\sum_{i=1}^{n_2} Z_{2i}}{\theta_1\theta_4 - \theta_2\theta_3} \right] = \frac{\frac{\theta_4^2}{n_1^2}\sum_{i=1}^{n_1} V(Z_{1i}) + \frac{\theta_2^2}{n_2^2}\sum_{i=1}^{n_2} V(Z_{2i})}{\left(\theta_1\theta_4 - \theta_2\theta_3\right)^2}$$

$$(1.18)$$

Now assume V_1 stands for the variance over the SRSWR design, and V_2 stands for the variance over the proposed randomizing device.
Then

$$V(Z_{1i}) = E_1 V_2(Z_{1i}) + V_1 E_2(Z_{1i})$$

$$= E_1 V_2\left[Y_{1i}S_1 + Y_{2i}S_2\right] + V_1 E_2\left[Y_{1i}S_1 + Y_{2i}S_2\right]$$

$$= E_1\left[Y_{1i}^2 V_2\left(S_1\right) + Y_{2i}^2 V_2\left(S_2\right)\right] + V_1\left[Y_{1i}E_2\left(S_1\right) + Y_{2i}E_2\left(S_2\right)\right]$$

$$= E_1\left[Y_{1i}^2\gamma_1^2 + Y_{2i}^2\gamma_2^2\right] + V_1\left[Y_{1i}\theta_1 + Y_{2i}\theta_2\right]$$

$$= \gamma_1^2 E_1\left(Y_{1i}^2\right) + \gamma_2^2 E_1\left(Y_{2i}^2\right) + \theta_1^2 V_1\left(Y_{1i}\right) + \theta_2^2 V_1\left(Y_{2i}\right) + 2Cov\left(\theta_1 Y_{1i}, \theta_2 Y_{2i}\right)$$

$$= \gamma_1^2\left(\sigma_{Y1}^2 + \mu_{Y1}^2\right) + \gamma_2^2\left(\sigma_{Y2}^2 + \mu_{Y2}^2\right) + \theta_1^2 \sigma_{Y1}^2 + \theta_2^2 \sigma_{Y2}^2 + 2\theta_1\theta_2\sigma_{Y_1Y_2} = \sigma_1^2 \text{ (say)}$$

$$(1.19)$$

where

$$\sigma_{Y_1Y_2} = Cov\left(Y_1, Y_2\right) \tag{1.20}$$

is the covariance between the two sensitive variables over the SRSWR design.
   Now,

$$V(Z_{2i}) = E_1 V_2(Z_{2i}) + V_1 E_2(Z_{2i})$$

$$= E_1 V_2\left[S_3 Y_{1i} + S_4 Y_{2i}\right] + V_1 E_2\left[S_3 Y_{1i} + S_4 Y_{2i}\right]$$

$$= E_1\left[Y_{1i}^2 V_2\left(S_3\right) + Y_{2i}^2 V_2\left(S_4\right)\right] + V_1\left[Y_{1i} E_2(S_3) + Y_{2i} E_2\left(S_4\right)\right]$$

$$= E_1\left[Y_{1i}^2 \gamma_3^2 + Y_{2i}^2 \gamma_4^2\right] + V_1\left[Y_{1i}\theta_3 + Y_{2i}\theta_4\right]$$

$$= \gamma_3^2 E_1\left(Y_{1i}^2\right) + \gamma_4^2 E_1\left(Y_{2i}^2\right) + \theta_3^2 V_1\left(Y_{1i}\right) + \theta_4^2 V_1\left(Y_{2i}\right) + 2\theta_3\theta_4 Cov\left(Y_{1i}, Y_{2i}\right)$$

$$= \gamma_3^2\left(\sigma_{Y1}^2 + \mu_{Y1}^2\right) + \gamma_4^2\left(\sigma_{Y2}^2 + \mu_{Y2}^2\right) + \theta_3^2 \sigma_{Y1}^2 + \theta_4^2 \sigma_{Y2}^2 + 2\theta_3\theta_4\sigma_{Y_1Y_2} = \sigma_2^2 \tag{1.21}$$

From (1.18), the variance of the estimator $\hat{\mu}_{Y_1}$ is given by

$$V(\hat{\mu}_{Y_1}) = \frac{\dfrac{\theta_4^2}{n_1^2}\sum_{i=1}^{n_1}\sigma_1^2 + \dfrac{\theta_2^2}{n_2^2}\sum_{i=1}^{n_2}\sigma_2^2}{(\theta_1\theta_4 - \theta_2\theta_3)^2} = \frac{1}{(\theta_1\theta_4 - \theta_2\theta_3)^2}\left[\frac{\theta_4^2\sigma_1^2}{n_1} + \frac{\theta_2^2\sigma_2^2}{n_2}\right] \tag{1.22}$$

which proves the theorem.

Theorem1.3. The variance of the estimator $\hat{\mu}_{Y_2}$ is given by

$$V(\hat{\mu}_{Y_2}) = \frac{1}{\left(\theta_1\theta_4 - \theta_2\theta_3\right)^2}\left[\frac{\theta_1^2\sigma_2^2}{n_2} + \frac{\theta_3^2\sigma_1^2}{n_1}\right] \qquad (1.23)$$

Proof. Due to independence of samples, we have

$$V(\hat{\mu}_{Y_2}) = V\left[\frac{\dfrac{\theta_1}{n_2}\sum_{i=1}^{n_2}Z_{2i} - \dfrac{\theta_3}{n_1}\sum_{i=1}^{n_1}Z_{1i}}{\theta_1\theta_4 - \theta_2\theta_3}\right] = \frac{\dfrac{\theta_1^2\sigma_2^2}{n_2} + \dfrac{\theta_3^2\sigma_1^2}{n_1}}{\left(\theta_1\theta_4 - \theta_2\theta_3\right)^2} \qquad (1.24)$$

which proves the theorem.

The variance expressions $V(\hat{\mu}_{Y_1})$ and $V(\hat{\mu}_{Y_2})$ are functions of the sample sizes n_1 and n_2. Thus it is difficult to make an optimal choice of the sample sizes n_1 and n_2. The optimal values of n_1 and n_2 will be different if one considers minimizing $V(\hat{\mu}_{Y_1})$ than if one considers the problem of minimization of $V(\hat{\mu}_{Y_2})$.

1.1 Optimal Sample Sizes for SRS Design

To find the optimal sample sizes for the case of SRSWR design, we consider the compromised function of $V(\hat{\mu}_{Y_1})$ and $V(\hat{\mu}_{Y_2})$, which is a convex combination of the two variances, and is given by

$$V_{SRSWR} = \alpha V(\hat{\mu}_{Y_1}) + \left(1-\alpha\right)V(\hat{\mu}_{Y_2})$$

$$= \frac{1}{\left(\theta_1\theta_4 - \theta_2\theta_3\right)^2}\left[\alpha\left\{\frac{\theta_4^2\sigma_1^2}{n_1} + \frac{\theta_2^2\sigma_2^2}{n_2}\right\} + \left(1-\alpha\right)\left\{\frac{\theta_1^2\sigma_2^2}{n_2} + \frac{\theta_3^2\sigma_1^2}{n_1}\right\}\right]$$

$$= \frac{1}{\left(\theta_1\theta_4 - \theta_2\theta_3\right)^2}\left[\frac{\alpha\theta_4^2\sigma_1^2 + \left(1-\alpha\right)\theta_3^2\sigma_1^2}{n_1} + \frac{\alpha\theta_2^2\sigma_2^2 + \left(1-\alpha\right)\theta_1^2\sigma_2^2}{n_2}\right]$$

$$= \frac{1}{\left(\theta_1\theta_4 - \theta_2\theta_3\right)^2}\left[\left\{\alpha\theta_4^2 + \left(1-\alpha\right)\theta_3^2\right\}\frac{\sigma_1^2}{n_1} + \left\{\alpha\theta_2^2 + \left(1-\alpha\right)\theta_1^2\right\}\frac{\sigma_2^2}{n_2}\right] = \frac{A}{n_1} + \frac{B}{n_2}$$

$$(1.25)$$

where

$$A = \frac{\left\{\alpha\theta_4^2 + \left(1-\alpha\right)\theta_3^2\right\}\sigma_1^2}{\left(\theta_1\theta_4 - \theta_2\theta_3\right)^2}$$

$$(1.26)$$

and

$$B = \frac{\left\{\alpha\theta_2^2 + \left(1-\alpha\right)\theta_1^2\right\}\sigma_2^2}{\left(\theta_1\theta_4 - \theta_2\theta_3\right)^2}$$

$$(1.27)$$

Let $n = n_1 + n_2$ be the total sample size. Then the associated Lagrange's function is given by

$$L = \frac{A}{n_1} + \frac{B}{n_2} + \lambda\left(n_1 + n_2 - n\right)$$

$$(1.28)$$

On setting

$$\frac{\partial L}{\partial n_1} = -\frac{A}{n_1^2} + \lambda = 0$$

We have

$$n_1^2\lambda = A \text{ or } n_1 = \frac{\sqrt{A}}{\sqrt{\lambda}}$$

$$(1.29)$$

On setting

$$\frac{\partial L}{\partial n_2} = -\frac{B}{n_2^2} + \lambda = 0$$

113

We get

$$n_2 = \frac{\sqrt{B}}{\sqrt{\lambda}} \qquad (1.30)$$

Note that we need total sample size as

$$n_1 + n_2 = n \qquad (1.31)$$

From (1.29), (1.30) and (1.31), we have

$$\frac{\sqrt{A}}{\sqrt{\lambda}} + \frac{\sqrt{B}}{\sqrt{\lambda}} = n \text{ or } \sqrt{\lambda} = \frac{\sqrt{A} + \sqrt{B}}{n} \qquad (1.32)$$

From (1.29), (1.30) and (1.32), the optimum value of n_1 and n_2 are given by

$$n_1 = \frac{n\sqrt{A}}{\sqrt{A} + \sqrt{B}} \qquad (1.33)$$

and

$$n_2 = \frac{n\sqrt{B}}{\sqrt{A} + \sqrt{B}} \qquad (1.34)$$

On substituting (1.33) and (1.34) into (1.25) the minimum compromised variance for SRSWR is given by

$$Min.V_{SRSWR} = \frac{A}{n_1} + \frac{B}{n_2} = \frac{A}{\dfrac{n\sqrt{A}}{\sqrt{A} + \sqrt{B}}} + \frac{B}{\dfrac{n\sqrt{B}}{\sqrt{A} + \sqrt{B}}}$$

$$= \frac{\sqrt{A}}{\dfrac{n}{\sqrt{A} + \sqrt{B}}} + \frac{\sqrt{B}}{\dfrac{n}{\sqrt{A} + \sqrt{B}}}$$

$$= \frac{1}{\left(\dfrac{n}{\sqrt{A}+\sqrt{B}}\right)}\left[\sqrt{A}+\sqrt{B}\right] = \frac{\left(\sqrt{A}+\sqrt{B}\right)^2}{n} \tag{1.35}$$

In the next section, we develop estimators for estimating the means of two sensitive variables for the case of Ranked Set Sampling (RSS) design.

2. RANKED SET SAMPLING

McIntyre (1952) was the pioneer developer of the Ranked Set Sampling (RSS) design which has been found to be more efficient than the SRSWR design. Following Bouza (2009) and Bouza *et al.* (2017), we consider selecting a sample s_1 on n_1 people from a population Ω by using RSS design. Note that we have two sensitive variables, Y_{1i} and Y_{2i} under study. It is not easy to rank a person based on both sensitive variables while doing RSS. Thus in the first sample s_1 of n_1 is selected by ranking the first variable $Y_{[1i]}$ and considering the second non-ranked variable $Y_{(2i)}$. Let $m_1 \times m_1$ be the subjects selected for ranking in a replication of m_1 cycles, and let r_1 be the total number of replications such that $n_1 = m_1 r_1$. Here we describe one replicating process of m_1 cycles of RSS design. In the first cycle, select an SRSWR of m_1 persons, do judgment ranking as $y_{[111]} \leq y_{[112]} \leq \ldots \leq y_{[11m_1]}$; in the second-cycle, select another independent SRSWR of m_1 subjects, again do judgment ranking as $y_{[211]} \leq y_{[212]} \leq \ldots \leq y_{[21m_1]}$; and in the m_1^{th} cycle, select an SRSWR of m_1 subjects, do judgment ranking as $y_{[m_111]} \leq y_{[m_112]} \leq \ldots \leq y_{[m_11m_1]}$. A tabulated display of such a cycle of RSS is shown in Figure 1.

Thus, in first-replication made of m_1 cycles, m_1 subjects are selected in the sample shown on the diagonal places in $m_1 \times m_1$ matrix. One can think, in the first-cycle of the first sample a subject ranked on the first sensitive variable as $y_{[111]}$, and an unranked on the second sensitive variable $y_{(121)}$ is selected. Likewise, in the second cycle of the first-sample, a subject of ranked value $y_{[212]}$ on the first variable and unranked value of $y_{(222)}$ on the second variable is selected, and in the m_1^{th} cycle a subject with a ranked of $y_{[m_1,m_1]}$ on the first variable and non-ranked value of $y_{(m_1,1,m_1)}$ is selected. For simplicity dropping the first identifier, on repeating these m_1 cycles r_1 times, it will form a RSS of $n_1 = m_1 r_1$ with their associated ranked, and unobserved ordered pairs as:

Figure 1. Cycle of Ranked Set Sampling in the first RSS

$y_{[111]}$ $y_{(121)}$	$y_{[112]}$ $y_{(122)}$	$\cdot$	$y_{[11m_1]}$ $y_{(12m_1)}$
$y_{[211]}$ $y_{(221)}$	$y_{[212]}$ $y_{(222)}$		$y_{[21m_1]}$ $y_{(22m_1)}$
$y_{[m_111]}$ $y_{(m_121)}$	$y_{[m_112]}$ $y_{(m_122)}$		$y_{[m_{11}m_1]}$ $y_{(m_12m_1)}$

$$(Y_{[11]}, Y_{(21)}), (Y_{[12]}, Y_{(22)}), ..., (Y_{[1n_1]}, Y_{(2n_1)}).$$

Note that

$$(Y_{[11]}, Y_{(21)}), (Y_{[12]}, Y_{(22)}), ..., (Y_{[1n_1]}, Y_{(2n_1)})$$

are the actual and unobservable sensitive variables of the subjects selected in a RSS s_1 of n_1 persons.

From each respondent selected in the first RSS, we collected scrambled responses as:

$$Z_{(1i)} = S_1 Y_{[1i]} + S_2 Y_{(2i)}, \quad i=1, 2, ..., n_1 \tag{2.1}$$

Likewise, we select another independent RSS s_2 of n_2 persons by ranking them on the second sensitive variable, and we collected the scrambled responses as:

$$Z_{(2i)} = S_3 Y_{(1i)} + S_4 Y_{[2i]}, \quad i=1,2,...,n_2 \tag{2.2}$$

On taking expected values on the both sides of (2.1) and (2.2), we get:

$$E\left(Z_{(1i)}\right) = E\left[S_1 Y_{[1i]} + S_2 Y_{(2i)}\right] = \theta_1 \mu_{Y1} + \theta_2 \mu_{Y2} \tag{2.3}$$

and

$$E\left(Z_{(2i)}\right) = E\left[S_3 Y_{(1i)} + S_4 Y_{[2i]}\right] = \theta_3 \mu_{Y1} + \theta_4 \mu_{Y2} \tag{2.4}$$

By the method of moments, the system of equations in (2.3) and (2.4) can be written as:

$$\begin{bmatrix} \theta_1 & \theta_2 \\ \theta_3 & \theta_4 \end{bmatrix} \begin{bmatrix} \hat{\mu}_{Y1}^{(RSS)} \\ \hat{\mu}_{Y2}^{(RSS)} \end{bmatrix} = \begin{bmatrix} \dfrac{1}{n_1} \sum_{i=1}^{n_1} Z_{(1i)} \\ \dfrac{1}{n_2} \sum_{i=1}^{n_2} Z_{(2i)} \end{bmatrix} \tag{2.5}$$

Applying the Cramer's Rule, from (2.5) we have

$$\Delta^* = det \begin{bmatrix} \theta_1 & \theta_2 \\ \theta_3 & \theta_4 \end{bmatrix} = \theta_1 \theta_4 - \theta_2 \theta_3 \tag{2.6}$$

$$\Delta_1^* = \begin{vmatrix} \dfrac{1}{n_1} \sum_{i=1}^{n_1} Z_{(1i)}, & \theta_2 \\ \dfrac{1}{n_2} \sum_{i=1}^{n_2} Z_{(2i)}, & \theta_4 \end{vmatrix} = \dfrac{\theta_4}{n_1} \sum_{i=1}^{n_1} Z_{(1i)} - \dfrac{\theta_2}{n_2} \sum_{i=1}^{n_2} Z_{(2i)} \tag{2.7}$$

$$\Delta_2^* = \begin{vmatrix} \theta_1, & \dfrac{1}{n_1} \sum_{i=1}^{n_1} Z_{(1i)} \\ \theta_3, & \dfrac{1}{n_2} \sum_{i=1}^{n_2} Z_{(2i)} \end{vmatrix} = \dfrac{\theta_1}{n_2} \sum_{i=1}^{n_2} Z_{(2i)} - \dfrac{\theta_3}{n_1} \sum_{i=1}^{n_1} Z_{(1i)} \tag{2.8}$$

From (2.6), (2.7) and (2.8) we have

$$\hat{\mu}_{Y1}^{(RSS)} = \frac{\Delta_1^*}{\Delta^*} = \frac{\left[\dfrac{\theta_4}{n_1}\sum_{i=1}^{n_1} Z_{(1i)} - \dfrac{\theta_2}{n_2}\sum_{i=1}^{n_2} Z_{(2i)}\right]}{\theta_1\theta_4 - \theta_2\theta_3} \tag{2.9}$$

and

$$\hat{\mu}_{Y2}^{(RSS)} = \frac{\Delta_2^*}{\Delta^*} = \frac{\left[\dfrac{\theta_1}{n_2}\sum_{i=1}^{n_2} Z_{(2i)} - \dfrac{\theta_3}{n_1}\sum_{i=1}^{n_1} Z_{(1i)}\right]}{\theta_1\theta_4 - \theta_2\theta_3} \tag{2.10}$$

We have the following theorem:

Theorem 2.1. The estimators $\hat{\mu}_{Y1}^{(RSS)}$ and $\hat{\mu}_{Y2}^{(RSS)}$ are unbiased estimators of μ_{Y_1} and μ_{Y_2}, respectively.

Proof. Assume E_1 stands for the expected value over the RSS design, and E_2 stands for the expected value over the proposed randomizing device. Taking expected values on both sides of $\hat{\mu}_{Y1}^{(RSS)}$, we have

$$E\left(\hat{\mu}_{Y1}^{(RSS)}\right) = E_1 E_2 \left[\frac{\dfrac{\theta_4}{n_1}\sum_{i=1}^{n_1} Z_{(1i)} - \dfrac{\theta_2}{n_2}\sum_{i=1}^{n_2} Z_{(2i)}}{\theta_1\theta_4 - \theta_2\theta_3}\right]$$

$$= E_1 \left[\frac{\dfrac{\theta_4}{n_1}\sum_{i=1}^{n_1} E_2(Z_{(1i)}) - \dfrac{\theta_2}{n_2}\sum_{i=1}^{n_2} E_2\left(Z_{(2i)}\right)}{\theta_1\theta_4 - \theta_2\theta_3}\right] \tag{2.11}$$

Now,

$$E_2(Z_{(1i)}) = E_2\left[S_1 Y_{[1i]} + S_2 Y_{(2i)}\right]$$

$$= Y_{[1i]} E_2 \left(S_1 \right) + Y_{(2i)} E_2 \left(S_2 \right)$$

$$= Y_{[1i]} \theta_1 + Y_{(2i)} \theta_2 \tag{2.12}$$

and

$$E_2 \left(Z_{(2i)} \right) = E_2 \left[S_3 Y_{(1i)} + S_4 Y_{[2i]} \right]$$

$$= Y_{(1i)} E_2 \left(S_3 \right) + Y_{[2i]} E_2 \left(S_4 \right)$$

$$= Y_{(1i)} \theta_3 + Y_{[2i]} \theta_4 \tag{2.13}$$

From (2.11), (2.12) and (2.13), we have

$$E \left(\hat{\mu}_{Y1}^{(RSS)} \right) = E_1 \left[\frac{ \dfrac{\theta_4}{n_1} \sum_{i=1}^{n_1} \left\{ Y_{[1i]} \theta_1 + Y_{(2i)} \theta_2 \right\} - \dfrac{\theta_2}{n_2} \sum_{i=1}^{n_2} \left\{ Y_{(1i)} \theta_3 + Y_{[2i]} \theta_4 \right\} }{ \theta_1 \theta_4 - \theta_2 \theta_3 } \right]$$

$$= \frac{ \theta_4 \left[\theta_1 E_1 \left(\dfrac{1}{n_1} \sum_{i=1}^{n_1} Y_{[1i]} \right) + \theta_2 E_1 \left(\dfrac{1}{n_1} \sum_{i=1}^{n_1} Y_{(2i)} \right) \right] - \theta_2 \left[\theta_3 E_1 \left(\dfrac{1}{n_2} \sum_{i=1}^{n_2} Y_{(1i)} \right) + \theta_4 E_1 \left(\dfrac{1}{n_2} \sum_{i=1}^{n_2} Y_{[2i]} \right) \right] }{ \theta_1 \theta_4 - \theta_2 \theta_3 }$$

$$= \left[\frac{ \theta_1 \theta_4 \mu_{Y_1} + \theta_2 \theta_4 \mu_{Y_2} - \theta_2 \theta_3 \mu_{Y_1} - \theta_2 \theta_4 \mu_{Y_2} }{ \theta_1 \theta_4 - \theta_2 \theta_3 } \right]$$

$$= \frac{ \left(\theta_1 \theta_4 - \theta_2 \theta_3 \right) \mu_{Y_1} }{ \left(\theta_1 \theta_4 - \theta_2 \theta_3 \right) } = \mu_{Y_1}$$

Thus $\hat{\mu}_{Y1}^{(RSS)}$ is unbiased for estimating μ_{Y_1}.

Now taking expected values on both sides of $\hat{\mu}_{Y2}^{(RSS)}$ as

$$E\left(\hat{\mu}_{Y2}^{(RSS)}\right) = E_1 E_2 \left[\frac{\dfrac{\theta_1}{n_2}\sum_{i=1}^{n_2} Z_{(2i)} - \dfrac{\theta_3}{n_1}\sum_{i=1}^{n_1} Z_{(1i)}}{\theta_1\theta_4 - \theta_2\theta_3}\right]$$

$$= E_1 \left[\frac{\dfrac{\theta_1}{n_2}\sum_{i=1}^{n_2} E_2(Z_{(2i)}) - \dfrac{\theta_3}{n_1}\sum_{i=1}^{n_1} E_2\left(Z_{(1i)}\right)}{\theta_1\theta_4 - \theta_2\theta_3}\right]$$

$$= E_1 \left[\frac{\dfrac{\theta_1}{n_2}\sum_{i=1}^{n_2}\left\{Y_{(1i)}\theta_3 + Y_{[2i]}\theta_4\right\} - \dfrac{\theta_3}{n_1}\sum_{i=1}^{n_1}\left\{Y_{[1i]}\theta_1 + Y_{(2i)}\theta_2\right\}}{\theta_1\theta_4 - \theta_2\theta_3}\right]$$

$$= E_1 \left[\frac{\dfrac{\theta_1\theta_3}{n_2}\sum_{i=1}^{n_2}Y_{(1i)} + \dfrac{\theta_1\theta_4}{n_2}\sum_{i=1}^{n_2}Y_{[2i]} - \dfrac{\theta_1\theta_3}{n_1}\sum_{i=1}^{n_1}Y_{[1i]} - \dfrac{\theta_2\theta_3}{n_1}\sum_{i=1}^{n_1}Y_{(2i)}}{\theta_1\theta_4 - \theta_2\theta_3}\right]$$

$$= \left[\frac{\theta_1\theta_3\mu_{Y_1} + \theta_1\theta_4\mu_{Y_2} - \theta_1\theta_3\mu_{Y_1} - \theta_2\theta_3\mu_{Y_2}}{\theta_1\theta_4 - \theta_2\theta_3}\right]$$

$$= \frac{(\theta_1\theta_4 - \theta_2\theta_3)\mu_{Y_2}}{(\theta_1\theta_4 - \theta_2\theta_3)} = \mu_{Y_2}$$

Thus the estimator $\hat{\mu}_{Y2}^{(RSS)}$ is unbiased for μ_{Y_2}.

Now, we develop the following Lemma:

Lemma 2.1. The variances of $Z_{(1i)}$ and $Z_{(2i)}$ are given by

$$\sigma_1^{*2} = \gamma_1^2 \left[\sigma_{Y1}^2 + \mu_{Y1}^2 - \frac{1}{m_1} \sum_{i=1}^{m_1} \left(\mu_{Y_{1[i]}} - \mu_{Y_1} \right)^2 \right] + \gamma_2^2 \left(\sigma_{Y2}^2 + \mu_{Y2}^2 \right)$$

$$+ \theta_1^2 \left[\sigma_{Y1}^2 - \frac{1}{m_1} \sum_{i=1}^{m_1} \left(\mu_{Y_{1[i]}} - \mu_{Y_1} \right)^2 \right] + \theta_2^2 \sigma_{Y2}^2 + 2\theta_1 \theta_2 \left[\sigma_{Y_1 Y_2} - \frac{1}{m_1} \sum_{i=1}^{m_1} \left(\mu_{Y_{1[i]}} - \mu_{Y_1} \right) \left(\mu_{Y_{2(i)}} - \mu_{Y_2} \right) \right]$$

$$(2.14)$$

and

$$\sigma_2^{*2} = \gamma_3^2 \left(\sigma_{Y1}^2 + \mu_{Y1}^2 \right) + \gamma_4^2 \left[\sigma_{Y2}^2 + \mu_{Y2}^2 - \frac{1}{m_2} \sum_{i=1}^{m_2} \left(\mu_{Y_{2[i]}} - \mu_{Y_2} \right)^2 \right]$$

$$+ \theta_3^2 \sigma_{Y1}^2 + \theta_4^2 \left[\sigma_{Y2}^2 - \frac{1}{m_2} \sum_{i=1}^{m_2} \left(\mu_{Y_{2[i]}} - \mu_{Y_2} \right)^2 \right] + 2\theta_3 \theta_4 \left[\sigma_{Y_1 Y_2} - \frac{1}{m_2} \sum_{i=1}^{m_2} \left(\mu_{Y_{1(i)}} - \mu_{Y_1} \right) \left(\mu_{Y_{2[i]}} - \mu_{Y_2} \right) \right]$$

$$(2.15)$$

Proof. Let V_1 denote the variance over the RSS design. Let V_2 denote the variance over the proposed randomizing device. Then the variance of $Z_{(1i)}$ is given by

$$V(Z_{(1i)}) = E_1 V_2 (Z_{(1i)}) + V_1 E_2 (Z_{(1i)})$$

$$= E_1 V_2 \left[Y_{[1i]} S_1 + Y_{(2i)} S_2 \right] + V_1 E_2 \left[Y_{[1i]} S_1 + Y_{(2i)} S_2 \right]$$

$$= E_1 \left[Y_{[1i]}^2 V_2 (S_1) + Y_{(2i)}^2 V_2 (S_2) \right] + V_1 \left[Y_{[1i]} E_2 (S_1) + Y_{(2i)} E_2 (S_2) \right]$$

$$= E_1 \left[Y_{[1i]}^2 \gamma_1^2 + Y_{(2i)}^2 \gamma_2^2 \right] + V_1 \left[Y_{[1i]} \theta_1 + Y_{(2i)} \theta_2 \right] \qquad (2.16)$$

We know that

$$V \left(Y_{(2i)} \right) = E \left(Y_{(2i)}^2 \right) - \left(E \left(Y_{(2i)} \right) \right)^2$$

$$E \left(Y_{(2i)}^2 \right) = \sigma_{Y2}^2 + \mu_{Y2}^2 \qquad (2.17)$$

and

$$V\left(Y_{[1i]}\right) = E\left(Y_{[1i]}^2\right) - \left(E\left(Y_{[1i]}\right)\right)^2$$

$$E\left[Y_{[1i]}^2\right] = V\left(Y_{[1i]}\right) + \left(E\left(Y_{[1i]}\right)\right)^2$$

$$= \sigma_{Y1}^2 - \frac{1}{m_1}\sum_{i=1}^{m_1}\left[\mu_{Y_{1[i]}} - \mu_{Y_1}\right]^2 + \mu_{Y1}^2 \tag{2.18}$$

So, we have

$$V(Z_{(1i)}) = \gamma_1^2\left[\sigma_{Y1}^2 + \mu_{Y1}^2 - \frac{1}{m_1}\sum_{i=1}^{m_1}\left(\mu_{Y_{1[i]}} - \mu_{Y_1}\right)^2\right]$$

$$+ r_2^2\left(\sigma_{Y2}^2 + \mu_{Y2}^2\right) + \theta_1^2 V_1\left(Y_{[1i]}\right) + \theta_2^2 V_1\left(Y_{(2i)}\right) + 2\theta_1\theta_2 Cov_1\left[Y_{[1i]}, Y_{(2i)}\right]$$

$$= \gamma_1^2\left[\sigma_{Y1}^2 + \mu_{Y1}^2 - \frac{1}{m_1}\sum_{i=1}^{m_1}\left(\mu_{Y_{1[i]}} - \mu_{Y_1}\right)^2\right] + \gamma_2^2\left(\sigma_{Y2}^2 + \mu_{Y2}^2\right)$$

$$+ \theta_1^2\left[\sigma_{Y1}^2 - \frac{1}{m_1}\sum_{i=1}^{m_1}\left(\mu_{Y_{1[i]}} - \mu_{Y_1}\right)^2\right] + \theta_2^2\sigma_{Y2}^2 + 2\theta_1\theta_2\left[\sigma_{Y_1Y_2} - \frac{1}{m_1}\sum_{i=1}^{m_1}\left(\mu_{Y_{1[i]}} - \mu_{Y_1}\right)\left(\mu_{Y_{2(i)}} - \mu_{Y_2}\right)\right] = \sigma_1^{*2}$$

$$\tag{2.19}$$

Likewise

$$V(Z_{(2i)}) = \gamma_3^2\left(\sigma_{Y1}^2 + \mu_{Y1}^2\right) + \gamma_4^2\left[\sigma_{Y2}^2 + \mu_{Y2}^2 - \frac{1}{m_2}\sum_{i=1}^{m_2}\left(\mu_{Y_{2[i]}} - \mu_{Y_2}\right)^2\right] + \theta_3^2\sigma_{Y1}^2$$

$$+ \theta_4^2\left[\sigma_{Y2}^2 - \frac{1}{m_2}\sum_{i=1}^{m_2}\left(\mu_{Y_{2[i]}} - \mu_{Y_2}\right)^2\right] + 2\theta_3\theta_4\left[\sigma_{Y_1Y_2} - \frac{1}{m_2}\sum_{i=1}^{m_2}\left(\mu_{Y_{1(i)}} - \mu_{Y_1}\right)\left(\mu_{Y_{2[i]}} - \mu_{Y_2}\right)\right] = \sigma_2^{*2}$$

$$\tag{2.20}$$

which proves the lemma.

Now we have the following theorems:

Theorem 2.2. The variances of the estimators $\hat{\mu}_{Y1}^{(RSS)}$ and $\hat{\mu}_{Y2}^{(RSS)}$ are, respectively, given by

$$V\left[\hat{\mu}_{Y1}^{(RSS)}\right] = \frac{\dfrac{\theta_4^2 \sigma_1^{*2}}{n_1} + \dfrac{\theta_2^2 \sigma_2^{*2}}{n_2}}{\left(\theta_1\theta_4 - \theta_2\theta_3\right)^2} \tag{2.21}$$

and

$$V\left[\hat{\mu}_{Y2}^{(RSS)}\right] = \frac{\dfrac{\theta_1^2 \sigma_2^{*2}}{n_2} + \dfrac{\theta_3^2 \sigma_1^{*2}}{n_1}}{\left(\theta_1\theta_4 - \theta_2\theta_3\right)^2} \tag{2.22}$$

where σ_1^{*2} and σ_2^{*2} are as defined in (2.14) and (2.15).

Proof. Note that both samples are taken independently by RSS, thus the variance of the proposed estimator $\hat{\mu}_{Y1}^{(RSS)}$ is given by

$$V\left[\hat{\mu}_{Y1}^{(RSS)}\right] = V\left[\frac{\dfrac{\theta_4}{n_1}\sum_{i=1}^{n_1} Z_{(1i)} - \dfrac{\theta_2}{n_2}\sum_{i=1}^{n_2} Z_{(2i)}}{\theta_1\theta_4 - \theta_2\theta_3}\right]$$

$$= \frac{\dfrac{\theta_4^2}{n_1^2}\sum_{i=1}^{n_1} V\left(Z_{(1i)}\right) + \dfrac{\theta_2^2}{n_2^2}\sum_{i=1}^{n_2} V\left(Z_{(2i)}\right)}{\left(\theta_1\theta_4 - \theta_2\theta_3\right)^2}$$

$$= \frac{\dfrac{\theta_4^2}{n_1^2}\sum_{i=1}^{n_1}\sigma_1^{*2} + \dfrac{\theta_2^2}{n_2^2}\sum_{i=1}^{n_2}\sigma_2^{*2}}{\left(\theta_1\theta_4 - \theta_2\theta_3\right)^2}$$

$$= \frac{\dfrac{\theta_4^2\sigma_1^{*2}}{n_1} + \dfrac{\theta_2^2\sigma_2^{*2}}{n_2}}{\left(\theta_1\theta_4 - \theta_2\theta_3\right)^2}$$

Similarly

$$V\left[\hat{\mu}_{Y2}^{(RSS)}\right] = \frac{\dfrac{\theta_1^2\sigma_2^{*2}}{n_2} + \dfrac{\theta_3^2\sigma_1^{*2}}{n_1}}{\left(\theta_1\theta_4 - \theta_2\theta_3\right)^2}$$

which proves the theorem.

The variance expressions $V(\hat{\mu}_{Y_1}^{(RSS)})$ and $V(\hat{\mu}_{Y_2}^{(RSS)})$ are functions of the sample sizes n_1 and n_2. Thus it is difficult to make an optimal choice of the sample sizes n_1 and n_2. The optimal values of n_1 and n_2 will be different if one considers minimizing $V(\hat{\mu}_{Y_1}^{(RSS)})$ than if one considers minimizing $V(\hat{\mu}_{Y_2}^{(RSS)})$.

2.1 Optimal Sample Sizes for RSS Design

To find the optimal sample sizes for the case of RSS design, we consider a compromised function of $V(\hat{\mu}_{Y_1}^{(RSS)})$ and $V(\hat{\mu}_{Y_2}^{(RSS)})$, which is a convex combination of the variances, is given by

$$V_{RSS} = \alpha V(\hat{\mu}_{Y_1}^{(RSS)}) + \left(1 - \alpha\right)V(\hat{\mu}_{Y_2}^{(RSS)})$$

$$= \frac{1}{\left(\theta_1\theta_4 - \theta_2\theta_3\right)^2}\left[\alpha\left\{\frac{\theta_4^2\sigma_1^{*2}}{n_1} + \frac{\theta_2^2\sigma_2^{*2}}{n_2}\right\} + \left(1 - \alpha\right)\left\{\frac{\theta_1^2\sigma_2^{*2}}{n_2} + \frac{\theta_3^2\sigma_1^{*2}}{n_1}\right\}\right]$$

$$= \frac{1}{\left(\theta_1\theta_4 - \theta_2\theta_3\right)^2}\left[\frac{\alpha\theta_4^2\sigma_1^{*2} + \left(1 - \alpha\right)\theta_3^2\sigma_1^{*2}}{n_1} + \frac{\alpha\theta_2^2\sigma_2^{*2} + \left(1 - \alpha\right)\theta_1^2\sigma_2^{*2}}{n_2}\right]$$

$$= \frac{1}{\left(\theta_1\theta_4 - \theta_2\theta_3\right)^2} \left[\left\{\alpha\theta_4^2 + \left(1-\alpha\right)\theta_3^2\right\}\frac{\sigma_1^{*2}}{n_1} + \left\{\alpha\theta_2^2 + \left(1-\alpha\right)\theta_1^2\right\}\frac{\sigma_2^{*2}}{n_2} \right]$$

$$= \frac{A^*}{n_1} + \frac{B^*}{n_2} \tag{2.21}$$

where

$$A^* = \frac{\left\{\alpha\theta_4^2 + \left(1-\alpha\right)\theta_3^2\right\}\sigma_1^{*2}}{\left(\theta_1\theta_4 - \theta_2\theta_3\right)^2} \tag{2.22}$$

and

$$B^* = \frac{\left\{\alpha\theta_2^2 + \left(1-\alpha\right)\theta_1^2\right\}\sigma_2^{*2}}{\left(\theta_1\theta_4 - \theta_2\theta_3\right)^2} \tag{2.23}$$

Let $n=n_1+n_2$ be the total sample size. Then the Lagrange's function is given by

$$L^* = \frac{A^*}{n_1} + \frac{B^*}{n_2} + \lambda^* \left(n_1 + n_2 - n\right) \tag{2.24}$$

On setting

$$\frac{\partial L^*}{\partial n_1} = -\frac{A^*}{n_1^2} + \lambda^* = 0$$

We have

$$n_1^2\lambda^* = A^* \text{ or } n_1 = \frac{\sqrt{A^*}}{\sqrt{\lambda^*}} \tag{2.25}$$

On setting

$$\frac{\partial L^*}{\partial n_2} = -\frac{B^*}{n_2^2} + \lambda^* = 0$$

We get

$$n_2 = \frac{\sqrt{B^*}}{\sqrt{\lambda^*}} \tag{2.26}$$

Note that we need total sample size as

$$n_1 + n_2 = n \tag{2.27}$$

From (2.25), (2.26) and (2.27), we have

$$\frac{\sqrt{A^*}}{\sqrt{\lambda^*}} + \frac{\sqrt{B^*}}{\sqrt{\lambda^*}} = n \text{ or } \sqrt{\lambda^*} = \frac{\sqrt{A^*} + \sqrt{B^*}}{n} \tag{2.28}$$

From (2.26), (2.27) and (2.28), the optimum value of n_1 and n_2 are given by

$$n_1 = \frac{n\sqrt{A^*}}{\sqrt{A^*} + \sqrt{B^*}} \tag{2.29}$$

and

$$n_2 = \frac{n\sqrt{B^*}}{\sqrt{A^*} + \sqrt{B^*}} \tag{2.30}$$

On substituting (2.29) and (2.30) into (2.21) the minimum compromised variance for RSS is given by

$$Min.V_{RSS} = \frac{A^*}{n_1} + \frac{B^*}{n_2} = \frac{A^*}{\frac{n\sqrt{A^*}}{\sqrt{A^*} + \sqrt{B^*}}} + \frac{B^*}{\frac{n\sqrt{B^*}}{\sqrt{A^*} + \sqrt{B^*}}}$$

$$= \frac{\dfrac{\sqrt{A^*}}{n}}{\sqrt{A^*}+\sqrt{B^*}} + \frac{\dfrac{\sqrt{B^*}}{n}}{\sqrt{A^*}+\sqrt{B^*}}$$

$$= \frac{1}{\left(\dfrac{n}{\sqrt{A^*}+\sqrt{B^*}}\right)}\left[\sqrt{A^*}+\sqrt{B^*}\right] = \frac{\left(\sqrt{A^*}+\sqrt{B^*}\right)^2}{n} \tag{2.31}$$

In the following section, we use a simulation study to investigate the performance of the suggested estimators under RSS design with respect to SRSWR design.

3. EMPIRICAL EVIDENCES: A SIMULATION

The percent relative efficiency (RE) of the RSS with respect to the SRSWR based on minimum compromised variance expressions is given by

$$RE = \frac{Min.V_{SRSWR}}{Min.V_{RSS}} \times 100\% = \frac{\left(\sqrt{A}+\sqrt{B}\right)^2}{\left(\sqrt{A^*}+\sqrt{B^*}\right)^2} \times 100\% \tag{3.1}$$

The value of RE in (3.1) does not depend on the value of n, however it is a function of several other parameters. In our interest of finding the magnitude of RE values, we did a simulation that we summarize as follows. The SAS codes used in producing the percent relative efficiency values are also given in Appendix-A. In order to investigate the magnitude of RE values of the use of RSS with respect to SRSWR, we simulated various situations and populations by generating various variables Y_{1i} and Y_{2i} having various values of correlation coefficient between them. The purpose of generating correlated variables Y_{1i} and Y_{2i} is to investigate whether the correlation between the two sensitive variables could be useful in increasing the value of RE of RSS compared to SRSWR. Thus following Singh and Horn (1998), we make the use of the following transformations to generate two sensitive quantitative variables as:

$$y_{1i} = \mu_{y_1^*} + \sqrt{\left(1 - \rho^2\right)} y_{1i}^* + \rho \frac{\sigma_{y_1}^*}{\sigma_{y_2}^*} y_{2i}^* \qquad (3.2)$$

and

$$y_{2i} = \mu_{y_2^*} + y_{2i}^* \qquad (3.3)$$

where y_{1i}^* and y_{2i}^* are independent Gamma variables generated within SAS. Here a_{y_1}, and b_{y_1} are shape and scale parameters, respectively, for the first sensitive variable y_{1i}^*, so that $\mu_{y_1^*} = E\left(y_{1i}^*\right) = a_{y_1^*} b_{y_1^*}$, $\sigma_{y_1^*}^2 = V\left(y_1^*\right) = a_{y_1^*} b_{y_1^*}^2$; $a_{y_2^*}$, and $b_{y_2^*}$ are shape and scale parameters, respectively, for the second sensitive variable y_{2i}^*, then $\mu_{y_2^*} = E\left(y_{2_i}^*\right) = a_{y_2^*} b_{y_2^*}$, $\sigma_{y_2^*}^2 = V\left(y_2^*\right) = a_{y_2^*} b_{y_2^*}^2$. By making use of (3.2) and (3.3), there will be a value of the correlation coefficient $\rho = Cov\left(y_{1i}^*, y_{2i}^*\right) / \left(\sigma_{y_1^*} \sigma_{y_2^*}\right)$ between the both sensitive variables Y_{1i} and Y_{2i}. For various values of shape parameters $a_{y_1^*}$ and $a_{y_2^*}$ and correlation coefficient ρ different populations were generated by using the SAS. Note that the percent relative efficiency also depends of the choice of compromising parameter α, and the randomization device parameters. In this study, we allowed α to vary between 0 and 1 with a jump of 0.2. The value of ρ was allowed to vary between -0.9 to 0.9 with a jump of 0.1. A huge number of sets of results can be obtained by executing the SAS codes for different choice of randomization device parameters. In this particular study we set $\theta_1=2$; $\theta_2=2.5$; $\theta_3=1.8$; $\theta_4=2.6$; $\gamma_1=2.1$; $\gamma_2=3.2$; $\gamma_3=2.6$; and $\gamma_4=1.8$. Also note that in practice the value of $R_{1[i]} = \mu_{Y_{1[i]}} / \mu_{Y_1}$ could be less than, equal to, or more than one. We consider RSS with $m_1=5$, so we consider five different forms of $R_{1[i]}$ as:

$$R_{1[1]} = 0.50 + 0.08 e_1 \qquad (3.4)$$

$$R_{1[2]} = 0.75 + 0.08 e_2 \qquad (3.5)$$

$$R_{1[3]} = 1.00 + 0.08 e_3 \qquad (3.6)$$

$$R_{1[4]} = 1.50 + 0.08e_4 \tag{3.7}$$

$$R_{1[5]} = 1.75 + 0.08e_5 \tag{3.8}$$

Likewise for the second study sensitive variable the value of $R_{2i} = \mu_{Y_{2[i]}} / \mu_{Y_2}$ could be less than, equal to, or greater than one. We again took RSS by taking $m_2=5$, thus again we made five different forms of $R_{2[i]}$ as:

$$R_{2[1]} = 0.50 + 0.07e_1 \tag{3.9}$$

$$R_{2[2]} = 0.75 + 0.07e_2 \tag{3.10}$$

$$R_{2[3]} = 1.00 + 0.07e_3 \tag{3.11}$$

$$R_{2[4]} = 1.50 + 0.07e_4 \tag{3.12}$$

$$R_{2[5]} = 1.75 + 0.07e_5 \tag{3.13}$$

where $e_i \sim N(0,1)$. For simplicity, we consider $R_{1[i]}=R_{1(i)}$ and $R_{2[i]}=R_{2(i)}$. Bollabonia et al. (2018), Salinas et al. (2018), Zong et al. (2018) and Singh et al. (2014) have also used similar ratios for doing their simulation studies. We created 19 different populations each of size 5000 units by changing the value of ρ between -0.9 to 0.9 with a skip of 0.1. Then we set six variations in α between 0 and 1 with a jump of 0.2, thus a total of 114 percent REs were observed as exhibited in Table 5 of the Appendix-A. (Online Supplementary Documented Material). A summary of RE for various values of ρ are given in Table 1, and those for different values of the compromising parameter α are given in Table 2.

Table 1. The average values of RE and standard deviation by ρ

Population	ρ	freq	μ_{RE}	σ_{RE}
1	-0.9	6	122.59	0.30
2	-0.8	6	131.38	0.05
3	-0.7	6	138.91	0.09
4	-0.6	6	136.04	0.18
5	-0.5	6	138.27	0.43
6	-0.4	6	136.94	0.47
7	-0.3	6	131.40	0.48
8	-0.2	6	128.76	0.44
9	-0.1	6	129.55	0.52
10	0.0	6	141.07	0.75
11	0.1	6	138.04	0.71
12	0.2	6	143.24	1.02
13	0.3	6	138.35	0.83
14	0.4	6	129.00	0.58
15	0.5	6	130.65	0.67
16	0.6	6	127.30	0.57
17	0.7	6	134.17	0.74
18	0.8	6	121.66	0.38
19	0.9	6	139.15	0.85

Table 2. The average values of RE and standard deviation by α

Situation	α	freq	μ_{RE}	σ_{RE}
1	0.0	19	132.74	5.87
2	0.2	19	133.15	5.99
3	0.4	19	133.45	6.10
4	0.6	19	133.70	6.18
5	0.8	19	133.90	6.25
6	1.0	19	134.06	6.31

From Table 1, it is observed that the average RE over all values of α, for the 19 possible values of correlation coefficients lies between 121.66% to 143.24%, with no clear trend as to whether the high or low value of correlation between two sensitive variables will change the efficiency of RSS with respect to SRSWR, although RSS is found to be more efficient than SRS in each situation considered. Note that in Tables 1 and 2, the column "freq" corresponds to the number of possible six values of α and nineteen values of ρ investigated in the simulation study.

Table 2 indicates that there is very slightly change in the average values of average

Figure 2. Visualization of RE in three-dimensional space.

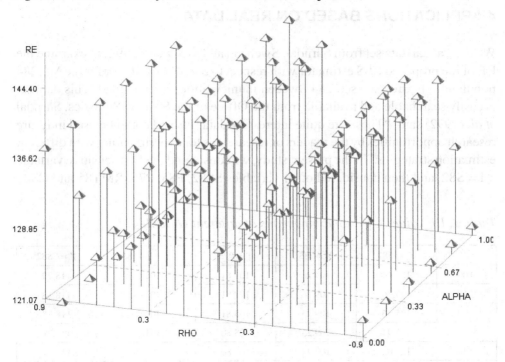

values of percent relative efficiency as the value of compromising parameter α changes between 0 and 1. This leads to an important message that the use of RSS shows same efficiency over the use of SRSWR irrespective of the fact if one wants to estimate the mean of the first or of the second sensitive variables. Thus, a choice of giving more or less importance to the first or the second sensitive variable is not crucial.

To make a graphical visualization of the results observed in the empirical evidences we provide a three dimensional graphical presentation in Figure 2.

From Figure 2, one can also conclude that a proper choice, as we considered in this study, of the proposed randomizing device parameters may lead to significantly efficient estimators while making use of RSS design with respect to the use of SRS design irrespective of the value of the correlation coefficient and importance to a variable.

In the following section, we discuss the RE of the RSS with respect to the SRS for secondary real data sets.

4 APPLICATIONS BASED ON REAL DATA

We used a real data set from Särndal, Swenson and Wretman (1992) to examine the RE of the proposed RSS estimator with respect to the SRS estimator for the MU284 population. In this data set, 284 Sweden municipalities are included. This data set is easily searchable and available from the Office of the Sweden Statistics. Särndal *et al.* (1992) said, "These are quite interesting data sets and could be used in future research opportunities by the readers or researchers for experimenting with different estimation strategies."In the present study, we considered the first sensitive variable Y1= S82, and then considered other variables SS82, P85, P75, RMT85 and CS82

Table 3. RE values for estimating means of different variables

α	$Y_2=SS82$	$Y_2=P85$	$Y_2=P75$	$Y_2=RMT85$	$Y_2=CS82$
0.00	125.64	109.26	108.81	102.04	118.29
0.10	125.76	109.26	108.81	102.02	118.48
0.20	125.86	109.25	108.81	102.00	118.65
0.30	125.94	109.25	108.80	101.99	118.79
0.40	126.02	109.24	108.80	101.97	118.92
0.50	126.08	109.24	108.79	101.96	119.04
0.60	126.14	109.24	108.79	101.95	119.14
0.70	126.20	109.23	108.79	101.94	119.23
0.80	126.24	109.23	108.79	101.93	119.31
0.90	126.29	109.23	108.79	101.92	119.39
1.00	126.33	109.23	108.78	101.91	119.46

as the second sensitive variables Y2. The variable S82 stands for total number of seats in municipal council, SS82 stands for number of Social-Democratic seats in municipal council, P85 stands for 1985 population (in thousands), P75 stands for 1975 population (in thousands), RMT85 stands for revenues from 1985 municipal

Table 4. Correlation between S82 and other five variables

	S82	SS82	P85	P75	RMT85	CS82
S82	1	0.7601	0.685	0.67068	0.58056	0.66682

taxation (in millions of kronor), and CS82 stands for number of Conservative seats in municipal council. We used the same SAS codes as we used for the case of simulation study as in the previous section. We found the RE values as reported in Table 3.

It is interesting to note that while considering the variables SS82 and CS82 as the second sensitive variables while considering S82 as the first sensitive variable, observed RE values are higher as compared to the other three variables: P85, P75, and RMT85.

From Table 4 there is again evidence that the higher value of the correlation between Y1=S82 and Y2=SS82 results in higher value of RE of RSS estimator with respect to SRSWR estimator. Thus, ultimately we conclude that the uses of RSS could be more fruitful while estimating means of two highly correlated sensitive variables. The original version of this chapter can be found in Chitneni (2020).

ACKNOWLEDGMENT

The authors are grateful to Prof. Bouza and the referees for very critical comments on the original version of this manuscript.

REFERENCES

Ahmed, S., Sedory, S. A., & Singh, S. (2018). Simultaneous estimation of means of two sensitive variables. *Communications in Statistics. Theory and Methods*, *47*(2), 324–343. doi:10.1080/03610926.2017.1303733

Ahmed, S., Sedory, S. A., & Singh, S. (2020). Forcibly Re-scrambled randomized response model for simultaneous estimation of means of two sensitive variables. *Communications in Mathematics and Statistics*, *8*(1), 23–45. doi:10.100740304-018-0156-7

Bollabonia, V., Sedory, S. A., & Singh, S. (2018). *Forced Quantitative Randomized Response Model Using Ranked Set Sampling. In Ranked Set Sampling: 65 Years Improving the Accuracy in Data Gathering//Introduction and Schedule*. Elsevier.

Bouza, C., Bracho, R., Santiago, A., & Sautto, J. M. (2017). Saha's randomized response technique under ranked set sampling. *RevistaInvestigacionOperacional*, *38*(5), 537–544.

Bouza, C. N. (2009). Ranked set sampling and randomized response procedure for estimating the mean of a sensitive quantitative character. *Metrika*, *70*(3), 267–277. doi:10.100700184-008-0191-6

Chitneni, R. S. (2020). *On estimating population means of two-sensitive variables with ranked set sampling design [Unpublished MS Project]*. Texas A&M University-Kingsville.

Eichhorn, B. H., & Hayre, L. S. (1983). Scrambled randomized response methods for obtaining sensitive quantitative data. *Journal of Statistical Planning and Inference*, *7*(4), 307–316. doi:10.1016/0378-3758(83)90002-2

Greenberg, B. G., Kuebler, R. R. Jr, Abernathy, J. R., & Horvitz, D. G. (1971). Application of the randomized response technique in obtaining quantitative data. *Journal of the American Statistical Association*, *66*(334), 243–250. doi:10.1080/0 1621459.1971.10482248

Himmelfarb, S., & Edgell, S. E. (1980). Additive constant model: A randomized response technique for eliminating evasiveness to quantitative response questions. *Psychological Bulletin*, *87*(3), 525–530. doi:10.1037/0033-2909.87.3.525

Horvitz, D.G., Shah, B.V., & Simmons, W.R. (1967). The unrelated question randomized response model. *Proc. of Social Statistics Section, Amer. Stat. Assoc.*, 65-72.

Salinas, V. I., Sedory, S. A., & Singh, S. (2018). Calibrated estimator of population mean using two-stage ranked set sampling. In Ranked Set Sampling: 65 Years Improving the Accuracy in Data Gathering// Introduction and Schedule. Elsevier.

Särndal, C. E., Swensson, B., & Wretman, J. H. (1992). *Model Assisted Survey Sampling*. Springer-Verlag. doi:10.1007/978-1-4612-4378-6

Singh, H. P., Tailor, R., & Singh, S. (2014). General procedure for estimating the population mean using ranked set sampling. *Journal of Simulation and Computation Statistics*, *84*(5), 931–945. doi:10.1080/00949655.2012.733395

Singh, S., & Horn, S. (1998). An alternative estimator in multi-character surveys. *Metrika*, 99–107.

Warner, S. L. (1965). Randomized response: A survey technique for eliminating evasive answer bias. *Journal of the American Statistical Association*, *60*(309), 63–69. doi:10.1080/01621459.1965.10480775 PMID:12261830

Zong, R., Sedory, S. A., & Singh, S. (2018). Construction of Strata Boundaries for Ranked Set Sampling. In Ranked Set Sampling: 65 Years Improving the Accuracy in Data Gathering//Introduction and Schedule. Elsevier.

APPENDIX

ONLINE PUBLISHABLE MATERIAL

Program A: SAS Codes Used to produce Empirical Evidences.

```
DATA DATA1;
CALL STREAMINIT(1234);
%LET AY_IN =2.5;
%LET BY_IN =3.5;
%LET AX_IN =2.2;
%LET BX_IN =1.5;
AY = &AY_IN;
BY = &BY_IN;
AX = &AX_IN;
BX = &BX_IN;
DO RHO = -0.9TOO.9BY0.1;
SDY = SQRT(AY*BY**2);
SDX = SQRT(AX*BX**2);
MEANY = AY*BY;
MEANX = AX*BX;
DO I = 1TO5000BY1;
YS = RAND('GAMMA', AY, BY);
XS = RAND('GAMMA', AX, BX);
OUTPUT;
END;
END;
DATA DATA2;
SET DATA1;
Y1 = MEANY + (SQRT(1-RHO**2))*YS+RHO*SDY*XS/SDX;
Y2 = MEANX + XS;
KEEP RHO Y1 Y2;
RUN;
PROC MEANS DATA = DATA2 NOPRINT;
VAR Y1 Y2;
BY RHO;
OUTPUTOUT = DATA3 MEAN=MEANY1 MEANY2 VAR = VARY1 VARY2 N=NP;
PROC SORT DATA = DATA2;
BY RHO;
PROC SORT DATA = DATA3;
```

```
BY RHO;
DATA DATA1000;
MERGE DATA2 (IN=ABC) DATA3 (IN=ABC);
BY RHO;
Y1Y2DEV = (Y1-MEANY1)*(Y2-MEANY2);
Y1DEV2 = (Y1-MEANY1)**2;
Y2DEV2 = (Y2-MEANY2)**2;
KEEP RHO Y1Y2DEV Y1DEV2 Y2DEV2;
RUN;
PROCMEANSDATA = DATA1000 NOPRINT;
VAR Y1Y2DEV Y1DEV2 Y2DEV2;
BY RHO;
OUTPUTOUT = COVY1Y2 MEAN = COVY1Y2 Y1DEV2 Y2DEV2;
DATA COVY1Y2;
SET COVY1Y2;
RHOXY = COVY1Y2/SQRT(Y1DEV2*Y2DEV2);
KEEP RHO RHOXY COVY1Y2;
RUN;
DATA DATA4;
SET DATA3;
SIGMAY1SQ = VARY1*(NP-1)/NP;
SIGMAY2SQ = VARY2*(NP-1)/NP;
CALL STREAMINIT(1234);
R11 = 0.50 + 0.08*RAND('NORMAL',0,1);
R12 = 0.75 + 0.08*RAND('NORMAL',0,1);
R13 = 1.00 + 0.08*RAND('NORMAL',0,1);
R14 = 1.50 + 0.08*RAND('NORMAL',0,1);
R15 = 1.70 + 0.08*RAND('NORMAL',0,1);
RDY1 = ((R11-1)**2 + (R12-1)**2+(R13-1)**2+(R14-
1)**2+(R15-1)**2)/5;
R21 = 0.50 + 0.07*RAND('NORMAL',0,1);
R22 = 0.75 + 0.07*RAND('NORMAL',0,1);
R23 = 1.00 + 0.07*RAND('NORMAL',0,1);
R24 = 1.50 + 0.07*RAND('NORMAL',0,1);
R25 = 1.70 + 0.07*RAND('NORMAL',0,1);
RDY2 = ((R21-1)**2 + (R22-1)**2+(R23-1)**2+(R24-
1)**2+(R25-1)**2)/5;
RDY12 =((R11-1)*(R21-1) +(R12-1)*(R22-1)+(R13-1)*(R23-1)
+(R14-1)*(R24-1)+(R15-1)*(R25-1))/5;
KEEP NP RHO MEANY1 MEANY2 SIGMAY1SQ SIGMAY2SQ RDY1 RDY2 RDY12;
```

```
PROCPRINTDATA=DATA4;
RUN;
DATA DATA5;
MERGE DATA4 COVY1Y2;
BY RHO;
DO ALPHA = 0.0TO1BY0.2;
TH1 = 2.0;
TH2 = 2.5;
TH3 = 1.8;
TH4 = 2.6;
GAM1 = 2.1;
GAM2 = 3.2;
GAM3 = 2.6;
GAM4 = 1.8;
SIGMA1SQ = GAM1**2*(SIGMAY1SQ+MEANY1**2)
        + GAM2**2*(SIGMAY2SQ+MEANY2**2)
              + TH1**2*SIGMAY1SQ+TH2**2*SIGMAY2SQ
              + 2*TH1*TH2*COVY1Y2;

SIGMA2SQ = GAM3**2*(SIGMAY1SQ+MEANY1**2)
        + GAM4**2*(SIGMAY2SQ+MEANY2**2)
        + TH3**2*SIGMAY1SQ + TH4**2*SIGMAY2SQ
        + 2*TH3*TH4*COVY1Y2;

DENO1 = (TH1*TH4-TH2*TH3)**2;
A = (ALPHA * TH4**2 + (1-ALPHA)*TH3**2)*SIGMA1SQ/DENO1;
B = (ALPHA * TH2**2 + (1-ALPHA)*TH1**2)*SIGMA2SQ/DENO1;
MIN_VAR_SRS = (SQRT(A)+SQRT(B))**2;
* RANKED SET SAMPLING;
SIGMA1SQ_STAR = GAM1**2*(SIGMAY1SQ+MEANY1**2-MEANY1**2*RDY1)
            + GAM2**2*(SIGMAY2SQ+MEANY2**2)
            + TH1**2*(SIGMAY1SQ-
MEANY1**2*RDY1)+TH2**2*SIGMAY2SQ
            + 2*TH1*TH2*(COVY1Y2-MEANY1*MEANY2*RDY12);
SIGMA2SQ_STAR = GAM3**2*(SIGMAY1SQ+MEANY1**2)
        + GAM4**2*(SIGMAY2SQ+MEANY2**2-MEANY2**2*RDY2)
        + TH3**2*SIGMAY1SQ + TH4**2*(SIGMAY2SQ-MEANY2**2*RDY2)
            + 2*TH3*TH4*(COVY1Y2-MEANY1*MEANY2*RDY12);
A_STAR = (ALPHA * TH4**2 + (1-ALPHA)*TH3**2)*SIGMA1SQ_STAR/
DENO1;
```

```
B_STAR = (ALPHA * TH2**2 + (1-ALPHA)*TH1**2)*SIGMA2SQ_STAR/
DENO1;
MIN_VAR_RSS = (SQRT(A_STAR)+SQRT(B_STAR))**2;
RE = MIN_VAR_SRS*100/MIN_VAR_RSS;
OUTPUT;
END;
KEEP RHO ALPHA RE;
DATA DATA6;
SET DATA5;
AY = &AY_IN;
BY = &BY_IN;
AX = &AX_IN;
BX = &BX_IN;
PROC PRINT DATA = DATA6;
VAR AY BY AX BX RHO ALPHA RE;
RUN;
PROC G3D DATA=DATA6;
SCATTER RHO*ALPHA=RE;
RUN;
PROC SORT DATA = DATA6;
BY RHO;
PROC MEANS DATA =DATA6 NOPRINT;
VAR RE;
BY RHO;
OUTPUTOUT = DATA7 MEAN=MEANRE STD=STDRE;
PROC SORT DATA = DATA6;
BY ALPHA;
PROC MEANS DATA =DATA6 NOPRINT;
VAR RE;
BY ALPHA;
OUTPUTOUT = DATA8 MEAN=MEANRE STD=STDRE;
PROC PRINT DATA=DATA7;
PROC PRINT DATA=DATA8;
RUN;
```

Table 5. Detailed results of RE values from the SAS output

ρ	α	RE	ρ	α	RE
-0.90	0.00	123.05	0.00	0.60	141.37
-0.90	0.20	122.80	0.00	0.80	141.67
-0.90	0.40	122.62	0.00	1.00	141.92
-0.90	0.60	122.47	0.10	0.00	136.94
-0.90	0.80	122.36	0.10	0.20	137.53
-0.90	1.00	122.26	0.10	0.40	137.98
-0.80	0.00	131.45	0.10	0.60	138.33
-0.80	0.20	131.41	0.10	0.80	138.62
-0.80	0.40	131.38	0.10	1.00	138.85
-0.80	0.60	131.36	0.20	0.00	141.67
-0.80	0.80	131.34	0.20	0.20	142.51
-0.80	1.00	131.32	0.20	0.40	143.15
-0.70	0.00	138.77	0.20	0.60	143.66
-0.70	0.20	138.85	0.20	0.80	144.07
-0.70	0.40	138.91	0.20	1.00	144.40
-0.70	0.60	138.95	0.30	0.00	137.08
-0.70	0.80	138.99	0.30	0.20	137.76
-0.70	1.00	139.02	0.30	0.40	138.28
-0.60	0.00	135.77	0.30	0.60	138.69
-0.60	0.20	135.91	0.30	0.80	139.02
-0.60	0.40	136.02	0.30	1.00	139.29
-0.60	0.60	136.11	0.40	0.00	128.10
-0.60	0.80	136.18	0.40	0.20	128.58
-0.60	1.00	136.24	0.40	0.40	128.95
-0.50	0.00	137.61	0.40	0.60	129.23
-0.50	0.20	137.96	0.40	0.80	129.47
-0.50	0.40	138.23	0.40	1.00	129.66
-0.50	0.60	138.44	0.50	0.00	129.62
-0.50	0.80	138.61	0.50	0.20	130.17
-0.50	1.00	138.75	0.50	0.40	130.59
-0.40	0.00	136.21	0.50	0.60	130.92
-0.40	0.20	136.60	0.50	0.80	131.18
-0.40	0.40	136.90	0.50	1.00	131.40
-0.40	0.60	137.13	0.60	0.00	126.42
-0.40	0.80	137.32	0.60	0.20	126.89
-0.40	1.00	137.47	0.60	0.40	127.25
-0.30	0.00	130.67	0.60	0.60	127.53
-0.30	0.20	131.06	0.60	0.80	127.76
-0.30	0.40	131.36	0.60	1.00	127.94
-0.30	0.60	131.59	0.70	0.00	133.03
-0.30	0.80	131.78	0.70	0.20	133.64
-0.30	1.00	131.94	0.70	0.40	134.11
-0.20	0.00	128.09	0.70	0.60	134.47
-0.20	0.20	128.45	0.70	0.80	134.77
-0.20	0.40	128.73	0.70	1.00	135.01
-0.20	0.60	128.94	0.80	0.00	121.07
-0.20	0.80	129.12	0.80	0.20	121.39
-0.20	1.00	129.26	0.80	0.40	121.63
-0.10	0.00	128.74	0.80	0.60	121.82
-0.10	0.20	129.17	0.80	0.80	121.97
-0.10	0.40	129.50	0.80	1.00	122.10
-0.10	0.60	129.76	0.90	0.00	137.83
-0.10	0.80	129.97	0.90	0.20	138.53
-0.10	1.00	130.14	0.90	0.40	139.07
0.00	0.00	139.91	0.90	0.60	139.49
0.00	0.20	140.53	0.90	0.80	139.84
0.00	0.40	141.00	0.90	1.00	140.12

Chapter 7
Stratified Ranked Set Sampling (SRSS) for Estimating the Population Mean With Ratio–Type Imputation of the Missing Values

Carmen Elena Viada- Gonzalez
Gestión de la Información, Clínica Centro de Inmunología Molecular, Cuba

Sira María Allende-Alonso
Facultad de Matemática y Computación, Universidad de La Habana, Cuba

ABSTRACT

In this chapter, the authors develop stratified ranked set sampling (RSS) under missing observations. Imputation based of ratio rules is used for completing the information for estimating the mean. They introduce the needed elements on imputation and on the sample selection procedures. They extend RSS models to imputation in stratified populations. A theory on ratio-based imputation rules for estimating the mean is presented. Some numerical studies, based on real-world problems, are developed for illustrating the behaviour of the accuracy of the estimators due to their proposals.

DOI: 10.4018/978-1-7998-7556-7.ch007

1. INTRODUCTION

The basic theory of survey sampling discuses how to derive estimation procedures for estimating population parameters effectively. Different models are available to select the sample from the population. The properties of the sampling models mainly depend upon the availability of observation units. The estimation process may be more reliable, if we utilize adequate and reliable auxiliary information. Its used the design or in the stage of estimation may increase the accuracy of the estimators.

In many applications we deal with indexes, which are measured repeatedly. Say that we are developing a longitudinal study. The indexes are measured initially in a census. A sample of the units is selected and some of them are not giving information in the second visit. Some examples are the following:

1. The satisfaction index of the customers is measured visiting all the establishments (hotels, restaurants etc.) The firm introduces new policies and periodic evaluations of the index are to be performed by selecting a sample of them and estimating the mean of the index.
2. The psoriasis affected areas of patients provides a index . A medicament is to be used and it is evaluated in a sample of patients. The mean of the index is estimated and the efficiency of the treatment is evaluated.
3. The index of assertiveness is calculated in a population of students. After some psychological massive treatment a sample is selected for evaluating its effect by estimating the mean of the index .

Note that in the examples the populations are naturally divided into strata.

Having census information of the index is possible to rank the units selected in a sample using a high correlated auxiliary variable. Therefore we may consider the use of ranked set sampling (RSS) for estimating the population mean.

Commonly samplers deal with the existence of missing observations (MO) . Using imputation methods may commonly solve this fact. Considering the existence of MO and using of Ranked Set Sampling (RSS). In this paper we develop a study of the estimation of a population mean using ratio based methods when we deal with a stratified population.

Ranked set sampling (RSS), was proposed by McIntyre (1952, 2005). It is a sampling strategy base on ranking the units previouslly to measuring the variable of interest. It has been obtained that this sampling design provides more efficient statistical inferences than simple random sampling (SRS).

In this paper we will develop stratified ranked sampling (SRSS) under missing observations. Imputation based of ratio rules is used for completing the information for estimating the mean.

In the next section we introduce the elements on imputation. The study of imputation is based on the developments presented in Little and Rubin (2002), Rubin (1987).

The third section is concerned with the sample selection procedures. The third section is concerned with the estimation of the mean. Recently to extend RSS models to stratified populations is receiving attention form theoreticians. For example see MacEachern, et al. (2004), Kadilar and Cingi (2003, 2005), Kamarulzaman et al. (2014), Samawi (1996), Samawi and Muttlak, (1996), Samawi and Saeid (2004), Samawi and Siam (2003), Saini and Kumar (2019).

In section 4 we are going to discuss on ratio based imputation for estimating the mean of Y using SRSS. Finally, some numerical studies are developed.

2. SOME IDEAS ON IMPUTATION

Almost all sampling based data sets collected contain missing data. Observations can be missing due to different reasons. The existence of missing values may spoil the inference procedures conveying to unreliable conclusions on the problem. There are three solutions to cope with this fact: to ignore the non-respondents, to subsample the non-respondents or to impute the missing values. Rarely, ignoring the non-responses is a good solution, as Y may be related with having very different values among respondents and non-respondents. A subsampling fixes the size of the subsample to be drawn from the set of non-respondents. Subsampling the non-respondents strategies are expensive and in any case some observational units may be difficulty to observe over time. Imputation is a usable procedure to impute the nonresponse. Imputation procedures depend on having an adequate model of the non-responses mechanism and reliable information for predicting Y for each non- respondent.

Rubin (1976) provided a comprehensive framework for explaining the mechanisms generating missing values and their pattern in available information. See detailed discussions in Rubin (2004). A general model for modeling imputation procedures is considering that we should use, in our study, a complete data set of the study variable $\widehat{Y}$ but that there is a set of missing data . In sampling $\widehat{Y}$ is the set of observations of Y in the sampled units. Say $\widehat{Y} = \left\{ Y_i \middle| i \in s \right\}$. The missing data is generated by a certain pattern deðned by the conditional distribution f($\widehat{X} \mid \widehat{Y}$, δ). δ is an unknown parameter. The '*Missing at Random*' (MAR) model considers that the missing data process depends on the observed data, but not unobserved data. That is f($\widehat{X} \mid \left\{ Y_i \middle| i \in s \right\}$, δ). When the missing values do not depend on Y it is f($\widehat{X} \mid \widehat{Y}$, δ)=f($\widehat{X} \mid$ δ). This model is called *Missing "Completely at Random"* (MCAR). Note that this assumption means that the missing values are independent of Y but not that they occurred at random . A more complicated pattern is denominated *'Non-ignorable non-response'* (NINR) which allows dependence on observed and unobserved data. Then, the parameters estimation based only on the observed data is typically biased. The extent of biasedness is depending on how strong is the relationship between the unobserved outcomes and the probability of non-response. Under NINR we must determine a model which always requires assuming some untestable assumptions.

Provided the imputation model is correct, the resulting estimates are consistent.

In finite population sampling the imputation procedures generally use some auxiliary information. Ratio, product and regression estimators are of wide use for imputing the missing values. Ahmed et al. (2006) provided some imputation procedures considering an auxiliary variable with known and unknown population parameters of the auxiliary variable. Recently Kadilar et al. (2009), Grover and Kaur (2011, 2014), Bouza-Herrera and Al-Omari (2011) considered the estimation of population mean. They used different sampling schemes and the proposed procedures appeared as more efficient when compared with other ones.

3. STRATIFIED RATIO-TYPE IMPUTATION UNDER SIMPLE RANDOM SAMPLING WITH REPLACEMENT (SSRSWR)

This modelling considers that the population is described as follows:

$$U = \{u_1, \ldots, u_N\}; U = \bigcup_{h=1}^{H} U_h, U_h \bigcap U_t = \emptyset, h \neq t$$

U_h is the h-th stratum. Independent samples s_j, j=1,..,H, are selected from each stratum. We know values of the auxiliary variable $X_1, \ldots, X_M$; $X_i = X(u_i)$, i=1,...,M. The variable of interest Y is to be measured in samples. We evaluate it and use the auxiliary variable in the development of the inferences.

In a population of size M the mean and variance of a variable Z are, denoted respectively:

$$\bar{Z} = \frac{1}{M} \sum_{i \in U} Z_i; \sigma_Z^2 = \frac{1}{M} \sum_{i \in U} \left(Z_i - \bar{Z} \right)^2$$

In the case of dealing with the auxiliary variable Z=X and in the case of the study variable Z=Y . The relationship between X and Y is measured Pearson`s correlation coefficient

144

$$\rho = \frac{\sigma_{X,Y}}{\sigma_X \sigma_Y} = \frac{\frac{1}{M}\sum_{i \in U}(X_i - \bar{X})(Y_i - \bar{Y})}{\sqrt{\left(\frac{1}{M}\sum_{i \in U}(X_i - \bar{X})^2\right)\left(\frac{1}{M}\sum_{i \in U}(Y_i - \bar{Y})^2\right)}}$$

Let us consider the selection of a sample of size m using simple random sampling with replacement (SRSWR) and that we observe $m(1)$ non-responding units out of the sampled ones. We also assume that the non responses (NR) are occurring randomly. Let us consider some imputation rules.

Rule 1: Use only the responses

Then, using only the responses we may calculate

$$\bar{y}_{s(1)} = \frac{1}{m(1)}\sum_{i=1}^{m(1)} y_i$$

as we assumed tan NR are generated by a 'response at random' mechanism equivalent to SRSWR and that for each unit the probability of obtaining a response at a visit is P_1 is the same for i=1,...,m(1) $E\left(\bar{y}_{s(1)}\right) = \bar{Y}$. Its conditional variance is

$$MSE\left(\bar{y}_{s(1)}|m(1)\right) = \frac{\sigma_Y^2}{m(1)}$$

Take

$$\bar{x}_{s(1)} = \frac{1}{m(1)}\sum_{i=1}^{m(1)} x_i; \bar{x}_s = \frac{1}{m}\sum_{i=1}^{m} x_i; V\left(\bar{x}_{s(1)}|m(1)\right) = \frac{\sigma_X^2}{m(1)}; V\left(\bar{x}_s\right) = \frac{\sigma_X^2}{m}$$

Rule 2: Impute the value of the sample mean by expanding through the ratio of the means of the auxiliary variable X in the whole sample to its mean in sub-sample of the respondents

The usual relation between X and Y suggests using the ratio-imputation estimator of the population mean given by:

$$\overline{y}_{r(1)} = \frac{\overline{y}_{s(1)}}{\overline{x}_{s(1)}} \overline{X}$$

being, $C_z^2 = \frac{\sigma_z^2}{\overline{Z}^2}$, $Z=X,Y$, $R = \frac{\overline{Y}}{\overline{X}}$, we have that

$$Bias\left(\overline{y}_{r(1)} \middle| m(1)\right) \cong \left(\frac{1}{m(1)} - \frac{1}{m}\right) \overline{Y}\left(C_x^2 - \rho C_y C_x\right)$$

$$MSE\left(\overline{y}_{r(1)} \middle| m(1)\right) \cong \frac{\sigma_x^2}{m} + \left(\frac{1}{m(1)} - \frac{1}{m}\right)\left(R^2\sigma_x^2 - 2R\sigma_{xy}\right),$$

Remark 1. $Bias\left(\overline{y}_{r(1)} \middle| m(1)\right) \cong 0$ *if* or $\dfrac{C_x}{C_y} \cong \rho$

Remark 2. $MSE\left(\overline{y}_{r(1)} \middle| m(1)\right) \cong V\left(\overline{y}\right)$ *if* $m(1) \cong m$.

Kadilar-Cingi (2009) developed ratio-type estimators that determine 3 other rules. They used the coefficient of regression of the respondents

$$b = \frac{S_{xy}}{S_x^2} = \frac{\dfrac{\sum_{i=1}^{m(1)}\left(x_i - \overline{x}_{s(1)}\right)\left(y_i - \overline{y}_s(1)\right)}{m(1)-1}}{\dfrac{\sum_{j=1}^{m}(x_i - \overline{x}_s)^2}{m-1}}$$

Rule 3. Impute the value of the sample mean of Y by predicting the error using the means of the respondents and the population of X and expanding by the factor $\dfrac{\overline{X}}{\overline{x}_{s(1)}}$.

This rule is implemented using

$$\bar{y}_{KC1} = \frac{\bar{y}_{s(1)} + b\left(\bar{X} - \bar{x}_s\right)}{\bar{x}_{s(1)}} \bar{X}$$

and uses an estimation of the regression coefficient b.

Rule 4. Impute the value of the sample mean of Y by predicting the error using b, the means of the sample and of the population of X and expanding by the factor $\dfrac{\bar{X}}{\bar{x}_s}$.

$$\bar{y}_{KC2} = \frac{\bar{y}_s + b\left(\bar{X} - \bar{x}_s\right)}{\bar{x}_s} \bar{X}$$

Rule 5. Impute the value of the sample mean of Y by predicting the error using b, the means of the whole sample and the subsample of the responects of X and expanding by the factor $\dfrac{\bar{x}}{\bar{x}_s}$.

The suggested estimator is given by

$$\bar{y}_{KC3} = \frac{\bar{y}_{s(1)} + b\left(\bar{x}_s - \bar{x}_{s(1)}\right)}{\bar{x}_s} \bar{x} ,$$

It can be used even if $\bar{X}$ is unknown.
Approximations to the corresponding biases are respectively

$$Bias\left(\bar{y}_{KC1}\right) \cong \frac{\bar{Y}C_x^2}{m},$$

$$Bias\left(\bar{y}_{KC2} | m(1)\right) \cong \left(\frac{1}{m(1)} - \frac{1}{m}\right)\bar{Y}C_x^2;$$

$$Bias\left(\bar{y}_{KC3} | m(1)\right) \cong \left(\frac{1}{m(1)} - \frac{1}{m}\right)\bar{Y}C_xC_y$$

$Bias\left(\overline{y}_{KC2}\big|m(1)\right)$ and $Bias\left(\overline{y}_{KC3}\big|m(1)\right)$ depend of m(1), which is a random variable with expectation mP_1, assuming valid the previous NR generation hypothesis. The conditional MSE`s are:

$$MSE\left(\overline{y}_{KC1}\big|m(1)\right) \cong \frac{\sigma_y^2}{m(1)} - \frac{\left(R^2 - B^2\right)\sigma_x^2}{m}\; ; MSE\left(\overline{y}_{KC2}\big|m(1)\right) \cong \frac{\sigma_y^2 - B\sigma_{xy} + B^2\sigma_x^2}{m(1)}\quad ;$$

$$MSE\left(\overline{y}_{KC3}\big|m(1)\right) \cong \frac{\sigma_y^2}{m(1)} + \left(\frac{1}{m(1)} - \frac{1}{m}\right)(R+B)\left[(R+B)\sigma_x^2 - 2\sigma_{xy}\right],$$

respectively, being $B = \dfrac{\sigma_{xy}}{\sigma_x^2} B = \dfrac{\tilde{A}_{xy}}{\tilde{A}_x^2} = \dfrac{\tilde{A}_{xy}}{\tilde{A}_x^2}$.

From the proposal of Stephan (1945) the second order development of *m(1)* is

$$E\left(\frac{1}{m(1)}\right) \cong \frac{1}{mP_1} + \frac{1-W_1}{m^2 P_1^2} \to \frac{1}{mP_1}\text{ for large values of m}.$$

Therefore, the expected biases are

$$E\left(Bias\left(\overline{y}_{r(1)}\big|m(1)\right)\right) \cong \left(\frac{1-P_1}{mP_1}\right)\overline{Y}\left(C_x^2 - \rho C_y C_x\right)$$

$$E\left[Bias\left(\overline{y}_{KC1}\right)\right] \cong \frac{\overline{Y}C_x^2}{m},$$

$$E\left[Bias\left(\overline{y}_{KC2}\big|m(1)\right)\right] \cong \left(\frac{1-P_1}{mP_1}\right)\overline{Y}C_x^2\;;$$

$$E\left[Bias\left(\overline{y}_{KC3}\big|m(1)\right)\right] \cong \left(\frac{1-P_1}{mP_1}\right)\overline{Y}C_x C_y$$

A similar analysis of the sampling errors yields that

$$MSE\left(\bar{y}_{s(1)}\middle|m(1)\right) \cong \frac{\sigma_Y^2}{mP_1}$$

$$E\left[MSE\left(\bar{y}_{r(1)}\middle|m(1)\right)\right] \cong \frac{\sigma_x^2}{mP_1} + \frac{1-P_1}{mP_1}\left(R^2\sigma_x^2 - 2R\sigma_{xy}\right)$$

$$E\left[MSE\left(\bar{y}_{KC1}\middle|m(1)\right)\right] \cong \frac{\sigma_y^2}{mP_1} - \frac{\left(R^2 - B^2\right)\sigma_x^2}{m};$$

$$E\left[MSE\left(\bar{y}_{KC2}\middle|m(1)\right)\right] \cong \frac{\sigma_y^2 - B\sigma_{xy} + B^2\sigma_x^2}{mP_1};$$

$$E\left[MSE\left(\bar{y}_{KC3}\middle|m(1)\right)\right] \cong \frac{\sigma_y^2}{mP_1} + \frac{1-P_1}{mP_1}(R+B)\left[(R+B)\sigma_x^2 - 2\sigma_{xy}\right].$$

Consider that the sampler is going to use a SSRWR for estimating the mean of the population. The population means may be written as

$$\bar{Z} = \frac{1}{M}\sum_{i\in U}Z_i = \sum_{h=1}^{H}W_h\left(\frac{1}{M_h}\sum_{i\in U_h}Z_i\right) = \sum_{h=1}^{H}W_h\bar{Z}_h; W_h = \frac{M_h}{M}, h = 1,..,H$$

Due to its linearity we have the following proposition:

Proposition. 1 Take the stratified population U and SSRSWR as the sampling design used for drawing independent samples $s_h \subseteq U_h, h = 1,\ldots,H$. Denote for each stratum

$$\bar{x}_{hs(1)} = \frac{1}{m_{h1}}\sum_{i=1}^{m_{h1}}x_{ih}; \bar{x}_{s(h)} = \frac{1}{m_h}\sum_{i=1}^{m_h}x_{ih}; \bar{X}_h = \frac{1}{M_h}\sum_{i=1}^{M_h}X_{ih}$$

$$C_z^2 = \frac{\sigma_z^2}{\bar{Z}^2}, Z=X,Y, R_h = \frac{\bar{Y}_h}{\bar{X}_h}$$

Define the class of predictors

$$\hat{\overline{Y}} = \left\{ \overline{y}_{I(t)} = \sum_{h=1}^{H} W_h \overline{y}_{hI} ; P_{1h} = probability\,of\,having\,a\,response\,in\,a\,unit\,of\,U_h \right\}$$

Under the hypothesis that $\overline{y}_{hI}$ *is* unbiased for the different rules, denoting

P_1 = probability of having a full-response

and accepting the validity of the approximation of Stephan (1945)

$$E\left(r(j)^{-k}\right) \cong \left[E\left(r(j)\right)\right]^{-k}.$$

Then, for the different imputation rules we have:

Rule 1: t=s(1)

$$\overline{y}_{hI} = \frac{1}{m_{h1}} \sum_{i=1}^{m_{h1}} y_i$$

This estimator is unbiased and its expected MSE is approximated by:

$$E\left[MSE\left(\overline{y}_{I(s(1))}|m(1,1),\ldots,m(1,H)\right)\right] \cong \sum_{h=1}^{H} W_h^2 \frac{\sigma_{Y_h}^2}{m_h P_{1h}}$$

Rule 2: t=r(1)

$$\overline{y}_{hI} = \left(\frac{\sum_{i=1}^{m_{h1}} y_i}{\sum_{i=1}^{m_{h1}} x_{ih}}\right)\left(\frac{1}{m_h}\sum_{i=1}^{m_h} x_{ih}\right)$$

it is biased and its approximated expected bias and MSE are:

$$E\left(Bias\left(\bar{y}_{I(r(1))}|m(1,1),\ldots,m(1,H)\right)\right) \cong \sum_{h=1}^{H} W_h \left(\frac{1-P_{1h}}{mP_{1h}}\right) \bar{Y}_h \left(C_{x_h}^2 - \rho_h C_{y_h} C_{x_h}\right)$$

$$E\left[MSE\left(\bar{y}_{I(r(1))}|m(1,1),\ldots,m(1,H)\right)\right] \cong \sum_{h=1}^{H} W_h^2 \left[\frac{\sigma_{x_h}^2}{m_h P_{1h}} + \frac{1-P_{1h}}{m_h P_{1h}}\left(R_h^2 \sigma_{x_h}^2 - 2R_h \sigma_{x_h y_h}\right)\right]$$

Rule 3: t=KC1.

$$\bar{y}_{hIt} = \frac{\frac{1}{M_h}\sum_{i \in U_h} X_i}{\frac{1}{m_{h1}}\sum_{i=1}^{m_{h1}} x_{ih}}\left[\frac{\sum_{i=1}^{m_{h1}} y_i}{m_{h1}} + \left(\frac{\frac{\sum_{i=1}^{m_{h1}}\left(x_i - \bar{x}_{hs(1)}\right)\left(y_i - \bar{y}_{hs}(1)\right)}{m_{h1}-1}}{\frac{\sum_{j=1}^{m_h}(x_i - \bar{x}_{hs})^2}{m_h - 1}}\right)\left(\frac{1}{M_h}\sum_{i \in U_i} X_i - \frac{1}{m_h}\sum_{i=1}^{m_h} x_{ih}\right)\right]$$

It is biased and its approximated expected bias is:

$$E\left[Bias\left(\bar{y}_{I(KC1)}|m(1,1),\ldots,m(1,H)\right)\right] \cong \sum_{h=1}^{H} W_h \frac{\bar{Y}_h C_{x_h}^2}{m_h}$$

Its approximated expected MSE is given by:

$$E\left[MSE\left(\bar{y}_{I(KC1)}|m(1,1),\ldots,m(1,H)\right)\right] \cong \sum_{h=1}^{H} W_h^2 \left[\frac{\sigma_{y_h}^2}{m_h P_{1h}} - \frac{\left(R_h^2 - B_h^2\right)\sigma_{x_h}^2}{m_h}\right]$$

Rule 4: t=KC2.

$$\overline{y}_{hIt} = \left(\frac{\frac{1}{M_h}\sum_{i\in U_h}X_i}{\frac{1}{m_h}\sum_{i=1}^{m_h}x_{ih}} \right)\left(C + \frac{\sum_{i=1}^{m_{h1}}y_i}{m_{h1}} \right)$$

with

$$C = \left(\frac{\frac{\sum_{i=1}^{m_{h1}}\left(x_i - \overline{x}_{hs(1)}\right)\left(y_i - \overline{y}_{hs}(1)\right)}{m_{h1}-1}}{\frac{\sum_{j=1}^{m_h}(x_i - \overline{x}_{hs})^2}{m_h-1}} \right)\left(\frac{1}{M_h}\sum_{i\in U_i}X_i - \frac{1}{m_h}\sum_{i=1}^{m_h}x_{ih} \right)$$

Its expected bias and MSE are given respectively by

$$E\left[Bias\left(\overline{y}_{I(KC2)}|m(1,1),\ldots,m(1,H) \right) \right] \cong \sum_{h=1}^{H}W_h\left(\frac{1-P_{1h}}{m_hP_{1h}} \right)\overline{Y}_hC_{x_h}^2$$

$$E\left[MSE\left(\overline{y}_{I(KC2)}|m(1,1),\ldots,m(1,H) \right) \right] \cong \sum_{h=1}^{H}W_h^2\left(\frac{\sigma_{y_h}^2 - B_h\sigma_{x_hy_h} + B_h^2\sigma_{x_h}^2}{m_hP_{1h}} \right)$$

Rule 5: t=KC3.

$$\overline{y}_{hIt} = \frac{\frac{1}{m_h}\sum_{i=1}^{m_h}x_{ih}}{\frac{1}{m_{h1}}\sum_{i=1}^{m_{h1}}x_{ih}}$$

$$\left[\frac{\sum_{i=1}^{m_{h1}} y_i}{m_{h1}} + \left(\frac{\dfrac{\sum_{i=1}^{m_{h1}} \left(x_i - \bar{x}_{hs(1)} \right)\left(y_i - \bar{y}_{hs}(1) \right)}{m_{h1} - 1}}{\dfrac{\sum_{j=1}^{m_h} (x_i - \bar{x}_{hs})^2}{m_h - 1}} \right) \left(\frac{1}{m_h} \sum_{i=1}^{m_h} x_{ih} - \frac{1}{m_{h1}} \sum_{i=1}^{m_{h1}} x_{ih} \right) \right]$$

It is biased and the formula of its approximated expected bias is given as

$$E\left[Bias\left(\bar{y}_{I(KC3)} | m(1,1), \ldots, m(1,H) \right) \right] \cong \sum_{h=1}^{H} W_h \left(\frac{1 - P_{1h}}{m_h P_{1h}} \right) \bar{Y}_h C_{x_h} C_{y_h}$$

The expected MSE is

$$E\left[MSE\left(\bar{y}_{I(KC3)} | m(1,1), \ldots, m(1,H) \right) \right] \cong \sum_{h=1}^{H} W_h^2 \frac{\sigma_{y_h}^2}{m_h P_{1h}} + \left[\frac{1 - P_{1h}}{m_h P_{1h}} \left(R_h + B_h \right) \left[\left(R_h + B_h \right) \sigma_{x_h}^2 - 2\sigma_{x_h y_h} \right] \right].$$

Proof:

From the results previously derived for SRSWR and the linearity of the predictors the expressions are easily obtained. ■

4. STRATIFIED RATIO-TYPE IMPUTATION UNDER RANKED SET SAMPLING (RSS)

Ranked set sampling (RSS) design was proposed in McIntyre (1952, 2005). His proposal was motivated by the need of estimating accurately the population mean in pasture and forage yields studies. He considered that RSS performed better than the usual simple random sampling design with replacement (SRWS). The mathematical theory for RSS was developed from the results of Takahasi-Wakimoto (1968). Dell et al. (1972) developed it further establishing that, even when there are ranking errors, it performs more efficiently than simple random sampling (SRS). MacEachern et al. (2002). The method is described in Figure 1.

In the sequel, we consider the existence of a variable A which is close related with X and Y. The ranking may be developed using the so called "judgmental ranking", see Arnold et al. (2009). A particular case is using $A=X$, as X is known. The RSS procedure is repeated r times independently; r is the number of cycles. Let $Z_{(j:t)h}$ be the j-th ($j=1,2,\ldots,m$) order statistics (OS) of $Z=X,Y$ in the t-th sample

Figure 1.

Step 1: Randomly select units from the target population. These units are randomly allocated into *m* sets, each of size *m*.
Step 2: The *m* units of each set are ranked visually or by any inexpensive method with
Step 3: From the first set of *m* units, the smallest ranked unit is measured; from the second set of *m* units the second ranked unit is measured. The process is continued in this way until the unit occupying the *j*th place is measured in the *j*th respect to the variable of interest.
Step 3: From the first set of *m* units, the smallest ranked unit is measured; from the second set of *m* units the second ranked unit is measured. The process is continued in this way until the unit occupying the *j*th place is measured in the *j*th sample up to the *m*th (the last) set. The whole process can be repeated *r* times to obtain *rm* RSS units.

($t=1,2,\ldots,m$) in the cycle h. Then, both variables are measured only in the site *j* of the ordered sample *j* of the cycle h. Therefore we measure

$$Z_{(1:1)h}, Z_{(2:2)h}, \ldots, Z_{(m:m)h}, h = 1, 2, \ldots, r .$$

The RSS mean of *Z* of the *n=mr* selected units is

$$\bar{Z}_{(RSS)} = \frac{1}{mr} \sum_{h=1}^{r} \sum_{j=1}^{m} Z_{(j:j)h} .$$

It is unbiased because

$$E\left(\frac{1}{m} \sum_{j=1}^{m} Z_{(j:j)r} \right) = \bar{Z}$$

Samawi-Muttlak (1996) proposed as estimator of the population ratio $r_{(RSS)} = \dfrac{\bar{y}_{(RSS)}}{\bar{x}_{(RSS)}}$ and the ratio estimator of the mean was $\bar{y}_{r(RSS)} \cong r_{(RSS)}\bar{X}$.

Using Taylor approximations up to the second degree we have that

$$\bar{y}_{r(RSS)} \cong \bar{y}_{(RSS)} - Q_1 \left(\bar{x}_{(RSS)} - \bar{X} \right) + Q_2 \left(\bar{x}_{(RSS)} - \bar{X} \right)^2 - Q_3 \left(\bar{x}_{(RSS)} - \bar{X} \right)\left(\bar{y}_{(RSS)} - \bar{Y} \right)$$

where $Q_1 = \dfrac{\bar{Y}}{\bar{X}}, Q_2 = \dfrac{\bar{Y}}{\bar{X}^2}$, and $Q_3 = \dfrac{1}{\bar{X}}$. The estimator is biased as

$$E\left(\overline{y}_{r(RSS)}\right) \cong \overline{Y} + \frac{R-B}{\overline{X}} Var\left(\overline{x}_{(RSS)}\right)$$

and

$$B\left(\overline{y}_{r(RSS)}\right) \cong \frac{R-B}{\overline{X}} Var\left(\overline{x}_{(RSS)}\right).$$

We may approximate the MSE of $\overline{y}_{r(RSS)}$ by

$$MSE\left(\overline{y}_{r(RSS)}\right) \cong Var\left(\overline{y}_{(RSS)}\right) + Q_2^2 Var\left(\overline{x}_{(RSS)}\right) - 2Q_3 Cov\left(\overline{x}_{(RSS)}, \overline{y}_{(RSS)}\right)$$

where

$$Cov\left(\overline{x}_{(RSS)}, \overline{y}_{(RSS)}\right) = E\left[\left(\overline{x}_{(RSS)} - \overline{X}\right)\left(\overline{y}_{(RSS)} - \overline{Y}\right)\right] = \rho \frac{\sigma_y}{\sigma_x} Var\left(\overline{x}_{(RSS)}\right).$$

We are studying the case of having missing observations and considering that we will have $r(j) \pounds r$ responses for the j-th OS. Following the line developed in the previous section it makes sense using

$$\overline{Z}'_{(RSS)} = \frac{1}{m} \sum_{j=1}^{m} \frac{\sum_{h=1}^{r(j)} Z_{(j:j)h}}{r(j)}.$$

$\overline{Z}'_{(RSS)}$ is an unbiased estimator of the population mean because

$$E\left(Z_{(j:j)h}\right) = \overline{Z}_{(j)} = \int_{-\infty}^{\infty} z f_{(j:j)}(z) dz, V\left(Z_{(j:j)h}\right) = \sigma_{(j)}^2 = \int_{-\infty}^{\infty} \left(z - \overline{Z}_{(j)}\right)^2 f_{(j:j)}(z) dz,$$

Therefore,

$$E\left(\overline{Z}'_{(RSS)}\right) = \frac{1}{m} \sum_{j=1}^{m} \frac{\sum_{h=1}^{r(j)} \overline{Z}_{(j)}}{r(j)} = \frac{\sum_{j=1}^{m} \overline{Z}_{(j)}}{m} = \overline{Z}.$$

$$V\left(\bar{Z}'_{(RSS)}\right) = \frac{1}{m^2} \sum_{j=1}^{m} \frac{\sum_{h=1}^{r(j)} \sigma^2_{(j)}}{r(j)^2}.$$

As $\sigma^2_{Z(j)} = \sigma^2_Z - D^2_{Z(j)}$, where $D_{Z(j)} = \bar{Z}_{(j)} - \bar{Z}$, we have that

$$V\left(\bar{Z}'_{(RSS)}\right) = \frac{\sigma^2_Z}{m^2} \sum_{j=1}^{m} \frac{1}{r(j)} - \frac{1}{m^2} \sum_{j=1}^{m} \frac{D^2_{Z(j)}}{r(j)}.$$

As P_1 denotes the probability of having a full-response, from the approximation of Stephan (1945), we may consider that $E\left(r(j)^{-k}\right) \cong \left[E\left(r(j)\right)\right]^{-k}$. Then

$$V\left(\bar{Z}'_{(RSS)}\right) \cong \frac{\sigma^2_Z}{nP_1} - \sum_{j=1}^{m} \frac{D^2_{Z(j)}}{nmP_1}, \qquad n = mr$$

Let us develop RSS rules for imputation .

RSS-Rule 1: use only the responses

We assumed that the NR are generated by a 'response at random' mechanism equivalent to SRSWR and that for each unit the probability of obtaining a response at a visit is P_1 is a known constant. As we are using only the responses, we are going to calculate

$$\bar{y}_{(RSSs(1))} = \frac{1}{m} \sum_{j=1}^{m} \frac{1}{r(h)} \sum_{j=1}^{r(j)} y_{(j:j)h}$$

As $E\left(y_{(j:j)h}\right) = \bar{Y}_{(j)}$.

$$E\left(\bar{y}_{(RSSs(1))} \big| r(1),\ldots,r(h)\right) = \frac{1}{m} \sum_{j=1}^{m} \bar{Y}_{(j)} = \bar{Y}$$

Its conditional variance is

$$V\left(\overline{y}_{(RSSs(1))}\middle|r(1),\ldots,r(h)\right)=\frac{1}{m^2}\sum_{j=1}^{m}\frac{\sigma_{Y_{(j)}}^2}{r(j)}=\frac{\sigma_Y^2}{m^2}\sum_{j=1}^{m}\frac{1}{r(j)}-\frac{1}{m^2}\sum_{j=1}^{m}\frac{D_{Y_{(j)}}^2}{r(j)}$$

Due to unbiasedness of the predictor we have that

$$E\left(MSE\left(\overline{y}_{(RSSs(1))}\right)\right)\cong EV\left(\overline{y}_{(RSSs(1))}\middle|r(1),\ldots,r(h)\right)=\frac{1}{m^2}\sum_{j=1}^{m}\frac{\sigma_{Y_{(j)}}^2}{r(j)}=\frac{\sigma_Y^2}{mrP_1}-\frac{1}{m^2rP_1}\sum_{j=1}^{m}D_{Y_{(j)}}^2$$

Denote

$$\overline{x}_{(RSSs(1))}=\frac{1}{m}\sum_{j=1}^{m}\frac{1}{r(h)}\sum_{j=1}^{r(j)}x_{(j:j)h};\; \overline{x}_{(RSS)}=\frac{1}{mr}\sum_{j=1}^{m}\sum_{j=1}^{r}x_{(j:j)h}$$

$$V\left(\overline{x}_{(RSSs(1))}\middle|r(1),\ldots,r(h)\right)=\frac{\sigma_X^2}{m^2}\sum_{j=1}^{m}\frac{1}{r(j)}-\frac{1}{m^2}\sum_{j=1}^{m}\frac{D_{X_{(j)}}^2}{r(j)}$$

$$V\left(\overline{x}_{(RSS)}\right)=\frac{\sigma_X^2}{rm}-\frac{1}{rm^2}\sum_{j=1}^{m}D_{X_{(j)}}^2$$

RSS-Rule 2: Impute the value of the sample mean by expanding through the RSS-ratios of the means of X in the whole sample to its RSS-mean in sub-sample of the respondents .

The usual relation in estimation theory suggests using the ratio-imputation estimator of the population mean given by:

$$\overline{y}_{RSS(2)}=\frac{\overline{y}_{(RSSs(1))}}{\overline{x}_{(RSSs(1))}}\overline{X}$$

The Taylor approximation, developed up to the second degree, is

$$\bar{y}_{RSS(2)} \cong \bar{y}_{RSS} - Q_1 \left(\bar{x}_{RSS} - \bar{X} \right) + Q_2 \left(\bar{x}_{RSS} - \bar{X} \right)^2 - Q_3 \left(\bar{x}_{RSS} - \bar{X} \right) \left(\bar{y}_{RSS} - \bar{X} \right)$$

where $Q_1 = \dfrac{\bar{Y}}{\bar{X}}, Q_2 = \dfrac{\bar{Y}}{\bar{X}^2}$ and $Q_3 = \dfrac{1}{\bar{X}}$. We have that, conditionally, the MSE of $\bar{y}_{RSS(1)}$ is approximated, in terms , by

$$MSE \left(\bar{y}_{RSS(2)} \middle| r(1), \ldots, r(h) \right)$$

$$\cong \frac{\sigma_Y^2}{m^2} \sum_{j=1}^{m} \frac{1}{r(j)} - \frac{1}{m^2} \sum_{j=1}^{m} \frac{D_{Y_{(j)}}^2}{r(j)} + Q_2^2 \left[\frac{\sigma_X^2}{m^2} \sum_{j=1}^{m} \frac{1}{r(j)} - \frac{1}{m^2} \sum_{j=1}^{m} \frac{D_{X_{(j)}}^2}{r(j)} \right]$$

$$-2Q_3 \left(\frac{\sigma_Y}{\sigma_X} \right) \left(\frac{\sigma_X^2}{rm} - \frac{1}{rm^2} \sum_{j=1}^{m} D_{X_{(j)}}^2 \right)$$

$$= \frac{\sigma_Y^2}{m^2} \sum_{j=1}^{m} \frac{1}{r(j)} + \frac{\sigma_X^2}{m^2} \left(Q_2^2 \sum_{j=1}^{m} \frac{1}{r(j)} - 2Q_3 \left(\frac{\sigma_Y}{\sigma_X} \right) \left(\frac{\sigma_X^2}{rm} - \frac{1}{rm^2} \sum_{j=1}^{m} D_{X_{(j)}}^2 \right) \right)$$

$$- \frac{1}{m^2} \sum_{j=1}^{m} \frac{D_{Y_{(j)}}^2}{r(j)} - \frac{Q_2^2}{m^2} \sum_{j=1}^{m} \frac{D_{X_{(j)}}^2}{r(j)} - 2Q_3 \left(\frac{\sigma_Y}{\sigma_X} \right) \frac{1}{rm^2} \sum_{j=1}^{m} D_{X_{(j)}}^2$$

As, see Alomari-Bouza (2015),

$$Cov \left(\left(\bar{x}_{RSS(1)}, \bar{y}_{RSS(1)} \middle| r(1), \ldots, r(h) \right) \right) = \left(\frac{\sigma_Y}{\sigma_X} \right) \rho_{X,Y} V \left(\bar{x}_{(RSS)} \right)$$

we have that the expected MSE, is denoted by

$$E \left[MSE \left(\bar{y}_{RSS(2)} \middle| r(1), \ldots, r(h) \right) \right] = \text{A-B}$$

where

$$A \cong \frac{\sigma_Y^2}{mrP_1} + \frac{\sigma_X^2}{mrP_1}\left(\frac{Q_2^2}{mrP_1} - 2Q_3\left(\frac{\sigma_Y}{\sigma_X} \right)\left(\frac{\sigma_X^2}{rm} - \frac{1}{rm^2}\sum_{j=1}^{m}D_{X_{(j)}}^2 \right) \right)$$

$$B = \left(\frac{1}{m^2 rP_1}\sum_{j=1}^{m}D_{Y_{(j)}}^2 + \frac{Q_2^2}{m^2 rP_1}\sum_{j=1}^{m}D_{X_{(j)}}^2 + 2Q_3\left(\frac{\sigma_Y}{\sigma_X} \right)\frac{1}{rm^2}\sum_{j=1}^{m}D_{X_{(j)}}^2 \right)$$

Let us develop a similar study with the proposal of Kadilar-Cingi (2009) . The RSS counterpart is

$$b_{RSS(1)} = \frac{s_{RSS(1),(X.Y)}}{s_{RSS(1),X}^2} = \frac{\frac{1}{m}\sum_{j=1}^{m}\frac{1}{r(h)}\sum_{j=1}^{r(j)}(y_{(j:j)h} - \overline{y}_{RSS(1)})(x_{(j:j)h} - \overline{x}_{RSS(1)})}{\frac{1}{m}\sum_{j=1}^{m}\frac{1}{r(h)}\sum_{j=1}^{r(j)}(x_{(j:j)h} - \overline{x}_{RSS(1)})^2}$$

The new imputation rule is described as follows:

RSS-Rule 3. Impute the value of the sample mean of Y by predicting the error using the means of the respondents and the population of X and expanding by the factor $\dfrac{\overline{X}}{\overline{x}_{s(1)}}$.

This rule is implemented using

$$\overline{y}_{KCRSS1} = \frac{\overline{y}_{RSSs(1)} + b\left(\overline{X} - \overline{x}_s \right)}{\overline{x}_{s(1)}}\overline{X}$$

It uses an estimation of the regression coefficient b.

RSS-Rule 4. Impute the value of the sample mean of Y by predicting the error using b, the means of the sample and of the population of X and expanding by the factor $\dfrac{\overline{X}}{\overline{x}_s}$.

$$\overline{y}_{KCRSS2} = \frac{\overline{y}_{KCRSS(1)} + b\left(\overline{X} - \overline{x}_s \right)}{\overline{x}_s}\overline{X}$$

RSS-Rule 5. Impute the value of the sample mean of Y by predicting the error using b, the means of the whole sample and the subsample of the respondents of X and expanding by the factor $\dfrac{\overline{x}}{\overline{x}_s}$.

The suggested estimator is given by

$$\overline{y}_{KCRSS3} = \frac{\overline{y}_{RSSs(1)} + b\left(\overline{x}_s - \overline{x}_{sRSS(1)}\right)}{\overline{x}_s} \, \overline{X} \, ,$$

It can be used even if $\overline{X}$ is unknown.

Approximations to the corresponding biases are, respectively,

$$Bias\left(\overline{y}_{KCRSS1}\right) \cong \frac{\overline{Y}C_x^2}{m} \, ,$$

$$Bias\left(\overline{y}_{KCRSS2}\,\middle|\,m(1)\right) \cong \left(\frac{1}{m(1)} - \frac{1}{m}\right)\overline{Y}C_x^2 \, ;$$

$$Bias\left(\overline{y}_{KCRSS3}\,\middle|\,m(1)\right) \cong \left(\frac{1}{m(1)} - \frac{1}{m}\right)\overline{Y}C_x C_y$$

The conditional MSE`s are:

$$MSE\left(\overline{y}_{KCRSS1}\,\middle|\,m(1)\right) \cong \frac{\sigma_y^2}{m(1)} - \frac{\left(R^2 - B^2\right)\sigma_x^2}{m} \, ;$$

$$MSE\left(\overline{y}_{KCRSS2}\,\middle|\,m(1)\right) \cong \frac{\sigma_y^2 - B\sigma_{xy} + B^2\sigma_x^2}{m(1)} \, ;$$

$$MSE\left(\overline{y}_{KCRSS3}\,\middle|\,m(1)\right) \cong \frac{\sigma_y^2}{m(1)} + \left(\frac{1}{m(1)} - \frac{1}{m}\right)(R+B)\left[(R+B)\sigma_x^2 - 2\sigma_{xy}\right],$$

respectively, being $B = \dfrac{\sigma_{xy}}{\sigma_x^2}$ $B = \dfrac{\tilde{A}_{xy}}{\tilde{A}_x^2}$ $B = \dfrac{\tilde{A}_{xy}}{\tilde{A}_x^2}$.

Note that some biases and MSE's depend of m(1). For deriving the expectation of them we rely on accepting the proposal of Stephan (1945) we have that the second order development of *m(1) is*

$$E\left(\frac{1}{m(1)}\right) \cong \frac{1}{mP_1} + \frac{1-W_1}{m^2 P_1^2} \to \frac{1}{mP_1}$$

for large values of m. Hence, assuming valid the previous NR generation hypothesis. We approximate the expected biases as follows:

$$E\left(Bias\left(\bar{y}_{r(1)}\big|m(1)\right)\right) \cong \left(\frac{1-P_1}{mP_1}\right)\bar{Y}\left(C_x^2 - \rho C_y C_x\right)$$

$$E\left[Bias\left(\bar{y}_{KCRSS1}\right)\right] \cong \frac{\bar{Y}C_x^2}{m},$$

$$E\left[Bias\left(\bar{y}_{KCRSS2}\big|m(1)\right)\right] \cong \left(\frac{1-P_1}{mP_1}\right)\bar{Y}C_x^2;$$

$$E\left[Bias\left(\bar{y}_{KCRSS3}\big|m(1)\right)\right] \cong \left(\frac{1-P_1}{mP_1}\right)\bar{Y}C_x C_y$$

A similar analysis of the sampling errors yields that

$$MSE\left(\bar{y}_{s(1)}\big|m(1)\right) \cong \frac{\sigma_Y^2}{mP_1}$$

$$E\left[MSE\left(\bar{y}_{r(1)}\big|m(1)\right)\right] \cong \frac{\sigma_x^2}{mP_1} + \frac{1-P_1}{mP_1}\left(R^2\sigma_x^2 - 2R\sigma_{xy}\right)$$

$$E\left[MSE\left(\bar{y}_{KCRSS1}\big|m(1)\right)\right] \cong \frac{\sigma_y^2}{mP_1} - \frac{\left(R^2 - B^2\right)\sigma_x^2}{m};$$

$$E\left[MSE\left(\bar{y}_{KCRSS2}\big|m(1)\right)\right] \cong \frac{\sigma_y^2 - B\sigma_{xy} + B^2\sigma_x^2}{mP_1};$$

$$E\left[MSE\left(\bar{y}_{KC3RSS}\big|m(1)\right)\right] \cong \frac{\sigma_y^2}{mP_1} + \frac{1-P_1}{mP_1}(R+B)\left[(R+B)\sigma_x^2 - 2\sigma_{xy}\right].$$

Consider that the sampler is going to use a SSRWR for estimating the mean of the population. The population means may be written as

$$\bar{Z} = \frac{1}{M}\sum_{i\in U}Z_i = \sum_{h=1}^{H}W_h\left(\frac{1}{M_h}\sum_{i\in U_h}Z_i\right) = \sum_{h=1}^{H}W_h\bar{Z}_h; W_h = \frac{M_h}{M}, h = 1,..,H$$

Due to its linearity we have the following proposition:

Proposition 2. Take the stratified population U and RSSWR as the sampling design used for drawing independent samples $s_h \subseteq U_h, h = 1,\ldots,H$. Denote for each stratum

$$\bar{x}_{hs(1)} = \frac{1}{m_{h1}}\sum_{i=1}^{m_{h1}}x_{ih}; \bar{x}_{s(h)} = \frac{1}{m_h}\sum_{i=1}^{m_h}x_{ih}; \bar{X}_h = \frac{1}{M_h}\sum_{i=1}^{M_h}X_{ih}$$

$$C_z^2 = \frac{\sigma_z^2}{\bar{Z}^2}, \ Z = X,Y, \ R_h = \frac{\bar{Y}_h}{\bar{X}_h},$$

$$Q_1 = \frac{\bar{Y}}{\bar{X}}, Q_2 = \frac{\bar{Y}}{\bar{X}^2} \text{ and } Q_3 = \frac{1}{\bar{X}}$$

$$Q_{1h} = \frac{\bar{Y}_h}{\bar{X}_h}, Q_{2h} = \frac{\bar{Y}_h}{\bar{X}_h^2} \text{ and } Q_{3h} = \frac{1}{\bar{X}_h}$$

Define the class of predictors

$$\widehat{\overline{Y}} = \left\{ \overline{y}_{SRSS(t)} = \sum_{h=1}^{H} W_h \overline{y}_{(t)} ; P_{1h} = probability\ of\ having\ a\ response\ in\ a\ unit\ of\ U_h \right\}$$

for the different rules we have:

RSS-Rule 1: t=SRSSs(1)

$$\overline{y}_{(SRSSs(1))} = \sum_{h=1}^{H} W_h \frac{1}{m} \sum_{j=1}^{m} \frac{1}{r(h)} \sum_{j=1}^{r(j)} y_{(j:j)h}$$

is unbiased and

$$E\left(MSE\left(\overline{y}_{(SRSSs(1))} \right) \right) \cong EV\left(\overline{y}_{(RSSSs(1))} \middle| r(1),...,r(h) \right) = \sum_{h=1}^{H} W_h^2 \sum_{j=1}^{m} \left(\frac{\sigma_{Y_{(j)}}^2}{mrP_{1h}} - \frac{1}{m^2 rP_{1h}} \sum_{j=1}^{m} D_{Y_{(j)}}^2 \right)$$

RSS-Rule 2: t=SRSSr(1)

$$\overline{y}_{(SRSSs(2))} = \sum_{h=1}^{H} W_h \overline{y}_{(RSSs(2)h)} = \sum_{h=1}^{H} W_h \left(\frac{\overline{y}_{(RSSs(1)h)}}{\overline{x}_{(RSSs(1)h)}} \overline{X}_h \right)$$

its approximated expected MSE is

$$\left[MSE\left(\overline{y}_{SRSS(2)} \middle| r(1),...,r(h) \right) \right] \cong \sum_{h=1}^{H} W_h^2 \left(V_h + R_h + O_h \right)$$

where

$$V_h = \frac{\sigma_{Y_h}^2}{m_h r_h P_{1h}}$$

$$R_h = -2Q_{3h}\left(\frac{\sigma_{Y_h}}{\sigma_{X_h}}\right)\left(\frac{\sigma_{X_h}^2}{r_h m_h} - \frac{1}{r_h m_h^2}\sum_{j=1}^{m}D_{X_{(j)h}}^2\right)$$

$$O_h = -\left(\frac{1}{m_h^2 r_h P_{1h}}\sum_{j=1}^{m_h}D_{Y_{(j)h}}^2 + \frac{Q_{2h}^2}{m_h^2 r_h P_{1h}}\sum_{j=1}^{m_h}D_{X_{(j)h}}^2 + 2Q_{3h}\left(\frac{\sigma_{Y_h}}{\sigma_{X_h}}\right)\frac{1}{r_h m_h^2}\sum_{j=1}^{m_h}D_{X_{(j)h}}^2\right)$$

RSS-Rule 3: t=SRSSKC1.

$$\bar{y}_{KCSRSS1} = \sum_{h=1}^{H}W_h\left(\frac{\bar{y}_{RSSs(1)h} + b_h\left(\bar{X}_h - \bar{x}_{s_h}\right)}{\bar{x}_{s(1)h}}\bar{X}_h\right)$$

$$E\left[Bias\left(\bar{y}_{KCSRSS1}|m(1,1),\ldots,m(1,H)\right)\right] \cong \sum_{h=1}^{H}W_h\frac{\bar{Y}_h C_{x_h}^2}{m_h P_{1h}},$$

$$E\left[MSE\left(\bar{y}_{KCSRSS1}|m(1,1),\ldots,m(1,H)\right)\right] \cong \sum_{h=1}^{H}W_h^2\left[\frac{\sigma_{x_h}^2}{m_h P_{1h}} + \frac{1-P_1}{m_h P_{1h}}\left(R_h^2\sigma_{x_h}^2 - 2R_h\sigma_{x_h y h}\right)\right]$$

RSS-Rule 4: t=SRSSKC2.

$$\bar{y}_{KCRSS2} = \sum_{h=1}^{H}W_h\frac{\bar{y}_{KCRSS(1)h} + b_h\left(\bar{X}_h - \bar{x}_{s_h}\right)}{\bar{x}_{sh}}\bar{X}_h$$

$$E\left[Bias\left(\bar{y}_{KCRSS2}|m(1,1),\ldots,m(1,H)\right)\right] \cong \sum_{h=1}^{H}W_h\left(\frac{1-P_1}{m_h P_{1h}}\right)\bar{Y}_h C_{x_h}^2$$

$$E\left[MSE\left(\bar{y}_{KCRSS2} | m\left(1,1\right),\ldots,m(1,H)\right)\right] \cong \sum_{h=1}^{H} W_h^2 \left(\frac{\sigma_{y_h}^2 - B_h \sigma_{x_h y_h} + B_h^2 \sigma_{x_h}^2}{m_h P_{1h}} \right)$$

RSS-Rule 5: t=SRSSKC3.

$$\bar{y}_{KCSRSS3} = \sum_{h=1}^{H} W_h \frac{\bar{y}_{RSSs(1)h} + b_h \left(\bar{x}_{s_h} - \bar{x}_{sRSS(1)h} \right)}{\bar{x}_{s_h}} \bar{X}_h,$$

$$E\left[Bias\left(\bar{y}_{KCSRSS3} | m\left(1,1\right),\ldots,m(1,H)\right)\right] \cong \sum_{h=1}^{H} W_h \left(\frac{1-P_{1h}}{m_h P_{1h}} \right) \bar{Y}_h C_{x_h} C_{y_h}$$

$$E\left[MSE\left(\bar{y}_{KCSRSS3} | m\left(1,1\right),\ldots,m(1,H)\right)\right] \cong \sum_{h=1}^{H} W_h^2 \frac{\sigma_{y_h}^2}{m_h P_{1h}} + \left(R_h + B_h \right)\left[\left(R_h + B_h \right) \sigma_{x_h}^2 - 2\sigma_{x_h y_h} \right].$$

Proof:
From the results derived previously for RSSWR for each stratum and the linearity of the predictors the expressions are easily obtained. ∎

4. NUMERICAL STUDIES

The SRSS models were compared with the SSRSWR counterparts evaluating the ratios

$$\gamma_{t,SRSSt} = \frac{\left[MSE\left(\bar{y}_v | m\left(1,1\right),\ldots,m(1,H)\right)\right]}{MSE\left(\bar{y}_u | m\left(1,1\right),\ldots,m(1,H)\right)},$$

v = s(1), r(1), KC1, KC2, KC3; u=SRSSs(1), SRSSr(1), SRSSKC1, SRSSKC2, SRSSKC3

The values of this index re ranked for each alternative using Kendall's consensus criteria: use the mean of the ranks.

1. The service quality expectations of hotels' customers, was examined in a population of hotels. They were stratified considering the expected quality of them. Four strata were naturally defined. The variables measured were:
    $Y=$ Customer Satisfaction Index of the hotel in the high season.
    $X=$ Customer Satisfaction Index of the hotel in the low season.
2. The assertiveness of a population of foreign students was measured before and after developing by a team of psychologists. They were stratified into 5 strata considering their nationality.
    $X=$ assertiveness at the before the training.
    $Y=$ assertiveness at the after the training.
3. The data of the population was obtained from a research, developed for determining the effect of AcM murino of isotope IgG2a, a medicament produced by Centro de Inmunología Molecular of Cuba. The interest was evaluating its effect in diminishing the area affected by psoriasis. See Viada et.al. (2004) for details. The index called *PASI* (Psoriasis Severity Index) was determined in each visit . We considered:
    $X=$ Value of the index at the first visit
    $Y=$ value of the index at the end of the treatment.

The set of measurements of *PASI* constituted an artificial population. It was partitioned using the area covered by psoriasis. Three strata were determined.

The values obtained from the population were used and we fixed $P_{ih}=0.25$, $h=1,...,H$.

See Table 1 for the results for estimating the mean of the Customer Satisfaction Index of the hotels in the high season. When the responses are used the ratio has the

Table 1. Results of $\gamma_{t,SRSSt}$ for a population of hotels, $Y=$ assertiveness at the after the training

	s(1)	r(1)	KC1	KC2	KC3	Consensus rank
SRSSs(1)	1,15	1,12	1,04	1,10	1,09	1
SRSSr(1)	1,71	1,46	1,48	1,45	1,42	4
SRSSKC1	1,81	1,16	1,13	1,72	1,44	2,5
SRSSKC2	2,72	1,41	2,07	2,13	2,22	5
SRSSKC3	1,95	1,18	1,99	1,12	1,29	2,5
Consensus Rank	1	2	3,5	5	3,5	

smallest values when SSRSWR is compared with the SRSS alternatives. The same conclusion is obtained when we compared the estimator based only in the responses obtained under SRSS with the other estimators. The ratios of the SSRSWR models when compared with their SRSS counterparts have moderate values. Looking to the consensus ranking obtained we have that the best SSRSWR estimator is KC2 and for SRSS was SRSSKC2.

Table 2 presents the results obtained when estimating the mean of the Customers Satisfaction Index of the hotels in the high season. Again using only the responses the ratio having the smallest values for the design SSRSWR is KC3. SRSS overcomes at large SSRSWR alternatives. The estimators based on SRSS are considerably more precise than the SSRSWR models. The best strategy for SRSS is using the imputation rule SRSSKC1.

Table 2. Results of $\gamma_{t,SRSSt}$ for a population of a population of foreign students, Y= assertiveness at the after the training

	s(1)	r(1)	KC1	KC2	KC3	Consensus rank
SRSSs(1)	1,61	1,68	2,52	2,61	2,82	1
SRSSr(1)	1,11	1,23	2,31	2,42	2,81	3
SRSSKC1	1,26	1,31	1,34	1,41	1,52	5
SRSSKC2	1,28	1,42	1,44	1,81	2,21	2
SRSSKC3	1,34	1,14	1,25	1,46	1,65	4
Consensus Rank	1	2	3	4	5	

The next Table is concerned with for the results for estimating the mean of the value of the psoriasis index at the end of the treatment. The imputation rule s(1) is the less precise again. The ratios of the MSE`s of the SSRSWR models when compared with their SRSS counterparts are always larger than 1. Hence RSS alternatives are to be preferred. Analyzing the consensus ranking we note that the best estimations are obtained for KC3 rules both in SSRSWR and SRSS

The results of the tables illustrate how, as expected, RSS performs considerably better than SSRSWR. The accuracy of KC3 rules appeared providing the larges gains in accuracy.

Table 3. Results of $\gamma_{t,SRSSt}$ for a population of a population of patients with psoriasis,. Y= value of the index at the end of the treatment

	s(1)	r(1)	KC1	KC2	KC3	Consensus rank
SRSSs(1)	1,10	1,87	1,26	1,39	1,78	1
SRSSr(1)	1,20	1,80	1,66	1,60	1,88	2
SRSSKC1	1,39	1,37	1,79	1,44	1,92	3
SRSSKC2	1,28	1,11	1,41	1,97	1,83	4
SRSSKC3	1,40	1,50	1,61	1,76	1,99	5
Consensus Rank	1	3,5	3,5	2	5	

ACKNOWLEDGMENT

This paper has been benefited by the suggestions of Prof. A. I. Alomari. These results have been supported by the project PN223LH010-005, Desarrollo de nuevos modelos y métodos matemáticos para la toma de decisiones.

This paper has been developed under the advisory of Prof. Dr. Carlos Bouza-Herrera.

REFERENCES

Al-Omari, A. I., & Bouza, C. N. (2014). Review of ranked set sampling: Modifications and applications. *Revista Investigación Operacional, 35,* 215–240.

Arnold, B. C., Castillo, E., & Sarabia, J. M. (2009). On multivariate order statistics. Application to ranked set sampling. *Computational Statistics & Data Analysis, 53*(12), 4555–4569. doi:10.1016/j.csda.2009.05.011

Dell, J. R., & And Clutter, J. N. (1972). Ranked sert sampling theory with order statititcs background. *Biometrics, 28*(2), 545–553. doi:10.2307/2556166

Kadilar, C., & Cingi, H. (2003). Ratio Estimators in Stratiðed Random Sampling. *Biometrical Journal. Biometrische Zeitschrift, 45*(2), 218–225. doi:10.1002/bimj.200390007

Kadilar, C., & Cingi, H. (2003). Ratio Estimators in Stratiðed Random Sampling. *Biometrical Journal, 45*(2), 218-225.

Kadilar, C., & Cingi, H. A. (2005). new ratio estimator in stratiðed random sampling. *Communications in Statistics. Theory and Methods, 34*(3), 597–602. doi:10.1081/STA-200052156

Kamarulzaman, I. M., Mandowara, V. L., & Mehta, N. (2014). Modiðed ratio estimators using stratiðed ranked set sampling. *Hacettepe Journal of Mathematics and Statistics, 43*, 461–471.

Little, R. J. A., & Rubin, D. B. (2002). *Statistical Analysis with Missing Data* (2nd ed.). Wiley. doi:10.1002/9781119013563

MacEachern, S. N., Stasny, E. A., & Wolfe, D. A. (2004). Stratiðcation with imprecise rankings. *Biometrics, 60*, 207–215. doi:10.1111/j.0006-341X.2004.00144.x PMID:15032791

McIntyre, G. A. (2005). A method for unbiased selective sampling using ranked set sampling. *The American Statistician, 59*, 230-232.

Rubin, R. B. (1976). Inference and missing data. *Biometrika, 63*(3), 581–592. doi:10.1093/biomet/63.3.581

Rubin, R. B. (1987). *Multiple imputation for non-response in surveys*. John Wiley. doi:10.1002/9780470316696

Saini, M. & Kumar, A. (2019). Ratio estimators using stratified random sampling and stratified ranked set sampling. *Life Cycle Reliab Saf Eng, 8*, 85-92.

Samawi, H. M. (1996). Stratiðed ranked set sample. *Pakistan Journal of Statistics, 12*, 9–16.

Samawi, H. M., & Muttlak, H. A. (1996). Estimation of ratio using ranked set sampling. *Biometrical Journal. Biometrische Zeitschrift, 38*(6), 753–764. doi:10.1002/bimj.4710380616

Samawi, H. M., & Saeid, L.-J. (2004). Stratified Extreme Ranked Set Sample With Application To Ratio Estimators. *Journal of Modern Applied Statistical Methods; JMASM, 3*(1), 117–133. doi:10.22237/jmasm/1083370320

Samawi, H. M., & Siam, M. I. (2003). Ratio estimation using stratiðed ranked set sample. *Metron, 61*, 75–90.

Stephan, F. F. (1945). The expected value and variance of the reciprocal and other negative power of a positive Binomial variate. *Ann. Math. Statistic., 16*(1), 50–61. doi:10.1214/aoms/1177731170

Takahashi, K., & Wakimoto, M. (1968). On unbiased estimates of the population mean based on the sample stratified by means ordering. *Annals of the Institute of Mathematical Statistics, 20*, 1031-1047.

Viada-González, C. E., Bouza-Herrera, C. N., Torres-Barbosa, F., & Torres-Gemeil, O. (2004). Estudio estadístico de ensayos clínicos de un medicamento para la psoriasis vulgar usando técnicas de imputación. *Revista Investigación Operacional, 25*, 243–255.

Chapter 8
A Review of Bootstrap Methods in Ranked Set Sampling

Arpita Chatterjee
Georgia Southern University, USA

Santu Ghosh
(iD) https://orcid.org/0000-0002-1420-3533
Augusta University, USA

ABSTRACT

This chapter provides a brief review of the existing resampling methods for RSS and its implementation to construct a bootstrap confidence interval for the mean parameter. The authors present a brief comparison of these existing methods in terms of their flexibility and consistency. To construct the bootstrap confidence interval, three methods are adopted, namely, bootstrap percentile method, bias-corrected and accelerated method, and method based on monotone transformation along with normal approximation. Usually, for the second method, the accelerated constant is computed by employing the jackknife method. The authors discuss an analytical expression for the accelerated constant, which results in reducing the computational burden of this bias-corrected and accelerated bootstrap method. The usefulness of the proposed methods is further illustrated by analyzing real-life data on shrubs.

INTRODUCTION

The sampling design is a fundamental part of any statistical inference. A well-developed sampling design plays a critical role in ensuring that data can capture the distinct characteristics of the population and are sufficient to draw the conclusions

DOI: 10.4018/978-1-7998-7556-7.ch008

needed. Choice of a sampling plan depends on many aspects, including but not limited to the purpose of the analysis, the rarity of the characteristics under study, the nature of the total population, the size of the area to be studied, and most importantly, the cost of the study. One of the most commonly cited sampling plans is the simple random sampling (SRS). In practice, a more structured sampling mechanism, such as stratified sampling or systematic sampling, may be obtained to achieve a representative sample of the population of interest. Ranked-set sampling (RSS) is an alternative data collection method and has been known as a cost-efficient sampling procedure for many years. This approach to data collection was first proposed by McIntyre (1952) to improve the precision of estimated pasture yield. Later, Takahasi and Wakimoto (1968) established a rigorous statistical foundation for the theory of RSS. The ranked set sampling (RSS) utilizes the basic intuitive properties associated with simple random sampling (SRS). However, it involves the extra structure induced through the judgment ranking and the independence of the resulting order statistics. As a result, the procedures based on RSS lead to more efficient estimators of population parameters than those based on an SRS with the same sample size. The existing literature also includes works on hypothesis testing and point and interval estimation under both parametric and nonparametric settings. The most basic version of RSS is the balanced RSS. The process of generating an RSS involves drawing k^2 units at random from the target population. These items are then randomly divided into k sets of k units each. Within each set, the units are then ranked by some means other than a direct measurement. For example, visually or using a concomitant measurement that is comparatively cheaper to measure and easy to obtain than the measurement of interest. Finally, one item from each set is chosen for actual quantification. To be more specific, from the first set, we select the item with the smallest judgment-rank for measurement, from the second set, we choose the item with the second smallest judgment-rank, and so on, until the unit ranked largest is selected from the kth set. This complete procedure, called a cycle, is repeated independently m times to obtain a ranked set sample of size mk. Therefore, a balanced RSS of size mk requires a total of mk^2 units to be selected, but only mk of them are measured. Hence, a more comprehensive range of the population can be covered while significantly reducing the sampling cost. According to Takahasi and Wakimoto (1968), for easy implementation of RSS, the set size k is usually kept as four or less. However, we can obtain a large sample by increasing the cycle size m. Another option is that of unbalanced RSS. In an unbalanced RSS, $n \times k$ units are selected at random from the target population. These items are then randomly divided into n sets of k units each. Units in each set are judgment ranked without measuring the actual units. In this setting, let m_r denote the number of sets allocated to measure units having the rth judgment-rank such that $n = \sum_{r=1}^{k} m_r$. The measured observations then constitute an unbalanced RSS of size n.

Recently, several bootstrap methods have been developed based on RSS. Hui et al. (2004) proposed a bootstrap confidence interval method for the population mean based on RSS via linear regression. They applied the bootstrap method to estimate the variance of the estimator of the population mean for constructing confidence intervals. In a similar vein, Modarres et al. (2006) developed many bootstrap procedures for balanced RSS and established their consistency for the sample mean. Drikvandi et al. (2011) proposed a bootstrap method to test for the symmetry of the distribution function about an unknown median based on RSS. Further, the bootstrap finds many applications in RSS. Many bootstrap methods (Frey (2007); Ozturk (2017); Ivković et al. (2019); Mahdizadeh et al. (2019, 2020); Biswas et al. (2020)) have been developed for constructing confidence intervals using the bootstrap method.

This chapter starts with a description of the existing resampling methods for RSS, namely, BRSSR (bootstrap RSS by row), BRSS (bootstrap RSS), and MRBRSS (mixed row bootstrap RSS). These three methods are commonly employed for resampling elements from an RSS. For example, the authors implemented the BRSSR method to construct bootstrap confidence intervals for the mean parameter.

RESAMPLING METHODS FOR RANKED SET SAMPLES

This section briefly describes the existing resampling methods, namely BRSSR (bootstrap RSS by row), BRSS (bootstrap RSS), and MRBRSS (mixed row bootstrap RSS). Let's consider an RSS

$$\zeta_{RSS} = \left\{ X_{(r),j}, sr = 1, 2, \cdots, k; j = 1, 2, \cdots m_r \right\}$$

drawn from the underlying distribution $F(x)$. For simplicity, let's assume $m_r = m$. Internally, an RSS sample can be viewed as a stratified sampling technique consisting of k strata. Suppose F_r denotes the distribution function of the rth order statistic from $F(x)$. Intuitively, the distribution function F can be expressed in terms of F_r as

$$F(t) = k^{-1} \sum_{r=1}^{k} F_r(t).$$

According to Stokes and Sager (1988), for each t, $F(t)$ is estimated as

$$\hat{F}(t) = k^{-1}\sum_{r=1}^{k}\hat{F}_r(t).$$

$\hat{F}_r(t)$ is the empirical distribution function based on, $\left\{X_{(r),1}, X_{(r),2}, \cdots, X_{(r),m}\right\}$,

the elements on the rth strata. That is, for each t, $\hat{F}_r(t) = m^{-1}\sum_{j=1}^{m}I(X_{(r),j} \leq t)$.

BRSSR (Bootstrap RSS by row)

The bootstrap RSS by row was introduced by Chen et al. (2004). Let's arrange the sampled data, χR_{SS} as a k×m matrix and call it the RSS data matrix. The $r t^h$ row, $\left\{X_{(r)1}, X_{(r)2}, \cdots, X_{(r)m}\right\}$, represents the m resulting units with rank r. The BRSSR method can be summed up as follows:

Step 1: Take a random sample of size m (with replacement) from the rth row of the RSS data matrix.
Step 2: Repeat step 1 for every rank, r=1,2,…,k.

Finally, the resulting bootstrap samples drawn independently and randomly with replacement from the k strata is denoted as $\left\{X^*_{(1),1}, \cdots, X^*_{(1),m}\right\}, \cdots, \left\{X^*_{(k),1}, \cdots, X^*_{(k),m}\right\}$. Replacing m with m_r in Step 1 leads to an unbalanced BRSSR. The next two methods were proposed by Modarres et al. (2006) for balanced RSS.

BRSS (Bootstrap RSS)

This approach ignores the concept of stratification by ranking as in BRSSR. On the contrary, the m resulting units from each rank are pooled together to obtain a large dataset with mk observations, initiating the sampling frame for the resampling method. The BRSS approach can be illustrated through the following steps.

Step 1: Select k^2 elements at random from the RSS χR_{SS}.
Step 2: Split them into k sets of k units each. Let's denote the elements in the rth set as $\left\{y_{r1}, \cdots, y_{rk}\right\}$.
Step 3: Sort them in ascending order to obtain $\left\{y_{r(1)}, \cdots, y_{r(k)}\right\}$.
Step 4: From the rth ordered set choose $y_{r(r)}$, the rth ordered entry, and rename it as

$$X^*_{(r),1}.$$

Step 5: Repeat Step 4 for every rank, $r=1,2,\ldots,k$.

Steps 1 through 5 completes one cycle of BRSS yielding $\left\{X^*_{(1),1},\cdots,X^*_{(k),1}\right\}$. Finally, the cycles are repeated m times to obtain $\left\{X^*_{(1),1},\cdots,X^*_{(1),m}\right\},\cdots,\left\{X^*_{(k),1},\cdots,X^*_{(k),m}\right\}$.

MRBRSS (Mixed Row Bootstrap RSS)

The mixed row bootstrap RSS is an extension of the bootstrap RSS by row method. Let's reconsider the rank-based stratification structure as outlined in the BRSSR. Based on the matrix representation of the RSS data matrix, with $\left\{X_{(r),1},\cdots,X_{(r),m}\right\}$ denoting the rth row, the MRBRSS approach can be described as follows:

Step 1: Randomly select one element from each row of the RSS data matrix. Let's call them $\{y_{1,\ldots,}k\}$.

Step 2: Arrange the sample in ascending order to produce an ordered list of elements, $\{y^*_{(1)},\cdots,y^*_{(k)}\}$. Retain the lowest ordered unit $y^*_{(1)}$ and call it $X^*_{(1),1}$.

Step 3: Repeat Steps 1 and 2 k times. At the jth repetition of the process, choose $y^*_{(j)}$, the element with the jth order.

This concludes one complete cycle of the bootstrap RSS, which gives $\left\{X^*_{(1),1},\cdots,X^*_{(k),1}\right\}$. Finally, the cycles are repeated m times to obtain $\left\{X^*_{(1),1},\cdots,X^*_{(1),m}\right\},\cdots,\left\{X^*_{(k),1},\cdots,X^*_{(k),m}\right\}$. Regardless of the above resampling criterion, the bootstrap empirical distribution function can be defined as,

$$\hat{F}^*(t) = k^{-1}\sum_{r=1}^{k}\hat{F}^*_r(t) = \frac{1}{mk}\sum_{r=1}^{k}\sum_{j=1}^{m}I\left(X^*_{(r),j}\leq t\right),$$

where $I\left(X^*_{(r),j}\leq t\right)$ is an indicator function.

The BRSS method consistently estimates the distribution of the sample mean under balanced RSS. However, BRSS may not be appropriate for unbalanced RSS as it may cause some bias (Modarres et al., 2006). The other resampling method MRBRSS is not quite appealing for RSS since it does not provide a consistent estimator for the distribution of the sample mean (Modarres et al., 2006). Out of the three resampling methods discussed above, BRSSR is the most flexible. It is applicable for both balanced and unbalanced cases, and it is a consistent method.

CONSTRUCTION OF BOOTSTRAP CONFIDENCE INTERVALS

This section presents a review of bootstrap confidence intervals for the mean parameter based on BRSSR. In this context, the authors adopt three confidence interval methods, namely, the bootstrap percentile (BP) method, the bias-corrected and accelerated (BC_a) method, and method based on monotone transformation.

RSS and Sample Mean

Let nk units be drawn randomly from a population with an unknown distribution $F(x)$. Let μ and $\sigma2$ be the mean and variance of F(x), respectively. These units are then randomly divided into n groups G1, $_{...}$,Gn $_o$f size k each. The rth^group Gr $_c$onsists of $\left\{ X_{r,1}, X_{r,2}, \cdots, X_{r,k} \right\}$. Then, the units in each n subgroups are ordered on the attribute of interest using some ranking process. Let mr be the number of actual measurements on units having rank r, $r=1,2,\ldots,k$, such that $n = \sum_{r=1}^{k} m_r$. Under the assumption of perfect ranking, let $X_{(r),j}$ denote the measurement on the jth unit having rank r and let the m_r resulting measurements on units with rank r be labeled as $\{X_{(r),1}, \cdots, X_{(r),m_r}\}$. The resulting

RSS of size n drawn from that underlying distribution $F(x)$ is given by

$$\mathcal{C}_{RSS} = \left\{ X_{(r),j}, r = 1, 2, \cdots, k; j = 1, 2, \cdots m_r \right\}.$$

When $m_r=m$, $r=1,\ldots,k$, RSS leads to the balanced ranked set sample of size mk.

Let $\{X_{(r),1}, \cdots, X_{(r),m_r}\}$ be a random sample from F_r where F_r denotes the distribution function of the rth order statistic from $F(x)$. Let μr denote the mean of Fr This chapter deals with the construction of confidence intervals for $\mu = k^{-1}\sum_{r=1}^{k}\mu_r$ based on $\chi R_{SS.}$ Dell and Clutter (1972) argued that the above identity holds under both perfect and imperfect rankings. An unbiased estimator of μ can be obtained as

$$\bar{X}_{RSS} = \frac{1}{k}\sum_{r=1}^{k}\bar{X}_r = \frac{1}{k}\sum_{r=1}^{k}\frac{1}{m_r}\sum_{j=1}^{m_r}\frac{1}{m_r}X_{(r),j},$$

where $\bar{X}_r$ is the sample mean based on $\{X_{(r),1}, \cdots, X_{(r),m_r}\}$. Let $\tau 2$ be the variance of $\bar{X}_{RSS}$ given by

$$\tau^2 = \frac{1}{k^2}\sum_{r=1}^{k}\frac{\sigma_r^2}{m_r},$$

where $\bar{A}_r^2$ is the variance of $X_{(r),j}$. Set $S_r^2 = m_r^{-1}\sum_{j=1}^{m_r}\left(X_{(r),j} - \bar{X}_r\right)^2$, a plug-in estimator for σ_r^2, so that the corresponding plug-in estimator for $\tau 2$ becomes $\hat{\tau}^2 = \frac{1}{k^2}\sum_{r=1}^{k}\frac{S_r^2}{m_r}.$

While seeking confidence intervals for μ, let $t_\P$ denote the ξt^h quantile of the distribution of the pivot

$$T_{RSS} = \frac{\left(\bar{X}_{RSS} - \mu\right)}{\hat{\tau}} = \frac{\sum_{r=1}^{k}(\bar{X}_r - \mu_r)}{\sqrt{\sum_{r=1}^{k}\frac{S_r^2}{m_r}}}$$

such that $P\left(T_{RSS} \leq t_\zeta\right) = \zeta.$ For the rest of this chapter, we consider α as the nominal coverage probability of a confidence interval. Then, $I_0 = \left[\bar{X}_{RSS} - t_\alpha\hat{\tau}, \infty\right),$ $I_1 = \left(-\infty, \bar{X}_{RSS} - t_{1-\alpha}\hat{\tau}\right],$ and $I_2 = \left[\bar{X}_{RSS} - t_{(1+\alpha)/2}\hat{\tau}, \bar{X}_{RSS} - t_{1-(1+\alpha)/2}\hat{\tau}\right]$ are the ideal lower, upper, and two-sided confidence intervals for μ, respectively. However, these intervals are unknown since $t_\P$ is unknown. Usually, these intervals are estimated by employing the normal approximation, based on the central limit theorem, to the distribution of T_{RSS}. An alternative method to the normal approximation is through bootstrap method, which has become a standard tool for estimating unknown confidence intervals.

Bootstrap Confidence Intervals for Mean Parameter

An accurate estimate of the uncertainty associated with parameter estimates is vital to prevent deceptive inference. This uncertainty is quantified based on a confidence interval or region containing the true value of a parameter with a specified probability, known as the confidence coefficient. The bootstrap plays a vital role in construction since the 1980s. The construction of bootstrap confidence intervals based on SRS has been studied extensively over the past few decades. A more straightforward method for computing confidence intervals is the bootstrap percentile method. Early criticism of the bootstrap percentile method (Efron, (1979)) led to several improvements of the methodology, including the bias-corrected method (Efron, (1981)), the bias-corrected and accelerated method (Efron, (1987)), and the studentized method (Efron, (1982)).

Confidence intervals for μ based on RSS can be easily constructed by extending Efron's (1979) bootstrap percentile method in the case of SRS. This method has some attractive features, such as it is invariant to monotone transformations, but it suffers from poor coverage probabilities. Efron (1987) proposed a correction to the percentile-method that reduces the coverage error while retaining the invariance property. The resulting confidence interval method is known as bias-corrected and accelerated (BCa) bootstrap. The authors (Ghosh et al. (2017)) extends Efron (1987)'s BCa confidence interval method to RSS scheme for μ, which is considered below.

Let $\left\{ X^*_{(1),1}, \cdots, X^*_{(1),m_1} \right\}, \cdots, \left\{ X^*_{(k),1}, \cdots, X^*_{(k),m_k} \right\}$ denote k bootstrap samples drawn independently and randomly with replacement from the k sets, $\left\{ X_{(1),1}, \cdots, X_{(1),m_1} \right\}, \cdots, \left\{ X_{(k),1}, \cdots, X_{(k),m_k} \right\}$, respectively. Then, the resulting bootstrap sample $\chi^*_{RSS} = \left\{ X^*_{(r),j}, r = 1, 2, \cdots, k; j = 1, 2, \cdots m_r \right\}$ is known as BRSSR.

Let us denote $\bar{X}^*_r = m_r^{-1} \sum_{j=1}^{m_r} X^*_{(r),j}$, and $S^{*2}_r = m_r^{-1} \sum_{j=1}^{m_r} \left(X^*_{(r),j} - \bar{X}^*_r \right)^2$. The bootstrap versions of $\bar{X}_{RSS}$ and $\hat{\tau}^2$ are then

$$\bar{X}^*_{RSS} = \frac{1}{k} \sum_{r=1}^{k} \bar{X}^*_r \text{ and } \hat{\tau}^{*2} = \frac{1}{k^2} \sum_{r=1}^{k} \frac{S^{*2}_r}{m_r}.$$

Define

$$\hat{u}_{¾} = \sup\{ u : P(\bar{X}^*_{RSS} \le u | \chi_{RSS}) \le ¾ \}.$$

Then, $I_{0,BP} = \left[\hat{u}_{1-\alpha}, \infty\right), I_{1,BP} = \left(-\infty, \hat{u}_{\alpha}\right],$ and $I_{2,BP} = \left[\hat{u}_{(1-\alpha)/2}, \hat{u}_{(1+\alpha)/2}\right]$ are the respective lower, upper, and both-sided percentile-method confidence intervals for μ. It can be shown that

$$P\left\{\mu \in I_{0,BP}\right\} = P\left\{\mu \in I_{1,BP}\right\} = \alpha + O\left(n^{-\frac{1}{2}}\right); \text{ and}$$

$$P\left\{\mu \in I_{2,BP}\right\} = \alpha + O\left(n^{-1}\right).$$

For constructing BC_a confidence intervals for μ based on RSS, we define

$$\hat{G}_{RSS}\left(x\right) = P\left(\bar{X}^*_{RSS} \le x \mid \chi_{RSS}\right),$$

the bootstrap distribution of $\bar{X}^*_{RSS}$. Put

$$\hat{d} = \gtrless^{-1}\left\{\hat{G}_{RSS}\left(\bar{X}_{RSS}\right)\right\},$$

$$I_{\hat{a}}\left(\alpha\right) = \Phi\left[\hat{d} + \left(\hat{d} + z_\alpha\right)\left\{1 - \hat{a}\left(\hat{d} + z_\alpha\right)\right\}^{-1}\right],$$

where $\hat{d}$ and $\hat{a}$ are called bias-correction and acceleration constant, respectively. Ghosh et al. (2017) define Efron's (1987) BC_a method confidence intervals for μ based on RSS as follows:

$$I_{0,BC_a} = \left[\hat{u}_{l_{\hat{a}}(1-\alpha)}, \infty\right),$$

$$I_{1,BC_a} = \left(-\infty, \hat{u}_{l_{\hat{a}}(\alpha)}\right],$$

and

$$I_{2,BC_a} = \left[\hat{u}_{l_{\hat{a}}((1-\alpha)/2)}, \hat{u}_{l_{\hat{a}}((1+\alpha)/2)}\right],$$

respectively. The bootstrap percentile and the bias-corrected methods can be viewed as special cases of BC_a, which can be obtained by letting $\hat{d} = \hat{a} = 0$ and $\hat{a} = 0$, respectively. In particular, the non-zero values of $\hat{d}$ and $\hat{a}$ change the quantiles used for BC_a. In practice, $\hat{d}$ is computed as

$$\hat{d} = \Phi^{-1}\left(\frac{\#\left\{\bar{X}^*_{RSS} \leq \bar{X}_{RSS}\right\}}{B}\right),$$

where B is the number of bootstrap samples. The acceleration constant $\hat{a}$ can be computed using the jackknife method (for details, see Efron, 1987; Efron and Tibshirani, 1993), which becomes computationally burdensome as the set size in RSS increases. This computational burden involved in BC_a method for RSS can be substantially reduced by letting

$$\hat{a} = \frac{1}{6}n^{-1/2}\hat{\eta}_1^{-3/2}\hat{\eta}_2 = \frac{1}{6}n^{-1/2}\left(\sum_{r=1}^{k}\frac{\hat{\sigma}_r^2}{\lambda_r}\right)^{-3/2}\sum_{r=1}^{k}\frac{\hat{\gamma}_r^2}{\lambda_r^2}.$$

Where $\lambda_r = \dfrac{m_r}{n}$, and $\hat{\gamma}_r$ is the sample skewness based on $\left\{X_{(r),1}, \cdots, X_{(r),m_1}\right\}$. The above formula for $\hat{a}$ is obtained by extending Hall's (1988) finding to the case of RSS. Then, I^*_{0,BC_a}, I^*_{1,BC_a}, and I^*_{2,BC_a} are versions of I_{0,BC_a}, I_{1,BC_a}, and I_{2,BC_a} based on the above expression for $\hat{a}$. The authors (Ghosh et al. (2017)) established the following result that shows the second-order accuracy of I^*_{0,BC_a}, I^*_{1,BC_a}, and I^*_{2,BC_a}.

Theorem 1: Under the assumptions on the smoothness of the population distribution and the finiteness of the first eight population moments,

$$P\left\{\mu \in I^*_{0,BC_a}\right\} = P\left\{\mu \in I^*_{1,BC_a}\right\} = P\left\{\mu \in I^*_{2,BC_a}\right\} = \alpha + O\left(n^{-1}\right).$$

The above Theorem shows that BC_a method-based lower and upper confidence intervals are more accurate than those based on normal approximation and bootstrap percentile-method, which provide a coverage error of order $O(n^{-1/2})$. However, for two sided-confidence intervals, normal approximation and bootstrap percentile methods are similar to BC_a method in terms of the coverage probability, as they all result in a coverage error of order $O(n^{-1})$. It is important to note that the normal approximation confidence intervals do not respect transformation.

Confidence Intervals Based on Monotone Transformations

Monotone transformations help reduce the effects of skewness of data on the distribution of an asymptotic pivot. Johnson (1978) proposed a modified one-sample *t* test based on a quadratic transformation that is less affected by the population skewness than the conventional *t* test. However, this quadratic transformation has some drawbacks in that it is not monotone and fails to correct adequately for skewness. For this reason, the authors adopt Hall's (1992) cubic transformation can be defined as

$$g\left(x\right) = x + n^{-1/2}\frac{1}{3}\hat{\eta}x^2 + n^{-1}\frac{1}{27}\hat{\eta}^2 x^3 + n^{-1/2}\frac{1}{6}\hat{\eta},$$

where $\hat{\eta} = \hat{\eta}_1^{-3/2}\hat{\eta}_2.\hat{\eta}$ is associated with the following Edgeworth expansion of the distribution function of T_{RSS}

$$P\left(T_{RSS} \leq x\right) = \Phi\left(x\right) + n^{-\frac{1}{2}}q_1\left(x\right)\phi\left(x\right) + O\left(n^{-1}\right),$$

where $\Phi(x)$ is the cdf of the standard normal distribution, and $p_1(x)$ and $q_1(x)$ are even polynomials of degree 2 having the expressions

$$p_1\left(x\right) = -\frac{1}{6}\eta_1^{-3/2}\eta_2\left(x^2 - 1\right),$$

$$q_1\left(x\right) = \frac{1}{6}\eta_1^{-3/2}\eta_2\left(2x^2 + 1\right),$$

with

$$\eta_1 = \sum_{r=1}^{k}\frac{\sigma_r^2}{\lambda_r}, \eta_2 = \sum_{r=1}^{k}\frac{\gamma_r^2}{\lambda_r^2}, and\ \gamma_r = E\left(X_{(r)} - \mu_r\right)^3.$$

Under the assumption of Theorem 1, $P\left\{g\left(T_{RSS}\right) \le x\right\} = \Phi(x) + O\left(n^{-1}\right)$; that is, the distribution of the transformed pivot, $g(T_{RSS})$, is more symmetric than that of T_{RSS}.

Let z_ζ be the ζth quantile of the standard normal distribution and define

$$I_{0,g} = \left[\bar{X}_{RSS} - g^{-1}(z_\alpha)\hat{\tau}, \infty\right),$$

$$I_{1,g} = \left(-\infty, \bar{X}_{RSS} - g^{-1}(z_{1-\alpha})\hat{\tau}\right], \text{ and}$$

$$I_{2,g} = \left[\bar{X}_{RSS} - g^{-1}(z_\beta)\hat{\tau}, \overline{X}_{RSS} - g^{-1}(z_{1-\beta})\hat{\tau}\right],$$

where $\beta = \frac{1}{2}(1+\alpha)$. Then, $I_{0,g}$, $I_{1,g}$, and $I_{2,g}$ are the respective lower, upper and two-sided confidence intervals for μ, based on the transformation g(.) with

$$g^{-1}(x) = n^{1/2}\left(\frac{1}{3}\hat{\eta}\right)^{-1}\left[\left\{1 + \hat{\eta}\left(n^{-1/2}x - \frac{1}{6}n^{-1}\hat{\eta}\right)\right\}^{1/3} - 1\right].$$

These transformation based confidence intervals are more accurate than the normal-approximation based confidence intervals as the coverage errors associated with the intervals $I_{0,g}$ and $I_{1,g}$ are of order $O(n^{-1})$. Whereas coverage errors associated with normal-approximation based one-sided confidence intervals are of order $O(n^{-1/2})$.

SIMULATION STUDY

Simulation studies were considered to compare the proposed confidence interval methods discussed above with three conventional confidence interval methods: the bootstrap percentile method, the bootstrap percentile-t method, and the normal approximation method. Lower, upper, and two-sided confidence intervals were constructed based on each of these methods. LCL, UCL, and TCL denote the lower, upper and two-sided confidence intervals to facilitate the discussion of the simulation results, respectively. The symbols N, BP, BT, BC_a stand for normal approximation method, bootstrap percentile method, bootstrap percentile-t method, and bias-corrected and accelerated method. Moreover, N_{g1} and N_{g2} denote the normal approximation along with transformations g1 and g2, respectively. These confidence interval methods are then compared with respect to their coverage probabilities, average lower confidence limits, average upper confidence limits, and average interval widths. The ranked set samples were generated based on several balanced RSS and unbalanced RSS designs with different sample sizes when the set sizes were chosen to be $k=2,3$. Data were generated from two underlying distributions with various degrees of skewness and kurtosis: a chi-square distribution with df $=$ 1 (χ_1^2), and the half-normal distribution denoted by HN (0, 1). The means are, respectively, 1, and $\sqrt{(2/\pi)}$. For every distribution and sample size combination, we generated 5000 simulated samples. The coverage probability for each method for each combination was then estimated by the proportion of times the method covered the true parameter of the underlying distribution. Based on the results in Table 1 and Table 2, we have the following findings: i) BC_a is the one the authors would recommend for the construction of lower confidence intervals, ii) BT method appears to be the best in terms of coverage accuracy for UCL when n is small, and iii) for large sample sizes, N_{g1} and N_{g2}, provide comparable coverages as BT in addition to being simple to compute and requiring less computational effort.

DATA EXAMPLE

In this section, the authors implemented the above-discussed bootstrap confidence intervals to a dataset involving 46 shrubs. These data were first reported by Muttlak and McDonald (1990). First, three transect lines were laid out across the area, and all shrubs intersecting each transect were sampled. Finally, the size of each shrub was measured. This technique is good for sampling a vast area relatively quickly. The original sample was broken into 15 groups, each containing three shrubs (leaving one out). The three shrubs in the first group were ranked based on their sizes, and the shortest of all was included in the sample. This process was repeated five times, which resulted in 5 replicates. For the next five groups, the ones with the second smallest size were included in the sample. Finally, from each of the remaining five groups, the largest shrubs were chosen. This process resulted in a balanced RSS with set size three and cycle size 5. The resulting confidence intervals for the mean shrub size are presented in Table 3.

It can be seen that the bootstrap percentile (BP) method gives the largest lower limit for the 90% lower confidence interval for the mean size of shrubs. The lower limit corresponding to the BC_a method is close to that of the BP method. The transformation based confidence interval method gives smaller lower limits than BP and BC_a methods.

Table 1. Coverage probabilities of 90% confidence intervals for mean of data

Methods:	$(k = 2, n = 10), (m_1 = 5, m_2 = 5)$			$(k = 2, n = 10), (m_1 = 4, m_2 = 6)$		
	LCL	UCL	TCL	LCL	UCL	TCL
N	0.938 (0.56)	0.773 (1.46)	0.798 (1.16)	0.943 (0.57)	0.768 (1.43)	0.793 (1.10)
BP	0.916 (0.61)	0.757 (1.42)	0.767 (1.05)	0.923 (0.62)	0.750(1.40)	0.762(0.99)
BT	0.937 (0.58)	0.835 (2.04)	0.889 (2.50)	0.938 (0.60)	0.852 (1.87)	0.896 (2.00)
BC_a	0.899 (0.64)	0.784 (1.51)	0.780 (1.09)	0.900 (0.65)	0.779 (1.47)	0.776 (1.04)
Ng_1	0.926 (0.60)	0.796 (1.54)	0.824 (1.30)	0.927 (0.61)	0.791 (1.51)	0.824 (1.24)
Ng_2	0.921 (0.61)	0.802 (1.56)	0.816 (1.23)	0.920 (0.63)	0.796 (1.52)	0.816 (1.17)
	$(k = 2, n = 60), (m_1 = 30, m_2 = 30)$			$(k = 2, n = 60), (m_1 = 25, m_2 = 35)$		
	LCL	UCL	TCL	LCL	UCL	TCL
N	0.929 (0.80)	0.840 (1.20)	0.872 (0.52)	0.925 (0.81)	0.851 (1.19)	0.873 (0.49)
BP	0.921 (0.80)	0.842 (1.20)	0.868 (0.51)	0.918 (0.82)	0.851 (1.20)	0.869 (0.49)
BT	0.901 (0.82)	0.887 (1.26)	0.897 (0.58)	0.908 (0.83)	0.894 (1.24)	0.905 (0.54)
BC_a	0.897 (0.82)	0.870 (1.23)	0.873 (0.53)	0.893 (0.84)	0.877 (1.22)	0.873 (0.50)
Ng_1	0.903 (0.82)	0.876 (1.24)	0.905 (0.58)	0.899 (0.83)	0.883 (1.23)	0.903 (0.55)
Ng_2	0.903 (0.82)	0.875 (1.24)	0.883 (0.54)	0.898 (0.83)	0.881 (1.23)	0.880 (0.52)
	$(k = 3, n = 10), (m_1 = 3, m_2 = 3, m_3 = 4)$			$(k = 3, n = 10), (m_1 = 4, m_2 = 3, m_3 = 3)$		
	LCL	UCL	TCL	LCL	UCL	TCL
N	0.940 (0.60)	0.760 (1.39)	0.785 (1.01)	0.933 (0.57)	0.748 (1.43)	0.756 (1.10)
BP	0.909 (0.66)	0.734 (1.34)	0.732 (0.86)	0.897 (0.64)	0.707 (1.36)	0.689 (0.86)
BT	0.942 (0.59)	0.844 (1.85)	0.902 (2.32)	0.951 (0.50)	0.841 (2.28)	0.878 (3.10)
BC_a	0.892 (0.68)	0.753 (1.39)	0.742 (0.90)	0.892 (0.66)	0.720 (1.38)	0.704 (0.94)
Ng_1	0.927 (0.64)	0.787 (1.46)	0.816 (1.15)	0.925 (0.60)	0.761 (1.48)	0.779 (1.19)
Ng_2	0.925 (0.64)	0.785 (1.45)	0.808 (1.07)	0.925 (0.60)	0.760 (1.48)	0.770 (1.14)

Table 2. Coverage probabilities of 90% confidence intervals for mean of data (Contd.)

	$(k = 3, n = 60), (m_1 = 20, m_2 = 20, m_3 = 20)$			$(k = 3, n = 60), (m_1 = 25, m_2 = 10, m_3 = 25)$		
	LCL	UCL	TCL	LCL	UCL	TCL
N	0.927 (0.81)	0.841 (1.18)	0.871 (0.48)	0.930 (0.81)	0.848 (1.18)	0.872 (0.47)
BP	0.920 (0.82)	0.839 (1.18)	0.862 (0.46)	0.922 (0.82)	0.845 (1.18)	0.862 (0.46)
BT	0.904 (0.83)	0.884 (1.24)	0.893 (0.54)	0.912 (0.83)	0.883 (1.23)	0.896 (0.52)
BC_a	0.896 (0.84)	0.865 (1.21)	0.863 (0.48)	0.896 (0.84)	0.871 (1.21)	0.864 (0.47)
Ng_1	0.903 (0.83)	0.874 (1.22)	0.901 (0.54)	0.905 (0.84)	0.880 (1.22)	0.897 (0.53)
Ng_2	0.902 (0.83)	0.873 (1.22)	0.877 (0.50)	0.904 (0.84)	0.879 (1.22)	0.875 (0.50)

For the 90% upper confidence limit, BP method produces the smallest upper limit, which is close to that of BC_a method. The transformation based confidence interval method gives larger upper limits than BP and BC_a methods.

For the 90% two-sided confidence interval, BC_a and BP methods have the shortest interval width as compared to the transformation based method.

DISCUSSION

RSS is an alternative data collection method and has been known as a cost-efficient sampling procedure for many years. Obtaining sampling distributions of statistics under RSS is often tricky. The bootstrap could be helpful in such cases. This chapter discusses different bootstrap methods for estimating the distributions of the mean based on an RSS sample and the construction of bootstrap confidence intervals for the mean parameter. Since RSS can be viewed as k independent random samples from k different distributions, BRSSR can therefore be easily implemented by drawing bootstrap samples independently from each of the k independent random samples. Among the bootstrap RSS methods, BRSSR can be easily extended for the unbalanced case. However, BRSS and MRBRSS are developed under the balanced case. Also, under the BRSSR scheme, the bootstrap distribution of the sample mean converges to its true distribution, making BRSSR a consistent method of resampling. The same is true for the BRSS method under the balanced case. However, the MRBRSS method lacks this quality since it does not provide a consistent estimator for the distribution of the sample mean.

Table 3. Coverage probabilities of 90% confidence intervals for mean of HN(0,1) data

Methods:	$(k = 2, n = 10), (m_1 = 5, m_2 = 5)$			$(k = 2, n = 10), (m_1 = 4, m_2 = 6)$		
	LCL	UCL	TCL	LCL	UCL	TCL
N	0.913 (0.60)	0.834 (0.99)	0.843 (0.50)	0.915(0.60)	0.837(0.99)	0.844 (0.49)
BP	0.889 (0.62)	0.818 (0.97)	0.802 (0.44)	0.884 (0.63)	0.813 (0.97)	0.808 (0.44)
BT	0.915 (0.60)	0.892 (1.07)	0.911 (0.69)	0.920 (0.58)	0.888 (1.08)	0.914 (0.73)
BC_a	0.890 (0.63)	0.831 (0.98)	0.812 (0.46)	0.893 (0.63)	0.830 (0.98)	0.814 (0.45)
Ng_1	0.908 (0.61)	0.852 (1.00)	0.857 (0.52)	0.913 (0.61)	0.845 (1.00)	0.856 (0.51)
Ng_2	0.908 (0.61)	0.852 (1.00)	0.852 (0.51)	0.913 (0.61)	0.847 (1.00)	0.852 (0.50)
	$(k = 2, n = 60), (m_1 = 30, m_2 = 30)$			$(k = 2, n = 60), (m_1 = 25, m_2 = 35)$		
	LCL	UCL	TCL	LCL	UCL	TCL
N	0.911 (0.71)	0.878 (0.88)	0.895 (0.21)	0.903 (0.72)	0.882 (0.88)	0.888 (0.21)
BP	0.906 (0.72)	0.877 (0.88)	0.889 (0.21)	0.898 (0.72)	0.879 (0.88)	0.884 (0.20)
BT	0.908 (0.72)	0.901 (0.89)	0.904 (0.22)	0.896 (0.72)	0.895 (0.89)	0.894 (0.21)
BC_a	0.896 (0.72)	0.886 (0.88)	0.896 (0.21)	0.894 (0.72)	0.889 (0.88)	0.886 (0.20)
Ng_1	0.900 (0.72)	0.890 (0.88)	0.908 (0.22)	0.893 (0.72)	0.895 (0.88)	0.900 (0.22)
Ng_2	0.900 (0.72)	0.889 (0.88)	0.900 (0.21)	0.893 (0.72)	0.895 (0.88)	0.892 (0.21)
	$(k = 3, n = 10), (m_1 = 3, m_2 = 3, m_3 = 4)$			$(k = 3, n = 10), (m_1 = 4, m_2 = 3, m_3 = 3)$		
	LCL	UCL	TCL	LCL	UCL	TCL
N	0.913 (0.63)	0.851 (0.97)	0.849 (0.43)	0.909 (0.62)	0.835 (0.97)	0.828 (0.45)
BP	0.867 (0.66)	0.816 (0.94)	0.784 (0.36)	0.863 (0.65)	0.802 (0.94)	0.76 (0.37)
BT	0.926 (0.61)	0.892 (1.03)	0.918 (0.63)	0.926 (0.58)	0.898 (1.06)	0.915 (0.72)
BC_a	0.892 (0.66)	0.826 (0.95)	0.788 (0.37)	0.894 (0.65)	0.811 (0.95)	0.761 (0.38)
Ng_1	0.899 (0.64)	0.859 (0.98)	0.858 (0.45)	0.896 (0.63)	0.844 (0.98)	0.835 (0.47)
Ng_2	0.898 (0.64)	0.858 (0.98)	0.852 (0.44)	0.895 (0.63)	0.844 (0.98)	0.830 (0.46)
	$(k = 3, n = 60), (m_1 = 20, m_2 = 20, m_3 = 20)$			$(k = 3, n = 60), (m_1 = 25, m_2 = 10, m_3 = 25)$		
	LCL	UCL	TCL	LCL	UCL	TCL
N	0.915 (0.73)	0.881 (0.87)	0.897 (0.19)	0.909 (0.72)	0.880 (0.87)	0.885 (0.19)
BP	0.909 (0.73)	0.875 (0.87)	0.889 (0.18)	0.902 (0.72)	0.873 (0.87)	0.872 (0.19)
BT	0.900 (0.73)	0.893 (0.88)	0.889 (0.19)	0.908 (0.72)	0.895 (0.88)	0.900 (0.21)
BC_a	0.901 (0.73)	0.888 (0.87)	0.891 (0.18)	0.895 (0.73)	0.885 (0.88)	0.878 (0.19)
Ng_1	0.909 (0.73)	0.894 (0.88)	0.907 (0.19)	0.899 (0.72)	0.893 (0.88)	0.896 (0.21)
Ng_2	0.909 (0.73)	0.894 (0.87)	0.899 (0.19)	0.899 (0.72)	0.892 (0.88)	0.888 (0.20)

The authors explore the bias-corrected and accelerated method and transformation method to construct a confidence interval for the mean parameter. It is worth exploring smoothed bootstrap to improve the coverage properties of confidence intervals using RSS. The authors feel that smoothed bootstrap approach does have advantages

Table 4. Summary of 90% LCL, UCL, and TCL for mean shrub size

Methods	LCL	UCL	TCL	Interval Length
BP	[0.906,¥)	(-¥,1.235]	(0.858,1.291)	0.433
BC$_a$	[0.900,¥)	(-¥,1.239]	(0.851,1.282)	0.432
Transformation based method	[0.884,¥)	(-¥,1.261]	(0.838,1.311)	0.473

beyond the correction of the coverage probabilities of confidence intervals. Perhaps the most critical issue is that of the finite sample characteristics of the percentile method confidence regions. Finite sample characteristics provide bounds on the actual coverage probabilities of percentile method confidence intervals. These bounds hold for any value of confidence coefficient, and therefore any correction of the coverage probability through the confidence coefficient will not change the bounds. The smoothed bootstrap is an effective method for correcting the coverage of the percentile method beyond these bounds.

REFERENCES

Biswas, A., Rai, A., & Ahmad, T. (2020). Rescaling bootstrap technique for variance estimation for ranked set samples in finite population. *Communications in Statistics. Simulation and Computation*, *10*(10), 2704–2718. doi:10.1080/03610918.2018.1527349

Chen, Z., Bai, Z., & Sinha, B. (2004). *Ranked Set Sampling: Theory and Applications*. Springer. doi:10.1007/978-0-387-21664-5

Dell, T. R., & Clutter, J. L. (1972). Ranked set sampling theory with order statistics background. *Biometrics*, *28*(2), 545–555. doi:10.2307/2556166

Drikvandi, R., Modarres, R., & Hui, T. P. (2011). A bootstrap test for symmetry based on ranked set samples. *Computational Statistics & Data Analysis*, *55*(4), 1807–1814. doi:10.1016/j.csda.2010.11.012

Efron, B. (1979). Bootstrap Methods: Another Look at the Jackknife. *Annals of Statistics*, *7*(1), 1–26. doi:10.1214/aos/1176344552

Efron, B. (1981). Nonparametric Standard Errors and Confidence Intervals (with discussion). *The Canadian Journal of Statistics*, *9*(2), 139–172. doi:10.2307/3314608

Efron, B. (1982). *The Jackknife, the Bootstrap, and Other Resampling Plans*. SIAM. doi:10.1137/1.9781611970319

Efron, B. (1987). Better Bootstrap Confidence Intervals. *Journal of the American Statistical Association*, 82(397), 171–200. doi:10.1080/01621459.1987.10478410

Efron, B., & Tibshirani, R. J. (1993). *An introduction to the bootstrap*. Chapman & Hall. doi:10.1007/978-1-4899-4541-9

Frey, J. (2007). Distribution-free statistical intervals via ranked-set sampling. *The Canadian Journal of Statistics*, 35(4), 585–596. doi:10.1002/cjs.5550350409

Ghosh, S., Chatterjee, A., & Balakrishnan, N. (2017). Nonparametric confidence intervals for ranked set samples. *Computational Statistics*, 32(4), 1689–1725. doi:10.100700180-017-0744-0

Hall, P. (1988). Theoretical Comparison of Bootstrap Confidence Intervals. *Annals of Statistics*, 16, 927–953.

Hall, P. (1992). On the removal of skewness by transformation. *Journal of the Royal Statistical Society. Series B. Methodological*, 54(1), 221–228. doi:10.1111/j.2517-6161.1992.tb01876.x

Hui, T. P., Modarres, R., & Zheng, G. (2004). Bootstrap confidence interval estimation of mean via ranked set sampling linear regression. *Journal of Statistical Computation and Simulation*, 75(7), 543–553. doi:10.1080/00949650412331286124

Ivković, I., & Rajić, V. (2019). *Better confidence intervals for the population coefficient of variation. Communications in Statistics - Simulation and Computation*. doi:10.1080/03610918.2019.1642482

Johnson, N. (1978). Modified t-tests and confidence intervals for asymmetrical populations. *Journal of the American Statistical Association*, 73(363), 536–554. doi:10.2307/2286597

Mahdizadeh, M., & Zamanzade, E. (2019). Confidence Intervals for Quantiles in Ranked Set Sampling. *Iranian Journal of Science and Technology. Transaction of Science*, 43(6), 3017–3028. doi:10.100740995-019-00790-6

Mahdizadeh, M., & Zamanzade, Z. (2020). *On interval estimation of the population mean in ranked set sampling. Communications in Statistics - Simulation and Computation*. doi:10.1080/03610918.2019.1700276

McIntyre, G. A. (1952). A method for unbiased selective sampling, using ranked sets. *Australian Journal of Agricultural Research*, 2(4), 385–390. doi:10.1071/AR9520385

Modarres, R., Hui, T. P., & Zheng, G. (2006). Resampling methods for ranked set samples. *Computational Statistics & Data Analysis, 51*(2), 1039–1050. doi:10.1016/j.csda.2005.10.010

Muttlak, H. A., & McDonald, L. L. (1990). Ranked set sampling with size-biased probability of selection. *Biometrics, 46*(2), 435–445. doi:10.2307/2531448

Ozturk, O. (2017). Statistical inference with empty strata in judgment post stratifed samples. *Annals of the Institute of Statistical Mathematics, 69*(5), 1029–1057. doi:10.100710463-016-0572-y

Stokes, S. L., & Sager, T. W. (1988). Characterization of a ranked set sample with application to estimating distribution functions. *Journal of the American Statistical Association, 83*(402), 374–381. doi:10.1080/01621459.1988.10478607

Takahasi, K., & Wakimoto, M. (1968). On unbiased estimates of the population mean based on the sample stratified by means ordering. *Annals of the Institute of Mathematical Statistics, 20*(1), 1031–1047. doi:10.1007/BF02911622

KEY TERMS AND DEFINITIONS

Asymptotic Pivot: It is pivot for diverging sample size.

Big-Oh: $a_n = O(b_n)$ if there exists a real constant $c < 0$ and there an integer constant $n_0 \geq 1$ such that $a_n \pounds cb_n$ for every integer $n \geq n_0$.

Coverage Error: The absolute difference between the true Coverage Probability and nominal overage Probability of confidence interval.

Coverage Probability: This term refers to the probability that a confidence region contains the true value of a parameter.

Nominal Coverage Probability: Desired coverage probability of confidence region.

Pivot: It is function of samples and unknown parameters whose probability distribution does not depends on the population characteristics.

Chapter 9
Fuzzy–Weighted Ranked Set Sampling Method

Bekir Cetintav
Burdur Mehmet Akif Ersoy University, Turkey

Selma Gürler
Dokuz Eylul University, Turkey

Neslihan Demirel
Dokuz Eylul University, Turkey

ABSTRACT

Sampling method plays an important role for data collection in a scientific research. Ranked set sampling (RSS), which was first introduced by McIntyre, is an advanced method to obtain data for getting information and inference about the population of interest. The main impact of RSS is to use the ranking information of the units in the sampling mechanism. Even though most of theoretical inferences are made based on exact measurement of the variable of interest, the ranking process is done with an expert judgment or concomitant variable (without exact measurement) in practice. Because of the ambiguity in discriminating the rank of one unit with another, ranking the units could not be perfect, and it may cause uncertainty. There are some studies focused on the modeling of this uncertainty with a probabilistic perspective in the literature. In this chapter, another perspective, a fuzzy-set-inspired approach, for the uncertainty in the ranking mechanism of RSS is introduced.

DOI: 10.4018/978-1-7998-7556-7.ch009

INTRODUCTION

Ranked set sampling (RSS) is first introduced by McIntyre (1952) in a biometric research. In simple terms, random sets are drawn from a population, the units in the sets are ranked with a ranking mechanism, and one of these ranked units is sampled from each set with a specific scheme in RSS procedure. The ranking mechanism can be the visual inspection of a human expert or a highly-correlated concomitant variable. When the actual measurement of the variable of interest is difficult or expensive than ranking the experimental units, RSS can be introduced as an easier and cheaper way to obtain a more representative sample. The main impact of RSS is to use the ranking information of units in the sampling mechanism. When the ranking is done properly, the inference based on RSS generally gives effective results comparing with simple random sampling (SRS) for both parametric and non-parametric cases.

The ranking mechanism is one of the major parts of RSS procedure. Ranking the units could not be perfect in practice because there is an ambiguity in discriminating the rank of one unit with another without actual measurement. Clearly, there is an uncertainty in the ranking mechanism of RSS in the cases of imperfect ranking. In the literature, several studies focused on the case of imperfect ranking. The main idea of these studies is to model the uncertainty in ranking mechanism and to search the impact of the imperfect ranking on inference. Dell and Clutter (1972) introduce a pioneering model for imperfect ranking with using an additive model of concerning and concomitant variable. Bohn and Wolfe (1994) propose expected spacings model for the probabilities of imperfect judgment rankings based on the expected differences of units in the set. They suggest constructing a single stochastic matrix consisting of specifying probabilities of units which are inversely proportional to the expected differences between the order statistics. Presnell and Bohn (1999) use this model to show that the RSS procedure is asymptotically at least as efficient as the SRS, even if the ranking is imperfect. Ozturk (2008) proposes inference techniques for RSS data in the case of imperfect ranking using the models of Bohn and Wolfe (1994) and Frey (2007). On the other hand, there are RSS inspired studies where new sampling procedures are defined using the main idea of ranking in RSS, but also the uncertainty in ranking mechanism is studied. MacEachern et al. (2004) introduced Judgment Post-Stratified (JPS) sampling method for a specific case where a simple random sample is already chosen. In JPS method, a random set is taken for each unit in the simple random sample and the units are ranked. Then the rank information of the units is used as an additional information for inference. Ozturk (2011a,b) introduce partially ranked ordered set (PROS) sampling design for a specific case of imperfect ranking. Rankers are allowed to declare any two or more units are tied in ranks whenever the units cannot be ranked with high confidence. In that study, *ties* are the cause of imprecise rank decisions in the sampling design and the tied units divide the probability equally among the assigned ranks.

In this chapter, we propose a fuzzy set perspective to dealing with the uncertainty occurring in the ranking process of RSS. The most important advantage of using fuzzy sets is to allow the units to belong to different sets with different membership degrees. When we use fuzzy sets, the units in the random sets could belong to not only the most possibly rank but also the other possible ranks. For this purpose, preliminaries for RSS and fuzzy set theory will be given at first. In the following section, fuzzy set inspired approach for modeling of the uncertainty in the ranking process will be introduced. Fuzzy inspired Ranked Set Sampling (FRSS) procedure for single ranker case is also given in this section. An extension for the FRSS procedure is also given to combine the information coming from multiple rankers. The estimator for the population mean based on the FRSS method is given, and some asymptotic properties are discussed. FRSS is also compared with simple random sampling (SRS), RSS and Multiple RSS via Monte Carlo simulation study. An application and a numerical study based on a real data set are conducted.

FUZZY-WEIGHTED RANKED SET SAMPLING

The advanced sampling methods provide increased assurances on the representativeness of the sample data by using some additional information. For example, stratified SRS uses the information coming from homogenous strata or cluster sampling uses the information coming from heterogeneous sets. From this aspect, RSS can be defined as the sampling method where the units are sampled from ranked sets which is randomly-chosen and the rank information of the sample units are used as an additional information. Thus, a ranked set sample is more likely to span the full range of values in the population than a simple random sample with the same size.

Fuzzy Set Approach for Uncertainty in
the Ranking Mechanism of RSS

Fuzzy set theory is introduced by Zadeh (1965) for representing and manipulating data when they are not precise. With a simple definition, it transforms the structure of membership in classical set theory from a binary categorization (0-1) into a flexible one which allows partial membership with a degree between 0 and 1. While a classical set has a *black or white* form, a fuzzy set can include the *grey zones*. Fuzzy set theory has transformed not only set theory but also logic, reasoning and inference by taking into account the human subjectivity and imprecision. Thus, there are a group of famous topics which are developed out of fuzzy set theory such as *fuzzy logic, approximate reasoning, fuzzy inference, possibility theory, soft computing,* etc. For detailed information about general fuzzy set theory, see Zimmermann (2001), the literature review of Kahraman et al. (2016) and the theoretical review of Zimmermann (2010).

A fuzzy set is a natural extension of a classical set. Thus it needs a reference set (called universe of discourse) which has always classical-crisp form. Let $X=x_1,x_2,\ldots,x_n$ be a classical set of units x_i. Then the fuzzy set is defined as follows.

Definition 1. Assume that $X=x_1,x_2,\ldots,x_n$ is the universe of discourse, then a fuzzy set $\tilde{A}$ is defined as a set of ordered pairs

$$\tilde{A} = \left(x_i, \mu_{\tilde{A}}(x_i) \right),$$

where $\mu_{\tilde{A}}$ is the membership function of $\tilde{A}$. Membership function allows the fuzzy approach to evaluate the membership degrees of the units for a fuzzy set.

Definition 2. Membership function is a mathematical function which defines the membership degree of a unit in the universe of discourse ($X=x_1,x_2,\ldots,x_n$) to a fuzzy set $\tilde{A}$ as,

$$\mu_{\tilde{A}} : X \rightarrow [0,1].$$

The degree of membership in a fuzzy set is represented by a number between 0 and 1. The membership degree 0 shows the unit is entirely not in the set, 1 shows the unit completely in the set and there are infinite number of membership degrees between 0 and 1. The main role of the membership function is to represent human perceptions and decisions as a member of a fuzzy set which is usually individual and subjective.

In application of RSS, ranking is performed via two main ways: i) one (or more) human ranker(s) can decide the rank of a unit in a set with visual inspection by taking the other units in the set into account, ii) one (or more) concomitant variable(s) can be used for ranking. In both ways, ranking must be done without actual measurement of variable of interest and ranking cost must be smaller than the cost to measure variable of interest. Since the ranker makes the decision of ranks without actual measurement, these decisions could not be always perfect even if ranking is done by powerful criteria with a high relation. Clearly, there is an uncertainty in ranking mechanism and it cause information loss. In our motivation, this problem can be discussed with a fuzzy set perspective. Suppose, there is a single human ranker to decide the rank of a unit in a random set. The ranker assigns the unit to the most likely rank based on his/her degree of believe. However, there could be some other possible ranks for that unit because of ranking without actual measurement. If we define fuzzy sets for all of the possible ranks, the units in the sets could belong to not only the most likely rank but also the other possible ranks.

Determination of Membership Degrees of Units for Possible Ranks

Fuzzy set theory overcomes the limitations of the classical set theory by allowing membership in a set to be a matter of degree. It provides a mechanism for measuring the membership degrees as a function $\mu(y)$, which represented by a real number in the range [0, 1]. Inspired by the fuzzy set concept, we define the assumptions of determination of the membership degrees in our sampling method as follows.

1. The ranker should be a real expert or a highly correlated concomitant variable.
2. The membership degree 1 is given for the most possible rank of a unit. The membership degrees degrade for the other possible ranks.
3. Tie is not allowed if there is one single ranker for determination of memberships.

According to the assumptions above, membership degrees can be determined visually (by a human expert) or with a concomitant variable. In the first way, the ranker can decide the membership degrees of the units with visual inspection by taking the other units in the set into account. In this case, the main role of the membership degrees is to represent human-ranker's perceptions on rank decisions. Let $r=1,2,\ldots,k$ be the rank number, $h=1,2,\ldots,k$ be the set size and $j=1,2,\ldots,n$ be the cycle number. The membership degree of hth ranked unit in a set of jth cycle to fuzzy set of rank r determined by the ranker is shown as $m_{h,j}(r)$. An example of the determined membership degrees by visual inspection is given for a random set of cycle j and the set size $k=3$ as follows (Figure 1).

Figure 1. Example for determination of membership degrees by visual inspection

$$\begin{bmatrix} m_{1,j}(1) & m_{1,j}(2) & m_{1,j}(3) \\ m_{2,j}(1) & m_{2,j}(2) & m_{2,j}(3) \\ m_{3,j}(1) & m_{3,j}(2) & m_{3,j}(3) \end{bmatrix} => \begin{bmatrix} 1 & 0.8 & 0.1 \\ 0.7 & 1 & 0.6 \\ 0.1 & 0.7 & 1 \end{bmatrix}$$

We can give an example for more explanation. Suppose that we have a random set from a specific population and it includes 3 units represented by the letters *A, B* and *C*. If we consider it is fully ranked by a human expert, each unit in the set is ordered. The ranker decides with his/her specific criteria that *unit A is the 1st, unit B* is the 2nd and *unit C* is the 3rd. Hence, he/she assigns rank 1 to *unit A* because he/she thinks 1st is the most possible rank for it. However, he/she think that 2nd rank is also possible (but not as likely as 1st rank) and that 3rd rank is the least (but not impossible). In the FRSS method, this ranker can determine the membership degrees as $m_{1,j}(1)=1$, $m_{1,j}(2)=0.8$ and $m_{1,j}(3)=0.1$.

We note that the determination of the membership degrees based on the visual inspection of a human expert may look like arbitrary to the researchers because of the uncertain nature of human reasoning. For example, a human ranker may determine different membership degree for the same unit in the same set at various times. Computing with words (CW) methodology in which words are used in place of numbers for computing and reasoning or other similar approaches may help to build a more consistent method for determination of the membership degrees by a human expert. The simulation of the determination of the memberships by human ranker also will be available if a CW or similar method is defined. However, using these kinds of methods will also increase the complexity of FRSS method and this could be a disadvantage for prefer-ability of FRSS in applications. Therefore, we propose to use the simplest method, determination of the membership degrees based on the visual inspection, for human ranker cases.

As a second way of ranking, a specific concomitant variable can be used for ranking the units in the sets. In that situation, a membership function is needed to determine the membership degrees. Let $Y_{(h)j}$ denote the value of the concomitant variable Y for hth ordered unit of the set in jth cycle. It is clear that the ranks of the units are determined more clearly and the accurately when the distances between the units based on the value of concomitant variable Y increase. Therefore, we introduce a new membership function where the memberships determined inversely proportional to the distance between the values of concomitant variables for each sampled unit in the set

$$m_{h,j}(r)=1-\frac{\left|Y_{(r)j}-Y_{(h)j}\right|}{\max\limits_{q}Y_{(q)j}-\min\limits_{q}Y_{(q)j}},\ q=1,2,\ldots,k \tag{1}$$

In practice, there may be some criteria in the human ranker's decisions or he/she may rank arbitrarily. In this case, the main role of the membership degrees is to represent the human ranker's perceptions on rank decisions and it really suits the main idea of fuzzy set theory. However, the fuzzy sets and the memberships in our approach is not totally same with fuzzy sets and memberships in fuzzy set theory because there is also concomitant variable option for determination of the membership degrees. The word of *fuzzy* in the topic is just for representing the main idea in our approach. The similar situation can be remembered in the topic *fuzzy c means* in data mining.

Combining the Ranking Information Coming from Multiple Rankers

Complement, intersection and union are the well-known operations of the classical set theory. Each of the operation is extended to a large class of operations in the flexible structure of fuzzy set theory. We give some basic definitions and famous operators in this section. One can see Zimmermann (2010) for a detailed information about fuzzy set operations.

In fuzzy set concept, the class of intersection operators is called t-norm (Triangular Norm). Zadeh (1965)'s min operator is the pioneer and the most famous one of this class.

Definition 3. Zadeh's intersection of two fuzzy sets $\tilde{A}$ and $\tilde{B}$ defined over the crisp set X is defined as

$$\tilde{A} \cap \tilde{B} : \mu_{\tilde{A} \cap \tilde{B}}(x_i) = \min\left(\mu_{\tilde{A}}(x_i), \mu_{\tilde{B}}(x_i)\right), \forall x_i \in X.$$

Drastic product, bounded difference and Einstein product are some other typical t-norms in the literature. In relation to t-norm operators, the class of union operators is called t-conorm (Triangular Conorm) or s-norm. Zadeh's max operator is the pioneer and the most famous one of this class.

Definition 4. Zadeh's union of two fuzzy sets $\tilde{A}$ and $\tilde{B}$ defined over the crisp set X is defined as

$$\tilde{A} \cup \tilde{B} : \mu_{\tilde{A} \cup \tilde{B}}(x_i) = \max\left(\mu_{\tilde{A}}(x_i), \mu_{\tilde{B}}(x_i)\right), \forall x_i \in X.$$

Drastic sum, bounded sum and Einstein sum are some other typical t-conorms in the literature. There is also an alternative class to t-norms and t-conorms, say averaging operators. Averaging operators are generally more optimistic than t-norm operators and more pessimistic than t-conorm operators. They are also known as to be better suited for modeling aggregation in a human decision environment than t-norm and t-conorm operators. Compensatory operators, Yager's OWA and arithmetic mean-average are the most famous ones in this class. In our approach, we suggest that one of these operators can be used to combine the ranking information coming from C $(C > 1)$ rankers for more accurate determination of membership degrees when we have more than one ranker (human or concomitant variable or both). In this study, we will use average operator to obtain the set of combined membership degree decisions of C $(C > 1)$ ranker. Let $c=1,2,\ldots,C$ be the number of ranker, then we define the combination of the membership degrees based on average as follows

$$m_{h,j}(r) = average\left(m_{h,j}^{1}(r), m_{h,j}^{2}(r), \ldots, m_{h,j}^{C}(r)\right), \tag{2}$$

where $m_{h,j}^{c}(r)$ represents the membership degree coming from the ranker c.

We should note that the membership degree matrix of a ranked set is not a stochastic matrix and the matrix notation is only for proper display of the membership degrees of the units in a ranked set. Only one row of the matrix (membership degrees of the unit which is chosen to the sample) is used in the procedure.

FRSS Procedure

Using the formula to determine membership degrees and the method to combine the information of multiple rankers given above, we introduce the sampling procedure of FRSS in a general form which can be used for both single and multiple ranker cases as follows.

Step 1: Select k units at random from a specified population.

Step 2: The ranker (each ranker if there is multiple rankers) ranks these k units without measuring them and determine the membership degrees of the units for each rank.

Step 3: Combine the membership degree decisions of each ranker. (This step is ignored for the single ranker case.)

Step 4: Choose the unit which has the highest membership degree for the rank in the first order and keep its membership degrees for each r ranks.

Step 5: Repeat the first four steps to choose the units which have the highest membership degrees for the ranks in the second, third, ..., kth orders, respectively.

Step 6: First five steps are repeated for n times to get n cycle and $k \times n$ observations.

Suppose that the ranking is done using a concomitant variable Y. $Y_{(h)j}$ means the value of the concomitant variable Y of hth unit in a specific set in the jth cycle and $X_{[h]j}$ means the hth ranked unit which is chosen to the sample from the jth cycle for $h = 1,2,...,k$ and $j = 1,2,...,n$. The first output of the procedure is $k \times n$ observations called as a fuzzy-ranked set sample. The second output is the membership degrees of the observations which represent the belongings degree to each rank. The chosen units from jth cycle are represented by a vector O_j and their membership degrees are given in a matrix M_j for clarity in the illustration given in Figure 2.

Figure 2. FRSS Procedure for a single ranker Y and set size k = 3

Cycle 1

$$\begin{bmatrix} Y_{(1)1} \leq Y_{(2)1} \leq Y_{(3)1} \\ Y_{(1)1} \leq Y_{(2)1} \leq Y_{(3)1} \\ Y_{(1)1} \leq Y_{(2)1} \leq Y_{(3)1} \end{bmatrix} \rightarrow O_1 = \begin{bmatrix} X_{[1]1} \\ X_{[2]1} \\ X_{[3]1} \end{bmatrix} ve \ M_1 = \begin{bmatrix} m_{1,1}(1) & m_{1,1}(2) & m_{1,1}(3) \\ m_{2,1}(1) & m_{2,1}(2) & m_{2,1}(3) \\ m_{3,1}(1) & m_{3,1}(2) & m_{3,1}(3) \end{bmatrix}$$

Cycle 2

$$\begin{bmatrix} Y_{(1)2} \leq Y_{(2)2} \leq Y_{(3)2} \\ Y_{(1)2} \leq Y_{(2)2} \leq Y_{(3)2} \\ Y_{(1)2} \leq Y_{(2)2} \leq Y_{(3)2} \end{bmatrix} \rightarrow O_2 = \begin{bmatrix} X_{[1]2} \\ X_{[2]2} \\ X_{[3]2} \end{bmatrix} ve \ M_2 = \begin{bmatrix} m_{1,2}(1) & m_{1,2}(2) & m_{1,2}(3) \\ m_{2,2}(1) & m_{2,2}(2) & m_{2,2}(3) \\ m_{3,2}(1) & m_{3,2}(2) & m_{3,2}(3) \end{bmatrix}$$

...

Cycle n

$$\begin{bmatrix} Y_{(1)n} \leq Y_{(2)n} \leq Y_{(3)n} \\ Y_{(1)n} \leq Y_{(2)n} \leq Y_{(3)n} \\ Y_{(1)n} \leq Y_{(2)n} \leq Y_{(3)n} \end{bmatrix} \rightarrow O_n = \begin{bmatrix} X_{[1]n} \\ X_{[2]n} \\ X_{[3]n} \end{bmatrix} ve \ M_n = \begin{bmatrix} m_{1,n}(1) & m_{1,n}(2) & m_{1,n}(3) \\ m_{2,n}(1) & m_{2,n}(2) & m_{2,n}(3) \\ m_{3,n}(1) & m_{3,n}(2) & m_{3,n}(3) \end{bmatrix}$$

It can be seen that the units chosen to sample are same in RSS and FRSS when there is a single ranker. However, there is an additional membership information about the ranks in FRSS procedure and this information will be used in the estimation procedure. We should note that the membership degree matrix of a ranked set is not a stochastic matrix and the matrix notation is only for proper display of the membership degrees of the units in a ranked set. Only one row of the matrix (membership degrees of the unit which is chosen to the sample) is used in the procedure.

Estimation of Population Mean

From the FRSS procedure, we obtain the observations (units chosen to sample) and the membership degree matrix consists of the membership degrees of the observations to each rank. In this study, we propose to use these membership degrees as the weights of the observations for calculation of the average of each rank.

Let $X_{[1]1}, X_{[2]1}, X_{[3]1}, ..., X_{[h]j}, ..., X_{[k]n}$ be the sample obtained via FRSS from the underlying distribution F having finite variance $\sigma^2 > 0$ Let the membership degrees,, for $h=, j=$ and $r=$ be determined considering the assumptions defined the previous section. The estimator for the population mean is introduced using the membership degrees as weights of the units obtained via FRSS procedure, as follows:

$$\bar{X}_{FRSS} = \frac{1}{k} \sum_{r=1}^{k} \bar{X}^r_{FwRSS},$$

where

$$\bar{X}^r_{FRSS} = \sum_{h=1}^{k} \sum_{j=1}^{n} \frac{m_{h,j}(r) X_{[h]j}}{\sum_{h=1}^{k} \sum_{j=1}^{n} m_{h,j}(r)}. \tag{3}$$

The new estimator $\bar{X}_{FwRSS}$ has the same settings with the prorated estimator given in MacEachern et al. (2004) and Ozturk (2011b, 2013) although the determination of weights has some differences. Similar to the prorated estimator in MacEachern et al. (2004), $m_{h,j}(r) X_{[h]j}$ assigns a proportion, i.e.

$\left(\dfrac{m_{h,j}(r) X_{[h]j}}{\sum_{h=1}^{k} \sum_{j=1}^{n} m_{h,j}(r)} \right)$, of $X_{[h]j}$ to post-stratum h in the estimation. Thus, one can

see that $\bar{X}_{FRSS}$ has some asymptotic properties such as asymptotic normality proved by Ozturk (2013).

SIMULATION STUDIES

In this section, we examine the performance of the new method with simulation studies for both single and multiple ranker cases. We first generate data sets from different symmetric and asymmetric distributions in order to compare the methods for single ranker case. The ranking mechanism is modeled through the Dell & Clutter (1972) method. Accuracy and efficiency of the proposed sampling design and former ones (SRS and RSS) are addressed. We have evaluated the estimators' unbiasedness for their accuracy and the mean squared errors for their efficiency. The relative efficiencies are defined in terms of mean squared errors (MSE) as follows.

$$RE_1 = \frac{MSE\left(\bar{X}_{SRS}\right)}{MSE\left(\bar{X}_{FRSS}\right)}, RE_2 = \frac{MSE\left(\bar{X}_{RSS}\right)}{MSE\left(\bar{X}_{FRSS}\right)}.$$

The set sizes are chosen as 2, 3, 4 and 6 for comparison of the performances of new estimators in chancing set sizes for fixed sample sizes. The R package *RSSampling* by Sevinc et al. (2019) is used for sampling and MATLAB is used for fuzzyfication.

According to Table 1, we can say that the new estimators perform quite well comparing with the estimators of SRS and RSS methods. The relative efficiencies are greater than 1 in most cases and increase as the correlation between the response and the concomitant variable increases. For fixed sample sizes, the efficiencies of the new estimators increase as the set size increases. This result indicates that the proposed estimators constructed based on FRSS can be more useful for the cases where the set sizes are relatively large.

Some of the remarkable results are as follows:

- For $N(10;5)$ case, relative efficiency rises to 4.042 in comparison to FRSS-SRS and to 1.232 in comparison to FRSS-RSS.
- For $Uni(0;1)$ case, relative efficiency rises to 3.889 in comparison to FRSS-SRS and to 1.111 in comparison to FRSS-RSS.
- For $Exp(1)$ case, the relative efficiency rises to 3.128 in comparison to FRSS-SRS and to 1.298 in comparison to FRSS-RSS.
- For $LogN(1; 2)$ case, relative efficiency rises to 2.968 in comparison to FRSS-SRS and to 1.880 in comparison to FRSS-RSS.
- For applications of symmetric distributions, relative efficiency generally increases when the sample size increases in the comparisons with FRSS-SRS and FRSS-RSS.
- For applications of asymmetric distributions, the relative efficiency generally decreases when the sample size increases in the comparisons with FRSS-SRS. However, the comparison with FRSS-RSS has a reverse situation.

Furthermore, the accuracy results are given in Table 2. We can say numerically that the new estimators give unbiased results where X and Y coming from symmetric-distributed populations. However, there are small amounts of biases for increasing set sizes in asymmetric distributions.

Another simulation study was conducted to draw conclusions about the performance of FRSS for multiple rankers case. Interested variable X and concomitant variables Y_1, Y_2 and Y_3 are generated from multivariate normal distribution (μ, Σ) where

Table 1. Relative efficiency results for FRSS comparing SRS and RSS

Distribution	S.Size	k	n	RE₁ $\rho=1.0$	$\rho=0.9$	$\rho=0.8$	$\rho=0.7$	$\rho=0.6$	RE₂ $\rho=1.0$	$\rho=0.9$	$\rho=0.8$	$\rho=0.7$	$\rho=0.6$
Normal (10,5)	12	2	6	1.425	1.321	1.242	1.206	1.165	1.000	1.000	1.000	1.000	1.000
		3	4	2.045	1.695	1.475	1.332	1.196	1.103	1.057	1.025	1.011	0.991
		4	3	2.756	1.966	1.641	1.411	1.259	1.180	1.093	1.041	1.017	1.003
		6	2	3.771	2.484	1.801	1.546	1.359	1.238	1.110	1.047	1.024	1.001
	24	2	12	1.487	1.328	1.280	1.167	1.136	1.000	1.000	1.000	1.000	1.000
		3	8	2.119	1.758	1.539	1.349	1.181	1.110	1.052	1.024	1.004	0.992
		4	6	2.676	2.005	1.616	1.380	1.282	1.166	1.083	1.042	1.014	0.998
		6	4	4.042	1.430	1.874	1.476	1.311	1.232	1.112	1.051	1.022	1.001
Uniform (0,1)	12	2	6	1.522	1.387	1.296	1.197	1.123	1.000	1.000	1.000	1.000	1.000
		3	4	2.121	1.776	1.529	1.299	1.176	1.061	1.041	1.015	0.991	0.987
		4	3	2.800	1.953	1.717	1.414	1.301	1.120	1.047	1.017	1.000	0.986
		6	2	3.737	2.486	1.907	1.538	1.373	1.053	1.057	1.019	1.000	0.993
	24	2	12	1.478	1.076	1.059	1.055	1.038	1.000	1.000	1.000	1.000	1.000
		3	8	2.188	1.140	1.039	1.026	0.984	1.063	1.040	1.029	1.000	0.987
		4	6	2.692	1.171	1.073	1.022	0.991	1.167	1.048	1.000	1.020	1.000
		6	4	3.889	1.218	1.106	0.998	1.013	1.111	1.000	1.000	1.000	1.000
Exponential (1)	12	2	6	1.363	1.274	1.180	1.121	1.077	1.000	1.000	1.000	1.000	1.000
		3	4	1.914	1.588	1.374	1.300	1.184	1.163	1.092	1.050	1.033	1.008
		4	3	2.425	1.971	1.593	1.418	1.198	1.280	1.151	1.090	1.048	1.025
		6	2	3.128	2.289	1.803	1.475	1.339	1.298	1.146	1.086	1.048	1.033
	24	2	12	1.359	1.242	1.169	1.162	1.092	1.000	1.000	1.000	1.000	1.000
		3	8	1.956	1.601	1.421	1.218	1.195	1.161	1.098	1.062	1.026	1.007
		4	6	2.364	1.904	1.524	1.311	1.240	1.205	1.126	1.071	1.034	1.019
		6	4	2.770	2.031	1.682	1.470	1.216	1.122	1.069	1.015	0.997	0.986
Log Normal (1,2)	12	2	6	1.147	1.154	1.068	1.169	1.035	1.000	1.000	1.000	1.000	1.000
		3	4	1.697	1.565	1.310	1.300	1.177	1.281	1.194	1.153	1.126	1.072
		4	3	2.272	1.872	1.502	1.414	1.201	1.608	1.299	1.205	1.143	1.095
		6	2	2.968	2.051	1.708	1.562	1.301	1.880	1.423	1.285	1.293	1.261
	24	2	12	1.142	1.113	1.122	1.063	1.066	1.000	1.000	1.000	1.000	1.000
		3	8	1.592	1.555	1.275	1.279	1.177	1.355	1.183	1.098	1.100	1.058
		4	6	2.153	1.797	1.535	1.421	1.249	1.395	1.296	1.230	1.169	1.075
		6	4	2.708	1.988	1.642	1.444	1.217	1.759	1.335	1.223	1.125	1.061

Table 2. Accuracy results for FRSS

S.Size	k	n	Normal (10,5)					Uniform (0,1)				
			ρ=1.0	ρ=0.9	ρ=0.8	ρ=0.7	ρ=0.6	ρ=1.0	ρ=0.9	ρ=0.8	ρ=0.7	ρ=0.6
12	2	6	0.00	0.00	0.00	0.00	0.00	0.00	0.00	0.00	0.00	0.00
	3	4	0.00	0.00	0.00	0.00	0.00	0.00	0.00	0.00	0.00	0.00
	4	3	0.00	0.00	0.00	0.00	0.00	0.00	0.00	0.00	0.00	0.00
	6	2	0.00	0.00	0.00	0.00	0.00	0.00	0.00	0.00	0.00	0.00
24	2	12	0.00	0.00	0.00	0.00	0.00	0.00	0.00	0.00	0.00	0.00
	3	8	0.00	0.00	0.00	0.00	0.00	0.00	0.00	0.00	0.00	0.00
	4	6	0.00	0.00	0.00	0.00	0.00	0.00	0.00	0.00	0.00	0.00
	6	4	0.00	0.00	0.00	0.00	0.00	0.00	0.00	0.00	0.00	0.00
S.Size			Exponential (1)					Log Normal (1,2)				
12	2	6	0.00	0.00	0.00	0.00	0.00	0.00	0.00	0.00	0.00	0.00
	3	4	0.02	0.02	0.02	0.02	0.02	0.04	0.04	0.04	0.04	0.04
	4	3	0.04	0.04	0.04	0.04	0.04	0.07	0.07	0.07	0.07	0.08
	6	2	0.07	0.07	0.07	0.07	0.07	0.11	0.10	0.11	0.12	0.11
24	2	12	0.00	0.00	0.00	0.00	0.00	0.00	0.00	0.00	0.00	0.00
	3	8	0.02	0.02	0.02	0.02	0.02	0.04	0.04	0.04	0.04	0.04
	4	6	0.04	0.04	0.04	0.04	0.04	0.06	0.07	0.07	0.07	0.07
	6	4	0.07	0.07	0.07	0.06	0.06	0.11	0.11	0.11	0.11	0.11

$$(\mu, \Sigma),\ \mu=[10,8,5,3] \text{ and } \Sigma = \begin{bmatrix} 5 & \sigma_{12} & \sigma_{13} & \sigma_{14} \\ \sigma_{21} & 5 & \sigma_{23} & \sigma_{24} \\ \sigma_{31} & \sigma_{32} & 3 & \sigma_{34} \\ \sigma_{41} & \sigma_{42} & \sigma_{43} & 3 \end{bmatrix}.$$

Covariances, $\sigma_{i,j}$'s, are computed from $\rho_{i,j} = \sigma_{i,j}/\sigma_i\sigma_j$ for various correlation levels. *FwRSS–Avg* represents the FRSS method where the information coming from multiple rankers is combined via average operator. *RSS1, RSS2* and *RSS3* represent the methods of classical RSS where the concomitant variable Y_1, Y_2 and Y_3 are used as single ranker, respectively. *RSS-M* represents the combination method and mean estimator defined by Ozturk (2011a). Empirical mean square errors are computed with 10,000 times reputation in the simulation study and the results are summarized in Table 3 in terms of the relative efficiencies, as follows.

$$RE_3 = \frac{MSE\left(\bar{X}_{SRS}\right)}{MSE\left(\bar{X}_{FRSS-Avg}\right)}, RE_4 = \frac{MSE\left(\bar{X}_{RSS1}\right)}{MSE\left(\bar{X}_{FRSS-Avg}\right)}$$

$$RE_5 = \frac{MSE\left(\bar{X}_{RSS2}\right)}{MSE\left(\bar{X}_{FRSS-Avg}\right)}, RE_6 = \frac{MSE\left(\bar{X}_{RSS3}\right)}{MSE\left(\bar{X}_{FRSS-Avg}\right)} RE_7 = \frac{MSE\left(\bar{X}_{RSS-M}\right)}{MSE\left(\bar{X}_{FRSS-Avg}\right)}$$

According to the results in Table 3, the idea of combining decisions of multiple rankers generally works well. Some of the discussions on combination operations based on the results in Table 3 are given below.

- For the average operation, the idea of combining the decisions of multiple rankers give efficient results even if one of them has a really low correlation level (95 - 90 - 30). The results of the FRSS estimator with multiple ranker are even better than the estimator based on RSS with a highly-correlated ranker.
- The combination of the rank information coming from 3 moderately-correlated (70 - 70 - 60) variables increases the efficiency more than 2.3 times compared with the SRS method, 1.6 times compared with the standard RSS methods and 1.1 times compared with the RSS-M method. The combination of the rank information coming from 3 low-correlated (30-30-30) variables enhances the efficiency more than 1.2, 1.1 and 1.08 times, respectively. These results encouraged us to promote our new method for cases where there are concomitant variables with only moderate or low correlation levels (this situation is more likely to be faced in real life applications).
- Combining the rank information coming from three concomitant variables which have similar correlation levels (95 - 95 - 95, 70 - 70 - 60 or 30 - 30 - 30) increases the efficiency of the estimator in comparison with the estimators based on single ranker RSS and RSS-M. These results indicate that our new method with the combination of rank decisions could be a good alternative for the cases such as the researcher has more than one concomitant variable having similar correlation levels.

REAL DATA APPLICATIONS

In this section, we applied the proposed procedure to a real data set for both single and multiple ranker cases. The real data set, called Abalone data set, is obtained from a biometrical study of Nash et al. (1994). The original study was conducted

Table 3. Relative efficiency results for multiple ranker case

Correlation			RE_3	RE_4	RE_5	RE_6	RE_7
ρ_1- ρ_2- ρ_3	*k*	*n*	ρ=1.0	ρ=0.9	ρ=0.8	ρ=0.7	ρ=0.6
(95-95-95)	2	6	1.538	1.108	1.111	1.110	1.000
	3	4	2.117	1.241	1.245	1.245	1.056
	4	3	2.858	1.351	1.349	1.368	1.089
	6	2	3.980	1.505	1.482	1.506	1.132
(95-90-30)	2	12	1.443	1.017	1.055	1.367	1.000
	3	8	1.864	1.067	1.148	1.803	1.040
	4	6	2.275	1.065	1.202	2.146	1.077
	6	4	2.770	1.057	1.220	2.668	1.158
(70-70-60)	2	6	1.398	1.170	1.165	1.244	1.000
	3	4	1.706	1.311	1.337	1.418	1.023
	4	3	1.986	1.436	1.421	1.580	1.090
	6	2	2.368	1.604	1.612	1.844	1.156
(95-65-30)	2	12	1.400	0.974	1.182	1.323	1.000
	3	8	1.762	0.975	1.344	1.704	1.058
	4	6	1.973	0.960	1.534	1.912	1.131
	6	4	2.456	0.938	1.731	2.279	1.284
(95-35-30)	2	6	1.261	0.901	1.188	1.233	1.000
	3	4	1.578	0.866	1.457	1.472	1.086
	4	3	1.730	0.839	1.633	1.646	1.185
	6	2	2.138	0.795	1.989	1.977	1.366
(30-30-30)	2	12	1.086	1.027	1.054	1.056	1.000
	3	8	1.086	1.093	1.094	1.047	1.024
	4	6	1.153	1.083	1.077	1.087	1.032
	6	4	1.218	1.110	1.117	1.111	1.081

to predict the age of abalones using physical measurements instead of ring method which is an expensive and time-consuming way. In their study, Nash et al. (1994) suggest using other physical measurements, which are easy to obtain, through a regression model to predict the age of abalones. The data set contains 4177 units with the variables, *sex, length (mm), diameter (mm), height (mm), whole weight (grams), shucked weight (grams), viscera weight (grams), shell weight (grams), rings* (integer +1.5 gives the age in years). We first give an application of proposed FRSS procedure and mean estimation for single ranker case where diameter is chosen as the concomitant variable Y and number of rings is chosen as the variable of interest, X. FRSS procedure is applied with settings $k=3$, $n=4$ as given in Table 4.

Table 4. An application of proposed FRSS procedure and mean estimation for single ranker case

Cycle (j)		Concomitant variable			Membership degree			Sample Unit
		Y_{1j}	Y_{2j}	Y_{3j}	rank1	rank2	rank3	(X)
1	Set1	0.315	0.335	0.405	1.000	0.778	0.000	7
	Set2	0.255	0.420	0.540	0.421	1.000	0.579	9
	Set3	0.270	0.440	0.570	0.000	0.567	1.000	9
2	Set1	0.185	0.430	0.460	1.000	0.109	0.000	4
	Set2	0.360	0.405	0.505	0.690	1.000	0.310	9
	Set3	0.360	0.450	0.525	0.000	0.546	1.000	11
3	Set1	0.400	0.460	0.495	1.000	0.368	0.000	9
	Set2	0.355	0.385	0.440	0.647	1.000	0.352	8
	Set3	0.440	0.470	0.495	0.000	0.546	1.000	13
4	Set1	0.305	0.435	0.495	1.000	0.316	0.000	10
	Set2	0.260	0.350	0.440	0.500	1.000	0.500	10
	Set3	0.310	0.420	0.475	0.000	0.546	1.000	18

$$\bar{X}_{RSS} = 9.750$$
$$\bar{X}_{FRSS} = 9.868$$

We also use the same data set to conduct a small simulation study to show the performance of the new method for multiple ranker cases. The settings are determined as $k = 4$, $n = 3$ and $C = 3$ and for two different objectives. Our first objective is to obtain the mean estimation of the *number of rings*, X, and *diameter, height* and *whole weight* are chosen as the concomitant variables, Y_1, Y_2 and Y_3, respectively. The correlation levels of the concomitants are 0.5747, 0.5575 and 0.5404 in this objective. In the second one, we want to obtain the mean estimation of the *viscera weight, X,* and *diameter, height* and *whole weight* chosen as the concomitant variables, respectively. The correlation levels of the concomitants are 0.9030, 0.8997 and 0.9664 in this objective. The relative efficiency results based on the empirical mean square errors computed with 10,000 times reputation are summarized for both two objectives in Table 5.

The results in Table 5 are compatible with the simulation study results in the previous section. The relative efficiency of the new estimator *based on FRSS* is

Table 5. Relative efficiency results of FRSS

Objective	RE_3	RE_4	RE_5	RE_6
1	1.1451	1.0129	1.0011	1.0122
2	2.0517	1.1090	1.0704	1.0486

greater than 1 for both of the objectives. For the second objective in which the highly correlated concomitant variables are used, it increases to 2.0517 and 1.1090 in comparison with *SRS* and *RSS*. These results encourage us to say that our new method can be a good alternative to the sampling methods.

CONCLUSION AND FUTURE RESEARCH DIRECTIONS

This study provides a fuzzy perspective for dealing with the uncertainty occurring in the ranking process of RSS. We introduced a sampling procedure to obtain sample units and their membership degrees. This new procedure can work for both single ranker and multiple ranker cases. An estimator for the population mean based on the proposed sampling procedure is introduced. The simulation studies for the cases single-ranker and multiple-ranker are conducted individually. The single-ranker case results show that the proposed sampling method allows us to increase efficiency of the RSS method without any change except the additional information of membership degrees. The relative efficiency increases with set sizes and the correlation levels and goes up to 4.04 in comparison with SRS and 1.88 in comparison with RSS for different cases. The multiple-ranker case results show that the idea of the combination of the membership degrees coming from multiple rankers performs quite well for the combining operator *average*. FRSS method for multiple ranker provides substantial improvement over the counterparts based on *SRS*, single rankers of *RSS* and *RSS - M*. The improvement generally maintains for different correlation levels of the rankers even if the ranking performance of one of the rankers is quite low. The numerical example and simulation study results based on a biometrical data set indicates that the new sampling method, *FRSS*, could be a useful alternative for the researchers in need of an efficient method for data collection.

Using our approach, further studies can proceed in different ways. Firstly, researchers can improve FRSS by using new functions for the determination of the memberships and/or new operations for the combination of the rank information coming from multiple rankers. In particular, introducing new operations for the *liberal* and the *conservative* combinations could be a good starting point. Based on FRSS, new statistical estimators for different population parameters such as variance and proportion can be defined. The density estimation, regression parameter estimation or other estimations and tests which are studied in the RSS literature can also be addressed. In another way, the FRSS procedure can be modified as in the procedures of Median RSS, Extreme RSS, Percentile RSS. Finally, the application of our new method to different real life problems can be beneficial for practitioners.

ACKNOWLEDGMENT

This research was supported by the Scientific and Technological Research Council of Turkey [TUBITAK-COST, Grant Number. 115F300].

REFERENCES

Bohn, L. L., & Wolfe, D. A. (1994). The effect of imperfect judgment rankings on properties of procedures based on the ranked-set samples analog of the mann-whitney-wilcoxon statistic. *Journal of the American Statistical Association, 89*(425), 168–176. doi:10.1080/01621459.1994.10476458

Dell, T. R., & Clutter, J. L. (1972). Ranked set sampling theory with order statistics background. *Biometrika, 28*(2), 545–555. doi:10.2307/2556166

Frey, J. (2007). New imperfect rankings models for ranked set sampling. *Journal of Statistical Planning and Inference, 137*(4), 1433–1445. doi:10.1016/j.jspi.2006.02.013

Kahraman, C., Öztayşi, B., & Çevik Onar, S. (2016). A comprehensive literature review of 50 years of fuzzy set theory. *International Journal of Computational Intelligence Systems, 9*(1, Supplement 1), 3–24. doi:10.1080/18756891.2016.1180817

MacEachern, S. N., Stasny, E. A., & Wolfe, D. A. (2004). Judgement post-stratification with imprecise rankings. *Biometrics, 60*(1), 207–215. doi:10.1111/j.0006-341X.2004.00144.x PMID:15032791

McIntyre, G. A. (1952). A method of unbiased selective sampling using ranked sets. *Australian Journal of Agricultural Research, 3*(4), 385–390. doi:10.1071/AR9520385

Nash, W. J., Sellers, T. L., Talbot, S. R., Cawthorn, A. J., & Ford, W. B. (1994). *The population biology of abalone. Technical report*. Sea Fisheries Division.

Ozturk, O. (2008). Inference in the presence of ranking error in ranked set sampling. *The Canadian Journal of Statistics, 36*(4), 577–594. doi:10.1002/cjs.5550360406

Ozturk, O. (2011a). Combining ranking information in judgment post stratified and ranked set sampling designs. *Environmental and Ecological Statistics*, *19*(1), 73–93. doi:10.100710651-011-0175-y

Ozturk, O. (2011b). Sampling from partially rank-ordered sets. *Environmental and Ecological Statistics*, *18*(4), 757–779. doi:10.100710651-010-0161-9

Ozturk, O. (2013). Combining multi-observer information in partially rank-ordered judgment post-stratified and ranked set samples. *The Canadian Journal of Statistics*, *41*(2), 304–324. doi:10.1002/cjs.11167

Presnell, B., & Bohn, L. L. (1999). U-statistics and imperfect ranking in ranked set sampling. *Journal of Nonparametric Statistics*, *10*(2), 111–126. doi:10.1080/10485259908832756

Sevinc, B., Cetintav, B., Esemen, M., & Gurler, S. (2019). A Pioneering Package for Ranked Set Sampling. *The R Journal*, *11*(1), 401–415. doi:10.32614/RJ-2019-039

Zadeh, L. A. (1965). Fuzzy sets. *Information and Control*, *8*(3), 338–353. doi:10.1016/S0019-9958(65)90241-X

Zimmermann, H.-J. (2001). *Fuzzy Set Theory—and Applications, 4th Rev*. Kluwer Academic Publishers. doi:10.1007/978-94-010-0646-0

Zimmermann, H.-J. (2010). Fuzzy set theory. *Wiley Interdisciplinary Reviews: Computational Statistics*, *2*(3), 317–332. doi:10.1002/wics.82

ADDITIONAL READING

Bilgiç, T., & Türkşen, I. B. (2000). *Measurement of Membership Functions: Theoretical and Empirical Work*. Springer US.

Cetintav, B., Ulutagay, G., Gurler, S., & Demirel, N. (2016). Mean estimation based on FWA using ranked set sampling with single and multiple rankers. In J. Carvalho, M. J. Lesot, U. Kaymak, S. Vieira, B. Bouchon-Meunier, & R. Yager (Eds.), *Information Processing and Management of Uncertainty in Knowledge-based Systems. IPMU 2016 Communications in Computer and Information Science* (pp. 611–616). doi:10.1007/978-3-319-40581-0_64

Dubois, D., & Prade, H. (1988). *Possibility theory: an approach to computerized processing of uncertainty* (1st ed.). Plenum Press. doi:10.1007/978-1-4684-5287-7

Chapter 10
Stratified Ranked Set Sampling With Missing Observations for Estimating the Difference

Carlos N. Bouza-Herrera
Universidad de La Habana, Cuba

ABSTRACT

The authors develop the estimation of the difference of means of a pair of variables X and Y when we deal with missing observations. A seminal paper in this line is due to Bouza and Prabhu-Ajgaonkar when the sample and the subsamples are selected using simple random sampling. In this this chapter, the authors consider the use of ranked set-sampling for estimating the difference when we deal with a stratified population. The sample error is deduced. Numerical comparisons with the classic stratified model are developed using simulated and real data.

1. INTRODUCTION

It is well known that the use of auxiliary information at the estimation stage improves the efficiency of the estimators of the population parameter such as mean or total. McIntyre in 1952 proposed ranked set sampling (RSS), see McIntyre (2005). He proposed that the sampled units may be ranked visually and noted that the method produced a gain in accuracy with respect simple random sampling with replacement (SRSWR). In many applications measuring the variable of interest Y in the sampled units is difficult, expensive, and/or time-consuming. The existence of an auxiliary variable X for ranking potential sample units which measurement may be made fairly easily and inexpensively. Take for example existent records, subjective prediction

DOI: 10.4018/978-1-7998-7556-7.ch010

of Y etc. In such cases RSS appears, as is a cost-efficient alternative SRS. Using as X expert`s judgment, a concomitant variable, or a combination of them provides an inexact ranking. RSS provides a structured samples and generally improves the efficiency of the estimation when compared with inference made on samples generated by SRS design. A good survey of the RSS literature in Wolfe (2012), Alomari-Bouza (2014).

RSS has been employed successfully in application in different areas. It appears to be appealing in applications in medicine, agricultural and environmental sciences as the researcher generally is able to straightforwardly identify the sampling units in the ðeld and a prediction of the exact measurements of the units is easy. See for example its use in environmental monitoring Al-Saleh-Al-Shrafat (2001) in the estimation of average milk yield (Kvam, 2003) medicine (Chen-Stasny-Wolfe 2005), auditing (Gemayel et al., 2012), fishery (Hatefi-Jafari-Jozani-Ozturk, 2015), Al-Omari, et al. (2016): in bioleaching studies, in medicine while studying (Bouza et al. 2017) persons infected with AIDS .

Some Basic Ideas on RSS

The basic mathematical theory was provided by Takahasi and Wakimoto (1968) while Dell et al. (1972) derived that RSS is more efficient than SRSR even when errors in ranking are present. More details see in MacEachern-Stasny-Wolfe (2004).

The implementation of RSS techniques relies in taking m independent random samples of size m. The researcher evaluates the sample units and ranks them using some quick and cheap method which provides an auxiliary variable X. Then, one unit is chosen and the variable of interest Y is precisely measured. The unit with the lowest rank among the m units is chosen in the ðrst sample. The unit with the second lowest rank is chosen from the second sample, and so on until the unit with the highest rank is chosen from the m-th sample. Then we have a sample of size m. This process is called balanced RSS, it is reported to be more efðcient than the classic simple random sampling with replacement .See full reviews of RSS in Chen, Bai, and Sinha (2004) .

The following code permits implementing the selection of a RSS-sample of size n

RSS Implementation

```
Input r, m
i=0 and t=0
      While t<r+1 do
          While i<m+1 do
```

```
          Select a sample s_i of size |s_i|=m using srswr
          Rank the sampled units with respect to the variable
of interest ξ=Y
          Measure Y in the unit with rank i (ξ_{i:m)t})
          i=i+1
     End
     t=t+1
End
```

The RSS sample generates a sequence of order statistics (OS) $\xi_{(1:1)t}, ..., \xi_{(m:m)t}$. The sub-index *(j:h)t* denotes the *j-th OS* in the *h-th* sample in the cycle *t=1,..,r*. Then we have *n=mr* observations, *r* of them are of the *i-th* OS, *i=1,...,m*. The classic RSS estimator of the mean of a variable of interest ξ_ξ is

$$\mu_{(rss)} = \frac{1}{rm} \sum_{t=1}^{r} \sum_{i=1}^{m} \xi_{(i:m)r} \tag{1.1}$$

and the estimator´s variance by

$$V\left(\mu_{(rss)}\right) = \frac{1}{rm^2} \sum_{t=1}^{r} \sigma_{(i:m)}^2 = \frac{\sigma^2}{rm} - \frac{1}{rm^2} \sum_{i=1}^{m} \Delta_{(i:m)}^2;$$

$$\sigma_{(i:m)}^2 = V\left(\xi_{(i:m)r}\right); \Delta_{(i:m)}^2 = \left[E\left(\xi_{(i:m)r} - \right)\right]^2; E\left(\xi_{(i:m)r}\right) = \mu_{\xi_{(i:m)}} \tag{1.2}$$

Stokes (1980) deduced the equality $\sigma_{(i:m)}^2 = \sigma^2 - \Delta_{(i:m)}^2$ from the statistical properties of order statistics (OS). The second term of $V\left(\mu_{(rss)}\right)$ measures the net gain in accuracy of RSS compared with SRSWR.

Take a finite population $U=\{u_1,...,u_N\}$. Comonly the sampler deals with the fact that the units may be classified into disjoint sub-populations. When independent sub-samples are selected from each sub-population they are identified as strata. A certain sampling design is used for selecting the samples. The sampling fraction may vary from stratum to stratum.

Let us give an useful definition, see Arnab (2017):

Definition 1. Take a population U of size N divided into L strata

$$U = \bigcup_{l=1}^{L} U_l, U_t \cap U_h = \varnothing, if \ t \neq h; U_t = N_t, U = N = \sum_{t=1}^{L} N_t$$

If a sample is selected independently for each stratum

$$s = \bigcup_{l=1}^{L} s_l, s_t \cap s_h = \varnothing, if \ t \neq h; s_t \subset U_t; s_t = n_t, s = n = \sum_{t=1}^{L} n_t$$

the sampling model is called Stratified Sampling. ■

The theory of stratification is discussed in detail in text books when simple random sampling (SRS) is used as sampling design. The population mean of random variable ξ is

$$\mu = E(\xi)$$

and the variance

$$\sigma2 = V(\xi) = E(\xi) - E(\xi)2$$

^{F}or each stratum the expectation and variances are respectively

$$\mu t = E(\xi|Ut)$$

and

$$\sigma_t^2 = V\left(\xi|U_t\right) = E\left(\xi - E\left(\xi|U_t\right)\right)^2$$

The probability of observing a unit of U, coming form the t-th stratum, when the selection is made with equal probabilities is $P\{u \in s|U_t\} = \dfrac{N_t}{N} = W_t$.

The usual models consider that μ is an estimable linear parameter

$$\mu = \sum_{t=1}^{L} W_t \mu_t$$

as, determining a set $\left\{\hat{\mu}_1, .., \hat{\mu}_L\right\}$ of unbiased estimtors of the strata's means

$$\hat{\mu} = \sum_{t=1}^{L} W_t \widehat{\mu_t}$$

it is an unbiased estimator, due to the linearity of the expectation. Selecting random independent samples $\{s_1,\ldots,s_L\}$ the variances of th estimator is

$$V\left(\hat{\mu}\right) = \sum_{t=1}^{L} W_t^2 V\left(\widehat{\mu_t}\right)$$

It is also an estimable linear parameter and

$$\hat{V}\left(\hat{\mu}\right) = \sum_{t=1}^{L} W_t^2 \hat{V}\left(\widehat{\mu_t}\right)$$

is an unbiased estimator.

Stratified Ranked Set Sampling (SRSS) improves the efficiency of the estimators, as it combines the advantages due to stratifying, and of having more structured samples within the strata, provided by selecting them using Ranked Set Sampling (RSS).

Our objective is studying the behavior of RSS in the estimation of the difference between the means of the variables X and Y: $D = \mu_X - \mu_Y$ when we have some missing observations. An antecedent is the paper of Pi-Ehr Lin (1971) who assumed the normality of X and Y. Bouza (1983) extended it to finite population sampling when SRS is used and is necessary to deal with the existence of missing observations due to non-responses. Bouza (2002) extended it to RSS following the results of Bouza and Prabhu-Ajgaonkar (1993). In these papers were assumed:

1. X and Y are dependent only within the units.
2. A response is obtained for least one of the variables in each sampled unit.

This paper is concerned with the development of a stratified RSS (SRSS) model under missing data. Section 2 presents the sample strategy for estimating D using the stratified SRS (SSRSWR) design and its RSS counterpart is presented in Section 3. A Monte Carlo experimentations, using real life data, are analyzed in Section 4. Section 5 presents the conclusions derived.

2. THE STRATIFIED SIMPLE RANDOM SAMPLING (SSRS) ESTIMATOR OF D

Let us consider that we select independent samples of size n_t from each strata U_t. The variables X and Y are measured in each unit and we interested in estimating the difference between the population means $D = \bar{Y} - \bar{X}$. We may write it as

$$D = \bar{Y} - \bar{X} = \sum_{l=1}^{L} W_l \left(\bar{Y}_l - \bar{X}_l \right)$$

where

$$\bar{Z}_l = \frac{1}{N_l} \sum_{i \in U_l} Z_{li}, Z = Y, X; W_l = \frac{N_l}{N}; l = 1, \dots, L$$

It is well known the unbiasedness of the sample means when the sample is selected using SRS

$$\bar{z}_l = \frac{1}{N_l} \sum_{i \in s_l} z_{li}, z = y, x; l = 1, \dots, L$$

Hence D is unbiasedly estimated by

$$\hat{D} = \bar{y}_e - \bar{x}_e = \sum_{l=1}^{L} W_l \left(\bar{y}_l - \bar{x}_l \right)$$

and the sampling error of the estimator is

$$V\left(\hat{D} \right) = \sum_{l=1}^{L} W_l^2 \left(\frac{\sigma_Y^2}{n_l} + \frac{\sigma_X^2}{n_l} - \frac{\sigma_{XY}}{n_l} \right)$$

these results are easily derived form the stratified SRSWR models discussed with detail in text books taking Z=Y-X.

The sampler may consider that both variables do not need to be evaluated in all the members of s. For example that is the case when we want to estimate the difference of the records of husband-wife, of patients evaluated in two occasions etc. in other occasions we have missing observations in one of the variables. We have an additional stratification criterion. That is we have, for each U_t

$$U_l = \bigcup_{t=1}^{3} U_{lt}, U_{lt} \cap U_{lh} = \varnothing, if \; t \neq h; U_{lt} = N_{lt}, U_l = N_l = \sum_{t=1}^{3} N_{lt}.$$

The units in the random sample s_l give their report as follows

A selected unit u_i reports $\begin{cases} X_i \; and \; Y_i \; if \; u_i \in U_{l1} \\ X_i \; if \; u_i \in U_{l2} \\ Y_i \; if \; u_i \in U_{l3} \end{cases}$

The sample s is partitioned as

$$s_l = \bigcup_{t=1}^{3} s_{lt}, s_{lt} \cap s_{lh} = \varnothing, if \; t \neq h; s_{lt} \subset U_{lt}; s_{lt} = n_{lt}, s_l = n_l = \sum_{t=1}^{3} n_{lt}$$

In this case the n_{lt}'s are random. Let us arrange the units in such way that:

$$s_{l1} = \{u_i \in s_l | 1 \leq i \leq n_{l1}\}; s_{l2} = \{u_i \in s_l | n_{l1} + 1 \leq i \leq n_{l1} + n_{l2}\}; s_{l3} = \{u_i \in s_l | n_{l1} + n_{l2} + 1 \leq i \leq n_l\}$$

Having evaluated the sample we may calculate

$$\overline{x}_{l1} = \frac{\sum_{i \in s_{l1}} x_i}{n_{l1}}, \overline{y}_{l1} = \frac{\sum_{i \in s_{l1}} y_i}{n_{l1}}, \overline{d}_{l1} = \frac{\sum_{i \in s_{l1}} (x_i - y_i)}{n_{l1}} = \frac{\sum_{i \in s_{l1}} d_i}{n_{l1}}, \overline{x}_{l2} = \frac{\sum_{i \in s_{l2}} x_i}{n_{l2}}, \overline{y}_{l3} = \frac{\sum_{i \in s_{l3}} y_i}{n_{l3}}$$

Based on this information we may propose using

$$\overline{y}_{el} - \overline{x}_{el} = \sum_{l=1}^{L} W_l \left[w_{l1} \overline{d}_{l1} + w_{l3} \overline{y}_{l3} - w_{l2} \overline{x}_{l2} \right]; w_{lt} = \frac{n_{lt}}{n_l}$$

The expectation of the terms into brackets is

$$E(d_{l1}) = \bar{Y}_l - \bar{X}_l; E(\bar{z}_{lt}|n_{lt}) = \bar{Z}_l; z = x, y; Z = X, Y$$

See that

$$E\left[w_{l1}d_{l1} + w_{l3}\bar{y}_{l3} - w_{l2}\bar{x}_{l2}|n_l\right] = \left(\frac{n_{l1}}{n_l} + \frac{n_{l3}}{n_l}\right)\bar{Y} - \left(\frac{n_{l1}}{n_l} + \frac{n_{l2}}{n_l}\right)\bar{X}$$

hence, $\bar{y}_{el} - \bar{x}_{el}$ is conditionally biased for D, but as

$$E\left(\hat{D}_{l1}|n_l\right) = E\left[\frac{w_{l1}\bar{y}_{l1} + w_{l3}\bar{y}_{l3}}{n_{l1} + n_{l3}} - \frac{w_{l1}\bar{x}_{l1} + w_{l2}\bar{x}_{l2}}{n_{l1} + n_{l2}}\middle|n_l\right] = \bar{Y}_l - \bar{X}_l$$

follows the unbiasedness of

$$\hat{D}_1 = \sum_{l=1}^{L} W_l \hat{D}_{l1}$$

$\hat{D}_1$ is linear estimator and there is impendence among the strata selections. We may write its variance as

$$V\left(\hat{D}_1\right) = \sum_{l=1}^{L} W_l^2 V\left(\hat{D}_{l1}\right)$$

Note that:

$$V\left(\hat{D}_{l1}\right) = VE\left(\hat{D}_{l1}|n_l\right) + EV\left(\hat{D}_{l1}|n_l\right) = EV\left(\hat{D}_{l1}|n_l\right)$$

The conditional variance is

$$V\left(\hat{D}_{l1}|n_l\right) = V\left(\frac{n_{l1}\bar{y}_{l1} + n_{l3}\bar{y}_{l3}}{n_{l1} + n_{l3}}|n_l\right) + V\left(\frac{n_{l1}\bar{x}_{l1} + n_{l2}\bar{x}_{l2}}{n_{l1} + n_{l2}}|n_l\right) - Cov\left(\frac{n_{l1}\bar{y}_{l1} + n_{l3}\bar{y}_{l3}}{n_{l1} + n_{l3}}, \frac{n_{l1}\bar{x}_{l1} + n_{l2}\bar{x}_{l2}}{n_{l1} + n_{l2}}|n_l\right)$$

$$V\left(\frac{n_{l1}\bar{y}_{l1} + n_{l3}\bar{y}_{l3}}{n_{l1} + n_{l3}}|n_l\right) + V\left(\frac{n_{l1}\bar{x}_{l1} + n_{l2}\bar{x}_{l2}}{n_{l1} + n_{l2}}|n_l\right) = \frac{\sigma_{Yl}^2}{n_{l1} + n_{l3}} + \frac{\sigma_{Xl}^2}{n_{l1} + n_{l2}}$$

The approximation of Stephan (1945) suggests considering appropriate that

$$E\left(\frac{\sigma_{Yl}^2}{n_{l1}+n_{l3}}+\frac{\sigma_{Xl}^2}{n_{l1}+n_{l2}}\right) \cong \frac{\sigma_{Yl}^2}{n_l\left(W_{l1}+W_{l3}\right)}+\frac{\sigma_{Xl}^2}{n_l\left(W_{l1}+W_{l2}\right)}$$

$$Cov\left(\frac{n_{l1}\bar{y}_{l1}+n_{l3}\bar{y}_{l3}}{n_{l1}+n_{l3}},\frac{n_{l1}\bar{x}_{l1}+n_{l2}\bar{x}_{l2}}{n_{l1}+n_{l2}}\Big|n_l\right)=\frac{\sigma_{X,Yl}}{\left(n_{l1}+n_{l2}\right)\left(n_{l1}+n_{l3}\right)}$$

The model an its properties is characterized in the following proposition

Proposition 2.1. Consider a stratified simple sampling random design with replacement design and the parameter of interest $D=\bar{Y}-\bar{X}$.

$$\hat{D}=\bar{y}_e-\bar{x}_e=\sum_{l=1}^{L}W_l\left(\bar{y}_l-\bar{x}_l\right)$$

is unbiased with variance

$$V\left(\hat{D}\right)=\sum_{l=1}^{L}W_l^2\left(\frac{\sigma_{Yl}^2}{n_l}+\frac{\sigma_{Xl}^2}{n_l}-\frac{\sigma_{XYl}}{n_l}\right)$$

$$\hat{D}_1=\sum_{l=1}^{L}W_l\hat{D}_{l1}$$

is unbiased with variance

$$V\left(\hat{D}_1\right)\cong\sum_{l=1}^{L}W_l^2\frac{\sigma_{Yl}^2}{n_l\left(W_{l1}+W_{l3}\right)}+\frac{\sigma_{Xl}^2}{n_l\left(W_{l1}+W_{l2}\right)}-\frac{\sigma_{X,Yl}}{n_l^2\left(W_{l1}+W_{l3}\right)\left(W_{l1}+W_{l2}\right)}\blacksquare$$

The estimators of the variances are easily derived form the results appearing in text books.

$$\hat{\sigma}_{Zl}^2=\frac{1}{n_l-1}\sum_{i=}^{n_l}\left(z_{il}-\bar{z}_l\right)^2\;;z=y,x$$

$$\hat{\sigma}_{X,Yl} = \frac{1}{n_l - 1} \sum_{i=}^{n_l} \left(x_{il} - \bar{x}\right)\left(y_{il} - \bar{y}\right)$$

3 STRATIFIED RSS (SRSS) ESTIMATION OF D

3.1. Some SRSS Models

One of the practical problems that arise when RSS is applied is to obtain an accurate and cheap ranking procedure. If it is not accurate we will have errors in the rankings. Dell-Clutter (1972) established that in such case we obtain not the i-th OS but the '*ith* – judgmental' one. The use of a concomitant variable is supported by the existence of a correlation between the true variable and the ranking variable. Stokes (1980) and Patil et. al (1995) studied the use of concomitant variables and used them for ranking.

Using RSS for selecting samples from the strata allows improving the efficiency of the usual model by combining the advantages of stratiõcation and RSS. A pillar in the development of estimators is that, auxiliary information at the estimation stage, generally allows developing more efficient estimators of the population parameters of Y. It is common knowing the population mean of the variable used for ranking. Then, some parameters of the distribution of X may be introduced in the selection and/or estimation stages for diminishing the bias and variance of the estimators, or even for deriving some optimality conditions. The extensions to SRSS is a theme of different papers.

A popular class of estimators of common use may be identified as "ratio-type estimators". When the auxiliary variable X is positively (high) correlated with the study variable Y, the use of a ratio estimator is quite effective

SRSS modeling was first suggested by Samawi-Muttlak (1996). The intention was improving the efficiency of the estimation of the population mean. Following the current theory on stratification Samawi -Siam (2003), Kadilar-Cingi (2003) among others developed SRSS-estimators counterparts of the SSRS.

A series of papers deal with the estimation using the information on the auxiliary variable. Then, different contributions are based on the development of ratio type estimators for SRSS. They pose the need of deriving convergence results which are obtained using a Taylor Series up to the õrst degree of approximation. Simulation studies of the proposals are used for sustaining that the estimators are more efficient when compared with competitors. Measures of the efficiency are developed using mainly Percentage Relative Efficiency (PRE), Percentage Relative Bias (PRB) .

Mandowara-Mehta (2014) have developed a SRSS model for increasing the efficiency of ratio-type estimators. Singh et al. [20] proposed ratio and product type estimators under SRSS. In the papers of Samawi-Saeid (2004), Khan-Shabbir-Gupta (2014) and Singh-Mehta-Pal (2014) Khan-Shabbir, J. (2015) were considered the performance of the Hartley-Ross unbiased ratio estimator, as well as combined and separate ratio estimates using SRSS. Theoretical and simulation study are presented. Results indicate that using SERSS for estimating the ratios is more efficient than using stratified simple random sample (SSRS) and simple random sample (SRS). In some cases, it is more efficient than ranked set sample (RSS) and stratified ranked set sample (SRSS), when the underlying distribution is symmetric.

Other extensions of RSS to stratification are due to Mahdizadeh-Zamanzade (2018) who introduced the use of the design pair SRSS; Saini-Kumar, A. (2019) who developed a comparison of ratio estimators using SSRS and SRSS

Commonly, in the evaluations of RSS alternatives, when there is not a clear expression for evaluating the performances of the proposed estimators, the authors develop simulation studies. The simulation generates bivariate random observations (X_h, Y_h), from a bivariate distribution for a fixed correlation and estimates of biases, variances mean squared errors etc., are computed under the stratiðed ranked sampling schemes. Estimators are compared in terms of some percentage relative efficiencies (PREs) as the relative or relative root mean square error (RRMSE). They are used for comparing the accuracy of different estimators. They allow to analyze the empirical bias, and/or to identify empirically an efficient estimator. When the developed models are application-oriented, data-bases coming from known studies are used for comparisons.

3.2. The SRSS Model for Estimating D

We will consider the case of sampling using RSS for estimating D. We assume that the sampler have a concomitant variable A with a high correlation with both X and Y. It is used for ranking. From the theory of RSS we derive the results supporting the following proposition

Proposition 3.1 When we use RSS an unbiased estimator of the difference of means is

$$d_{rss} = \frac{1}{rm} \sum_{t=1}^{r} \sum_{i=1}^{m} y_{(i:m)t} - x_{(i:m)t} = \frac{1}{rm} \sum_{t=1}^{r} \sum_{i=1}^{m} d_{(i:m)t}$$

with variance

$$V(d_{rss}) = \frac{\sigma_d^2}{rm} - \frac{1}{rm^2}\sum_{i=1}^{m}\Delta_{d(i:m)}^2 = \frac{\sigma_d^2}{n} - \frac{\Delta_d^2}{nm}$$

$$\sigma_d^2 = \frac{1}{N}\sum_{j=1}^{N}(Y_i - X_i)^2 \, ; \Delta_{d(i:m)} = \left(\bar{Y}_{(i:m)} - \bar{X}_{(i:m)}\right) - D$$

as rm=n.

Proof:

From the results on the unbiasedness of the RSS mean due to the fact that

$$E\left(\hat{\mu}_{Zrss}\right) = E\left(\frac{1}{rm}\sum_{t=1}^{r}\sum_{i=1}^{m}z_{(i:m)t}\right) = \frac{1}{r}\sum_{t=1}^{r}E\left(\frac{1}{m}\sum_{i=1}^{m}z_{(i:m)t}\right) = \frac{1}{m}\sum_{i=1}^{m}\mu_{z(i:m)} = \mu_Z$$

follows that

$$E\left(\frac{1}{rm}\sum_{t=1}^{r}\sum_{i=1}^{m}d_{(i:m)t}\right) = \frac{1}{m}\sum_{i=1}^{m}\mu_{d(i:m)} = D = \bar{Y} - \bar{X}\,.$$

As the RSS-samples are independent

$$V(d_{rss}) = \frac{1}{r^2 m^2}\sum_{t=1}^{r}\sum_{i=1}^{m}V(y_{(i:m)t} - x_{(i:m)t}) = \frac{1}{rm^2}\sum_{i=1}^{m}\sigma_{(i:m)}^2$$

noting that, see Stokes (1980),

$$V(\hat{\mu}_{Zrss}) = \frac{\sigma_z^2}{rm} - \frac{1}{rm^2}\sum_{i=1}^{m}\Delta_{Z(i:m)}^2 = \frac{\sigma_z^2}{n} - \frac{\Delta_z^2}{nm}$$

then taking Z=D the proposition is proved. ∎

Remark 2.1: As $\Delta_d^2 \geq 0$ we should prefer d_{rss} to the classic SRS estimator

$$d_{srs} = \frac{1}{n} \sum_{i=1}^{n} y_i - x_i$$

based on SRS.

The estimation of the variance σ_Z^2 using RSS has various alternatives. Bouza et al. (2017) analyzed the different estimators and recommend selecting between

$$\hat{\sigma}_{1Z(rss)}^2 = \frac{1}{rm} \sum_{t=1}^{r} \sum_{i=1}^{m} \left(z_{(i:i)t} - \bar{z}_{t(rss)} \right)^2 + \frac{m}{m(r-1)} \sum_{t=1}^{r} \left(\bar{z}_{t(rss)} - \frac{1}{r} \sum_{t=1}^{r} \bar{z}_{t(rss)} \right)^2, \bar{z}_{t(rss)} = \frac{1}{m} \sum_{i=1}^{m} z_{(i:i)t}$$

and

$$\hat{\sigma}_{2Z(rss)}^2 = \frac{m - m + 1}{rm^2} \sum_{t=1}^{r} \sum_{i=1}^{m} \left(z_{(i:i)t} - \bar{z}_i \right)^2 + \frac{r}{mr} \sum_{t=1}^{r} \left(\bar{z}_i - \frac{1}{m} \sum_{t=1}^{r} \bar{z}_i \right)^2, \bar{z}_i = \frac{1}{r} \sum_{t=1}^{r} z_{(i:i)t}$$

See also Perron-Sinha (2004).

Then we have that the errors may be estimated using Z=Y-X and substituting in the above estimator of the variance.

Let us present a code describing the selection in SRSS.

Implementation of the Selection of a Stratified Sampling using RSS

```
Input L
For q=1,…,L Input r_q, m_q
   While l<L do
      l=0,   i=0 and t=0
         While t<r_q+1 do
            While i<m_q+1 do
               Select a sample s_li of size m_l using SRSWR
               Rank the sampled units using auxiliary variable of
interest A
                  Measure Y in the unit with rank i (A_{i:m)t})
               i=i+1
            End
               t=t+1
```

221

```
End
        q=q+1
    End
        l=l+1
END
```

Let us develop the estimation of D using SRSS.
When we use SSRS an estimator of the difference of the means is

$$\hat{D}_{e(rss)} = \bar{y}_{e(rss)} - \bar{x}_{e(rss)} = \sum_{l=1}^{L} W_l \left(\bar{y}_{l(rss)} - \bar{x}_{l(rss)} \right), \bar{z}_{l(rss)} = \frac{1}{r_l m_l} \sum_{t=1}^{r_l} \sum_{i=1}^{m_l} z_{(i:m_l)t}$$

It is unbiased as

$$E\left(\bar{y}_{l(rss)} \right) - E\left(\bar{x}_{l(rss)} \right) = \bar{Y}_l - \bar{X}_l$$

From the results of Proposition 3.1 we have that

$$V(\hat{D}_{e(rss)}) = \sum_{l=1}^{L} W_l^2 \left(\frac{\sigma_{ld}^2}{r_l m_l} - \frac{\Delta_{ld}^2}{r_l m_l^2} \right),$$

where

$$\sigma_{ld}^2 = \frac{1}{N_l} \sum_{j=1}^{N_l} \left(Y_{lj} - X_{lj} \right)^2$$

$$\Delta_{l(i:m)d} = \left(\bar{Y}_{(i:m_l)} - \bar{Y}_l \right) + \left(\left(\bar{X}_{(i:m_l)} - \bar{X}_l \right); \quad \Delta_{ld}^2 = \frac{1}{r_j m_j^2} \sum_{i=1}^{m_l} \Delta_{l(i:m_l)d}^2 \right)$$

Let us again consider that the RSS-sample is divided into three subsamples. One of them reports (X, Y), another only Y and the other only X. We have that

$$\bar{z}_{lj(i:m_l)} = \frac{\sum_{t=1}^{r_l} \sum_{i=1}^{m_l} z_{(i:m_l)t}}{r_l m_l}, j = 2(3) \text{ if } z = x(y)$$

is conditionally unbiased for a fixed sub-sample size $n_l = r_l m_l$. Mimicking the structure used for proposing an estimator in case of SRS we propose the use as estimator of the difference within the l-th stratum.

$$\hat{D}_{l(rssNR)} = \frac{1}{r_{1l} m_{1l}} \sum_{t=1}^{r_{1l}} \sum_{i=1}^{m_{1l}} y_{1(i:m_{1l})t} - x_{1(i:m_{1l})t} + \frac{1}{r_{3l} m_{3l}} \sum_{t=1}^{r_{1l}} \sum_{i=1}^{m_{1l}} y_{3(i:m_{3l})t}$$

$$-\frac{1}{r_{2l} m_{2l}} \sum_{t=1}^{r_{1l}} \sum_{i=1}^{m_{1l}} x_{2(i:m_{2l})t} = \frac{r_{1l} m_{1l} \bar{y}_{1l(rss)} + r_{3l} m_{3l} \bar{y}_{3l(rss)}}{r_{1l} m_{1l} + r_{3l} m_{3l}} - \frac{r_{1l} m_{1l} \bar{x}_{1l(rss)} + r_{2l} m_{2l} \bar{x}_{2l(rss)}}{r_{1l} m_{1l} + r_{2l} m_{2l}}$$

its expectation is

$$E(\hat{D}_{l(rss)} \big| r_{1l} m_{1l}, r_{3l} m_{3l}, r_{2l} m_{3l})$$

$$= \frac{r_{1l} m_{1l} E(\bar{y}_{1l(rss)} \big| r_{1l} m_{1l}) + r_{3l} m_{3l} E\left(\bar{y}_{3l(rss)} \big| r_{3l} m_{3l}\right)}{r_{1l} m_{1l} + r_{3l} m_{3l}}$$

$$- \frac{r_{1l} m_{1l} E\left(\bar{x}_{1l(rss)} \big| r_{1l} m_{1l}\right) + r_{2l} m_{2l} \left(\bar{x}_{2l(rss)} \big| r_{2l} m_{2l}\right)}{r_{1l} m_{1l} + r_{2l} m_{2l}} = \bar{Y} - \bar{X}$$

. Hence it is unbiased for the difference of means and its variance is to be calculated using the relationship

$$VE(\hat{D}_{l(rss)} \big| r_{1l} m_{1l}, r_{3l} m_{3l}, r_{2l} m_{3l}) + EV(\hat{D}_{l(rss)} \big| r_{1l} m_{1l}, r_{3l} m_{3l}, r_{2l} m_{3l})$$

As

$$E(\hat{D}_{l(rss)} \big| r_{1l} m_{1l}, r_{3l} m_{3l}, r_{2l} m_{3l}).$$

is constant the sampling error depends only of the second term.

$$V\left(\frac{r_{1l}m_{1l}\bar{y}_{1l(rss)}+r_{3l}m_{3l}\bar{y}_{3l(rss)}}{r_{1l}m_{1l}+r_{3l}m_{3l}}-\frac{r_{1l}m_{1l}\bar{x}_{1l(rss)}+r_{2l}m_{2l}\bar{x}_{2l(rss)}}{r_{1l}m_{1l}+r_{2l}m_{2l}}\middle|\middle|r_{1l}m_{1l},r_{3l}m_{3l},r_{2l}m_{3l}\right)$$

$$=\frac{\sigma^2_{ly(rss)}}{r_{1l}m_{1l}+r_{3l}m_{3l}}+\frac{\sigma^2_{lx(rss)}}{r_{1l}m_{1l}+r_{2l}m_{2l}}-\frac{\sigma_{x,yl(rss)}}{\left(r_{1l}m_{1l}+r_{3l}m_{3l}\right)\left(r_{1l}m_{1l}+r_{2l}m_{2l}\right)}$$

Without losing in generality take $r_{tl}=r_l$ in the sequel. The gain in accuracy due to the use of RSS samples is given by

$$\Delta_{Zl(rss)}=\left(\bar{Z}_{(i:m_{1l})}-\bar{Z}_l\right);Z=Y,X;t=\begin{cases}3\;if\;Z=Y\\2\;if\;Z=X\end{cases}\Delta^2_{lz}=\frac{1}{r\,n^2}\sum^{m_{zl}}\Delta^2_{l(i:m_l)y},$$

$$n_{zl}=\begin{cases}m_{1l}+\;m_{3l}\;if\;Z=Y\\m_{1l}+m_{2l}\;if\;Z=X\end{cases}$$

Applying the approximation of Stephan (1945) we have that

$$E\left(r_{1l}m_{1l}+r_{3l}m_{3l}\right)^{-1}\cong\frac{1}{r_l\left(W_{1l}+W_{3l}\right)};E\left(r_{1l}m_{1l}+r_{2l}m_{3l}\right)^{-1}\cong\frac{1}{r_l\left(W_{1l}+W_{2l}\right)}$$

$$E\left(\frac{1}{r_{tl}n^2_{zl}}\right)\cong\frac{1}{r_{tl}n^2_{zl}}=\frac{1}{n_l\left(W_1\left(1-W_1\right)+W_t\left(1-W_t\right)+W_1^2W_t^2n_l^2\right)}=\frac{1}{M_t};$$

taking

$$t=\begin{cases}3\;if\;Z=Y\\2\;if\;Z=X\end{cases}$$

We must calculate the expectation of the conditional variance. It is

$$EV(\hat{D}_{l(rss)}\left|r_{1l}m_{1l},r_{3l}m_{3l},r_{2l}m_{3l}\right.)$$

$$\cong \sum_{l=1}^{L}W_l^2\left(\frac{\sigma_{Yl}^2}{r_l\left(W_{1l}+W_{3l}\right)}+\frac{\sigma_{Xl}^2}{r_l\left(W_{1l}+W_{2l}\right)}\right)-\sum_{l=1}^{L}W_l^2\left(\frac{\Delta_{Yl}^2}{r_lM_{3l}}+\frac{\Delta_{Xl}^2}{r_lM_{2l}}-\frac{\sigma_{X,Yl}}{r_l^2M_{3l}M_{2l}}\right)$$

Then we have proved the validity of

Proposition 3.2. Under the described RSS design and if H1-H2 hold the estimator

$$\hat{D}_{l(rssNR)}\sum_{l=1}^{L}W_l\left(\frac{r_{1l}m_{1l}\overline{y}_{1l(rss)}+r_{3l}m_{3l}\overline{y}_{3l(rss)}}{r_{1l}m_{1l}+r_{3l}m_{3l}}-\frac{r_{1l}m_{1l}\overline{x}_{1l(rss)}+r_{2l}m_{2l}\overline{x}_{2l(rss)}}{r_{1l}m_{1l}+r_{2l}m_{3l}}\right)$$

is unbiased being its expected variance

$$\sum_{l=1}^{L}W_l^2\left(\frac{\sigma_{Yl}^2}{n_lr_lM_{3l}}+\frac{\sigma_{Xl}^2}{n_lr_lM_{2l}}\right)-\sum_{l=1}^{L}W_l^2\left(\frac{\Delta_{Yl}^2}{n_lM_{3l}}+\frac{\Delta_{Xl}^2}{n_lM_{2l}}+\frac{\sigma_{X,Yl}}{r_l^2M_{3l}M_{2l}}\right)\blacksquare$$

Remark 3.1: The last term of the expression is always positive whenever for any stratum $\rho X_{Yl>}0$ and represents the gain in accuracy due to selecting the subsamples using RSS. Hence, the use of RSS for subsampling the NR when D is estimated is a better alternative than the SRSWR strategy when X and Y are positively correlated.

Remark 3.2: If ρX_{Yl} is not positive for all the strata SRSS is also more efficient than SRSS whenever for any stratum holds the inequalities

$$\frac{\Delta_{Yl}^2}{n_lM_3}+\frac{\Delta_{Xl}^2}{n_lM_2}>\rho_{XY(rss)l}\sqrt{\left(\frac{\sigma_{Yl}^2}{n_lr_lM_3}-\frac{\Delta_{Yl}^2}{n_lM_3}\right)\left(\frac{\sigma_{Xl}^2}{n_lr_lM_{2l}}-\frac{\Delta_{Xl}^2}{n_lM_{3l}}\right)}$$

4. NUMERICAL COMPARISON OF SSRS AND SRSS MONTE CARLO EXPERIMENT

We will compare the accuracy of the proposed RSS sampling strategy with its SRS counterpart.

Real problem 1. A large medical study was developed for determining the effect of *a* treatment of psoriasis. A population of 1210 patients was evaluated in a longitudinal survey. They were stratified in terms of the severity of the psoriasis in 3 levels. The index called PASI (Psoriasis Severity Index), see Laupracis et.al. (1988), was calculated in each visit. We considered:

$A=$ Initial value of PASI
$Y=$ Value of PASI at the first visit after treatment
$X=$ Value of PASI at the end of the treatment.

Real problem 2. The assertiveness of a population of 932 foreign students was measured during 3 years before and after developing training under the guidance of a team of psychologists. They were stratified into 5 strata considering their nationality.

$A=$Intelligence coefficient
$Y=$ assertiveness at the before the training.
$X=$ assertiveness at the after the training.

Real problem 3. The availability of pastures was measured before and after the grazing of a herd of cattle. The pastures were of 5 kinds and 2560 plots were evaluated. They determined the strata

$A=$eye estimation of the availability
$Y=$ measured availability before the grazing.
$X=$ measured availability after the grazing.

Real problem 4. The motivation of students was evaluated in a population of 1198 students in the subjects of Probability and Statistics during 5 years. They were stratified by sex.

$A=$obtained note in the final test
$Y=$ motivation index for Probability subjects.
$X=$ motivation index for Statistics subjects.

Real problem 5. A population of 2567 couples was inquired and a questionnaire permitted to compute an index of racial prejudices. The difference of the means of wife and husband was of interest. The population was stratified into 6 strata: both Asiatic, both Black, both White, mixed Asiatic -Black, mixed Asiatic- White, mixed Black-White.

A=Index of familiar disagreement
Y= index of racial prejudices of the wife.
X= index of racial prejudices of the wife..

The set of measurements of X and Y constituted an artificial population. It was randomly partitioned using $W_{tl}=W_l=0.5, t=2.3$ for generating the non-responses strata U_{2l} and U_{3l} in each stratum U_l. 1000 samples were generated with common sample fractions 0,10, 0,20 and 0,50 in the selection of the within strata samples using SSRS and SRSS. *D* was computed and estimated SRSS and SRSS . The evaluation of mean relative accuracy of the estimators is made computing

$$G_{SSRS,SRSS} = \frac{\sum_{s=1}^{1000} \dfrac{\left|\hat{D}_{eRSS} - D\right|_s}{1000}}{\sum_{s=1}^{1000} \dfrac{\left|\hat{D}_{eSRS} - D\right|_s}{1000}}$$

It was computed for the five problems and the results appear in Table 1.

Table 1. $G_{SSRS,SRSS}$ *: Relative Accuracy in 5 real life problems*

	sampling	fractions	
	0,1	0,2	0,5
Real problem 1	0,34	0,34	0,32
Real problem 2	0,57	0,50	0,45
Real problem 3	0,36	0,32	0,26
Real problem 4	0,42	0,43	0,32
Real problem 5	0,29	0,22	0,19

SRSS provided more accurate estimations than SSRS, as expected. The gain was considerably large for Problem 5. In both cases their relative accuracy was no seriously affected by the increase in sub-sampling fractions.

For evaluating the effect of the correlation between X and Y we are going to generate them using a bivariate probability density probability function f(x, y). We are going to use the bivariate normal standard distribution (BN), the bivariate uniform density (BU) in $(0,1)^2$ and the bivariate exponential density (BE) with vector parameter $\vec{\theta} = (1,1)^{-1}$. We generated them using high $\rho X_{,Y=} \mp 0.95$, medium $\rho X_{,Y=0}.5$ and small $\rho X, Y_{=\mp 0}.05$ correlation. The NR were generated fixing the corresponding percentiles of order 0,05, 01, 0,9 and 0,95 of the variables. Five strata were conformed as follows

$$If\ X_h \in \left]-\infty, \lambda_{0,05}\right] \cup \left[\lambda_{0,95}, \infty\right[\ and\ Y_h \notin \left]-\infty, \lambda_{0,10}\right] \cup \left[\lambda_{0,90}, \infty\right[\ then\ u_h \in U_2$$

$$If\ X_h \in \left]-\infty, \lambda_{0,10}\right] \cup \left[\lambda_{0,90}, \infty\right[\ and\ Y_h \notin \left]-\infty, \lambda_{0,05}\right] \cup \left[\lambda_{0,95}, \infty\right[\ then\ u_h \in U_3$$

$$If\ Y_h \in \left]-\infty, \lambda_{0,05}\right] \cup \left[\lambda_{0,95}, \infty\right[\ and\ X_h \notin \left]-\infty, \lambda_{0,10}\right] \cup \left[\lambda_{0,90}, \infty\right[\ then\ u_h \in U_3$$

$$If\ Y_h \in \left]-\infty, \lambda_{0,10}\right] \cup \left[\lambda_{0,90}, \infty\right[\ and\ X_h \notin \left]-\infty, \lambda_{0,05}\right] \cup \left[\lambda_{0,95}, \infty\right[\ then\ u_h \in U_4$$

Else $u_h \hat{I} U_1$

Their weights were computed using the corresponding pdf. We generated 5000 samples and computed

$$G_{SSRS,SRSS} = \frac{\sum_{s=1}^{5000} \frac{\left|\hat{D}_{eRSS} - D\right|_s}{5000}}{\sum_{s=1}^{5000} \frac{\left|\hat{D}_{eSRS} - D\right|_s}{5000}}$$

We used W_{tl}=0.5, t=2.3 and common sample fractions 0,10, 0,20 and 0,50 for generating NR.

Table 2 illustrates that having large negative correlations allows preferring SSRS. For small negative correlation coefficients SRSS is more efficient. As deduced theoretically, for positive correlation coefficients SRSS outperforms SSRS. Note that, for normal variables and ρ= -0.95, the efficiency of SRSS is very bad but the

Table 2. $G_{SSRS,SRSS}$: Relative Accuracy Simulated populations

	sampling	fractions		sampling	fractions		sampling	fractions	
	0,1	0,2	0,5	0,1	0,2	0,5	0,1	0,2	0,5
ρ		BN			NU			NU	
-0,95	1,72	1,75	1,81	1,83	1,90	1,94	1,41	1,40	1,38
-0,05	0,77	0,79	0,74	0,90	0,83	1,08	1,07	1,05	1,03
0,05	0,67	0,66	0,63	0,88	0,81	0,77	0,92	0,94	0,91
0,50	0,50	0,48	0,62	0,61	0,55	0,46	0,92	0,91	0,88
0,95	0,48	0,45	0,33	0,57	0,49	0,45	0,89	0,89	0,88

efficiency is rapidly improved for larger values. A similar behavior is observed in the other distributions except for the bivariate exponential. In this case SRSS is more efficient only for positive correlation coefficients.

5. CONCLUSION

We may mention some theoretical results, which should be taken into account for using the proposed RSS model:

1. Generally the use of the proposed RSS model is more accurate than the classic SRS one.
2. The proposed model relies on assumptions on the behavior of the independence of the involved variables and not on the size of the population and on properties of the subsample sizes.

The use of RSS in the estimation of a difference with non-responses seems to be a natural approach because, having information on one of the variables allows to rank without an extra effort the non-respondents obtaining an increase in the accuracy of the estimators.

ACKNOWLEDGMENT

This paper was presented in 2020 at XIIIth International Conference on Operations Research the author thanks the referees for their suggestions. They allowed improving the quality of this paper.

REFERENCES

Al-Hadhrami, S. A. (2010). Estimation of the Population Variance Using Ranked Set Sampling with Auxiliary Variable Int. *J. Contemp. Math. Sciences*, *5*, 2567–2576.

Al-Omari, A. I., & Bouza, C. N. (2014). Review Of Ranked Set Sampling: Modifications And Applications. *Revista Investigación Operacional*, *35*, 215–240.

Al-Omari, A. I., Bouza, C. N., Covarrubias, D., & Pal, R. (2016). A New Estimator of the Population Mean: An Application to Bioleaching Studies. *Journal of Modern Applied Statistical Methods; JMASM*, *15*(2), 9. Advance online publication. doi:10.22237/jmasm/1478002020

Al-Saleh, M. F., & Al-Shrafat, K. (2001). Estimation of average milk yield using ranked set sampling. *Environmetrics*, *12*(4), 395–399. doi:10.1002/env.478

Arnab, R. (2017). *Survey Sampling Theory and Applications*. Academic Press, Elsevier.

Bouza, C. N. (1983). Estimation of the difference of population means with missing observations. *Biometrical J.*, *25*(2), 123–128. doi:10.1002/bimj.19830250203 PMID:31466424

Bouza, C. N., & Jose, F. (2017). Variance estimation of persons infected with AIDS under ranked set sampling. *Clinical Epidemiology and Global Health*. doi:10.1016/j.cegh.2017.12.002

Bouza, C. N., & Prhabu-Ajgaonkar, S. G. (1993). Estimation of the difference of population means when observations are missing. *Biometrical Journal. Biometrische Zeitschrift*, *35*, 245–252. doi:10.1002/bimj.4710350217

Dell, J. R., & And Clutter, J. N. (1972). Ranked sert sampling theory eith order statititcs background. *Biometrics*, *28*(2), 545–553. doi:10.2307/2556166

Ibrahi, K., Syam, M., & Al-Omari, A. I. (2012). The Efficiency of Stratified Quartile Ranked Set Sampling in Estimating the Population Mean. *Tamsui Oxford Journal of Information and Mathematical Sciences*, *28*, 175–190.

Kadilar, C., & Cingi, H. (2003). Ratio Estimators in Stratiðed Random Sampling. *Biometrical Journal. Biometrische Zeitschrift*, *45*(2), 218–225. doi:10.1002/bimj.200390007

Kadilar, C., & Cingi, H. (2005). A new ratio estimator in stratiðed random sampling. *Communications in Statistics. Theory and Methods*, *34*(3), 597–602. doi:10.1081/STA-200052156

Kadilar, C., & Cingi, H. (2012). Ratio Estimators in Stratiðed Random Sampling. *Biometrical Journal. Biometrische Zeitschrift*, *45*(2), 218–225. doi:10.1002/bimj.200390007

Khan, L., & Shabbir, J. (2015). A class of Hartley-Ross type unbiased estimators for population mean using ranked set sampling. *Hacettepe Journal of Mathematics and Statistics*. doi:10.15672/HJMS.20156210579

Khan, L., Shabbir, J., & Gupta, S. (2014). Unbiased Ratio Estimators of the Mean in Stratiðed Ranked Set Sampling. *Hacettepe Journal of Mathematics and Statistics*, *43*, 461–471.

Laupracis, A., & Sackett, D. L. (1988). An Assessment Of Clinically Useful measures of the consequences of a treatment. *The New England Journal of Medicine*, *318*(26), 1728–1733. doi:10.1056/NEJM198806303182605 PMID:3374545

MacEachern, S. N., Stasny, E. A., & Wolfe, D. A. (2004). Stratiðcation with imprecise rankings. *Biometrics*, *60*(1), 207–215. doi:10.1111/j.0006-341X.2004.00144.x PMID:15032791

Mahdizadeh, M., & Zamanzade, E. (2018). Stratiðed pair ranked set sampling. *Communications in Statistics. Theory and Methods*, *47*, 5904–5410.

Mandowara, V. L., & Mehta, N. (2014). Modiðed ratio estimators using stratiðed ranked set sampling. *Hacettepe Journal of Mathematics and Statistics*, *43*, 461–471.

McIntyre, G. A. (2005). A method for unbiased selective sampling using ranked set sampling. *The American Statistician*, *59*, 230-232.

Ozturk & Demirel. (2014). Estimation of Population Variance from Multi-Ranker Ranked Set Sampling Designs. *Communications in Statistics. Simulation and Computation*. Advance online publication. doi:10.1080/03610918.2014.948191

Patil, G. P., Sinha, A. K., & And Taillie, C. (1995). Ranked Set Sampling Coherent Ranking And Size Biased permutations. *Journal of Statistical Planning and Inference*, *63*(2), 311–324. doi:10.1016/S0378-3758(97)00030-X

Perron, F., & Sinha, B. K. (2004). Estimation of variance based on a ranked set sample. *Journal of Statistical Planning and Inference*, *120*(1-2), 21–28. doi:10.1016/S0378-3758(02)00497-4

Pi-Ehr, L. (1971). Estimation Procedures For The Difference Of Means With Missing Observations. *Journal of the American Statistical Association*, *41*, 517–553.

Saini, M. & Kumar, A. (2019). Ratio estimators using stratified random sampling and stratified ranked set sampling. *Life Cycle Reliab Saf Eng, 8*, 85-92.

Samawi, H. M. (1996). Stratiðed ranked set sample. *Pakistan Journal of Statistics, 12*, 9–16.

Samawi, H. M., & Muttlak, H. A. (1996). Estimation of ratio using ranked set sampling. *Biometrical Journal. Biometrische Zeitschrift, 38*(6), 753–764. doi:10.1002/bimj.4710380616

Samawi, H. M., & Saeid, L.-J. (2004). Stratified Extreme Ranked Set Sample With Application To Ratio Estimators. *Journal of Modern Applied Statistical Methods; JMASM, 3*(1), 117–133. doi:10.22237/jmasm/1083370320

Samawi, H. M., & Siam, M. I. (2003). Ratio estimation using stratiðed ranked set sample. *Metron, 61*, 75–90.

Singh, H. P., Mehta, V., & Pal, S.K. (2004). Dual to ratio and product type estimators using stratiðed ranked set sampling. *Journal of Basic and Applied Engineering Research, 1*, 7-12.

Singh, H. P., Mehta, V., & Pal, S. K. (2014). Dual to ratio and product type estimators using stratiðed ranked set sampling. *Journal of Basic and Applied Engineering Research, 1*, 7–12.

Stokes, S. L. (1980). Estimation of variance using judgment ordered ranked set samples. Encyclopedia of Statistical Sciences, 36, 35-42. doi:10.2307/2530493

Takahashi, K., & Wakimoto, M. (1968). On Unbiased Estimates Of The Population Mean Based On The sample stratified by means ordering. *Annals of the Institute of Mathematical Statistics, 20*, 1031-1047.

Wolfe, D. A. (2012). *Ranked set sampling: its relevance and impact on statistical inference*. ISRN Probability and Statistics.

Compilation of References

Abd Elgawad, M. A., Alawady, M. A., Barakat, H. M., & Xiong, S. (2020). Concomitants of generalized order statistics from Huang–Kotz Farlie–Gumbel–Morgenstern bivariate distribution: Some information measures. *Bulletin of the Malaysian Mathematical Sciences Society*, *43*(3), 2627–2645. doi:10.100740840-019-00822-9

Abo-Eleneen, Z. A., & Nagaraja, H. N. (2002). Fisher information in an order statistic and its concomitant. *Annals of the Institute of Statistical Mathematics*, *54*(3), 667–680. doi:10.1023/A:1022479514859

Adatia, A. (2000). Estimation of parameters of the half-logistic distribution using generalized ranked set sampling. *Computational Statistics & Data Analysis*, *33*(1), 1–13. doi:10.1016/S0167-9473(99)00035-3

Ahmed, S., Sedory, S. A., & Singh, S. (2018). Simultaneous estimation of means of two sensitive variables. *Communications in Statistics. Theory and Methods*, *47*(2), 324–343. doi:10.1080/03610926.2017.1303733

Ahmed, S., Sedory, S. A., & Singh, S. (2020). Forcibly Re-scrambled randomized response model for simultaneous estimation of means of two sensitive variables. *Communications in Mathematics and Statistics*, *8*(1), 23–45. doi:10.100740304-018-0156-7

Alawady, M. A., Barakat, H. M., & Abd Elgawad, M. A. (2021). Concomitants of Generalized Order Statistics from Bivariate Cambanis Family of Distributions Under a General Setting. *Bulletin of the Malaysian Mathematical Sciences Society*, *44*(5), 3129–3159. Advance online publication. doi:10.100740840-021-01102-1

Al-Hadhrami, S. A. (2010). Estimation of the Population Variance Using Ranked Set Sampling with Auxiliary Variable Int. *J. Contemp. Math. Sciences*, *5*, 2567–2576.

Al-Omari, A.I., Ibrahim, K., & JEMAIN, A.A. (2009). New ratio estimators of the mean using simple random sampling and ranked set sampling methods. *Revista Investigacion Operacional*, *30*, 97–108.

Al-Omari, A. I., & Al-Nasser, A. D. (2018). Ratio estimation using multistage median ranked set sampling approach. *Journal of Statistical Theory and Practice*, *12*(3), 512–529. doi:10.1080/15598608.2018.1425168

Al-Omari, A. I., & Bouza, C. N. (2014). Review of ranked set sampling: Modifications and applications. *Investigación Operacional, 35*(3), 215–235.

Al-Omari, A. I., & Bouza, C. N. (2014). Review of ranked set sampling: Modifications and applications. *Revista Investigación Operacional, 35*, 215–240.

Al-Omari, A. I., & Bouza, C. N. (2014). Review Of Ranked Set Sampling: Modifications And Applications. *Revista Investigación Operacional, 35*, 215–240.

Al-Omari, A. I., Bouza, C. N., Covarrubias, D., & Pal, R. (2016). A New Estimator of the Population Mean: An Application to Bioleaching Studies. *Journal of Modern Applied Statistical Methods; JMASM, 15*(2), 9. Advance online publication. doi:10.22237/jmasm/1478002020

Al-Omari, A. I., Jaber, K., & Al-Omari, A. (2008). Modified ratio-type estimators of the mean using extreme ranked set sampling. *Journal of Mathematics and Statistics, 4*(3), 150–155. doi:10.3844/jmssp.2008.150.155

Al-Omari, A. I., & Zamanzade, E. (2017). Goodness of-fit-tests for Laplace distribution in ranked set sampling. *Revista Investigación Operacional, 38*(4), 366–276.

Al-Saleh, M. F. (2004). Steady-state ranked set sampling and parametric inference. *Journal of Statistical Planning and Inference, 123*(1), 83–95. doi:10.1016/S0378-3758(03)00139-3

Al-Saleh, M. F., & Al-Kadiri, M. (2000). Double ranked set sampling. *Statistics & Probability Letters, 48*(2), 205–212. doi:10.1016/S0167-7152(99)00206-0

Al-Saleh, M. F., & Al-Omari, A. (2002). Multistage ranked set sampling. *Journal of Statistical Planning and Inference, 102*(2), 273–286. doi:10.1016/S0378-3758(01)00086-6

Al-Saleh, M. F., & Al-Shrafat, K. (2001). Estimation of milk yield using ranked set sampling. *Environmetrics, 12*(4), 395–399. doi:10.1002/env.478

Arnab, R. (2017). *Survey Sampling Theory and Applications*. Academic Press, Elsevier.

Arnold, B. C., Castillo, E., & Sarabia, J. M. (2009). On multivariate order statistics. Application to ranked set sampling. *Computational Statistics & Data Analysis, 53*(12), 4555–4569. doi:10.1016/j.csda.2009.05.011

Bain, L. J. (1978). *Statistical analysis of reliability and life testing models: theory and methods*. Marcel Dekker.

Bai, Z. D., & Chen, Z. (2003). On the theory of ranked set sampling *and* its ramifications. *Journal of Statistical Planning and Inference, 109*(1-2), 81–99. doi:10.1016/S0378-3758(02)00302-6

Barnett, V., & Moore, K. (1997). Best linear unbiased estimates in ranked-set sampling with particular reference to imperfect ordering. *Journal of Applied Statistics, 24*(6), 697–710. doi:10.1080/02664769723431

Biswas, A., Rai, A., & Ahmad, T. (2020). Rescaling bootstrap technique for variance estimation for ranked set samples in finite population. *Communications in Statistics. Simulation and Computation, 10*(10), 2704–2718. doi:10.1080/03610918.2018.1527349

Blair, G., & Imai, K. (2012). Statistical analysis of list experiments. *Political Analysis, 20*(1), 47–77. doi:10.1093/pan/mpr048

Bohn, L. L., & Wolfe, D. A. (1994). The effect of imperfect judgment rankings on properties of procedures based on the ranked-set samples analog of the mann-whitney-wilcoxon statistic. *Journal of the American Statistical Association, 89*(425), 168–176. doi:10.1080/01621459.1994.10476458

Bollabonia, V., Sedory, S. A., & Singh, S. (2018). *Forced Quantitative Randomized Response Model Using Ranked Set Sampling. In Ranked Set Sampling: 65 Years Improving the Accuracy in Data Gathering//Introduction and Schedule.* Elsevier.

Bouza, C. N. (1983). Estimation of the difference of population means with missing observations. *Biometrical J., 25*(2), 123–128. doi:10.1002/bimj.19830250203 PMID:31466424

Bouza, C. N. (2001). Model assisted ranked survey sampling. *Biometrical Journal. Biometrische Zeitschrift, 43*(2), 249–259. doi:10.1002/1521-4036(200105)43:2<249::AID-BIMJ249>3.0.CO;2-U

Bouza, C. N. (2009). Ranked set sampling and randomized response procedure for estimating the mean of a sensitive quantitative character. *Metrika, 70*(3), 267–277. doi:10.100700184-008-0191-6

Bouza, C. N., & Al-Omari, A. I. (2018). *Ranked Set Sampling, 65 Years Improving the Accuracy in Data Gathering.* Elsevier.

Bouza, C. N., & Jose, F. (2017). Variance estimation of persons infected with AIDS under ranked set sampling. *Clinical Epidemiology and Global Health.* doi:10.1016/j.cegh.2017.12.002

Bouza, C. N., & Prhabu-Ajgaonkar, S. G. (1993). Estimation of the difference of population means when observations are missing. *Biometrical Journal. Biometrische Zeitschrift, 35,* 245–252. doi:10.1002/bimj.4710350217

Bouza, C., Bracho, R., Santiago, A., & Sautto, J. M. (2017). Saha's randomized response technique under ranked set sampling. *RevistaInvestigacionOperacional, 38*(5), 537–544.

Chacko, M., & Thomas, P. Y. (2008). Estimation of parameter of Morgenstern type bivariate exponential distribution by ranked set sampling. *Annals of the Institute of Statistical Mathematics, 60*(2), 301–318. doi:10.100710463-006-0088-y

Chaudhuri, A., & Stenger, H. (1992). *Sampling Survey.* Marcel Dekker.

Chen, H. (2008). Alternative ranked set sample estimators for the variance of a sample proportion. *Applied Statistics Research Progress, 35.*

Chen, Z., Bai, Z., & Sinha, B. K. (2004). Ranked set sampling: theory and applications. In Lectures Notes in Statistics (vol. 176). Springer.

Chen, H., Stasny, E. A., & Wolfe, D. A. (2005). Ranked set sampling for efficient estimation of a population proportion. *Statistics in Medicine*, *24*(21), 3319–3329. doi:10.1002im.2158 PMID:16100735

Chen, Z. (2000). The efficiency of ranked-set sampling relative to simple random sampling under multi-parameter families. *Statistica Sinica*, *10*, 247–263.

Chen, Z., & Bai, Z. (2000). The optimal ranked set sampling scheme for parametric families. *Sankhya Series A*, *46*, 178–192.

Chen, Z., Bai, Z., & Sinha, B. K. (2004). *Lecture notes in statistics, ranked set sampling, theory and applications*. Springer. doi:10.1007/978-0-387-21664-5

Chitneni, R. S. (2020). *On estimating population means of two-sensitive variables with ranked set sampling design [Unpublished MS Project]*. Texas A&M University-Kingsville.

David, H. A., & Nagaraja, H. N. (2003). *Order Statistics* (3rd ed.). John Wiley & sons, Inc.

Deka, D., Das, B., Deka, U., & Baruah, B. K. (2021). Bivariate transmuted exponentiated Gumbel distribution (BTEGD) and concomitants of its order statistics. *J. Math. Comput. Sci.*, *11*(3), 3563–3593.

Dell, T. R., & Clutter, J. L. (1972). Ranked set sampling theory with order statistics background. *Biometrics*, *28*, 545–555.

Dell, T. R., & Clutter, J. L. (1972). Ranked set sampling theory with order statistics Background. *Biometrika*, *28*(2), 545–555. doi:10.2307/2556166

Drikvandi, R., Modarres, R., & Hui, T. P. (2011). A bootstrap test for symmetry based on ranked set samples. *Computational Statistics & Data Analysis*, *55*(4), 1807–1814. doi:10.1016/j.csda.2010.11.012

Droitcour, J. A., & Larson, E. M. (2002). An innovative technique for asking sensitive questions: The three-card method. *Bulletin of Sociological Methodology*, *75*(1), 5–23. doi:10.1177/075910630207500103

Efron, B. (1979). Bootstrap Methods: Another Look at the Jackknife. *Annals of Statistics*, *7*(1), 1–26. doi:10.1214/aos/1176344552

Efron, B. (1981). Nonparametric Standard Errors and Confidence Intervals (with discussion). *The Canadian Journal of Statistics*, *9*(2), 139–172. doi:10.2307/3314608

Efron, B. (1982). *The Jackknife, the Bootstrap, and Other Resampling Plans*. SIAM. doi:10.1137/1.9781611970319

Efron, B. (1987). Better Bootstrap Confidence Intervals. *Journal of the American Statistical Association*, *82*(397), 171–200. doi:10.1080/01621459.1987.10478410

Efron, B., & Tibshirani, R. J. (1993). *An introduction to the bootstrap*. Chapman & Hall. doi:10.1007/978-1-4899-4541-9

Eichhorn, B. H., & Hayre, L. S. (1983). Scrambled randomized response methods for obtaining sensitive quantitative data. *Journal of Statistical Planning and Inference*, *7*(4), 307–316. doi:10.1016/0378-3758(83)90002-2

Frey, J. (2007). Distribution-free statistical intervals via ranked-set sampling. *The Canadian Journal of Statistics*, *35*(4), 585–596. doi:10.1002/cjs.5550350409

Frey, J. (2007). New imperfect rankings models for ranked set sampling. *Journal of Statistical Planning and Inference*, *137*(4), 1433–1445. doi:10.1016/j.jspi.2006.02.013

Ghosh, S., Chatterjee, A., & Balakrishnan, N. (2017). Nonparametric confidence intervals for ranked set samples. *Computational Statistics*, *32*(4), 1689–1725. doi:10.100700180-017-0744-0

Gibson, M. A., Gurmu, E., Cobo, B., Rueda, M. M., & Scott, I. M. (2018). Indirect questioning method reveals hidden support for female genital cutting in Southern Ethiopia. *PLoS One*, *13*(5), e0193985. doi:10.1371/journal.pone.0193985 PMID:29718908

Gjestvang, C. R., & Singh, S. (2006). A new randomized response model. *J.R. Statist. B*, *68*, 523–530.

Gjestvang, C., & Singh, S. (2009). An improved randomized response model: Estimation of mean. *Journal of Applied Statistics*, *36*(12), 1361–1367.

Glynn, A. N. (2013). What can we learn with statistical truth serum? Design and analysis of the list experiment. *Public Opinion Quarterly*, *77*(S1), 159–172. doi:10.1093/poq/nfs070

Greenberg, B. G., Kuebler, R. R. Jr, Abernathy, J. R., & Horvitz, D. G. (1971). Application of the randomized response technique in obtaining quantitative data. *Journal of the American Statistical Association*, *66*(334), 243–250. doi:10.1080/01621459.1971.10482248

Hall, L. K., & Dell, T. R. (1996). Trials of ranked set sampling for forage yields. *Forest Sc*, *121*, 22–26.

Hall, P. (1988). Theoretical Comparison of Bootstrap Confidence Intervals. *Annals of Statistics*, *16*, 927–953.

Hall, P. (1992). On the removal of skewness by transformation. *Journal of the Royal Statistical Society. Series B. Methodological*, *54*(1), 221–228. doi:10.1111/j.2517-6161.1992.tb01876.x

Haq, A., Brown, J., Moltchanova, E., & Al-Omari, A. I. (2015). Improved exponentially weighted moving average control charts for monitoring process mean and dispersion. *Quality and Reliability Engineering International*, *31*(2), 217–237. doi:10.1002/qre.1573

Himmelfarb, S., & Edgell, S. E. (1980). Additive constant model: A randomized response technique for eliminating evasiveness to quantitative response questions. *Psychological Bulletin*, *87*(3), 525–530. doi:10.1037/0033-2909.87.3.525

Horvitz, D.G., Shah, B.V., & Simmons, W.R. (1967). The unrelated question randomized response model. *Proc. of Social Statistics Section, Amer. Stat. Assoc.*, 65-72.

Horvitz, D. G., & Thompson, D. J. (1952). A generalization of sampling without replacement from a finite universe. *Journal of the American Statistical Association, 47*(260), 663–685. doi: 10.1080/01621459.1952.10483446

Hui, T. P., Modarres, R., & Zheng, G. (2004). Bootstrap confidence interval estimation of mean via ranked set sampling linear regression. *Journal of Statistical Computation and Simulation, 75*(7), 543–553. doi:10.1080/00949650412331286124

Ibrahi, K., Syam, M., & Al-Omari, A. I. (2012). The Efficiency of Stratified Quartile Ranked Set Sampling in Estimating the Population Mean. *Tamsui Oxford Journal of Information and Mathematical Sciences, 28*, 175–190.

Irshad, M. R., Maya, R. K., & Arun, S. P. (2019). Estimation of a Parameter of Morgenstern Type Bivariate Lindley Distribution by Ranked Set Sampling. *ISTAT˙IST˙IK: Journal of the Turkish Statistical Association, 12*(1-2), 25–34.

Ivković, I., & Rajić, V. (2019). *Better confidence intervals for the population coefficient of variation. Communications in Statistics - Simulation and Computation.* doi:10.1080/0361091 8.2019.1642482

Jasti, S. (2020). A study of Gjestvang and Singh randomized response model using ranked set Sampling [Unpublished MS project]. Department of Mathematics, Texas A&M University-Kingsville, Kingsville, TX.

Johnson, N. (1978). Modified t-tests and confidence intervals for asymmetrical populations. *Journal of the American Statistical Association, 73*(363), 536–554. doi:10.2307/2286597

Kadilar, C. & Cingi, H. (2003). Ratio estimators in stratified random sampling. *Biometrical Journal. Biometrische Zeitschrift, 45*, 218–225.

Kadilar, C., & Cingi, H. (2003). Ratio Estimators in Stratiðed Random Sampling. *Biometrical Journal, 45*(2), 218-225.

Kadilar, C., & Cingi, H. (2003). Ratio Estimators in Stratiðed Random Sampling. *Biometrical Journal. Biometrische Zeitschrift, 45*(2), 218–225. doi:10.1002/bimj.200390007

Kadilar, C., & Cingi, H. (2005). A new ratio estimator in stratified random sampling. Communications in Statistics. *Theory and Methods, 34*, 597–602.

Kadilar, C., & Cingi, H. A. (2005). new ratio estimator in stratiðed random sampling. *Communications in Statistics. Theory and Methods, 34*(3), 597–602. doi:10.1081/STA-200052156

Kahraman, C., Öztayşi, B., & Çevik Onar, S. (2016). A comprehensive literature review of 50 years of fuzzy set theory. *International Journal of Computational Intelligence Systems, 9*(1, Supplement 1), 3–24. doi:10.1080/18756891.2016.1180817

Kamarulzaman, I. M., Mandowara, V. L., & Mehta, N. (2014). Modiðed ratio estimators using stratiðed ranked set sampling. *Hacettepe Journal of Mathematics and Statistics, 43*, 461–471.

Khan, L., & Shabbir, J. (2015). A class of Hartley-Ross type unbiased estimators for population mean using ranked set sampling. *Hacettepe Journal of Mathematics and Statistics*. doi:10.15672/HJMS.20156210579

Khan, L., Shabbir, J., & Gupta, S. (2014). Unbiased Ratio Estimators of the Mean in Stratiðed Ranked Set Sampling. *Hacettepe Journal of Mathematics and Statistics, 43*, 461–471.

Kotz, S., Balakrishnan, N., & Johnson, N. L. (2000). *Distributions in statistics:continuous multivariate distributions*. Wiley. doi:10.1002/0471722065

Lam, K., Sinha, B. K., & Wu, Z. (1995). Estimation of location and scale parameters of a logistic distribution using ranked set sample. In: H. N. Nagaraja, P. K. Sen, & D. F. Morrison (Eds.), Statistical theory and applications: papers in honor of Herbert A. David. New York: Springer.

Lam, K., Sinha, B. K., & Wu, Z. (1994). Estimation of a two-parameter exponential distribution using ranked set sample. *Annals of the Institute of Statistical Mathematics, 46*(4), 723–736. doi:10.1007/BF00773478

Laupracis, A., & Sackett, D. L. (1988). An Assessment Of Clinically Useful measures of the consequences of a treatment. *The New England Journal of Medicine, 318*(26), 1728–1733. doi:10.1056/NEJM198806303182605 PMID:3374545

Little, R. J. A., & Rubin, D. B. (2002). *Statistical Analysis with Missing Data* (2nd ed.). Wiley. doi:10.1002/9781119013563

MacEachern, S. N., Stasny, E. A., & Wolfe, D. A. (2004). Stratiðcation with imprecise rankings. *Biometrics, 60*, 207–215. doi:10.1111/j.0006-341X.2004.00144.x PMID:15032791

Mahdizadeh, M., & Zamanzade, E. (2018). Stratiðed pair ranked set sampling. *Communications in Statistics. Theory and Methods, 47*, 5904–5410.

Mahdizadeh, M., & Zamanzade, E. (2019). Confidence Intervals for Quantiles in Ranked Set Sampling. *Iranian Journal of Science and Technology. Transaction of Science, 43*(6), 3017–3028. doi:10.100740995-019-00790-6

Mahdizadeh, M., & Zamanzade, Z. (2020). *On interval estimation of the population mean in ranked set sampling. Communications in Statistics - Simulation and Computation*. doi:10.1080/03610918.2019.1700276

McIntyre, G. A. (2005). A method for unbiased selective sampling using ranked set sampling. *The American Statistician, 59*, 230-232.

McIntyre, G. A. (1952). A method for unbiased selective sampling using ranked sets. *Australian Journal of Agricultural Research, 3*, 385–390.

McIntyre, G. A. (1952). A method for unbiased selective sampling, using ranked sets. *Australian Journal of Agricultural Research*, *3*(4), 385–390. doi:10.1071/AR9520385

McIntyre, G. A. (1952). A method of unbiased selective sampling using ranked sets. *Australian Journal of Agricultural Research*, *3*, 385–390.

Mehta, V. (2018a). A New Morgenstern Type Bivariate Exponential Distribution With Known Coefficient Of Variation By Ranked Set Sampling. In Ranked Set Sampling: 65 years improving the accuracy in Data Gathering. Elsevier.

Mehta, V. (2018b). Shrinkage Estimators Of Scale Parameter Towards An Interval Of Morgenstern Type Bivariate Uniform Distribution Using Ranked Set Sampling. In Ranked Set Sampling: 65 years improving the accuracy in Data Gathering . Elsevier.

Mehta, V. (2017). Shrinkage estimator of the parameters of normal distribution based on K-record values. *Int. J. Sci. Res. Math. Stat. Sci.*, *4*(1), 1–5.

Mehta, V., & Singh, H. P. (2014). Shrinkage estimators of parameters of Morgenstern type bivariate logistic distribution using ranked set sampling. *J. Basic Appl. Eng. Res.*, *1*(13), 1–6.

Mehta, V., & Singh, H. P. (2015). *Minimum mean square error estimation of parameters in bivariate normal distribution using concomitants of record values. In Statistics and Informatics in Agricultural Research*. Indian Society of Agricultural Statistics, Excel India Publishers.

Miller, J. D. (1984). *A New Survey Technique for Studying Deviant Behavior* [Ph.D. Thesis]. The George Washington University.

Miller, J. D. (1985). The Nominative Technique: A New Method of Estimating Heroin Prevalence. *NIDA Research Monograph*, *57*, 104–124. PMID:3929108

Modarres, R., Hui, T. P., & Zheng, G. (2006). Resampling methods for ranked set samples. *Computational Statistics & Data Analysis*, *51*(2), 1039–1050. doi:10.1016/j.csda.2005.10.010

Modarres, R., & Zheng, G. (2004). Maximum likelihood estimation of dependence parameter using ranked set sampling. *Statistics & Probability Letters*, *68*(3), 315–323. doi:10.1016/j.spl.2004.04.003

Muttlak, H. A., & McDonald, L. L. (1990). Ranked set sampling with size-biased probability of selection. *Biometrics*, *46*(2), 435–445. doi:10.2307/2531448

Nash, W. J., Sellers, T. L., Talbot, S. R., Cawthorn, A. J., & Ford, W. B. (1994). *The population biology of abalone. Technical report*. Sea Fisheries Division.

Ozturk & Demirel. (2014). Estimation of Population Variance from Multi-Ranker Ranked Set Sampling Designs. *Communications in Statistics. Simulation and Computation*. Advance online publication. doi:10.1080/03610918.2014.948191

Ozturk, O. (2008). Inference in the presence of ranking error in ranked set sampling. *The Canadian Journal of Statistics*, *36*(4), 577–594. doi:10.1002/cjs.5550360406

Ozturk, O. (2011a). Combining ranking information in judgment post stratified and ranked set sampling designs. *Environmental and Ecological Statistics, 19*(1), 73–93. doi:10.100710651-011-0175-y

Ozturk, O. (2011b). Sampling from partially rank-ordered sets. *Environmental and Ecological Statistics, 18*(4), 757–779. doi:10.100710651-010-0161-9

Ozturk, O. (2013). Combining multi-observer information in partially rank-ordered judgment post-stratified and ranked set samples. *The Canadian Journal of Statistics, 41*(2), 304–324. doi:10.1002/cjs.11167

Ozturk, O. (2017). Statistical inference with empty strata in judgment post stratifed samples. *Annals of the Institute of Statistical Mathematics, 69*(5), 1029–1057. doi:10.100710463-016-0572-y

Patil, G. P. (2002). Ranked Set Sampling. In A. H. El-Shaarawy & W. W. Piegorsch (Eds.), *Encyclopedia of Environmetrics*. John Wiley and Sons.

Patil, G. P., Sinha, A. K., & And Taillie, C. (1995). Ranked Set Sampling Coherent Ranking And Size Biased permutations. *Journal of Statistical Planning and Inference, 63*(2), 311–324. doi:10.1016/S0378-3758(97)00030-X

Pelle, E., & Perri, P. F. (2018). Improving mean estimation in ranked set sampling using the Rao regression-type estimator. *Brazilian Journal of Probability and Statistics, 32*(3), 467–496. doi:10.1214/17-BJPS350

Perron, F., & Sinha, B. K. (2004). Estimation of variance based on a ranked set sample. *Journal of Statistical Planning and Inference, 120*(1-2), 21–28. doi:10.1016/S0378-3758(02)00497-4

Pi-Ehr, L. (1971). Estimation Procedures For The Difference Of Means With Missing Observations. *Journal of the American Statistical Association, 41*, 517–553.

Presnell, B., & Bohn, L. L. (1999). U-statistics and imperfect ranking in ranked set sampling. *Journal of Nonparametric Statistics, 10*(2), 111–126. doi:10.1080/10485259908832756

Raghavarao, D., & Federer, W. F. (1979). Block total response as an alternative to the randomized response method in survey. *Journal of the Royal Statistical Society. Series B. Methodological, 41*(1), 40–45. doi:10.1111/j.2517-6161.1979.tb01055.x

Ranked set estimation with imputation of the missing observations: The median estimator. (2011). *Revista Investigación Operacional, 32*, 30-37.

Rubin, R. B. (1976). Inference and missing data. *Biometrika, 63*(3), 581–592. doi:10.1093/biomet/63.3.581

Rubin, R. B. (1987). *Multiple imputation for non-response in surveys*. John Wiley. doi:10.1002/9780470316696

Saini, M. & Kumar, A. (2019). Ratio estimators using stratified random sampling and stratified ranked set sampling. *Life Cycle Reliab Saf Eng, 8*, 85-92.

Salinas, V. I., Sedory, S. A., & Singh, S. (2018). Calibrated estimator of population mean using two-stage ranked set sampling. In Ranked Set Sampling: 65 Years Improving the Accuracy in Data Gathering// Introduction and Schedule. Elsevier.

Salinas, V. I., Sedory, S. A., & Singh, S. (2018). Calibrated estimator of population mean using two-stage ranked set sampling. In Ranked Set Sampling: 65 Years Improving the Accuracy in Data Gathering//Introduction and Schedule. Elsevier.

Samawi, H. M. (1996). Stratiðed ranked set sample. *Pakistan Journal of Statistics, 12*, 9–16.

Samawi, H. M., & Muttlak, H. A. (1996). Estimation of ratio using ranked set sampling. *Biometrical Journal. Biometrische Zeitschrift, 38*(6), 753–764. doi:10.1002/bimj.4710380616

Samawi, H. M., & Saeid, L.-J. (2004). Stratified Extreme Ranked Set Sample With Application To Ratio Estimators. *Journal of Modern Applied Statistical Methods; JMASM, 3*(1), 117–133. doi:10.22237/jmasm/1083370320

Samawi, H. M., & Siam, M. I. (2003). Ratio estimation using stratiðed ranked set sample. *Metron, 61*, 75–90.

Santiago, A., Sautto, J. M., & Bouza, C. N. (2019). Randomized estimation a proportion using ranked set sampling and Warner's. *Investigação Operacional, 40*(3), 356–361.

Särndal, C. E., Swensson, B., & Wretman, J. H. (1992). *Model Assisted Survey Sampling*. Springer-Verlag.

Scaria, J., & Mohan, S. (2021). Dependence Concepts and Reliability Application of Concomitants of Order Statistics from the Morgenstern Family. *Journal of Statistical Theory and Applications: JSTA, 20*(2), 193. Advance online publication. doi:10.2991/jsta.d.210325.001

Scaria, J., & Nair, N. U. (1999). On concomitants of order statistics from Morgenstern family. *Biometrical Journal. Biometrische Zeitschrift, 41*(4), 483–489. doi:10.1002/(SICI)1521-4036(199907)41:4<483::AID-BIMJ483>3.0.CO;2-2

Searls, D. T. (1964). The utilization of a know coefficient of variation in the estimation procedure. *Journal of the American Statistical Association, 59*(308), 1225–1226. doi:10.1080/01621459.1964.10480765

Searls, D. T., & Intarapanich, P. (1990). A note on the estimator for the variance that utilizes the kurtosis. *The American Statistician, 44*, 295–296.

Sevinc, B., Cetintav, B., Esemen, M., & Gurler, S. (2019). A Pioneering Package for Ranked Set Sampling. *The R Journal, 11*(1), 401–415. doi:10.32614/RJ-2019-039

Singh, H. P., & Mehta, V. (2017). Improved estimation of the scale parameter for log-logistic distribution using balanced ranked set sampling. Stat. Trans: New Ser., 18(1), 53-74.

Singh, H. P., Mehta, V., & Pal, S.K. (2004). Dual to ratio and product type estimators using stratiðed ranked set sampling. *Journal of Basic and Applied Engineering Research, 1*, 7-12.

Singh, H.P. & Mehta, V. (2014b). An alternative estimation of the scale parameter for Morgenstern type bivariate log-logistic distribution using ranked set sampling. *J. Reliab. Stat. Stud., 7*(1), 19-29.

Singh, H. P., & Mehta, V. (2013). An improved estimation of parameters of Morgenstern type bivariate logistic distribution using ranked set sampling. *Statistica, 73*(4), 437–461.

Singh, H. P., & Mehta, V. (2014a). Linear shrinkage estimator of scale parameter of Morgenstern type bivariate logistic distribution using ranked set sampling. *Model Assisted Statistics and Applications: An International Journal, 9*(4), 295–307. doi:10.3233/MAS-140301

Singh, H. P., & Mehta, V. (2015). Estimation of scale parameter of a Morgenstern type bivariate uniform distribution using censored ranked set samples. *Model Assisted Statistics and Applications: An International Journal, 10*(2), 139–153. doi:10.3233/MAS-140315

Singh, H. P., & Mehta, V. (2016a). Improved estimation of scale parameter of Morgenstern type bivariate uniform distribution using ranked set sampling. *Communications in Statistics. Theory and Methods, 45*(5), 1466–1476. doi:10.1080/03610926.2013.864767

Singh, H. P., & Mehta, V. (2016b). Some classes of shrinkage estimators in the Morgenstern type bivariate exponential distribution using ranked set sampling. *Hacettepe Journal of Mathematics and Statistics, 45*(2), 575–591. doi:10.15672/HJMS.201611415693

Singh, H. P., & Mehta, V. (2016c). A class of shrinkage estimators of scale parameter of uniform distribution based on K-record values. *National Academy Science Letters, 39*(3), 221–227. doi:10.100740009-016-0438-0

Singh, H. P., Mehta, V., & Pal, S. K. (2014). Dual to ratio and product type estimators using stratiðed ranked set sampling. *Journal of Basic and Applied Engineering Research, 1*, 7–12.

Singh, H. P., Tailor, R., & Singh, S. (2014). General procedure for estimating the population mean using ranked set sampling. *Journal of Simulation and Computation Statistics, 84*, 931–945.

Singh, H. P., Tailor, R., & Tailor, R. (2010). On ratio and product methods with certain known population parameters of auxiliary variable in sample surveys. *SORT (Barcelona), 34*, 157–180.

Singh, J., Pandey, B. N., & Hirano, K. (1973). On the utilization of known coefficient of kurtosis in the estimation procedure of variance. *Annals of the Institute of Statistical Mathematics, 25*(1), 51–55. doi:10.1007/BF02479358

Singh, S. (2020). Reply to the correction by Grover and Kaur: A new randomized response model. *J.R. Statist., Series B, 82*(3), 865–868.

Singh, S., & Horn, S. (1998). An alternative estimator in multi-character surveys. *Metrika*, 99–107.

Stephan, F. F. (1945). The expected value and variance of the reciprocal and other negative power of a positive Binomial variate. *Ann. Math. Statistic., 16*(1), 50–61. doi:10.1214/aoms/1177731170

Stokes, S. L. (1980). Estimation of variance using judgment ordered ranked set samples. Encyclopedia of Statistical Sciences, 36, 35-42. doi:10.2307/2530493

Stokes, S.L. (1977). Ranked set sampling with concomitant variables. *Communications in Statistics – Theory & Methods A, 6*(12), 1207-1211.

Stokes, S. L. (1977). Ranked set sampling with concomitant variables. *Communications in Statistics. Theory and Methods, 6*(12), 1207–1211. doi:10.1080/03610927708827563

Stokes, S. L. (1980). Inference on the correlation coefficient in bivariate normal populations from ranked set samples. *Journal of the American Statistical Association, 75*(372), 989–995. doi:10.1080/01621459.1980.10477584

Stokes, S. L. (1995). Parametric ranked set sampling. *Annals of the Institute of Statistical Mathematics, 47*, 465–482.

Stokes, S. L., & Sager, T. W. (1988). Characterization of a ranked set sample with application to estimating distribution functions. *Journal of the American Statistical Association, 83*(402), 374–381. doi:10.1080/01621459.1988.10478607

Takahashi, K., & Wakimoto, M. (1968). On unbiased estimates of the population mean based on the sample stratified by means ordering. *Annals of the Institute of Mathematical Statistics, 20*, 1031-1047.

Takahashi, K., & Wakimoto, M. (1968). On Unbiased Estimates Of The Population Mean Based On The sample stratified by means ordering. *Annals of the Institute of Mathematical Statistics, 20*, 1031-1047.

Takahasi, K., & Wakimoto, K. (1968). On the unbiased estimates of the population mean based on the sample stratified by means of ordering. *Annals of the Institute of Statistical Mathematics, 20*, 1–31.

Takahasi, K., & Wakimoto, M. (1968). On unbiased estimates of the population mean based on the sample stratified by means ordering. *Annals of the Institute of Mathematical Statistics, 20*(1), 1031–1047. doi:10.1007/BF02911622

Tian, G.L., & Tang, M.L. (2014). *Incomplete Categorical Data Design: Non-Randomized Response Techniques for Sensitive Questions in Surveys.* Chapman & Hall/CRC (Statistics in the Social and Behavioral Sciences).

Viada-González, C. E., Bouza-Herrera, C. N., Torres-Barbosa, F., & Torres-Gemeil, O. (2004). Estudio estadístico de ensayos clínicos de un medicamento para la psoriasis vulgar usando técnicas de imputación. *Revista Investigación Operacional, 25*, 243–255.

Warner, S. L. (1965). Randomized response: A survey technique for eliminating evasive answer bias. *Journal of the American Statistical Association, 60*(309), 63–69. doi:10.1080/01621459.1965.10480775 PMID:12261830

Wolfe, D. A. (2012). Ranked set sampling: Its relevance and impact on statistical inference. *ISRN Probability and Statistics.*

Compilation of References

Wolfe, D. A. (2012). *Ranked set sampling: its relevance and impact on statistical inference.* ISRN Probability and Statistics.

Wu, C., & Thompson, M. E. (2020). *Sampling Theory and Practice.* Springer Nature, Switzerland AG.

Zadeh, L. A. (1965). Fuzzy sets. *Information and Control, 8*(3), 338–353. doi:10.1016/S0019-9958(65)90241-X

Zamanzade, E., & Vock, M. (2018). Parametric tests of perfect judgment ranking based on ordered ranked set samples. *Revista de Statistica, 16*(4), 463–474.

Zheng, G., & Modarres, R. (2006). A robust estimate of correlation coefficient for bivariate normal distribution using ranked set sampling. *Journal of Statistical Planning and Inference, 136*(1), 298–309. doi:10.1016/j.jspi.2004.06.006

Zimmermann, H.-J. (2001). *Fuzzy Set Theory—and Applications, 4th Rev.* Kluwer Academic Publishers. doi:10.1007/978-94-010-0646-0

Zimmermann, H.-J. (2010). Fuzzy set theory. *Wiley Interdisciplinary Reviews: Computational Statistics, 2*(3), 317–332. doi:10.1002/wics.82

Zong, R., Sedory, S. A., & Singh, S. (2018). Construction of Strata Boundaries for Ranked Set Sampling. In Ranked Set Sampling: 65 Years Improving the Accuracy in Data Gathering// Introduction and Schedule. Elsevier.

Related References

To continue our tradition of advancing information science and technology research, we have compiled a list of recommended IGI Global readings. These references will provide additional information and guidance to further enrich your knowledge and assist you with your own research and future publications.

Aasi, P., Rusu, L., & Vieru, D. (2017). The Role of Culture in IT Governance Five Focus Areas: A Literature Review. *International Journal of IT/Business Alignment and Governance, 8*(2), 42-61. doi:10.4018/IJITBAG.2017070103

Abdrabo, A. A. (2018). Egypt's Knowledge-Based Development: Opportunities, Challenges, and Future Possibilities. In A. Alraouf (Ed.), *Knowledge-Based Urban Development in the Middle East* (pp. 80–101). Hershey, PA: IGI Global. doi:10.4018/978-1-5225-3734-2.ch005

Abu Doush, I., & Alhami, I. (2018). Evaluating the Accessibility of Computer Laboratories, Libraries, and Websites in Jordanian Universities and Colleges. *International Journal of Information Systems and Social Change, 9*(2), 44–60. doi:10.4018/IJISSC.2018040104

Adeboye, A. (2016). Perceived Use and Acceptance of Cloud Enterprise Resource Planning (ERP) Implementation in the Manufacturing Industries. *International Journal of Strategic Information Technology and Applications, 7*(3), 24–40. doi:10.4018/IJSITA.2016070102

Adegbore, A. M., Quadri, M. O., & Oyewo, O. R. (2018). A Theoretical Approach to the Adoption of Electronic Resource Management Systems (ERMS) in Nigerian University Libraries. In A. Tella & T. Kwanya (Eds.), *Handbook of Research on Managing Intellectual Property in Digital Libraries* (pp. 292–311). Hershey, PA: IGI Global. doi:10.4018/978-1-5225-3093-0.ch015

Related References

Adhikari, M., & Roy, D. (2016). Green Computing. In G. Deka, G. Siddesh, K. Srinivasa, & L. Patnaik (Eds.), *Emerging Research Surrounding Power Consumption and Performance Issues in Utility Computing* (pp. 84–108). Hershey, PA: IGI Global. doi:10.4018/978-1-4666-8853-7.ch005

Afolabi, O. A. (2018). Myths and Challenges of Building an Effective Digital Library in Developing Nations: An African Perspective. In A. Tella & T. Kwanya (Eds.), *Handbook of Research on Managing Intellectual Property in Digital Libraries* (pp. 51–79). Hershey, PA: IGI Global. doi:10.4018/978-1-5225-3093-0.ch004

Agarwal, R., Singh, A., & Sen, S. (2016). Role of Molecular Docking in Computer-Aided Drug Design and Development. In S. Dastmalchi, M. Hamzeh-Mivehroud, & B. Sokouti (Eds.), *Applied Case Studies and Solutions in Molecular Docking-Based Drug Design* (pp. 1–28). Hershey, PA: IGI Global. doi:10.4018/978-1-5225-0362-0.ch001

Ali, O., & Soar, J. (2016). Technology Innovation Adoption Theories. In L. Al-Hakim, X. Wu, A. Koronios, & Y. Shou (Eds.), *Handbook of Research on Driving Competitive Advantage through Sustainable, Lean, and Disruptive Innovation* (pp. 1–38). Hershey, PA: IGI Global. doi:10.4018/978-1-5225-0135-0.ch001

Alsharo, M. (2017). Attitudes Towards Cloud Computing Adoption in Emerging Economies. *International Journal of Cloud Applications and Computing, 7*(3), 44–58. doi:10.4018/IJCAC.2017070102

Amer, T. S., & Johnson, T. L. (2016). Information Technology Progress Indicators: Temporal Expectancy, User Preference, and the Perception of Process Duration. *International Journal of Technology and Human Interaction, 12*(4), 1–14. doi:10.4018/IJTHI.2016100101

Amer, T. S., & Johnson, T. L. (2017). Information Technology Progress Indicators: Research Employing Psychological Frameworks. In A. Mesquita (Ed.), *Research Paradigms and Contemporary Perspectives on Human-Technology Interaction* (pp. 168–186). Hershey, PA: IGI Global. doi:10.4018/978-1-5225-1868-6.ch008

Anchugam, C. V., & Thangadurai, K. (2016). Introduction to Network Security. In D. G., M. Singh, & M. Jayanthi (Eds.), Network Security Attacks and Countermeasures (pp. 1-48). Hershey, PA: IGI Global. doi:10.4018/978-1-4666-8761-5.ch001

Anchugam, C. V., & Thangadurai, K. (2016). Classification of Network Attacks and Countermeasures of Different Attacks. In D. G., M. Singh, & M. Jayanthi (Eds.), Network Security Attacks and Countermeasures (pp. 115-156). Hershey, PA: IGI Global. doi:10.4018/978-1-4666-8761-5.ch004

Anohah, E. (2016). Pedagogy and Design of Online Learning Environment in Computer Science Education for High Schools. *International Journal of Online Pedagogy and Course Design*, 6(3), 39–51. doi:10.4018/IJOPCD.2016070104

Anohah, E. (2017). Paradigm and Architecture of Computing Augmented Learning Management System for Computer Science Education. *International Journal of Online Pedagogy and Course Design*, 7(2), 60–70. doi:10.4018/IJOPCD.2017040105

Anohah, E., & Suhonen, J. (2017). Trends of Mobile Learning in Computing Education from 2006 to 2014: A Systematic Review of Research Publications. *International Journal of Mobile and Blended Learning*, 9(1), 16–33. doi:10.4018/IJMBL.2017010102

Assis-Hassid, S., Heart, T., Reychav, I., & Pliskin, J. S. (2016). Modelling Factors Affecting Patient-Doctor-Computer Communication in Primary Care. *International Journal of Reliable and Quality E-Healthcare*, 5(1), 1–17. doi:10.4018/IJRQEH.2016010101

Bailey, E. K. (2017). Applying Learning Theories to Computer Technology Supported Instruction. In M. Grassetti & S. Brookby (Eds.), *Advancing Next-Generation Teacher Education through Digital Tools and Applications* (pp. 61–81). Hershey, PA: IGI Global. doi:10.4018/978-1-5225-0965-3.ch004

Balasubramanian, K. (2016). Attacks on Online Banking and Commerce. In K. Balasubramanian, K. Mala, & M. Rajakani (Eds.), *Cryptographic Solutions for Secure Online Banking and Commerce* (pp. 1–19). Hershey, PA: IGI Global. doi:10.4018/978-1-5225-0273-9.ch001

Baldwin, S., Opoku-Agyemang, K., & Roy, D. (2016). Games People Play: A Trilateral Collaboration Researching Computer Gaming across Cultures. In K. Valentine & L. Jensen (Eds.), *Examining the Evolution of Gaming and Its Impact on Social, Cultural, and Political Perspectives* (pp. 364–376). Hershey, PA: IGI Global. doi:10.4018/978-1-5225-0261-6.ch017

Banerjee, S., Sing, T. Y., Chowdhury, A. R., & Anwar, H. (2018). Let's Go Green: Towards a Taxonomy of Green Computing Enablers for Business Sustainability. In M. Khosrow-Pour (Ed.), *Green Computing Strategies for Competitive Advantage and Business Sustainability* (pp. 89–109). Hershey, PA: IGI Global. doi:10.4018/978-1-5225-5017-4.ch005

Basham, R. (2018). Information Science and Technology in Crisis Response and Management. In M. Khosrow-Pour, D.B.A. (Ed.), Encyclopedia of Information Science and Technology, Fourth Edition (pp. 1407-1418). Hershey, PA: IGI Global. doi:10.4018/978-1-5225-2255-3.ch121

Batyashe, T., & Iyamu, T. (2018). Architectural Framework for the Implementation of Information Technology Governance in Organisations. In M. Khosrow-Pour, D.B.A. (Ed.), Encyclopedia of Information Science and Technology, Fourth Edition (pp. 810-819). Hershey, PA: IGI Global. doi:10.4018/978-1-5225-2255-3.ch070

Bekleyen, N., & Çelik, S. (2017). Attitudes of Adult EFL Learners towards Preparing for a Language Test via CALL. In D. Tafazoli & M. Romero (Eds.), *Multiculturalism and Technology-Enhanced Language Learning* (pp. 214–229). Hershey, PA: IGI Global. doi:10.4018/978-1-5225-1882-2.ch013

Bennett, A., Eglash, R., Lachney, M., & Babbitt, W. (2016). Design Agency: Diversifying Computer Science at the Intersections of Creativity and Culture. In M. Raisinghani (Ed.), *Revolutionizing Education through Web-Based Instruction* (pp. 35–56). Hershey, PA: IGI Global. doi:10.4018/978-1-4666-9932-8.ch003

Bergeron, F., Croteau, A., Uwizeyemungu, S., & Raymond, L. (2017). A Framework for Research on Information Technology Governance in SMEs. In S. De Haes & W. Van Grembergen (Eds.), *Strategic IT Governance and Alignment in Business Settings* (pp. 53–81). Hershey, PA: IGI Global. doi:10.4018/978-1-5225-0861-8.ch003

Bhatt, G. D., Wang, Z., & Rodger, J. A. (2017). Information Systems Capabilities and Their Effects on Competitive Advantages: A Study of Chinese Companies. *Information Resources Management Journal*, 30(3), 41–57. doi:10.4018/IRMJ.2017070103

Bogdanoski, M., Stoilkovski, M., & Risteski, A. (2016). Novel First Responder Digital Forensics Tool as a Support to Law Enforcement. In M. Hadji-Janev & M. Bogdanoski (Eds.), *Handbook of Research on Civil Society and National Security in the Era of Cyber Warfare* (pp. 352–376). Hershey, PA: IGI Global. doi:10.4018/978-1-4666-8793-6.ch016

Boontarig, W., Papasratorn, B., & Chutimaskul, W. (2016). The Unified Model for Acceptance and Use of Health Information on Online Social Networks: Evidence from Thailand. *International Journal of E-Health and Medical Communications*, 7(1), 31–47. doi:10.4018/IJEHMC.2016010102

Brown, S., & Yuan, X. (2016). Techniques for Retaining Computer Science Students at Historical Black Colleges and Universities. In C. Prince & R. Ford (Eds.), *Setting a New Agenda for Student Engagement and Retention in Historically Black Colleges and Universities* (pp. 251–268). Hershey, PA: IGI Global. doi:10.4018/978-1-5225-0308-8.ch014

Burcoff, A., & Shamir, L. (2017). Computer Analysis of Pablo Picasso's Artistic Style. *International Journal of Art, Culture and Design Technologies*, 6(1), 1–18. doi:10.4018/IJACDT.2017010101

Byker, E. J. (2017). I Play I Learn: Introducing Technological Play Theory. In C. Martin & D. Polly (Eds.), *Handbook of Research on Teacher Education and Professional Development* (pp. 297–306). Hershey, PA: IGI Global. doi:10.4018/978-1-5225-1067-3.ch016

Calongne, C. M., Stricker, A. G., Truman, B., & Arenas, F. J. (2017). Cognitive Apprenticeship and Computer Science Education in Cyberspace: Reimagining the Past. In A. Stricker, C. Calongne, B. Truman, & F. Arenas (Eds.), *Integrating an Awareness of Selfhood and Society into Virtual Learning* (pp. 180–197). Hershey, PA: IGI Global. doi:10.4018/978-1-5225-2182-2.ch013

Carlton, E. L., Holsinger, J. W. Jr, & Anunobi, N. (2016). Physician Engagement with Health Information Technology: Implications for Practice and Professionalism. *International Journal of Computers in Clinical Practice, 1*(2), 51–73. doi:10.4018/IJCCP.2016070103

Carneiro, A. D. (2017). Defending Information Networks in Cyberspace: Some Notes on Security Needs. In M. Dawson, D. Kisku, P. Gupta, J. Sing, & W. Li (Eds.), Developing Next-Generation Countermeasures for Homeland Security Threat Prevention (pp. 354-375). Hershey, PA: IGI Global. doi:10.4018/978-1-5225-0703-1.ch016

Cavalcanti, J. C. (2016). The New "ABC" of ICTs (Analytics + Big Data + Cloud Computing): A Complex Trade-Off between IT and CT Costs. In J. Martins & A. Molnar (Eds.), *Handbook of Research on Innovations in Information Retrieval, Analysis, and Management* (pp. 152–186). Hershey, PA: IGI Global. doi:10.4018/978-1-4666-8833-9.ch006

Chase, J. P., & Yan, Z. (2017). Affect in Statistics Cognition. In *Assessing and Measuring Statistics Cognition in Higher Education Online Environments: Emerging Research and Opportunities* (pp. 144–187). Hershey, PA: IGI Global. doi:10.4018/978-1-5225-2420-5.ch005

Chen, C. (2016). Effective Learning Strategies for the 21st Century: Implications for the E-Learning. In M. Anderson & C. Gavan (Eds.), *Developing Effective Educational Experiences through Learning Analytics* (pp. 143–169). Hershey, PA: IGI Global. doi:10.4018/978-1-4666-9983-0.ch006

Chen, E. T. (2016). Examining the Influence of Information Technology on Modern Health Care. In P. Manolitzas, E. Grigoroudis, N. Matsatsinis, & D. Yannacopoulos (Eds.), *Effective Methods for Modern Healthcare Service Quality and Evaluation* (pp. 110–136). Hershey, PA: IGI Global. doi:10.4018/978-1-4666-9961-8.ch006

Cimermanova, I. (2017). Computer-Assisted Learning in Slovakia. In D. Tafazoli & M. Romero (Eds.), *Multiculturalism and Technology-Enhanced Language Learning* (pp. 252–270). Hershey, PA: IGI Global. doi:10.4018/978-1-5225-1882-2.ch015

Cipolla-Ficarra, F. V., & Cipolla-Ficarra, M. (2018). Computer Animation for Ingenious Revival. In F. Cipolla-Ficarra, M. Ficarra, M. Cipolla-Ficarra, A. Quiroga, J. Alma, & J. Carré (Eds.), *Technology-Enhanced Human Interaction in Modern Society* (pp. 159–181). Hershey, PA: IGI Global. doi:10.4018/978-1-5225-3437-2.ch008

Cockrell, S., Damron, T. S., Melton, A. M., & Smith, A. D. (2018). Offshoring IT. In M. Khosrow-Pour, D.B.A. (Ed.), Encyclopedia of Information Science and Technology, Fourth Edition (pp. 5476-5489). Hershey, PA: IGI Global. doi:10.4018/978-1-5225-2255-3.ch476

Coffey, J. W. (2018). Logic and Proof in Computer Science: Categories and Limits of Proof Techniques. In J. Horne (Ed.), *Philosophical Perceptions on Logic and Order* (pp. 218–240). Hershey, PA: IGI Global. doi:10.4018/978-1-5225-2443-4.ch007

Dale, M. (2017). Re-Thinking the Challenges of Enterprise Architecture Implementation. In M. Tavana (Ed.), *Enterprise Information Systems and the Digitalization of Business Functions* (pp. 205–221). Hershey, PA: IGI Global. doi:10.4018/978-1-5225-2382-6.ch009

Das, A., Dasgupta, R., & Bagchi, A. (2016). Overview of Cellular Computing-Basic Principles and Applications. In J. Mandal, S. Mukhopadhyay, & T. Pal (Eds.), *Handbook of Research on Natural Computing for Optimization Problems* (pp. 637–662). Hershey, PA: IGI Global. doi:10.4018/978-1-5225-0058-2.ch026

De Maere, K., De Haes, S., & von Kutzschenbach, M. (2017). CIO Perspectives on Organizational Learning within the Context of IT Governance. *International Journal of IT/Business Alignment and Governance, 8*(1), 32-47. doi:10.4018/IJITBAG.2017010103

Demir, K., Çaka, C., Yaman, N. D., İslamoğlu, H., & Kuzu, A. (2018). Examining the Current Definitions of Computational Thinking. In H. Ozcinar, G. Wong, & H. Ozturk (Eds.), *Teaching Computational Thinking in Primary Education* (pp. 36–64). Hershey, PA: IGI Global. doi:10.4018/978-1-5225-3200-2.ch003

Deng, X., Hung, Y., & Lin, C. D. (2017). Design and Analysis of Computer Experiments. In S. Saha, A. Mandal, A. Narasimhamurthy, S. V, & S. Sangam (Eds.), Handbook of Research on Applied Cybernetics and Systems Science (pp. 264-279). Hershey, PA: IGI Global. doi:10.4018/978-1-5225-2498-4.ch013

Denner, J., Martinez, J., & Thiry, H. (2017). Strategies for Engaging Hispanic/Latino Youth in the US in Computer Science. In Y. Rankin & J. Thomas (Eds.), *Moving Students of Color from Consumers to Producers of Technology* (pp. 24–48). Hershey, PA: IGI Global. doi:10.4018/978-1-5225-2005-4.ch002

Devi, A. (2017). Cyber Crime and Cyber Security: A Quick Glance. In R. Kumar, P. Pattnaik, & P. Pandey (Eds.), *Detecting and Mitigating Robotic Cyber Security Risks* (pp. 160–171). Hershey, PA: IGI Global. doi:10.4018/978-1-5225-2154-9.ch011

Dores, A. R., Barbosa, F., Guerreiro, S., Almeida, I., & Carvalho, I. P. (2016). Computer-Based Neuropsychological Rehabilitation: Virtual Reality and Serious Games. In M. Cruz-Cunha, I. Miranda, R. Martinho, & R. Rijo (Eds.), *Encyclopedia of E-Health and Telemedicine* (pp. 473–485). Hershey, PA: IGI Global. doi:10.4018/978-1-4666-9978-6.ch037

Doshi, N., & Schaefer, G. (2016). Computer-Aided Analysis of Nailfold Capillaroscopy Images. In D. Fotiadis (Ed.), *Handbook of Research on Trends in the Diagnosis and Treatment of Chronic Conditions* (pp. 146–158). Hershey, PA: IGI Global. doi:10.4018/978-1-4666-8828-5.ch007

Doyle, D. J., & Fahy, P. J. (2018). Interactivity in Distance Education and Computer-Aided Learning, With Medical Education Examples. In M. Khosrow-Pour, D.B.A. (Ed.), Encyclopedia of Information Science and Technology, Fourth Edition (pp. 5829-5840). Hershey, PA: IGI Global. doi:10.4018/978-1-5225-2255-3.ch507

Elias, N. I., & Walker, T. W. (2017). Factors that Contribute to Continued Use of E-Training among Healthcare Professionals. In F. Topor (Ed.), *Handbook of Research on Individualism and Identity in the Globalized Digital Age* (pp. 403–429). Hershey, PA: IGI Global. doi:10.4018/978-1-5225-0522-8.ch018

Eloy, S., Dias, M. S., Lopes, P. F., & Vilar, E. (2016). Digital Technologies in Architecture and Engineering: Exploring an Engaged Interaction within Curricula. In D. Fonseca & E. Redondo (Eds.), *Handbook of Research on Applied E-Learning in Engineering and Architecture Education* (pp. 368–402). Hershey, PA: IGI Global. doi:10.4018/978-1-4666-8803-2.ch017

Estrela, V. V., Magalhães, H. A., & Saotome, O. (2016). Total Variation Applications in Computer Vision. In N. Kamila (Ed.), *Handbook of Research on Emerging Perspectives in Intelligent Pattern Recognition, Analysis, and Image Processing* (pp. 41–64). Hershey, PA: IGI Global. doi:10.4018/978-1-4666-8654-0.ch002

Related References

Filipovic, N., Radovic, M., Nikolic, D. D., Saveljic, I., Milosevic, Z., Exarchos, T. P., ... Parodi, O. (2016). Computer Predictive Model for Plaque Formation and Progression in the Artery. In D. Fotiadis (Ed.), *Handbook of Research on Trends in the Diagnosis and Treatment of Chronic Conditions* (pp. 279–300). Hershey, PA: IGI Global. doi:10.4018/978-1-4666-8828-5.ch013

Fisher, R. L. (2018). Computer-Assisted Indian Matrimonial Services. In M. Khosrow-Pour, D.B.A. (Ed.), Encyclopedia of Information Science and Technology, Fourth Edition (pp. 4136-4145). Hershey, PA: IGI Global. doi:10.4018/978-1-5225-2255-3.ch358

Fleenor, H. G., & Hodhod, R. (2016). Assessment of Learning and Technology: Computer Science Education. In V. Wang (Ed.), *Handbook of Research on Learning Outcomes and Opportunities in the Digital Age* (pp. 51–78). Hershey, PA: IGI Global. doi:10.4018/978-1-4666-9577-1.ch003

García-Valcárcel, A., & Mena, J. (2016). Information Technology as a Way To Support Collaborative Learning: What In-Service Teachers Think, Know and Do. *Journal of Information Technology Research*, *9*(1), 1–17. doi:10.4018/JITR.2016010101

Gardner-McCune, C., & Jimenez, Y. (2017). Historical App Developers: Integrating CS into K-12 through Cross-Disciplinary Projects. In Y. Rankin & J. Thomas (Eds.), *Moving Students of Color from Consumers to Producers of Technology* (pp. 85–112). Hershey, PA: IGI Global. doi:10.4018/978-1-5225-2005-4.ch005

Garvey, G. P. (2016). Exploring Perception, Cognition, and Neural Pathways of Stereo Vision and the Split–Brain Human Computer Interface. In A. Ursyn (Ed.), *Knowledge Visualization and Visual Literacy in Science Education* (pp. 28–76). Hershey, PA: IGI Global. doi:10.4018/978-1-5225-0480-1.ch002

Ghafele, R., & Gibert, B. (2018). Open Growth: The Economic Impact of Open Source Software in the USA. In M. Khosrow-Pour (Ed.), *Optimizing Contemporary Application and Processes in Open Source Software* (pp. 164–197). Hershey, PA: IGI Global. doi:10.4018/978-1-5225-5314-4.ch007

Ghobakhloo, M., & Azar, A. (2018). Information Technology Resources, the Organizational Capability of Lean-Agile Manufacturing, and Business Performance. *Information Resources Management Journal*, *31*(2), 47–74. doi:10.4018/IRMJ.2018040103

Gianni, M., & Gotzamani, K. (2016). Integrated Management Systems and Information Management Systems: Common Threads. In P. Papajorgji, F. Pinet, A. Guimarães, & J. Papathanasiou (Eds.), *Automated Enterprise Systems for Maximizing Business Performance* (pp. 195–214). Hershey, PA: IGI Global. doi:10.4018/978-1-4666-8841-4.ch011

Gikandi, J. W. (2017). Computer-Supported Collaborative Learning and Assessment: A Strategy for Developing Online Learning Communities in Continuing Education. In J. Keengwe & G. Onchwari (Eds.), *Handbook of Research on Learner-Centered Pedagogy in Teacher Education and Professional Development* (pp. 309–333). Hershey, PA: IGI Global. doi:10.4018/978-1-5225-0892-2.ch017

Gokhale, A. A., & Machina, K. F. (2017). Development of a Scale to Measure Attitudes toward Information Technology. In L. Tomei (Ed.), *Exploring the New Era of Technology-Infused Education* (pp. 49–64). Hershey, PA: IGI Global. doi:10.4018/978-1-5225-1709-2.ch004

Grace, A., O'Donoghue, J., Mahony, C., Heffernan, T., Molony, D., & Carroll, T. (2016). Computerized Decision Support Systems for Multimorbidity Care: An Urgent Call for Research and Development. In M. Cruz-Cunha, I. Miranda, R. Martinho, & R. Rijo (Eds.), *Encyclopedia of E-Health and Telemedicine* (pp. 486–494). Hershey, PA: IGI Global. doi:10.4018/978-1-4666-9978-6.ch038

Gupta, A., & Singh, O. (2016). Computer Aided Modeling and Finite Element Analysis of Human Elbow. *International Journal of Biomedical and Clinical Engineering*, *5*(1), 31–38. doi:10.4018/IJBCE.2016010104

H., S. K. (2016). Classification of Cybercrimes and Punishments under the Information Technology Act, 2000. In S. Geetha, & A. Phamila (Eds.), *Combating Security Breaches and Criminal Activity in the Digital Sphere* (pp. 57-66). Hershey, PA: IGI Global. doi:10.4018/978-1-5225-0193-0.ch004

Hafeez-Baig, A., Gururajan, R., & Wickramasinghe, N. (2017). Readiness as a Novel Construct of Readiness Acceptance Model (RAM) for the Wireless Handheld Technology. In N. Wickramasinghe (Ed.), *Handbook of Research on Healthcare Administration and Management* (pp. 578–595). Hershey, PA: IGI Global. doi:10.4018/978-1-5225-0920-2.ch035

Hanafizadeh, P., Ghandchi, S., & Asgarimehr, M. (2017). Impact of Information Technology on Lifestyle: A Literature Review and Classification. *International Journal of Virtual Communities and Social Networking*, *9*(2), 1–23. doi:10.4018/IJVCSN.2017040101

Harlow, D. B., Dwyer, H., Hansen, A. K., Hill, C., Iveland, A., Leak, A. E., & Franklin, D. M. (2016). Computer Programming in Elementary and Middle School: Connections across Content. In M. Urban & D. Falvo (Eds.), *Improving K-12 STEM Education Outcomes through Technological Integration* (pp. 337–361). Hershey, PA: IGI Global. doi:10.4018/978-1-4666-9616-7.ch015

Haseski, H. İ., Ilic, U., & Tuğtekin, U. (2018). Computational Thinking in Educational Digital Games: An Assessment Tool Proposal. In H. Ozcinar, G. Wong, & H. Ozturk (Eds.), *Teaching Computational Thinking in Primary Education* (pp. 256–287). Hershey, PA: IGI Global. doi:10.4018/978-1-5225-3200-2.ch013

Hee, W. J., Jalleh, G., Lai, H., & Lin, C. (2017). E-Commerce and IT Projects: Evaluation and Management Issues in Australian and Taiwanese Hospitals. *International Journal of Public Health Management and Ethics*, 2(1), 69–90. doi:10.4018/IJPHME.2017010104

Hernandez, A. A. (2017). Green Information Technology Usage: Awareness and Practices of Philippine IT Professionals. *International Journal of Enterprise Information Systems*, 13(4), 90–103. doi:10.4018/IJEIS.2017100106

Hernandez, A. A., & Ona, S. E. (2016). Green IT Adoption: Lessons from the Philippines Business Process Outsourcing Industry. *International Journal of Social Ecology and Sustainable Development*, 7(1), 1–34. doi:10.4018/IJSESD.2016010101

Hernandez, M. A., Marin, E. C., Garcia-Rodriguez, J., Azorin-Lopez, J., & Cazorla, M. (2017). Automatic Learning Improves Human-Robot Interaction in Productive Environments: A Review. *International Journal of Computer Vision and Image Processing*, 7(3), 65–75. doi:10.4018/IJCVIP.2017070106

Horne-Popp, L. M., Tessone, E. B., & Welker, J. (2018). If You Build It, They Will Come: Creating a Library Statistics Dashboard for Decision-Making. In L. Costello & M. Powers (Eds.), *Developing In-House Digital Tools in Library Spaces* (pp. 177–203). Hershey, PA: IGI Global. doi:10.4018/978-1-5225-2676-6.ch009

Hossan, C. G., & Ryan, J. C. (2016). Factors Affecting e-Government Technology Adoption Behaviour in a Voluntary Environment. *International Journal of Electronic Government Research*, 12(1), 24–49. doi:10.4018/IJEGR.2016010102

Hu, H., Hu, P. J., & Al-Gahtani, S. S. (2017). User Acceptance of Computer Technology at Work in Arabian Culture: A Model Comparison Approach. In M. Khosrow-Pour (Ed.), *Handbook of Research on Technology Adoption, Social Policy, and Global Integration* (pp. 205–228). Hershey, PA: IGI Global. doi:10.4018/978-1-5225-2668-1.ch011

Huie, C. P. (2016). Perceptions of Business Intelligence Professionals about Factors Related to Business Intelligence input in Decision Making. *International Journal of Business Analytics, 3*(3), 1–24. doi:10.4018/IJBAN.2016070101

Hung, S., Huang, W., Yen, D. C., Chang, S., & Lu, C. (2016). Effect of Information Service Competence and Contextual Factors on the Effectiveness of Strategic Information Systems Planning in Hospitals. *Journal of Global Information Management, 24*(1), 14–36. doi:10.4018/JGIM.2016010102

Ifinedo, P. (2017). Using an Extended Theory of Planned Behavior to Study Nurses' Adoption of Healthcare Information Systems in Nova Scotia. *International Journal of Technology Diffusion, 8*(1), 1–17. doi:10.4018/IJTD.2017010101

Ilie, V., & Sneha, S. (2018). A Three Country Study for Understanding Physicians' Engagement With Electronic Information Resources Pre and Post System Implementation. *Journal of Global Information Management, 26*(2), 48–73. doi:10.4018/JGIM.2018040103

Inoue-Smith, Y. (2017). Perceived Ease in Using Technology Predicts Teacher Candidates' Preferences for Online Resources. *International Journal of Online Pedagogy and Course Design, 7*(3), 17–28. doi:10.4018/IJOPCD.2017070102

Islam, A. A. (2016). Development and Validation of the Technology Adoption and Gratification (TAG) Model in Higher Education: A Cross-Cultural Study Between Malaysia and China. *International Journal of Technology and Human Interaction, 12*(3), 78–105. doi:10.4018/IJTHI.2016070106

Islam, A. Y. (2017). Technology Satisfaction in an Academic Context: Moderating Effect of Gender. In A. Mesquita (Ed.), *Research Paradigms and Contemporary Perspectives on Human-Technology Interaction* (pp. 187–211). Hershey, PA: IGI Global. doi:10.4018/978-1-5225-1868-6.ch009

Jamil, G. L., & Jamil, C. C. (2017). Information and Knowledge Management Perspective Contributions for Fashion Studies: Observing Logistics and Supply Chain Management Processes. In G. Jamil, A. Soares, & C. Pessoa (Eds.), *Handbook of Research on Information Management for Effective Logistics and Supply Chains* (pp. 199–221). Hershey, PA: IGI Global. doi:10.4018/978-1-5225-0973-8.ch011

Jamil, G. L., Jamil, L. C., Vieira, A. A., & Xavier, A. J. (2016). Challenges in Modelling Healthcare Services: A Study Case of Information Architecture Perspectives. In G. Jamil, J. Poças Rascão, F. Ribeiro, & A. Malheiro da Silva (Eds.), *Handbook of Research on Information Architecture and Management in Modern Organizations* (pp. 1–23). Hershey, PA: IGI Global. doi:10.4018/978-1-4666-8637-3.ch001

Janakova, M. (2018). Big Data and Simulations for the Solution of Controversies in Small Businesses. In M. Khosrow-Pour, D.B.A. (Ed.), Encyclopedia of Information Science and Technology, Fourth Edition (pp. 6907-6915). Hershey, PA: IGI Global. doi:10.4018/978-1-5225-2255-3.ch598

Jha, D. G. (2016). Preparing for Information Technology Driven Changes. In S. Tiwari & L. Nafees (Eds.), *Innovative Management Education Pedagogies for Preparing Next-Generation Leaders* (pp. 258–274). Hershey, PA: IGI Global. doi:10.4018/978-1-4666-9691-4.ch015

Jhawar, A., & Garg, S. K. (2018). Logistics Improvement by Investment in Information Technology Using System Dynamics. In A. Azar & S. Vaidyanathan (Eds.), *Advances in System Dynamics and Control* (pp. 528–567). Hershey, PA: IGI Global. doi:10.4018/978-1-5225-4077-9.ch017

Kalelioğlu, F., Gülbahar, Y., & Doğan, D. (2018). Teaching How to Think Like a Programmer: Emerging Insights. In H. Ozcinar, G. Wong, & H. Ozturk (Eds.), *Teaching Computational Thinking in Primary Education* (pp. 18–35). Hershey, PA: IGI Global. doi:10.4018/978-1-5225-3200-2.ch002

Kamberi, S. (2017). A Girls-Only Online Virtual World Environment and its Implications for Game-Based Learning. In A. Stricker, C. Calongne, B. Truman, & F. Arenas (Eds.), *Integrating an Awareness of Selfhood and Society into Virtual Learning* (pp. 74–95). Hershey, PA: IGI Global. doi:10.4018/978-1-5225-2182-2.ch006

Kamel, S., & Rizk, N. (2017). ICT Strategy Development: From Design to Implementation – Case of Egypt. In C. Howard & K. Hargiss (Eds.), *Strategic Information Systems and Technologies in Modern Organizations* (pp. 239–257). Hershey, PA: IGI Global. doi:10.4018/978-1-5225-1680-4.ch010

Kamel, S. H. (2018). The Potential Role of the Software Industry in Supporting Economic Development. In M. Khosrow-Pour, D.B.A. (Ed.), Encyclopedia of Information Science and Technology, Fourth Edition (pp. 7259-7269). Hershey, PA: IGI Global. doi:10.4018/978-1-5225-2255-3.ch631

Karon, R. (2016). Utilisation of Health Information Systems for Service Delivery in the Namibian Environment. In T. Iyamu & A. Tatnall (Eds.), *Maximizing Healthcare Delivery and Management through Technology Integration* (pp. 169–183). Hershey, PA: IGI Global. doi:10.4018/978-1-4666-9446-0.ch011

Kawata, S. (2018). Computer-Assisted Parallel Program Generation. In M. Khosrow-Pour, D.B.A. (Ed.), Encyclopedia of Information Science and Technology, Fourth Edition (pp. 4583-4593). Hershey, PA: IGI Global. doi:10.4018/978-1-5225-2255-3.ch398

Khanam, S., Siddiqui, J., & Talib, F. (2016). A DEMATEL Approach for Prioritizing the TQM Enablers and IT Resources in the Indian ICT Industry. *International Journal of Applied Management Sciences and Engineering, 3*(1), 11–29. doi:10.4018/IJAMSE.2016010102

Khari, M., Shrivastava, G., Gupta, S., & Gupta, R. (2017). Role of Cyber Security in Today's Scenario. In R. Kumar, P. Pattnaik, & P. Pandey (Eds.), *Detecting and Mitigating Robotic Cyber Security Risks* (pp. 177–191). Hershey, PA: IGI Global. doi:10.4018/978-1-5225-2154-9.ch013

Khouja, M., Rodriguez, I. B., Ben Halima, Y., & Moalla, S. (2018). IT Governance in Higher Education Institutions: A Systematic Literature Review. *International Journal of Human Capital and Information Technology Professionals, 9*(2), 52–67. doi:10.4018/IJHCITP.2018040104

Kim, S., Chang, M., Choi, N., Park, J., & Kim, H. (2016). The Direct and Indirect Effects of Computer Uses on Student Success in Math. *International Journal of Cyber Behavior, Psychology and Learning, 6*(3), 48–64. doi:10.4018/IJCBPL.2016070104

Kiourt, C., Pavlidis, G., Koutsoudis, A., & Kalles, D. (2017). Realistic Simulation of Cultural Heritage. *International Journal of Computational Methods in Heritage Science, 1*(1), 10–40. doi:10.4018/IJCMHS.2017010102

Korikov, A., & Krivtsov, O. (2016). System of People-Computer: On the Way of Creation of Human-Oriented Interface. In V. Mkrttchian, A. Bershadsky, A. Bozhday, M. Kataev, & S. Kataev (Eds.), *Handbook of Research on Estimation and Control Techniques in E-Learning Systems* (pp. 458–470). Hershey, PA: IGI Global. doi:10.4018/978-1-4666-9489-7.ch032

Köse, U. (2017). An Augmented-Reality-Based Intelligent Mobile Application for Open Computer Education. In G. Kurubacak & H. Altinpulluk (Eds.), *Mobile Technologies and Augmented Reality in Open Education* (pp. 154–174). Hershey, PA: IGI Global. doi:10.4018/978-1-5225-2110-5.ch008

Lahmiri, S. (2018). Information Technology Outsourcing Risk Factors and Provider Selection. In M. Gupta, R. Sharman, J. Walp, & P. Mulgund (Eds.), *Information Technology Risk Management and Compliance in Modern Organizations* (pp. 214–228). Hershey, PA: IGI Global. doi:10.4018/978-1-5225-2604-9.ch008

Related References

Landriscina, F. (2017). Computer-Supported Imagination: The Interplay Between Computer and Mental Simulation in Understanding Scientific Concepts. In I. Levin & D. Tsybulsky (Eds.), *Digital Tools and Solutions for Inquiry-Based STEM Learning* (pp. 33–60). Hershey, PA: IGI Global. doi:10.4018/978-1-5225-2525-7.ch002

Lau, S. K., Winley, G. K., Leung, N. K., Tsang, N., & Lau, S. Y. (2016). An Exploratory Study of Expectation in IT Skills in a Developing Nation: Vietnam. *Journal of Global Information Management, 24*(1), 1–13. doi:10.4018/JGIM.2016010101

Lavranos, C., Kostagiolas, P., & Papadatos, J. (2016). Information Retrieval Technologies and the "Realities" of Music Information Seeking. In I. Deliyannis, P. Kostagiolas, & C. Banou (Eds.), *Experimental Multimedia Systems for Interactivity and Strategic Innovation* (pp. 102–121). Hershey, PA: IGI Global. doi:10.4018/978-1-4666-8659-5.ch005

Lee, W. W. (2018). Ethical Computing Continues From Problem to Solution. In M. Khosrow-Pour, D.B.A. (Ed.), Encyclopedia of Information Science and Technology, Fourth Edition (pp. 4884-4897). Hershey, PA: IGI Global. doi:10.4018/978-1-5225-2255-3.ch423

Lehto, M. (2016). Cyber Security Education and Research in the Finland's Universities and Universities of Applied Sciences. *International Journal of Cyber Warfare & Terrorism, 6*(2), 15–31. doi:10.4018/IJCWT.2016040102

Lin, C., Jalleh, G., & Huang, Y. (2016). Evaluating and Managing Electronic Commerce and Outsourcing Projects in Hospitals. In A. Dwivedi (Ed.), *Reshaping Medical Practice and Care with Health Information Systems* (pp. 132–172). Hershey, PA: IGI Global. doi:10.4018/978-1-4666-9870-3.ch005

Lin, S., Chen, S., & Chuang, S. (2017). Perceived Innovation and Quick Response Codes in an Online-to-Offline E-Commerce Service Model. *International Journal of E-Adoption, 9*(2), 1–16. doi:10.4018/IJEA.2017070101

Liu, M., Wang, Y., Xu, W., & Liu, L. (2017). Automated Scoring of Chinese Engineering Students' English Essays. *International Journal of Distance Education Technologies, 15*(1), 52–68. doi:10.4018/IJDET.2017010104

Luciano, E. M., Wiedenhöft, G. C., Macadar, M. A., & Pinheiro dos Santos, F. (2016). Information Technology Governance Adoption: Understanding its Expectations Through the Lens of Organizational Citizenship. *International Journal of IT/Business Alignment and Governance, 7*(2), 22-32. doi:10.4018/IJITBAG.2016070102

Mabe, L. K., & Oladele, O. I. (2017). Application of Information Communication Technologies for Agricultural Development through Extension Services: A Review. In T. Tossy (Ed.), *Information Technology Integration for Socio-Economic Development* (pp. 52–101). Hershey, PA: IGI Global. doi:10.4018/978-1-5225-0539-6.ch003

Manogaran, G., Thota, C., & Lopez, D. (2018). Human-Computer Interaction With Big Data Analytics. In D. Lopez & M. Durai (Eds.), *HCI Challenges and Privacy Preservation in Big Data Security* (pp. 1–22). Hershey, PA: IGI Global. doi:10.4018/978-1-5225-2863-0.ch001

Margolis, J., Goode, J., & Flapan, J. (2017). A Critical Crossroads for Computer Science for All: "Identifying Talent" or "Building Talent," and What Difference Does It Make? In Y. Rankin & J. Thomas (Eds.), *Moving Students of Color from Consumers to Producers of Technology* (pp. 1–23). Hershey, PA: IGI Global. doi:10.4018/978-1-5225-2005-4.ch001

Mbale, J. (2018). Computer Centres Resource Cloud Elasticity-Scalability (CRECES): Copperbelt University Case Study. In S. Aljawarneh & M. Malhotra (Eds.), *Critical Research on Scalability and Security Issues in Virtual Cloud Environments* (pp. 48–70). Hershey, PA: IGI Global. doi:10.4018/978-1-5225-3029-9.ch003

McKee, J. (2018). The Right Information: The Key to Effective Business Planning. In *Business Architectures for Risk Assessment and Strategic Planning: Emerging Research and Opportunities* (pp. 38–52). Hershey, PA: IGI Global. doi:10.4018/978-1-5225-3392-4.ch003

Mensah, I. K., & Mi, J. (2018). Determinants of Intention to Use Local E-Government Services in Ghana: The Perspective of Local Government Workers. *International Journal of Technology Diffusion*, *9*(2), 41–60. doi:10.4018/IJTD.2018040103

Mohamed, J. H. (2018). Scientograph-Based Visualization of Computer Forensics Research Literature. In J. Jeyasekar & P. Saravanan (Eds.), *Innovations in Measuring and Evaluating Scientific Information* (pp. 148–162). Hershey, PA: IGI Global. doi:10.4018/978-1-5225-3457-0.ch010

Moore, R. L., & Johnson, N. (2017). Earning a Seat at the Table: How IT Departments Can Partner in Organizational Change and Innovation. *International Journal of Knowledge-Based Organizations*, *7*(2), 1–12. doi:10.4018/IJKBO.2017040101

Mtebe, J. S., & Kissaka, M. M. (2016). Enhancing the Quality of Computer Science Education with MOOCs in Sub-Saharan Africa. In J. Keengwe & G. Onchwari (Eds.), *Handbook of Research on Active Learning and the Flipped Classroom Model in the Digital Age* (pp. 366–377). Hershey, PA: IGI Global. doi:10.4018/978-1-4666-9680-8.ch019

Mukul, M. K., & Bhattaharyya, S. (2017). Brain-Machine Interface: Human-Computer Interaction. In E. Noughabi, B. Raahemi, A. Albadvi, & B. Far (Eds.), *Handbook of Research on Data Science for Effective Healthcare Practice and Administration* (pp. 417–443). Hershey, PA: IGI Global. doi:10.4018/978-1-5225-2515-8.ch018

Na, L. (2017). Library and Information Science Education and Graduate Programs in Academic Libraries. In L. Ruan, Q. Zhu, & Y. Ye (Eds.), *Academic Library Development and Administration in China* (pp. 218–229). Hershey, PA: IGI Global. doi:10.4018/978-1-5225-0550-1.ch013

Nabavi, A., Taghavi-Fard, M. T., Hanafizadeh, P., & Taghva, M. R. (2016). Information Technology Continuance Intention: A Systematic Literature Review. *International Journal of E-Business Research*, *12*(1), 58–95. doi:10.4018/IJEBR.2016010104

Nath, R., & Murthy, V. N. (2018). What Accounts for the Differences in Internet Diffusion Rates Around the World? In M. Khosrow-Pour, D.B.A. (Ed.), Encyclopedia of Information Science and Technology, Fourth Edition (pp. 8095-8104). Hershey, PA: IGI Global. doi:10.4018/978-1-5225-2255-3.ch705

Nedelko, Z., & Potocan, V. (2018). The Role of Emerging Information Technologies for Supporting Supply Chain Management. In M. Khosrow-Pour, D.B.A. (Ed.), Encyclopedia of Information Science and Technology, Fourth Edition (pp. 5559-5569). Hershey, PA: IGI Global. doi:10.4018/978-1-5225-2255-3.ch483

Ngafeeson, M. N. (2018). User Resistance to Health Information Technology. In M. Khosrow-Pour, D.B.A. (Ed.), Encyclopedia of Information Science and Technology, Fourth Edition (pp. 3816-3825). Hershey, PA: IGI Global. doi:10.4018/978-1-5225-2255-3.ch331

Nozari, H., Najafi, S. E., Jafari-Eskandari, M., & Aliahmadi, A. (2016). Providing a Model for Virtual Project Management with an Emphasis on IT Projects. In C. Graham (Ed.), *Strategic Management and Leadership for Systems Development in Virtual Spaces* (pp. 43–63). Hershey, PA: IGI Global. doi:10.4018/978-1-4666-9688-4.ch003

Nurdin, N., Stockdale, R., & Scheepers, H. (2016). Influence of Organizational Factors in the Sustainability of E-Government: A Case Study of Local E-Government in Indonesia. In I. Sodhi (Ed.), *Trends, Prospects, and Challenges in Asian E-Governance* (pp. 281–323). Hershey, PA: IGI Global. doi:10.4018/978-1-4666-9536-8.ch014

Odagiri, K. (2017). Introduction of Individual Technology to Constitute the Current Internet. In *Strategic Policy-Based Network Management in Contemporary Organizations* (pp. 20–96). Hershey, PA: IGI Global. doi:10.4018/978-1-68318-003-6.ch003

Okike, E. U. (2018). Computer Science and Prison Education. In I. Biao (Ed.), *Strategic Learning Ideologies in Prison Education Programs* (pp. 246–264). Hershey, PA: IGI Global. doi:10.4018/978-1-5225-2909-5.ch012

Olelewe, C. J., & Nwafor, I. P. (2017). Level of Computer Appreciation Skills Acquired for Sustainable Development by Secondary School Students in Nsukka LGA of Enugu State, Nigeria. In C. Ayo & V. Mbarika (Eds.), *Sustainable ICT Adoption and Integration for Socio-Economic Development* (pp. 214–233). Hershey, PA: IGI Global. doi:10.4018/978-1-5225-2565-3.ch010

Oliveira, M., Maçada, A. C., Curado, C., & Nodari, F. (2017). Infrastructure Profiles and Knowledge Sharing. *International Journal of Technology and Human Interaction*, *13*(3), 1–12. doi:10.4018/IJTHI.2017070101

Otarkhani, A., Shokouhyar, S., & Pour, S. S. (2017). Analyzing the Impact of Governance of Enterprise IT on Hospital Performance: Tehran's (Iran) Hospitals – A Case Study. *International Journal of Healthcare Information Systems and Informatics*, *12*(3), 1–20. doi:10.4018/IJHISI.2017070101

Otunla, A. O., & Amuda, C. O. (2018). Nigerian Undergraduate Students' Computer Competencies and Use of Information Technology Tools and Resources for Study Skills and Habits' Enhancement. In M. Khosrow-Pour, D.B.A. (Ed.), Encyclopedia of Information Science and Technology, Fourth Edition (pp. 2303-2313). Hershey, PA: IGI Global. doi:10.4018/978-1-5225-2255-3.ch200

Özçınar, H. (2018). A Brief Discussion on Incentives and Barriers to Computational Thinking Education. In H. Ozcinar, G. Wong, & H. Ozturk (Eds.), *Teaching Computational Thinking in Primary Education* (pp. 1–17). Hershey, PA: IGI Global. doi:10.4018/978-1-5225-3200-2.ch001

Pandey, J. M., Garg, S., Mishra, P., & Mishra, B. P. (2017). Computer Based Psychological Interventions: Subject to the Efficacy of Psychological Services. *International Journal of Computers in Clinical Practice*, *2*(1), 25–33. doi:10.4018/IJCCP.2017010102

Parry, V. K., & Lind, M. L. (2016). Alignment of Business Strategy and Information Technology Considering Information Technology Governance, Project Portfolio Control, and Risk Management. *International Journal of Information Technology Project Management*, *7*(4), 21–37. doi:10.4018/IJITPM.2016100102

Patro, C. (2017). Impulsion of Information Technology on Human Resource Practices. In P. Ordóñez de Pablos (Ed.), *Managerial Strategies and Solutions for Business Success in Asia* (pp. 231–254). Hershey, PA: IGI Global. doi:10.4018/978-1-5225-1886-0.ch013

Patro, C. S., & Raghunath, K. M. (2017). Information Technology Paraphernalia for Supply Chain Management Decisions. In M. Tavana (Ed.), *Enterprise Information Systems and the Digitalization of Business Functions* (pp. 294–320). Hershey, PA: IGI Global. doi:10.4018/978-1-5225-2382-6.ch014

Paul, P. K. (2016). Cloud Computing: An Agent of Promoting Interdisciplinary Sciences, Especially Information Science and I-Schools – Emerging Techno-Educational Scenario. In L. Chao (Ed.), *Handbook of Research on Cloud-Based STEM Education for Improved Learning Outcomes* (pp. 247–258). Hershey, PA: IGI Global. doi:10.4018/978-1-4666-9924-3.ch016

Paul, P. K. (2018). The Context of IST for Solid Information Retrieval and Infrastructure Building: Study of Developing Country. *International Journal of Information Retrieval Research*, 8(1), 86–100. doi:10.4018/IJIRR.2018010106

Paul, P. K., & Chatterjee, D. (2018). iSchools Promoting "Information Science and Technology" (IST) Domain Towards Community, Business, and Society With Contemporary Worldwide Trend and Emerging Potentialities in India. In M. Khosrow-Pour, D.B.A. (Ed.), Encyclopedia of Information Science and Technology, Fourth Edition (pp. 4723-4735). Hershey, PA: IGI Global. doi:10.4018/978-1-5225-2255-3.ch410

Pessoa, C. R., & Marques, M. E. (2017). Information Technology and Communication Management in Supply Chain Management. In G. Jamil, A. Soares, & C. Pessoa (Eds.), *Handbook of Research on Information Management for Effective Logistics and Supply Chains* (pp. 23–33). Hershey, PA: IGI Global. doi:10.4018/978-1-5225-0973-8.ch002

Pineda, R. G. (2016). Where the Interaction Is Not: Reflections on the Philosophy of Human-Computer Interaction. *International Journal of Art, Culture and Design Technologies*, 5(1), 1–12. doi:10.4018/IJACDT.2016010101

Pineda, R. G. (2018). Remediating Interaction: Towards a Philosophy of Human-Computer Relationship. In M. Khosrow-Pour (Ed.), *Enhancing Art, Culture, and Design With Technological Integration* (pp. 75–98). Hershey, PA: IGI Global. doi:10.4018/978-1-5225-5023-5.ch004

Poikela, P., & Vuojärvi, H. (2016). Learning ICT-Mediated Communication through Computer-Based Simulations. In M. Cruz-Cunha, I. Miranda, R. Martinho, & R. Rijo (Eds.), *Encyclopedia of E-Health and Telemedicine* (pp. 674–687). Hershey, PA: IGI Global. doi:10.4018/978-1-4666-9978-6.ch052

Qian, Y. (2017). Computer Simulation in Higher Education: Affordances, Opportunities, and Outcomes. In P. Vu, S. Fredrickson, & C. Moore (Eds.), *Handbook of Research on Innovative Pedagogies and Technologies for Online Learning in Higher Education* (pp. 236–262). Hershey, PA: IGI Global. doi:10.4018/978-1-5225-1851-8.ch011

Radant, O., Colomo-Palacios, R., & Stantchev, V. (2016). Factors for the Management of Scarce Human Resources and Highly Skilled Employees in IT-Departments: A Systematic Review. *Journal of Information Technology Research*, *9*(1), 65–82. doi:10.4018/JITR.2016010105

Rahman, N. (2016). Toward Achieving Environmental Sustainability in the Computer Industry. *International Journal of Green Computing*, *7*(1), 37–54. doi:10.4018/IJGC.2016010103

Rahman, N. (2017). Lessons from a Successful Data Warehousing Project Management. *International Journal of Information Technology Project Management*, *8*(4), 30–45. doi:10.4018/IJITPM.2017100103

Rahman, N. (2018). Environmental Sustainability in the Computer Industry for Competitive Advantage. In M. Khosrow-Pour (Ed.), *Green Computing Strategies for Competitive Advantage and Business Sustainability* (pp. 110–130). Hershey, PA: IGI Global. doi:10.4018/978-1-5225-5017-4.ch006

Rajh, A., & Pavetic, T. (2017). Computer Generated Description as the Required Digital Competence in Archival Profession. *International Journal of Digital Literacy and Digital Competence*, *8*(1), 36–49. doi:10.4018/IJDLDC.2017010103

Raman, A., & Goyal, D. P. (2017). Extending IMPLEMENT Framework for Enterprise Information Systems Implementation to Information System Innovation. In M. Tavana (Ed.), *Enterprise Information Systems and the Digitalization of Business Functions* (pp. 137–177). Hershey, PA: IGI Global. doi:10.4018/978-1-5225-2382-6.ch007

Rao, Y. S., Rauta, A. K., Saini, H., & Panda, T. C. (2017). Mathematical Model for Cyber Attack in Computer Network. *International Journal of Business Data Communications and Networking*, *13*(1), 58–65. doi:10.4018/IJBDCN.2017010105

Rapaport, W. J. (2018). Syntactic Semantics and the Proper Treatment of Computationalism. In M. Danesi (Ed.), *Empirical Research on Semiotics and Visual Rhetoric* (pp. 128–176). Hershey, PA: IGI Global. doi:10.4018/978-1-5225-5622-0.ch007

Raut, R., Priyadarshinee, P., & Jha, M. (2017). Understanding the Mediation Effect of Cloud Computing Adoption in Indian Organization: Integrating TAM-TOE- Risk Model. *International Journal of Service Science, Management, Engineering, and Technology*, *8*(3), 40–59. doi:10.4018/IJSSMET.2017070103

Regan, E. A., & Wang, J. (2016). Realizing the Value of EHR Systems Critical Success Factors. *International Journal of Healthcare Information Systems and Informatics*, *11*(3), 1–18. doi:10.4018/IJHISI.2016070101

Rezaie, S., Mirabedini, S. J., & Abtahi, A. (2018). Designing a Model for Implementation of Business Intelligence in the Banking Industry. *International Journal of Enterprise Information Systems*, *14*(1), 77–103. doi:10.4018/IJEIS.2018010105

Rezende, D. A. (2016). Digital City Projects: Information and Public Services Offered by Chicago (USA) and Curitiba (Brazil). *International Journal of Knowledge Society Research*, *7*(3), 16–30. doi:10.4018/IJKSR.2016070102

Rezende, D. A. (2018). Strategic Digital City Projects: Innovative Information and Public Services Offered by Chicago (USA) and Curitiba (Brazil). In M. Lytras, L. Daniela, & A. Visvizi (Eds.), *Enhancing Knowledge Discovery and Innovation in the Digital Era* (pp. 204–223). Hershey, PA: IGI Global. doi:10.4018/978-1-5225-4191-2.ch012

Riabov, V. V. (2016). Teaching Online Computer-Science Courses in LMS and Cloud Environment. *International Journal of Quality Assurance in Engineering and Technology Education*, *5*(4), 12–41. doi:10.4018/IJQAETE.2016100102

Ricordel, V., Wang, J., Da Silva, M. P., & Le Callet, P. (2016). 2D and 3D Visual Attention for Computer Vision: Concepts, Measurement, and Modeling. In R. Pal (Ed.), *Innovative Research in Attention Modeling and Computer Vision Applications* (pp. 1–44). Hershey, PA: IGI Global. doi:10.4018/978-1-4666-8723-3.ch001

Rodriguez, A., Rico-Diaz, A. J., Rabuñal, J. R., & Gestal, M. (2017). Fish Tracking with Computer Vision Techniques: An Application to Vertical Slot Fishways. In M. S., & V. V. (Eds.), Multi-Core Computer Vision and Image Processing for Intelligent Applications (pp. 74-104). Hershey, PA: IGI Global. doi:10.4018/978-1-5225-0889-2.ch003

Romero, J. A. (2018). Sustainable Advantages of Business Value of Information Technology. In M. Khosrow-Pour, D.B.A. (Ed.), Encyclopedia of Information Science and Technology, Fourth Edition (pp. 923-929). Hershey, PA: IGI Global. doi:10.4018/978-1-5225-2255-3.ch079

Romero, J. A. (2018). The Always-On Business Model and Competitive Advantage. In N. Bajgoric (Ed.), *Always-On Enterprise Information Systems for Modern Organizations* (pp. 23–40). Hershey, PA: IGI Global. doi:10.4018/978-1-5225-3704-5.ch002

Rosen, Y. (2018). Computer Agent Technologies in Collaborative Learning and Assessment. In M. Khosrow-Pour, D.B.A. (Ed.), Encyclopedia of Information Science and Technology, Fourth Edition (pp. 2402-2410). Hershey, PA: IGI Global. doi:10.4018/978-1-5225-2255-3.ch209

Rosen, Y., & Mosharraf, M. (2016). Computer Agent Technologies in Collaborative Assessments. In Y. Rosen, S. Ferrara, & M. Mosharraf (Eds.), *Handbook of Research on Technology Tools for Real-World Skill Development* (pp. 319–343). Hershey, PA: IGI Global. doi:10.4018/978-1-4666-9441-5.ch012

Roy, D. (2018). Success Factors of Adoption of Mobile Applications in Rural India: Effect of Service Characteristics on Conceptual Model. In M. Khosrow-Pour (Ed.), *Green Computing Strategies for Competitive Advantage and Business Sustainability* (pp. 211–238). Hershey, PA: IGI Global. doi:10.4018/978-1-5225-5017-4.ch010

Ruffin, T. R. (2016). Health Information Technology and Change. In V. Wang (Ed.), *Handbook of Research on Advancing Health Education through Technology* (pp. 259–285). Hershey, PA: IGI Global. doi:10.4018/978-1-4666-9494-1.ch012

Ruffin, T. R. (2016). Health Information Technology and Quality Management. *International Journal of Information Communication Technologies and Human Development*, 8(4), 56–72. doi:10.4018/IJICTHD.2016100105

Ruffin, T. R., & Hawkins, D. P. (2018). Trends in Health Care Information Technology and Informatics. In M. Khosrow-Pour, D.B.A. (Ed.), Encyclopedia of Information Science and Technology, Fourth Edition (pp. 3805-3815). Hershey, PA: IGI Global. doi:10.4018/978-1-5225-2255-3.ch330

Safari, M. R., & Jiang, Q. (2018). The Theory and Practice of IT Governance Maturity and Strategies Alignment: Evidence From Banking Industry. *Journal of Global Information Management*, 26(2), 127–146. doi:10.4018/JGIM.2018040106

Sahin, H. B., & Anagun, S. S. (2018). Educational Computer Games in Math Teaching: A Learning Culture. In E. Toprak & E. Kumtepe (Eds.), *Supporting Multiculturalism in Open and Distance Learning Spaces* (pp. 249–280). Hershey, PA: IGI Global. doi:10.4018/978-1-5225-3076-3.ch013

Sanna, A., & Valpreda, F. (2017). An Assessment of the Impact of a Collaborative Didactic Approach and Students' Background in Teaching Computer Animation. *International Journal of Information and Communication Technology Education*, *13*(4), 1–16. doi:10.4018/IJICTE.2017100101

Savita, K., Dominic, P., & Ramayah, T. (2016). The Drivers, Practices and Outcomes of Green Supply Chain Management: Insights from ISO14001 Manufacturing Firms in Malaysia. *International Journal of Information Systems and Supply Chain Management*, *9*(2), 35–60. doi:10.4018/IJISSCM.2016040103

Scott, A., Martin, A., & McAlear, F. (2017). Enhancing Participation in Computer Science among Girls of Color: An Examination of a Preparatory AP Computer Science Intervention. In Y. Rankin & J. Thomas (Eds.), *Moving Students of Color from Consumers to Producers of Technology* (pp. 62–84). Hershey, PA: IGI Global. doi:10.4018/978-1-5225-2005-4.ch004

Shahsavandi, E., Mayah, G., & Rahbari, H. (2016). Impact of E-Government on Transparency and Corruption in Iran. In I. Sodhi (Ed.), *Trends, Prospects, and Challenges in Asian E-Governance* (pp. 75–94). Hershey, PA: IGI Global. doi:10.4018/978-1-4666-9536-8.ch004

Siddoo, V., & Wongsai, N. (2017). Factors Influencing the Adoption of ISO/IEC 29110 in Thai Government Projects: A Case Study. *International Journal of Information Technologies and Systems Approach*, *10*(1), 22–44. doi:10.4018/IJITSA.2017010102

Sidorkina, I., & Rybakov, A. (2016). Computer-Aided Design as Carrier of Set Development Changes System in E-Course Engineering. In V. Mkrttchian, A. Bershadsky, A. Bozhday, M. Kataev, & S. Kataev (Eds.), *Handbook of Research on Estimation and Control Techniques in E-Learning Systems* (pp. 500–515). Hershey, PA: IGI Global. doi:10.4018/978-1-4666-9489-7.ch035

Sidorkina, I., & Rybakov, A. (2016). Creating Model of E-Course: As an Object of Computer-Aided Design. In V. Mkrttchian, A. Bershadsky, A. Bozhday, M. Kataev, & S. Kataev (Eds.), *Handbook of Research on Estimation and Control Techniques in E-Learning Systems* (pp. 286–297). Hershey, PA: IGI Global. doi:10.4018/978-1-4666-9489-7.ch019

Simões, A. (2017). Using Game Frameworks to Teach Computer Programming. In R. Alexandre Peixoto de Queirós & M. Pinto (Eds.), *Gamification-Based E-Learning Strategies for Computer Programming Education* (pp. 221–236). Hershey, PA: IGI Global. doi:10.4018/978-1-5225-1034-5.ch010

Sllame, A. M. (2017). Integrating LAB Work With Classes in Computer Network Courses. In H. Alphin Jr, R. Chan, & J. Lavine (Eds.), *The Future of Accessibility in International Higher Education* (pp. 253–275). Hershey, PA: IGI Global. doi:10.4018/978-1-5225-2560-8.ch015

Smirnov, A., Ponomarev, A., Shilov, N., Kashevnik, A., & Teslya, N. (2018). Ontology-Based Human-Computer Cloud for Decision Support: Architecture and Applications in Tourism. *International Journal of Embedded and Real-Time Communication Systems*, 9(1), 1–19. doi:10.4018/IJERTCS.2018010101

Smith-Ditizio, A. A., & Smith, A. D. (2018). Computer Fraud Challenges and Its Legal Implications. In M. Khosrow-Pour, D.B.A. (Ed.), Encyclopedia of Information Science and Technology, Fourth Edition (pp. 4837-4848). Hershey, PA: IGI Global. doi:10.4018/978-1-5225-2255-3.ch419

Sohani, S. S. (2016). Job Shadowing in Information Technology Projects: A Source of Competitive Advantage. *International Journal of Information Technology Project Management*, 7(1), 47–57. doi:10.4018/IJITPM.2016010104

Sosnin, P. (2018). Figuratively Semantic Support of Human-Computer Interactions. In *Experience-Based Human-Computer Interactions: Emerging Research and Opportunities* (pp. 244–272). Hershey, PA: IGI Global. doi:10.4018/978-1-5225-2987-3.ch008

Spinelli, R., & Benevolo, C. (2016). From Healthcare Services to E-Health Applications: A Delivery System-Based Taxonomy. In A. Dwivedi (Ed.), *Reshaping Medical Practice and Care with Health Information Systems* (pp. 205–245). Hershey, PA: IGI Global. doi:10.4018/978-1-4666-9870-3.ch007

Srinivasan, S. (2016). Overview of Clinical Trial and Pharmacovigilance Process and Areas of Application of Computer System. In P. Chakraborty & A. Nagal (Eds.), *Software Innovations in Clinical Drug Development and Safety* (pp. 1–13). Hershey, PA: IGI Global. doi:10.4018/978-1-4666-8726-4.ch001

Srisawasdi, N. (2016). Motivating Inquiry-Based Learning Through a Combination of Physical and Virtual Computer-Based Laboratory Experiments in High School Science. In M. Urban & D. Falvo (Eds.), *Improving K-12 STEM Education Outcomes through Technological Integration* (pp. 108–134). Hershey, PA: IGI Global. doi:10.4018/978-1-4666-9616-7.ch006

Related References

Stavridi, S. V., & Hamada, D. R. (2016). Children and Youth Librarians: Competencies Required in Technology-Based Environment. In J. Yap, M. Perez, M. Ayson, & G. Entico (Eds.), *Special Library Administration, Standardization and Technological Integration* (pp. 25–50). Hershey, PA: IGI Global. doi:10.4018/978-1-4666-9542-9. ch002

Sung, W., Ahn, J., Kai, S. M., Choi, A., & Black, J. B. (2016). Incorporating Touch-Based Tablets into Classroom Activities: Fostering Children's Computational Thinking through iPad Integrated Instruction. In D. Mentor (Ed.), *Handbook of Research on Mobile Learning in Contemporary Classrooms* (pp. 378–406). Hershey, PA: IGI Global. doi:10.4018/978-1-5225-0251-7.ch019

Syväjärvi, A., Leinonen, J., Kivivirta, V., & Kesti, M. (2017). The Latitude of Information Management in Local Government: Views of Local Government Managers. *International Journal of Electronic Government Research, 13*(1), 69–85. doi:10.4018/IJEGR.2017010105

Tanque, M., & Foxwell, H. J. (2018). Big Data and Cloud Computing: A Review of Supply Chain Capabilities and Challenges. In A. Prasad (Ed.), *Exploring the Convergence of Big Data and the Internet of Things* (pp. 1–28). Hershey, PA: IGI Global. doi:10.4018/978-1-5225-2947-7.ch001

Teixeira, A., Gomes, A., & Orvalho, J. G. (2017). Auditory Feedback in a Computer Game for Blind People. In T. Issa, P. Kommers, T. Issa, P. Isaías, & T. Issa (Eds.), *Smart Technology Applications in Business Environments* (pp. 134–158). Hershey, PA: IGI Global. doi:10.4018/978-1-5225-2492-2.ch007

Thompson, N., McGill, T., & Murray, D. (2018). Affect-Sensitive Computer Systems. In M. Khosrow-Pour, D.B.A. (Ed.), Encyclopedia of Information Science and Technology, Fourth Edition (pp. 4124-4135). Hershey, PA: IGI Global. doi:10.4018/978-1-5225-2255-3.ch357

Trad, A., & Kalpić, D. (2016). The E-Business Transformation Framework for E-Commerce Control and Monitoring Pattern. In I. Lee (Ed.), *Encyclopedia of E-Commerce Development, Implementation, and Management* (pp. 754–777). Hershey, PA: IGI Global. doi:10.4018/978-1-4666-9787-4.ch053

Triberti, S., Brivio, E., & Galimberti, C. (2018). On Social Presence: Theories, Methodologies, and Guidelines for the Innovative Contexts of Computer-Mediated Learning. In M. Marmon (Ed.), *Enhancing Social Presence in Online Learning Environments* (pp. 20–41). Hershey, PA: IGI Global. doi:10.4018/978-1-5225-3229-3.ch002

Tripathy, B. K. T. R., S., & Mohanty, R. K. (2018). Memetic Algorithms and Their Applications in Computer Science. In S. Dash, B. Tripathy, & A. Rahman (Eds.), *Handbook of Research on Modeling, Analysis, and Application of Nature-Inspired Metaheuristic Algorithms* (pp. 73-93). Hershey, PA: IGI Global. doi:10.4018/978-1-5225-2857-9.ch004

Turulja, L., & Bajgoric, N. (2017). Human Resource Management IT and Global Economy Perspective: Global Human Resource Information Systems. In M. Khosrow-Pour (Ed.), *Handbook of Research on Technology Adoption, Social Policy, and Global Integration* (pp. 377–394). Hershey, PA: IGI Global. doi:10.4018/978-1-5225-2668-1.ch018

Unwin, D. W., Sanzogni, L., & Sandhu, K. (2017). Developing and Measuring the Business Case for Health Information Technology. In K. Moahi, K. Bwalya, & P. Sebina (Eds.), *Health Information Systems and the Advancement of Medical Practice in Developing Countries* (pp. 262–290). Hershey, PA: IGI Global. doi:10.4018/978-1-5225-2262-1.ch015

Vadhanam, B. R. S., M., Sugumaran, V., V., V., & Ramalingam, V. V. (2017). Computer Vision Based Classification on Commercial Videos. In M. S., & V. V. (Eds.), *Multi-Core Computer Vision and Image Processing for Intelligent Applications* (pp. 105-135). Hershey, PA: IGI Global. doi:10.4018/978-1-5225-0889-2.ch004

Valverde, R., Torres, B., & Motaghi, H. (2018). A Quantum NeuroIS Data Analytics Architecture for the Usability Evaluation of Learning Management Systems. In S. Bhattacharyya (Ed.), *Quantum-Inspired Intelligent Systems for Multimedia Data Analysis* (pp. 277–299). Hershey, PA: IGI Global. doi:10.4018/978-1-5225-5219-2.ch009

Vassilis, E. (2018). Learning and Teaching Methodology: "1:1 Educational Computing. In K. Koutsopoulos, K. Doukas, & Y. Kotsanis (Eds.), *Handbook of Research on Educational Design and Cloud Computing in Modern Classroom Settings* (pp. 122–155). Hershey, PA: IGI Global. doi:10.4018/978-1-5225-3053-4.ch007

Wadhwani, A. K., Wadhwani, S., & Singh, T. (2016). Computer Aided Diagnosis System for Breast Cancer Detection. In Y. Morsi, A. Shukla, & C. Rathore (Eds.), *Optimizing Assistive Technologies for Aging Populations* (pp. 378–395). Hershey, PA: IGI Global. doi:10.4018/978-1-4666-9530-6.ch015

Wang, L., Wu, Y., & Hu, C. (2016). English Teachers' Practice and Perspectives on Using Educational Computer Games in EIL Context. *International Journal of Technology and Human Interaction, 12*(3), 33–46. doi:10.4018/IJTHI.2016070103

Watfa, M. K., Majeed, H., & Salahuddin, T. (2016). Computer Based E-Healthcare Clinical Systems: A Comprehensive Survey. *International Journal of Privacy and Health Information Management*, 4(1), 50–69. doi:10.4018/IJPHIM.2016010104

Weeger, A., & Haase, U. (2016). Taking up Three Challenges to Business-IT Alignment Research by the Use of Activity Theory. *International Journal of IT/Business Alignment and Governance, 7*(2), 1-21. doi:10.4018/IJITBAG.2016070101

Wexler, B. E. (2017). Computer-Presented and Physical Brain-Training Exercises for School Children: Improving Executive Functions and Learning. In B. Dubbels (Ed.), *Transforming Gaming and Computer Simulation Technologies across Industries* (pp. 206–224). Hershey, PA: IGI Global. doi:10.4018/978-1-5225-1817-4.ch012

Williams, D. M., Gani, M. O., Addo, I. D., Majumder, A. J., Tamma, C. P., Wang, M., ... Chu, C. (2016). Challenges in Developing Applications for Aging Populations. In Y. Morsi, A. Shukla, & C. Rathore (Eds.), *Optimizing Assistive Technologies for Aging Populations* (pp. 1–21). Hershey, PA: IGI Global. doi:10.4018/978-1-4666-9530-6.ch001

Wimble, M., Singh, H., & Phillips, B. (2018). Understanding Cross-Level Interactions of Firm-Level Information Technology and Industry Environment: A Multilevel Model of Business Value. *Information Resources Management Journal, 31*(1), 1–20. doi:10.4018/IRMJ.2018010101

Wimmer, H., Powell, L., Kilgus, L., & Force, C. (2017). Improving Course Assessment via Web-based Homework. *International Journal of Online Pedagogy and Course Design*, 7(2), 1–19. doi:10.4018/IJOPCD.2017040101

Wong, Y. L., & Siu, K. W. (2018). Assessing Computer-Aided Design Skills. In M. Khosrow-Pour, D.B.A. (Ed.), Encyclopedia of Information Science and Technology, Fourth Edition (pp. 7382-7391). Hershey, PA: IGI Global. doi:10.4018/978-1-5225-2255-3.ch642

Wongsurawat, W., & Shrestha, V. (2018). Information Technology, Globalization, and Local Conditions: Implications for Entrepreneurs in Southeast Asia. In P. Ordóñez de Pablos (Ed.), *Management Strategies and Technology Fluidity in the Asian Business Sector* (pp. 163–176). Hershey, PA: IGI Global. doi:10.4018/978-1-5225-4056-4.ch010

Yang, Y., Zhu, X., Jin, C., & Li, J. J. (2018). Reforming Classroom Education Through a QQ Group: A Pilot Experiment at a Primary School in Shanghai. In H. Spires (Ed.), *Digital Transformation and Innovation in Chinese Education* (pp. 211–231). Hershey, PA: IGI Global. doi:10.4018/978-1-5225-2924-8.ch012

Yilmaz, R., Sezgin, A., Kurnaz, S., & Arslan, Y. Z. (2018). Object-Oriented Programming in Computer Science. In M. Khosrow-Pour, D.B.A. (Ed.), Encyclopedia of Information Science and Technology, Fourth Edition (pp. 7470-7480). Hershey, PA: IGI Global. doi:10.4018/978-1-5225-2255-3.ch650

Yu, L. (2018). From Teaching Software Engineering Locally and Globally to Devising an Internationalized Computer Science Curriculum. In S. Dikli, B. Etheridge, & R. Rawls (Eds.), *Curriculum Internationalization and the Future of Education* (pp. 293–320). Hershey, PA: IGI Global. doi:10.4018/978-1-5225-2791-6.ch016

Yuhua, F. (2018). Computer Information Library Clusters. In M. Khosrow-Pour, D.B.A. (Ed.), Encyclopedia of Information Science and Technology, Fourth Edition (pp. 4399-4403). Hershey, PA: IGI Global. doi:10.4018/978-1-5225-2255-3.ch382

Zare, M. A., Taghavi Fard, M. T., & Hanafizadeh, P. (2016). The Assessment of Outsourcing IT Services using DEA Technique: A Study of Application Outsourcing in Research Centers. *International Journal of Operations Research and Information Systems*, 7(1), 45–57. doi:10.4018/IJORIS.2016010104

Zhao, J., Wang, Q., Guo, J., Gao, L., & Yang, F. (2016). An Overview on Passive Image Forensics Technology for Automatic Computer Forgery. *International Journal of Digital Crime and Forensics*, 8(4), 14–25. doi:10.4018/IJDCF.2016100102

Zimeras, S. (2016). Computer Virus Models and Analysis in M-Health IT Systems: Computer Virus Models. In A. Moumtzoglou (Ed.), *M-Health Innovations for Patient-Centered Care* (pp. 284–297). Hershey, PA: IGI Global. doi:10.4018/978-1-4666-9861-1.ch014

Zlatanovska, K. (2016). Hacking and Hacktivism as an Information Communication System Threat. In M. Hadji-Janev & M. Bogdanoski (Eds.), *Handbook of Research on Civil Society and National Security in the Era of Cyber Warfare* (pp. 68–101). Hershey, PA: IGI Global. doi:10.4018/978-1-4666-8793-6.ch004

About the Contributors

Sira Allende was born in La Habana in 1949. In 1972 she got her BSc. In Mathematics at Havana University and started to teach at this center. In 1980 she got her Ph. D. at Humboldt University in Berlin. Since 1994 she is full professor at Havana University. She reads lectures of the Optimization courses for BSc students of Mathematics and Computer Science as well as for Master Students. Her research focuses in the area of optimization, mainly in the study of the optimization models appearing when solving logistics and statistical problems. Now she is Consultant Professor at the Havana University

Bekir Cetintav is a researcher at the Department of Statistics, Burdur Mehmet Akif Ersoy University, Turkey. He received his PhD degree in Statistics from Dokuz Eylul University in 2018. His research interests are biostatistics/biometrics, fuzzy logic, data science and applied statistics.

Arpita Chatterjee is an associate professor at the Department of Mathematical Sciences at Georgia Southern University.

Shivacharan Rao Chitneni recently graduated with MS degree in Statistical Analytics, Computing and Modeling from Texas A&M University-Kingsville, Kingsville, TX, USA.

Beatriz Cobo, PhD, is Assistant Professor in the Department of Quantitative Methods for the Economy and Business at the University of Granada. Her research focuses on the use of indirect questioning techniques for sensitive issues, sampling theory, estimation with auxiliary information, and their computational treatment.

Neslihan Demirel works as an Associate Professor at the Department of Statistics, Dokuz Eylul University, Izmir, Turkey. She received her PhD degree in Statistics from Dokuz Eylul University in 2007 and completed her post-doctoral study at The

Ohio State University, USA. Her research interests are regression analysis, ranked set sampling, applied statistics and machine learning.

Santu Ghosh is an assistant professor at the Department of Population Health Sciences at Augusta University.

Selma Gürler is a Professor at the Department of Statistics, Dokuz Eylul University, Izmir, Turkey. She received her PhD degree in Statistics from Dokuz Eylul University in 2006 and did her post-doctoral study at RWTH Aachen University, Germany. Her research interests are reliability theory, applied probability and statistics.

Shravya Jasti recently graduated with MS in Statistical Analytics, Computing and Modeling, Department of Mathematics, Texas A&M University-Kingsville.

Vishal Mehta working as an Assistant Professor at Department of Agricultural Statistics, College of Agriculture, Acharya Narendra Deva University Of Agriculture And Technology (ANDUAT), Kumarganj, Ayodhya, Uttar Pradesh, India. He has more than Nine years of research and more than six years of teaching experiences. He has published quality Research Paper at National and International journal of repute.

Elvira Pelle, PhD, is Assistant Professor of Social Statistics at the Department of Communication and Economics at the University of Modena and Reggio Emilia, Italy. Her current interests focus on randomized responses theory for sensitive attributes, social network analysis, sampling theory for finite populations, estimation with auxiliary information.

Stephen A. Sedory is a Professor of Mathematics at Texas A&M University-Kingsville, Kingsville, TX, USA.,

Sarjinder Singh is a Professor of Statistics at Texas A&M University-Kingsville, Kingsville, TX, USA.

Index

A

Asymptotic Pivot 181, 189

B

bias 1, 5, 7-10, 13, 15, 17, 35-38, 41, 44, 49, 52, 62, 66-69, 71-72, 75-80, 82, 101, 105, 135, 150-153, 175, 218-219
bias-correction and acceleration 179
Big-Oh 189

C

confidence interval 171, 173, 176-178, 182-183, 185-186, 188-189
coverage error 171, 178, 180-181, 189
coverage probability 177, 180, 183, 187, 189

D

difference of means 209, 219, 223, 231

E

Edgeworth expansion 181
Estimation of Population Mean 144, 198

F

fuzzy sets 190, 192, 194, 196, 208

I

Indirect questioning techniques 26, 30

M

mean estimation 40, 190, 204-205, 208
Minimum Mean Square Error Estimator 1
missing data 85, 143, 169, 213
missing observations 60, 84, 141-142, 155, 209, 213, 215, 230-231
monotone transformation 171, 176
Morgenstern type bivariate exponential distribution 1, 3, 18, 22-24
multiple ranker 197, 199, 203-206

N

Nominal Coverage Probability 177, 189
normal approximation 171, 177, 180-182

O

order statistics 21-23, 28, 39, 47, 60, 73-74, 77, 84, 153, 168, 172, 187, 191, 207, 211

P

percentile method 171, 178, 182, 187
pivot 177, 181-182, 189
Privacy Protection 26

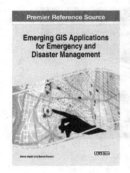

IGI Global Author Services

Providing a high-quality, affordable, and expeditious service, IGI Global's Author Services enable authors to streamline their publishing process, increase chance of acceptance, and adhere to IGI Global's publication standards.

Benefits of Author Services:

- **Professional Service:** All our editors, designers, and translators are experts in their field with years of experience and professional certifications.
- **Quality Guarantee & Certificate:** Each order is returned with a quality guarantee and certificate of professional completion.
- **Timeliness:** All editorial orders have a guaranteed return timeframe of 3-5 business days and translation orders are guaranteed in 7-10 business days.
- **Affordable Pricing:** IGI Global Author Services are competitively priced compared to other industry service providers.
- **APC Reimbursement:** IGI Global authors publishing Open Access (OA) will be able to deduct the cost of editing and other IGI Global author services from their OA APC publishing fee.

Author Services Offered:

English Language Copy Editing
Professional, native English language copy editors improve your manuscript's grammar, spelling, punctuation, terminology, semantics, consistency, flow, formatting, and more.

Scientific & Scholarly Editing
A Ph.D. level review for qualities such as originality and significance, interest to researchers, level of methodology and analysis, coverage of literature, organization, quality of writing, and strengths and weaknesses.

Figure, Table, Chart & Equation Conversions
Work with IGI Global's graphic designers before submission to enhance and design all figures and charts to IGI Global's specific standards for clarity.

Translation
Providing 70 language options, including Simplified and Traditional Chinese, Spanish, Arabic, German, French, and more.

Hear What the Experts Are Saying About IGI Global's Author Services

"Publishing with IGI Global has been *an amazing experience* for me for sharing my research. The *strong academic production* support ensures quality and timely completion." – **Prof. Margaret Niess, Oregon State University, USA**

"The service was *very fast, very thorough, and very helpful* in ensuring our chapter meets the criteria and requirements of the book's editors. I was *quite impressed and happy* with your service." – **Prof. Tom Brinthaupt, Middle Tennessee State University, USA**

Easily Identify, Acquire, and Utilize Published Peer-Reviewed Articles in Support of Your Current Research.

Printed in the United States
by Baker & Taylor Publisher Services